Silicon Triangle

A report of the Working Group on
Semiconductors and the Security of the
United States and Taiwan, a joint project of
the Hoover Institution and the Asia Society
Center on U.S.-China Relations

Silicon Triangle

THE UNITED STATES, TAIWAN, CHINA, AND GLOBAL SEMICONDUCTOR SECURITY

Editors

LARRY DIAMOND,

JAMES O. ELLIS JR.,

AND ORVILLE SCHELL

Executive Editor

David Fedor

Contributors

Robert Daly	Matthew Pottinger
Christopher Ford	Don Rosenberg
Edlyn V. Levine	David J. Teece
Greg Linden	Kharis Templeman
Mary Kay Magistad	Glenn Tiffert
Oriana Skylar Mastro	Matthew Turpin
Jim Plummer	H.-S. Philip Wong

HOOVER INSTITUTION PRESS
STANFORD UNIVERSITY   STANFORD, CALIFORNIA

Hoover Institution

With its eminent scholars and world-renowned library and archives, the Hoover Institution seeks to improve the human condition by advancing ideas that promote economic opportunity and prosperity, while securing and safeguarding peace for America and all mankind. The views expressed in its publications are entirely those of the authors and do not necessarily reflect the views of the staff, officers, or Board of Overseers of the Hoover Institution.

hoover.org

Asia Society Center on U.S.-China Relations

In seeking new ways of building mutual understanding between the United States and China, the Asia Society Center on U.S.-China Relations undertakes projects and events which explore areas of common interest and divergent views between the two countries, focusing on policy, culture, business, media, economics, energy, and the environment. The Center on U.S.-China Relations and the Asia Society take no institutional positions on matters of public policy and other issues addressed in the reports and publications they sponsor. All statements of fact and expressions of opinion contained in this report are the sole responsibility of its authors and may not reflect the views of the organization and its board, staff, and supporters.

AsiaSociety.org

Hoover Institution Press Publication No. 735
Hoover Institution at Leland Stanford Junior University,
Stanford, California 94305-6003

First printing 2023
29 28 27 26 25 24 23   7 6 5 4 3 2 1

Manufactured in the United States of America
Printed on acid-free, archival-quality paper

Library of Congress Control Number: 2023941785

ISBN 978-08179-2615-1 (pbk)
ISBN 978-08179-2616-8 (epub)
ISBN 978-08179-2618-2 (PDF)

CONTENTS

EXECUTIVE SUMMARY

The United States, Taiwan, and China are bound within a "silicon triangle." Semiconductors link our geopolitics, our ongoing economic prosperity, and our technological competitiveness. The more than two dozen participants in this working group have worked together for eighteen months to better understand this strategic triangle. The questions we considered include these:

- How can the United States mitigate the risks of semiconductor supply chain disruptions and become an even more competitive player in this foundational critical technology?
- How can this be done in a way that preserves Taiwan's self-governing democracy, underpins its prosperity and our partnership, and promotes stability in the Taiwan Strait?
- How can we work with global partners to respond to new vulnerabilities stemming from China's state-driven global semiconductor ambitions?

Despite significant policy efforts on these issues to date, we believe more needs to be done. As with other critical technologies where economic and national security interests will increasingly intersect, ensuring continued semiconductor security will require continuous policy adaptation as the US-China relationship changes.

1. Near-Term Domestic Resilience

We appear to be moving toward a world of intensified trade among like-minded nations and sharply reduced dependence on adversaries for critical supply chains and technologies. The United States should therefore seek to make it attractive for friendly states to participate in this emerging trading network.

The United States should ensure that its imports of finished semiconductors and key inputs in the supply chain come from reliable and broadly ideologically compatible trading partners, such as current foreign industry leaders Taiwan, South Korea, and Japan.

The United States should pursue efficiencies and growth through trade and increased market access within this network, while also investing in a major new effort to revive US domestic production of semiconductors from design to fabrication. Even if this approach succeeds, the United States will still be heavily dependent on international partners for its semiconductor supply chain—but this approach will also leave us less vulnerable to pressure from unreliable suppliers.

To address the vulnerability of our supply chains to disruption or extortion and to strengthen the US industrial base in semiconductors, we recommend that the US government pursue a near-term "insurance policy" that includes the following:

- A realistic degree of onshoring of semiconductor supply chains, incentivized by policy initiatives such as the CHIPS and Science Act of 2022. The onshoring process should be open to foreign firms of partner nations and should not impose additional regulatory requirements.
- Improved semiconductor supply chain information sharing, data analysis, and economic modeling, akin to the Energy Information Administration of the Department of Energy

- Multiyear block buys by the Department of Defense to stockpile semiconductors for critical weapons platforms, and a new tax credit to encourage the private sector to build up its own inventories of chips beyond normal commercial needs
- Trade deals that offer increased market access to US partners that share common values

2. Business Environment

The United States is seeking new capabilities in the semiconductor supply chain, especially in areas where it is no longer cost-competitive with other global trading partners. To attract investment from partners that command significant semiconductor supply chain strengths and expertise, the United States must forge and maintain a welcoming business environment. The federal government subsidies in the CHIPS Act will help here, but investment-friendly incentives should extend beyond the five-year time frame of the Act. Ensuring fair business opportunities and US market access for partner nations' technology firms will not only invigorate the US-based semiconductor industry, but also further incentivize partner governments to align with otherwise costly controls on commerce with China.

To that end, US federal and state governments should take steps to reduce the costs of doing business domestically in this and other critical-technology sectors, including through these measures:

- Federal tax efficiency to encourage the deployment of private capital, at levels well beyond public subsidies, to the semiconductor sector
- Streamlining of federal environmental regulations—such as the National Environmental Policy Act—that could considerably delay and increase the cost of domestic semiconductor projects
- Promotion of business environments, nationally and in individual states, that encourage cost efficiencies through regional industrial clustering, as used in Taiwan

3. Long-Term Technological Competitiveness

The United States should pursue comprehensive, market-oriented industrial policy measures as part of a long-term critical-technology global competitiveness agenda. To achieve strategic autonomy by means of technology and economic leadership, these policies should invest in US research capacity (a traditional US strength) as well as applied engineering and manufacturing activities (a growing US weakness). And they should strengthen the global intellectual property (IP) regime—through domestic reforms and in consultation with allies and partners—to counter China's systematic theft of the IP and technologies of open societies. We recommend these measures:

- Increasing retention of skilled immigrants educated in the United States through H-1B visas for all foreign STEM (science, technology, engineering, mathematics) graduates of US universities
- Policies to boost take-home pay for US citizens working in the semiconductor industry
- Comprehensive investments in our K–12 educational system to produce the engineers that our country will need to maintain global critical-technology leadership
- More federal funding for applied research and development, not just basic science
- Incorporating national security implications into US federal regulatory agency decision making, to acknowledge that corporate activity in technological fields can advance national security priorities
- Inbound and outbound investment screening in critical technologies that favors partner countries over unreliable competitor countries
- Legal and technology measures to strengthen the US intellectual property system, protect tacit knowledge, and incentivize private sector US innovation

4. Taiwan's Stability

Taiwan is one of Asia's most prosperous and successful liberal democracies, the world's leading innovator in and producer of semiconductors, and a trusted partner in critical supply chains. While Taiwan stands at the center of the global semiconductor economy, its lack of diplomatic recognition and formal alliances contributes to its existential vulnerability to being invaded or otherwise involuntarily absorbed into the People's Republic of China (PRC).

We believe it is in the interest not only of Taiwan's twenty-four million people, but also of the United States and the entire Indo-Pacific region, to deter PRC aggression against the island. We strongly endorse US efforts toward this end, including appropriate arms sales to strengthen Taiwan's defenses in a so-called porcupine strategy, and improving coordination and training among willing defense forces in the Indo-Pacific.

We also endorse a variety of steps to create an environment that fosters deeper business-to-business, research, academic, individual, and civil ties between the United States and Taiwan on the semiconductor front, including these:

- R&D collaboration between Taiwan's semiconductor firms and research organizations and their US peers
- Increased workforce and educational people-to-people exchanges between Taiwan and the United States
- Joint evaluations of mutual semiconductor supply chain vulnerabilities
- Increased statistical and technical collaboration between Taiwan and the US Department of Energy and national labs on energy security and infrastructure resilience
- Broad reduction of US-Taiwan economic frictions through a tax treaty to avoid dual income taxation of expatriate workers and the conclusion of a US-Taiwan free-trade deal
- Establishment of a US-hosted industry and government working group to overcome barriers to US-Taiwan defense industry coproduction and codevelopment in Taiwan

5. Dealing with China

US dependence on China for critical components and products in the global semiconductor supply chain puts it at considerable strategic and economic risk. Mitigating this risk must be an urgent priority for US policy. China has its own semiconductor agenda: to reduce its dependence on imports, improve its ability to make a variety of chips, and compete globally with leading semiconductor manufacturers so as to increase other countries' dependence on its own semiconductors. PRC government subsidies to China's semiconductor firms increase the odds that these firms will undercut the pricing of established semiconductor firms in the United States and its trading partners, unfairly harming US or partner producers and, over time, creating new US or partner dependencies on China-based supply chains.

The United States and its allies should also consider how to use their strengths in the semiconductor supply chain—and China's current reliance on them—as a form of economic deterrence against PRC aggression and intimidation in achieving its geopolitical goals. US and allied policy stances to deny China technological supremacy should remain flexible and preserve options for both escalation and deescalation, based upon principles of reciprocity and adherence to a rules-based order. Steps should include these:

- Creating a nimble multilateral export control regime. This regime should include semiconductor-specific efforts and frameworks more appropriate for broader critical technologies—allowing US technology export controls to have greater impact at a lower domestic cost.
- Avoiding future US government or critical-infrastructure dependence on chips, software, or services from state-oriented firms in China
- More funding and technical staffing so the Department of Commerce's Bureau of Industry and Security can effectively enforce its expanded rules
- Expanding export control blacklists to include China's semiconductor equipment–manufacturing firms and subsidiaries

- Considering creative and more proactive trade rules, including import restriction and antidumping measures, to forestall a likely oversupply of below-cost mature chips from China
- Given that the focus of China's semiconductor subsidies likely will be on mature nodes, the US should consider elevating export restrictions of US and partner semiconductor equipment to the 28nm range, in order to restrain China's ability to gain market power and coercive leverage in that important part of the global supply chain.

In sum, if the United States is to retain and strengthen its global leadership in semiconductors, or even to preserve its most vital economic and national security interests in this sector, it will need to revive the competitiveness of its workforce and business environment. It is not enough to simply constrain China. It is not even enough to innovate in design. The United States must run faster, harder, and with longer-term vision.

And in this increasingly globalized world, it cannot run alone. Restoring US leadership requires close cooperation with reliable partner countries. It also requires an international talent pool of scientists and engineers from around the world, with immigration rules that welcome and retain this talent.

To win this race, we will need both vigilance and agility. We will need focus and enhanced information systems to detect important new trend lines, as well as the agility to respond to these changing forces as quickly as possible. And we will need the flexibility and humility to understand that our partners will sometimes hold different views, and that their policies will sometimes evolve at a different pace from our own. The key for the United States will be to deepen and nurture these cooperative relationships while enabling innovation to thrive through multilateral collaboration. In so doing, we can make our supply chains for semiconductors and other critical technologies secure and resilient against actions by adversaries and enable open societies to win the technological competition with dictatorships.

INTRODUCTION

Washington, Taipei, and Beijing— The Silicon Triangle

ORVILLE SCHELL, LARRY DIAMOND, AND JAMES O. ELLIS JR.

This report is the result of an eighteen-month study of the triangular relationship among the United States, China, and Taiwan as seen through the lens of the rapidly evolving and increasingly strategic global trade in semiconductors. Our Working Group on Semiconductors and the Security of the United States and Taiwan, convened by the Hoover Institution and Asia Society's Center on US-China Relations, and led by Hoover fellows Larry Diamond and Adm. James Ellis (USN, Ret.) and Asia Society's Orville Schell, drew together economists, military strategists, industry players, and regional policy experts to assess how best to enhance the economic and military security of both the United States and Taiwan, while minimizing supply chain disruptions as much as possible.

This multidisciplinary working group held numerous roundtables, dialogues, and scenario-planning exercises to track and analyze this confluence of colliding interests. The working group sought a balanced view of how US and partner policies on semiconductors can increase the resilience of semiconductor supply chains and contribute to deterrence of conflict in the Taiwan Strait.

Over the course of our study, the stakes have only increased. Both US industry and government are acting to strengthen the country's capabilities in semiconductor manufacturing and, working with partners, to reshape the global chip trade. China, meanwhile, is also focused on advancing its own domestic capabilities across the full semiconductor supply chain, both to relieve its dependence on US and other imports and to strengthen and expand its role as a global supplier of essential semiconductors, including older legacy chips.

Taiwan excels especially at the leading edge of semiconductor manufacturing. Taiwan Semiconductor Manufacturing Company (TSMC) alone makes more than 90 percent of the world's supply of such chips and is now opening a fabrication ("fab") facility in Arizona. At the facility's December 2022 "tool-in" ceremony, TSMC founder and chairman Morris Chang described the moment as "the end of the beginning." The reference was not only to TSMC's bold move to construct its first semiconductor fab in the United States, but also to the rapidly shifting geopolitical contours of the global semiconductor supply chain.

It is also not lost on us that Chang's choice of words to describe a commercial construction project evoked those of a wartime Winston Churchill reflecting on Britain's 1942 victories in North Africa. The intersection of commerce and national security is an uneasy one, but the policy questions this intersection poses have become increasingly central on agendas in Washington, DC, and they will not resolve themselves anytime soon. One of those questions is how the United States can work with trusted partners to make the global chip supply chain and the economy it undergirds more robust and resilient, while at the same time acting to protect Taiwan, both as a crucial source of leading-edge semiconductors and as a flourishing democracy.

The Silicon Triangle

In the summer of 2022, when Speaker of the US House of Representatives Nancy Pelosi visited Taipei, Beijing retaliated by launching an unprecedented fusillade of six live-fire exercises and naval and air deployments in Taiwan's surrounding waters. Pelosi rejected China's claim that her visit was an unwarranted provocation. Instead she insisted she was simply making "an unequivocal statement that America stands with Taiwan, our democratic partner, as it defends herself and its freedom."[1] And she told Taiwan's president, Tsai Ing-wen, her visit was designed "to make unequivocally clear that we will not abandon Taiwan."[2]

What Pelosi did not explicitly mention, however, was how important Taiwan's semiconductor industry has become to the United States and to other countries, feeding a global industry valued at more than $500 billion annually.[3] Whether in kitchens, cars, offices, transportation systems, communication networks, or complex military capabilities, almost anything powered by electricity now increasingly depends on microchips. The Semiconductor Industry Association reports that global semiconductor sales in 2021 were $556 billion, a record high, and that sales in China were $193 billion, a 27 percent increase over the previous year. As a result, China is now the world's largest consumer of semiconductors, many of which find their way into products for global export. Others also become critical components in weapons systems deployed by China's rapidly expanding military.

As with the rest of the world, the United States has become deeply dependent on foreign production processes to fabricate these chips. The United States once led the world in both the design and fabrication of microchips, producing 37 percent of the global supply in 1999. Now, however, while most leading-edge logic chips, such as those featuring lithography smaller than 16nm, are still designed in the United States, the percentage of chips actually fabricated in the United States has slid to 12 percent.[4]

In fact, no country now has a completely autonomous chip supply chain. Instead, each national production cycle now involves an extremely complex, multinational collaboration. Software tools and design are largely done in the United States. Extremely sophisticated manufacturing tools, such as lithography machines, are mainly produced in the United States, the Netherlands, and Japan. Manufacturing and packaging are centered in Taiwan and Korea. Testing is largely done in China and Southeast Asia, and the assembly of finished devices is predominantly centered in China, along with some recent migration to Vietnam and India. One industry executive told our working group that the inputs and components of a typical finished chip may involve hundreds of national border crossings.

With the United States now accounting for only 4 percent of global fabrication of memory chips, it is highly dependent on other nations such as South Korea, home to Samsung and SK hynix.[5] Meanwhile, Taiwan's ultramodern and well-run foundry system has enabled the island to produce more than 90 percent of the world's leading-edge logic chips and more than 20 percent of its legacy chips,[6] which together contribute almost 40 percent of the world's added increment of computing power each year.[7]

China's leaders have, over the past two decades, increasingly pursued greater self-sufficiency in key technologies including semiconductors. The Indigenous Innovation initiative of 2005 eventually led to the "Made in China 2025 Green Paper on Technological Innovation in Key Areas: Technology Roadmap," which came out in 2015 and was updated two years later. It highlights the urgency of supporting "national champion" firms to help China secure the technologies it needs at home and to compete more robustly abroad.[8]

The year before, the Chinese government's National Integrated Circuit Plan called on China's domestic semiconductor industry to expand capacity, so China could onshore 70 percent of its semiconductor needs by 2025 and reach design and production parity with foreign chip companies by 2030.[9] A report issued by the US Trade Representative (USTR) described the strategy as "creating a closed loop semiconductor manufacturing ecosystem with self-sufficiency at every stage of the manufacturing process—from integrated circuit (IC) design and manufacturing to packaging and testing, and the production of related materials and equipment."[10]

Ever since, President and Chinese Communist Party (CCP) General Secretary Xi Jinping has urged Chinese researchers, state enterprises, and private entrepreneurs to strive for greater chip independence, as part of his goal of "rejuvenating" China.[11] "We must take the technology lifeline in our own hands," he declared in June of 2022 while visiting a Wuhan semiconductor plant.[12]

To attain this goal, Xi's government has made an estimated $180 billion[13] available to People's Republic of China (PRC) companies, including Semiconductor Manufacturing International Corp. (SMIC), Yangtze Memory Technologies Co. (YMTC), and Huawei's HiSilicon. Fifty billion dollars came through China's National Integrated Circuit

Industry Investment Fund,[14] which became known as the "Big Fund" after its launch in 2014.[15] Success was mixed. Tens of billions of dollars flowed through the ill-fated Tsinghua Unigroup, which went heavily into debt and faced bankruptcy.[16] Other high-profile fund-backed startups landed their executives in jail for corruption.[17] Yet, tens of thousands of domestic semiconductor firms have been created across every step of the supply chain. Despite such efforts, some industry analysts predict that China will remain dependent on foreign firms for more than half of its semiconductor supply until at least 2026. Indeed, China must import hundreds of billions of dollars' worth of chips each year, with it spending twice as much on semiconductors as it spent importing oil in 2020.[18]

Meanwhile, Taiwan firms TSMC and United Microelectronics Corporation (UMC), along with South Korea's Samsung, continue to dominate the fab sector, with TSMC the clear global leader in making the most-advanced chips.[19] As of 2022, TSMC alone accounted for 54 percent of the global contract-foundry market, in which chips are produced to meet client designs,[20] with record revenues of $76 billion, up 42.6 percent from the previous year.[21]

The irony is that both the United States and China have long depended on Taiwan's semiconductor fabrication capabilities. Even in an era of increased US-China tensions, they remain each other's biggest customers, as well as their biggest competitors and threats.[22]

Many iconic US brands are still deeply dependent on China's domestic market and businesses for parts and labor. For example, because of China's superior supply lines and low costs, Apple continues to embrace complex manufacturing and assembly in China, with its iPhones and iPads mainly assembled in massive factories in mainland China—although by Taiwan companies such as Foxconn and Pegatron and powered by TSMC's chips from Taiwan. Some 90 percent of iPhones, iPads, and Macs are made in China, with China-based component suppliers now outnumbering those from Taiwan.[23]

While it is true that Apple has started to diversify, opening factories in India and Vietnam, a full disengagement from China's efficient supply chains, should one be sought, will take a long time.

The End of the Beginning

As China has ramped up military operations in disputed maritime areas over which it claims sovereignty, officials in the Obama, Trump, and Biden administrations have all focused on how to preserve stability in the Indo-Pacific. They have also pondered how they might begin to economically disentangle the United States from China, to reduce China's geopolitical leverage over the United States in a potential conflict scenario, and to mitigate economic damages should a conflict occur.

In August 2022, President Biden signed the game-changing bipartisan CHIPS and Science Act of 2022, pumping $52.7 billion into the US semiconductor industry to encourage the construction of new fabs and to support research and development within the United States.[24] At the time, Intel's CEO Patrick Gelsinger, whose firm stood to benefit handsomely from the bill's subsidies, proclaimed the legislation "the most important piece of industrial policy since the Second World War."[25]

Building on that momentum, TSMC announced in December 2022 that in addition to its semiconductor "Fab 21," which it was already building in Arizona to begin production of 4–5nm chips in 2024, it would start construction on a second fab, scheduled to begin production of leading-edge 3nm chips in 2026. TSMC said its overall investment in these two fabs would be about $40 billion, one of the largest foreign direct investments in US history. To mark the importance of this investment, President Biden flew to Phoenix for the fab's tool-in ceremony.[26]

In other efforts to build semiconductor capacity within the United States, thirty-five private companies have announced plans to invest another $200 billion in US-based chip research and manufacturing facilities.[27] And more than twenty other corporate[28] commitments have been made to locate new chip facilities across sixteen US states.[29]

Meanwhile, the Biden administration has moved to limit the sale of key US chip technologies to China, particularly for chips that could be useful for military purposes. These export controls both restrict the ability of China's chip manufacturers to use US chipmaking equipment in their most-advanced fabs and make it difficult for China's fabless chip designers to have their most advanced products made at TSMC in Taiwan.[30] (A "fabless" company is one that designs its own microchips but, rather than owning its own factory, contracts out their production.)

Then, in December 2022, the US Department of Commerce put an additional thirty-six China-based semiconductor companies on its "Entity List." Those on this list are required to apply for special licenses to buy US-made technologies. Commerce has also applied the more stringent "foreign direct product rule" to twenty-one other entities in China, prohibiting even third parties, such as companies in other countries, from exporting US physical or intellectual property to China. Against this background, Apple quietly shelved plans to buy memory chips from Yangtze Memory Technologies Co.,[31] causing Beijing to protest that the United States was attempting to impose a "technological blockade" on China.[32]

The win-win promise of globalization—which encouraged governments to embrace cross-national supply chains that provide quality, low prices, and fast delivery without fully considering possible geopolitical risks—is now ending. So too is the US policy of "engagement," which had assumed that if China and the United States embraced each other through more trade, civil society interactions, and scientific and cultural exchanges, China would eventually become more open so that political differences become less disturbing. Engagement and globalization were win-win visions that promised a peaceful pathway forward, not only for the United States and China, but also for Taiwan and the world. But as the advent of "Xi Jinping Thought on Socialism with Chinese Characteristics for a New Era"[33] ushered in a far more antagonistic relationship with the United States and its allies, those pathways were foreclosed.

In his speeches and writings, Xi often describes a vision of a peaceful and harmonious world. However, it's one in which China is at the center and strategically positions itself by creating political leverage through trade, investments, and diplomacy. And it includes such efforts as Xi's very personalized global Belt and Road Initiative that has seen China give almost $1 trillion in loans to build infrastructure, but also promote China's technologies, engineering, and excess commodities, as well as its preferred rules and standards.

All this is part of President Xi Jinping's grandiose effort to attain what he has called the "China Dream," not only to make China prosperous at home and powerful throughout the world, but also to compel Taiwan to become a legal, internationally recognized part of the People's Republic of China, under the direct control of the Chinese Communist Party. In attempting to make such a forced marriage more palatable to Taiwanese, China's leaders have, over the years, floated the idea that the island could enjoy a "One Country, Two Systems" deal, like the one Hong Kong was granted when it reverted from UK to Chinese control in 1997. However, after the PRC's recent crackdown on free speech and assembly in Hong Kong, few Taiwanese now have much confidence in such a formula.

With China now facing a slowing economy and a contracting workforce and population, Xi may see a finite and closing window in which to achieve the goal of bringing Taiwan into "the embrace of the motherland" before the PRC's hundredth anniversary in 2049.

Speculation has increased about whether and under what circumstances Xi would order China's military to enforce China's claim over Taiwan. The global blowback would be fierce. But Xi has said that "no one should underestimate the Chinese people's staunch determination, firm will, and strong ability to defend national sovereignty and territorial integrity" because "the historical task of the complete reunification of the motherland must be fulfilled, and will definitely be fulfilled."[34]

The Taiwanese people are hardly receptive to such a future. An overwhelming majority of them prefer a maintenance of the status quo that allows Taiwan to remain a self-governing, robust democracy that enthusiastically embraces freedom of speech and assembly. Should the People's Liberation Army move against Taiwan, they will confront an enormous challenge when they try to put boots on the ground, and a far greater challenge to ever win the hearts, minds, and allegiance of the Taiwanese people.

The United States and China are at inflection points where the policy verities of the past—such as "engagement," "win-win," and "peaceful evolution"—no longer satisfy. As Morris Chang bluntly observed in his tool-in speech at TSMC's new Arizona plant, "Globalization is *almost* dead and free trade is *almost* dead."[35] The question is, What will replace them?

Uneasy Questions

How can the United States and its global partners manage the increasingly tense and consequential triangular US-China-Taiwan relationship, in which global supply chains and a vibrant democracy hang in the balance and military conflict is an increasingly real possibility?

As part of our working group's assessment of this question, we embarked on a multimonth strategic scenario-planning exercise that tested assumptions and provoked robust discussion about the implications of plausible futures, each playing out over a ten-year period. To create four distinctly different futures, we considered different combinations of two variables: whether global trade would remain open or become balkanized, and whether global leadership in critical technologies would come from China or from the United States and its allies.

Scenario planning helps participants understand the risks, opportunities, and other implications of different kinds of futures, while recognizing that actual events may play out in ways that move from one scenario to another, or bring in elements of several. The purpose is to actively think early on in that evolution about strategies that improve the odds of protecting one's interests and achieving one's goals. In this case, our working group considered America's interests in the US-Taiwan-China "Silicon Triangle."

Thus far, we are seeing coalescence of a world in which goods, technologies, intellectual property (IP), services, people, and capital are increasingly flowing *within* voluntary networks of like-minded nations—and less so *across* the two gathering US/China blocs. A key question we considered is: How can the United States and its like-minded partners take advantage of this shift from the "flat," rapidly globalizing world of the 1990s to one in which economic relationships are increasingly informed by strategic interests?

Our scenario work suggests that the relative attractiveness of each network—and therefore its broader economic performance, growth, and prosperity—will be shaped by the strength and sophistication of its systems and technologies, particularly of emerging critical technologies like semiconductors. The separation between commercial and security considerations is becoming murkier.

But many questions remained. For example, do Taiwan's fabs provide a "silicon shield" that makes it less likely China will attack the island? Or do they make an attack more likely because the PRC may believe that if it can take control of them, not only will China benefit from Taiwan's technical prowess, but at the same time this resource will be denied to the West? Our working group's participants did not generally accept that Taiwan's chip industry provides a meaningful "silicon shield" for Taiwan. Instead, our sense is that in assessing the risks and possible costs of an invasion, China's leaders will make their own calculations, based on goals and leadership imperatives that will go far beyond semiconductors.

As US-China trade continues, Treasury Secretary Janet Yellen stated in April 2023 that the United States seeks a "constructive and fair economic relationship with China" and that China's economic growth "need not be incompatible with US economic leadership." Nonetheless, the Biden administration has also launched policies and initiatives "to ensure that emerging technologies work for, not against, our democracies and security," as National Security Advisor Jake Sullivan said in prepared remarks at a White House briefing in September 2022.[36]

The US government has, for security reasons, already restricted the ability of US or partner firms to supply technologies to China's Huawei and ZTE given their use in establishing 5G telecom systems around the world. So, a question for our working group was: Should Washington for security reasons ban the sale of US design and manufacturing technologies that would enable China's semiconductor firms to supply its military or to displace Western firms by establishing significant global market shares?

There was disagreement on this. Many industry executives from the United States and Taiwan, as well as those in Japan, Korea, and Europe, argue that it makes good sense to continue selling technologies and manufacturing equipment for older legacy chips (in the higher nanometer range), and to block only leading-edge chips (in the lower nanometer range). Many others insist that Washington should thwart the development of China's entire chip industry lest we feed a critical, enabling industry in a country with whom conflict is no longer unthinkable.

And, already, there is some movement in the latter direction in Washington. In December 2022, the UK chip group Arm, owned by Japan's Softbank, denied China's Alibaba use of its Neoverse V-series chip because its high performance capacity was developed by the United States.[37] And when US National Security Advisor Jake Sullivan addressed the question of export controls in a late 2022 speech, he said, "We have to revisit the long-standing premise of maintaining 'relative' advantages over competitors in certain key technologies. We previously maintained a 'sliding scale' approach that said we need to stay only a couple of generations ahead. That is not the strategic environment we are in today. Given the foundational nature of certain technologies, such as advanced-logic and memory chips, we must maintain as large of a lead as possible."[38]

Financial Times columnist Edward Luce commented in October 2022 that it was beginning to seem as if "America was now pledged to do everything short of fighting an actual war to stop China's rise."[39] A few months later, in January 2023, he wrote: "The uncertainty is no longer about whether the US-China decoupling will happen, but how far it will go. Whatever its pace over the present year, the US-China relationship is heading in an ominous direction. Businesses, countries, regions and the world are only just starting to grapple with the potential consequences."[40]

Unless China, the United States, and Taiwan find some significant new accommodation, the trend lines do not look good—either for maintaining existing microchip supply chains or for generating enough self-sufficiency for any party to stand alone.

So, given this contradiction, what is to be done? If maintaining the current global microchip ecosystem is uncertain or impossible, governments and companies alike must formulate consistent and collaborative new rules to guide them in realigning a new global industry supply chain order. Most would, of course, prefer to maintain, or perhaps modify, the current system rather than see it completely dismantled, whether by design or by conflict. But sustaining this status quo appears increasingly out of reach, with radical change already under way. Policy choices, economic subsidies, hedging opportunities, and geopolitical realignments are all a part of the current dialogue, many occurring in an uncoordinated fashion.

The balance between national security and free markets is a matter of sensitivity and judgment, and our working group does not have a unanimous view on this matter. But this shift has profound implications for relations among US partners, and for the task of domestic governance. And these implications have not yet been fully appreciated in semiconductors or in other critical sectors where principles of economic freedom and national security intersect.

Deterrence

There are two lenses through which the United States must look at the broader problem. The first allows us to judge which policies best protect our technological competitiveness and the global supply chain of microchips. The second allows us to judge which policies best protect Taiwan's people, their autonomy, and their liberal democracy from the PRC's ambition to directly govern and control Taiwan. While these two imperatives are not in conflict, they are also not coterminous. The best preemptive policy for attaining both goals is developing an effective deterrence strategy that will discourage and, if necessary, prevent the PRC from taking military action to make China's long-standing claims of sovereignty over Taiwan a physical reality.

The former secretary general of NATO, Anders Fogh Rasmussen, described the strategy this way: "Deterring an attack by China relies on the credible belief that any invasion would come at an immense cost. . . . So spelling out the consequences of an attack in advance can act as a powerful deterrent." And, he added, "To be an effective deterrent, we should give Taiwan the weapons it needs to defend itself now. Xi Jinping must calculate that the cost of an invasion is simply too high. . . . The best way to preserve peace is to make clear you are ready to go to war."[41]

At stake is not just the world's largest traded industry—and, moreover, Taiwan's democracy.[42] A US-China conflict in the Taiwan Strait would implicate the entire Indo-Pacific, with stakes so high that they are difficult to even imagine. Still, the implications must be considered, debated, and ultimately acted upon.

•   •   •

Each chapter in this report reflects the richness of experience and expertise brought by a group of interdisciplinary contributors. While their work stands on its own, our collective thinking is informed by group deliberation, argument, and joint education over the past year and a half as we have conferred with various business, security, and policy stakeholders in the United States and in Taiwan.

In chapter 1, former China correspondent Mary Kay Magistad, now with Asia Society's Center on US-China Relations, draws from our scenario-planning exercise to examine four scenarios that may play out over the next decade, and the driving forces that underpin them, which are referenced throughout the rest of the report.

Chapter 2 takes a deep dive into the current structure of the global semiconductor industry, and underlying trends of how the core technologies are progressing. Authors H.-S. Philip Wong and Jim Plummer, Stanford professors of electrical engineering and leading technical experts on semiconductors, describe this industry as extremely dynamic and fast moving, which has implications for what policy can and cannot reasonably expect to accomplish in this space.

Chapter 3, written by international security scholar and former arms control negotiator Christopher Ford, focuses on resilience measures the United States should take, given its current reliance on fragile global semiconductor supply chains. Ford looks at measures that could reduce the cost of doing business, improve supply chain information and analysis capabilities, and provide incentives for stockpiling and/or extended inventory management.

In chapter 4, physicist and risk capital investor Edlyn V. Levine and longtime semiconductor industry leader Don Rosenberg argue that the United States should pursue security- and market-oriented industrial policy measures that are mindful of the interests of US partners. They propose a long-term US global technological competitiveness strategy that also includes building a voluntary network of like-minded nations, with US leadership in critical technologies such as semiconductors attracting participation by other countries and contributing to collective prosperity.

Chapter 5 focuses on the importance of protecting Taiwan's stability, prosperity, and democracy. Taiwan specialist Kharis Templeman and China military scholar Oriana Skylar Mastro describe how Taiwan became a trusted partner in critical supply chains despite its broader political isolation from the international community, and they offer ways in which a shared interest in semiconductors provides a rich platform for further US-Taiwan business-to-business, people-to-people, and policy exchange. They argue that deepening these relationships enhances deterrence toward those who would seek to challenge Taiwan's stability.

In chapter 6, organizational economists and global supply chain experts David J. Teece and Greg Linden explore the relative strengths and ambitions of potential global partners for the United States in the effort to ensure that US imports of semiconductors and key inputs in the supply chain come from reliable, ideologically compatible trading partners, such as the current foreign industry leaders Taiwan, Korea, and Japan, and new entrants such as India.

In chapter 7, Indo-Pacific security scholar and former deputy national security advisor Matthew Pottinger asks what the United States and its allies and partners could achieve together through a strategy that not only seeks mutual economic gains, but also recognizes the potential strategic role of critical-technology supply chains as a tool to deter China's leadership from using force or coercion to achieve its geopolitical goals.

Chapter 8, written by historian and analyst of modern China Glenn Tiffert, looks at China's historic efforts to build its semiconductor sector, and its progress to date. He examines why China remains in a relatively weak position as a semiconductor manufacturer, despite significant efforts to emerge as a global leader in this sector.

In chapter 9, US-China policy experts Robert Daly and Matthew Turpin examine how anticompetitive behavior by semiconductor firms in China could unfairly harm those of the United States or its partners—for example, in the production of legacy chips. The authors point to ways to mitigate the risk of new dependencies on China-based chip supply chains, and thus avoid compromising future US strategic autonomy.

The concluding chapter presents our policy recommendations in five areas: US domestic resilience, the US business environment, long-term US technological competitiveness, Taiwan's stability, and dealing with China. Generally, these policy recommendations derive from the preceding chapters, which were drafted by the individual authors in consideration of our collective deliberations. But the recommendations have been extensively discussed and debated by the members of the working group, and unless otherwise noted, they represent the broad consensus of the group. As the project leaders and editors of this report, we have acted as the final arbiters and synthesizers of these recommendations.

NOTES

1. Nancy Pelosi, "Why I'm Leading a Congressional Delegation to Taiwan," *Washington Post*, August 2, 2022.
2. Yimou Lee and Sarah Wu, "Pelosi Lauds Taiwan, Says China's Fury Cannot Stop Visits by World Leaders," Reuters, August 3, 2022.
3. Suranjana Tewari, "US-China Chip War: America Is Winning," *BBC News*, January 13, 2023.
4. Gillian Tett, "The Semiconductor Chip Pendulum Is Slowly Swinging West," *Financial Times*, July 21, 2022.
5. Don Clark and Ana Swanson, "US Pours Money into Chips, but Even Soaring Spending Has Limits," *New York Times*, January 1, 2023.
6. Clark and Swanson, "US Pours Money."
7. Chris Miller, *Chip War: The Fight for the World's Most Critical Technology* (New York: Scribner, 2022), xxv.

8. Chinese Academy of Engineering, "Made in China 2025 Green Paper on Technological Innovation in Key Areas: Technology Roadmap," September 29, 2015 (2015 version as translated and archived by the Center for Security and Emerging Technology).

9. Dan Kim and John VerWey, "The Potential Impacts of the Made in China 2025 Roadmap on the Integrated Circuit Industries in the US, EU and Japan" (Washington, DC: Office of Industries Working Paper ID-061, August 2019). For the plan, see State Council of the PRC, "Guideline for the Promotion of the Development of the National Integrated Circuit Industry," June 24, 2014 (in Chinese).

10. Office of the United States Trade Representative, 2017 Special 301 Report (Washington, DC: USTR, 2017), 113.

11. Li Yuan, "Xi Jinping's Vision for Tech Self-Reliance in China Runs into Reality," *New York Times*, August 29, 2022.

12. Yuan, "Xi Jinping's Vision."

13. *Wall Street Journal*, "US vs. China: The Race to Develop the Most Advanced Chips," January 11, 2023.

14. Eduardo Jaramillo, "After a Year of Corruption Scandals, China's National Chip Fund Forges Ahead," *China Project*, January 4, 2023.

15. Brent Crane, "The Semiconductor Madman," *The Wire: China*, January 8, 2023.

16. Crane, "Semiconductor Madman."

17. Edward White and Qianer Liu, "China's Big Fund Corruption Probe Casts Shadow over Chip Sector," *Financial Times*, September 28, 2022; and Yuan, "Xi Jinping's Vision."

18. Richard Cronin, "Semiconductors and Taiwan's 'Silicon Shield': A Wild Card in US-China Technological and Geopolitical Competition," Stimson, August 16, 2022.

19. Jung Song, "Samsung Seeks to Reassure Markets over Semiconductor Competitiveness," *Financial Times*, July 30, 2022.

20. *Wall Street Journal*, "US vs. China."

21. Jeff Su, "4Q 2022 Quarterly Management Report," TSMC Investor Relations Division, January 12, 2023.

22. Andrew Hill, "The Great Chip War—and the Challenge for Global Diplomacy," review of *Chip War: The Fight for the World's Most Critical Technology*, by Chris Miller, *Financial Times*, December 12, 2022.

23. Cheng Ting-Fang and Lauly Li, "China Ousts Taiwan as Apple's Biggest Source of Suppliers," *Nikkei Asia*, June 2, 2021.

24. The White House, "FACT SHEET: CHIPS and Science Act Will Lower Costs, Create Jobs, Strengthen Supply Chains, and Counter China," August 9, 2022.

25. Richard Waters, "Chipmakers Battle for Slice of US Government Support," *Financial Times*, August 3, 2022.

26. Katherine Hille, "TSMC Triples Arizona Chip Investment to $40bn," *Financial Times*, December 7, 2022.

27. Clark and Swanson, "US Pours Money."

28. Demetri Sevastopulo, Kathrin Hille, and Qianer Liu, "US Adds 36 Chinese Companies to Trade Blacklist," *Financial Times*, December 15, 2022.

29. Clark and Swanson, "US Pours Money."

30. Bloomberg, "TSMC Halts Work for China Firm," *Taipei Times*, October 24, 2022.

31. Siu Han and Willis Ke, "Apple Reportedly to Have Samsung Replace YMTC for iPhone-Use NAND Flash Supply in 2023," *DIGITIMES Asia*, November 21, 2022.

32. Edward White and Kana Inakagi, "China Starts 'Surgical' Retaliation against Foreign Companies after US-led Tech Blockade," *Financial Times*, April 16, 2023.

33. Chris Buckley, "Xi Jinping Thought Explained: A New Ideology for a New Era," *New York Times*, February 26, 2018.

34. Vincent Ni, "Xi Jinping Vows to Fulfil Taiwan 'Reunification' with China by Peaceful Means," *The Guardian*, October 9, 2021.

35. Cheng Ting-Fang, "TSMC Founder Morris Chang Says Globalization 'Almost Dead,'" *Nikkei Asia*, December 7, 2022 (emphasis added).

36. The White House, "Remarks by National Security Advisor Jake Sullivan at the Special Competitive Studies Project Global Emerging Technologies Summit," September 16, 2022.

37. Qianer Liu, Anna Gross, and Demetri Sevastopulo, "Export Controls Hit China's Access to Arm's Leading-Edge Chip Designs," *Financial Times*, December 13, 2022.

38. Jake Sullivan, "Remarks by National Security Advisor Jake Sullivan at the Special Competitive Studies Project Global Emerging Technologies Summit," The White House, September 16, 2022.

39. Edward Luce, "Containing China Is Biden's Explicit Goal," *Financial Times*, October 19, 2022.

40. Edward Luce, "US-China Relations Pursue an Ominous Path," *Financial Times*, January 17, 2023.

41. Anders Fogh Rasmussen, "Taiwan Must Not Suffer the Same Fate as Ukraine," *Financial Times*, January 12, 2023.

42. Hermann-P. Rapp and Jochen Möbert, "Semiconductors or Petroleum—Which Is Traded Most?," Deutsche Bank Research, Germany Monitor, November 23, 2022.

CHAPTER ONE

Scenarios for Future US-China Competition

MARY KAY MAGISTAD

Forming a strategy on semiconductors depends on one's expectations about the future nature of US-China relations, the motivations of other global participants in critical supply chains within that context, and Taiwan's own environment. Today's analysts—including those among our working group—unsurprisingly hold different expectations about how these futures will unfold.

We therefore begin our analysis by creating a scenario-planning framework to consider what the key drivers of the US-China-Taiwan relationship may be over the next decade—and the different futures they may yield. In particular, we focus on the impact of (a) global trade decisions and (b) the locus of leadership in critical technologies.

This chapter describes four resulting scenarios for the United States', China's, and Taiwan's roles in the world—some appealing, and some less so—and the implications of those potential futures for (1) what the United States should do to reduce current vulnerabilities to semiconductor supply chain disruptions; (2) how that can be done in a way that promotes stability in the Taiwan Strait; and, in doing so, (3) guard against new vulnerabilities as China further develops its own semiconductor industry. A key lesson is that if we look to be heading toward one of those worlds, we can take tailored policy steps to improve our security and our prosperity within it—or we can shape the drivers of that future to avoid it altogether.

• • •

Many of the most consequential shifts in recent decades have defied assumptions and expectations. From the fall of the Berlin Wall and the "end of history" to the more recent global resurgence of authoritarianism accented by the first major war in Europe in seventy years, conventional wisdom has sometimes proven to be too conventional and not nearly wise enough. That has certainly been true in relation to China's transformation of its economy and its role in the world, from the dawn of Deng Xiaoping's era of "reform and opening up," through China's rapid economic and political rise, to Xi Jinping's tighter control at home and pursuit of greater wealth, power, and influence abroad.

Today's observers can reasonably hold quite different expectations about the future of US-China relations, the reordering of global trade and technology leadership, the status of Taiwan, and the future of the liberal international order.

In global trade and technology, semiconductors now play a pivotal role. US policy makers increasingly recognize the need for a reliable and resilient supply chain of semiconductors for the United States and its partners.

Most semiconductors are now fabricated in East Asia, with almost all leading-edge semiconductors fabricated by Taiwan Semiconductor Manufacturing Company (TSMC) in Taiwan. China has, in recent years, become more aggressive in asserting its claims of sovereignty over Taiwan—just when China, like the United States, needs the kind of leading-edge semiconductors TSMC makes, but has not yet developed the capability to make them domestically.

In the face of all this, prudent planning requires not just deterrence against aggressive action from China but also a collaborative strategy for a more robust and resilient global semiconductor supply chain. Such planning also requires consideration of how key variables may play out in the near term. Our working group scenario team has used a timeline of ten years to consider how alternative futures could affect global semiconductor supply chains.

Scenario planning requires contemplating what is plausible, not making hard predictions about what "will" happen. Our participants identified critical uncertainties and then imagined futures in which different combinations of those variables may shape different—even opposite— possible futures. The group then considered the actionable implications in each scenario. This process was done with the recognition that the *actual* future may include elements of some or all of the imagined scenarios, or may move from one scenario to another. The point was to think and prepare in a way that optimizes the outcome for each scenario while also identifying actions that may be common to more than one.

Scenario planning has been used by organizations, companies, and governments for over forty years, enabling them to remain open-minded and to hedge against risks. The technique was pioneered by Shell Oil and made prominent by the Global Business Network's founders Stewart Brand, Napier Collyns, Jay Ogilvy, Peter Schwartz, and Lawrence Wilkinson.

Wilkinson himself led this report's working group through a scenario-planning deep dive. We aimed to develop answers to our key questions, with related implications, and then to produce a set of recommendations that would be effective in all the futures we thought were plausible.

To do this, a small subgroup composed of retired senior military officers, China specialists, economists, semiconductor specialists, strategists, and others met regularly over three months in 2022, reporting back regularly to the larger group. This subgroup thought about the forces that could influence how we answer three main strategic questions:

1. What should the United States do in the near term to reduce current vulnerabilities to semiconductor supply chain disruptions, and over time to create more assured and durable access to the types of semiconductors needed, when they are needed?
2. How can this be done in a way that preserves Taiwan's current self-governing status, underpins its prosperity and innovative vitality, and promotes stability in the Taiwan Strait?
3. How can the United States and its allies guard against new vulnerabilities as China further develops its own semiconductor industry, and anticipate the next strategically important technology industry competition?

To imagine different plausible futures, our full working group of over two dozen experts came up with more than two hundred driving forces that could shape the next decade. Our scenarios subgroup narrowed the list down to forty driving forces and then, finally, down to just two driving forces, considered by the subgroup to be the most relevant to the three main strategic questions. These are shown in figure 1.1.

1. *Global Economy:* Whether the global economy becomes more integrated and "flat" or more hived up into blocs.

2. *Technology and Innovation:* Whether the United States continues to lead in technology in general, and semiconductors in particular, or China takes the lead.

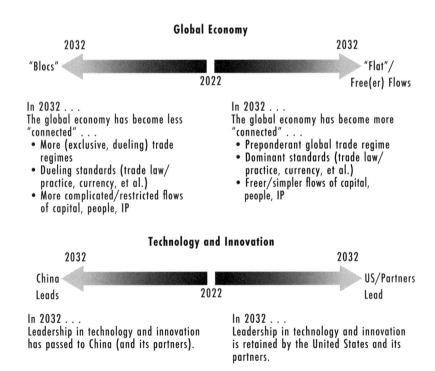

Global Economy

2032   2032

"Blocs"   "Flat"/
                                    2022   Free(er) Flows

In 2032 . . .   In 2032 . . .
The global economy has become less   The global economy has become more
"connected" . . .   "connected" . . .
• More (exclusive, dueling) trade   • Preponderant global trade regime
  regimes   • Dominant standards (trade law/
• Dueling standards (trade law/   practice, currency, et al.)
  practice, currency, et al.)   • Freer/simpler flows of capital,
• More complicated/restricted flows   people, IP
  of capital, people, IP

Technology and Innovation

2032   2032

China   US/Partners
Leads   2022   Lead

In 2032 . . .   In 2032 . . .
Leadership in technology and innovation Leadership in technology and innovation
has passed to China (and its partners). is retained by the United States and its
                                         partners.

Figure 1.1. Scenario Logics

The two chosen variables can be visually presented as a four-quadrant grid, as shown in figure 1.2, in which each quadrant represents a distinctly different future.

Each of these futures pushes as far as we can plausibly go in our ten-year time frame, and each uses "outside-in" thinking—that is, understanding external dynamics and drivers that might affect the issues at hand. This approach illustrates the range of challenges and opportunities the United States and its allies might face, given the variables we chose.

Scenario planning can help decision makers think in advance about what they would do if they saw early signs indicating movement in a particular direction, and what that direction means for their interests. It may signal that they should seize opportunities or take defensive action. Some actions and strategies are "robust"—ones that make sense in any of the imagined plausible futures. Others are "contingent"—beneficial in some futures, harmful in others.

Early in this process, subgroup participants were asked to think back to what the world looked like a decade ago, and to share what they were sure would happen that didn't and what did happen that surprised them. Everyone had something to contribute on both counts. And, of course, the same is likely to manifest in the next decade as well.

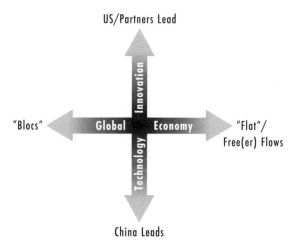

Figure 1.2. Scenario Logics Applied to Two Axes

The world may become more multipolar and multialigned. New players may arise in the technology space in general, and in the semiconductor sector in particular. Whatever happens, the scenarios we created can be updated and adjusted as the future unfolds, allowing implications to evolve that can better inform strategy in a changing environment.

Driving Forces

The following driving forces are what our scenario team felt could most likely impact US-Taiwan-China relations, especially pertaining to semiconductors, over the next decade. The forces below are listed in rough order from most to least influential, according to the scenario team:

1. War or other disruptive conflict or action

In a large-scale conflict involving Taiwan, semiconductor manufacturing, along with a variety of other industries, would be catastrophically disrupted, and the US economy would suffer negative downstream effects. More limited hostile actions, such as a cyberattack on TSMC, would have similar effects.[1] Other conflicts in the region or beyond could have downstream effects on the global semiconductor industry, such as sanctions against an aggressor.

2. Degree of policy coordination among the United States, Europe, and Asia on security and economic competition with China

The United States is increasingly coordinating with its partners to compete with China. Such efforts include the Quadrilateral Security Dialogue ("Quad") among the United States, Japan, Australia, and India; the AUKUS security pact among the United States, United Kingdom, and Australia; the G7's "Build Back Better World" (B3W) developing world infrastructure financing initiative[2]; the EU-US Trade and Technology Council (TTC), and other efforts at EU-US strategic cooperation[3]; the Clean Network initiative for safeguarding communications and network traffic from People's Republic of China (PRC) vendors such as Huawei[4]; and the Chip 4 Alliance of the United States,

Japan, South Korea, and Taiwan. Most recently, the US CHIPS and Science Act has codified dozens of incentives, subsidies, restrictions, and new or expanded partnerships.

3. Rate of technological progress in strategic sectors

A dozen key advanced technologies relevant to US national security are detailed in the National Science and Technology Council's February 2022 update of its Critical and Emerging Technologies List.[5]

4. TSMC's degree of regional diversification of production

Most of TSMC's manufacturing sites ("fabs") are currently in Taiwan, with two smaller fabs in China and one in the United States (Camas, Washington). TSMC is in the process of building two advanced-logic fabs in Arizona,[6] and another fab in Japan through a joint venture with Sony.[7]

5. Use of public policy tools to increase research and development (R&D) spending and innovation on semiconductors in the US private sector

The CHIPS and Science Act of 2022 offers $39 billion in federal subsidies for semiconductor foundry construction, including loan guarantees and a federal-to-state or local subsidy match program; in addition, it creates a 25 percent investment tax credit for semiconductor manufacturing facilities and equipment. Further, the CHIPS Act appropriates significant new R&D funding through the Department of Commerce—$11 billion—for novel public-private R&D programs including a National Semiconductor Technology Center and a Manufacturing USA Semiconductor Institute, plus a federal National Advanced Packaging Manufacturing Program.

6. Choices on sales destinations made by semiconductor manufacturing equipment vendors, or their host governments, such as the Dutch company Advanced Semiconductor Materials Lithography (ASML)

ASML's extreme ultraviolet (EUV) lithography machines are a critical piece of the advanced-semiconductor manufacturing process, because they are used to etch integrated circuit designs into silicon wafers at the smallest scales. ASML, Canon, Nikon, and others produce deep ultraviolet (DUV) lithography machines to make chips one or two generations behind the leading edge.[8] A decision by ASML, other equipment firms, or their governments to refuse selling to China—or to other countries willing to sell to China—would limit China's ability to compete globally on this front.

7. Extent to which regionalization replaces globalization

Populist nationalism or the weakening of multilateral institutions such as the International Monetary Fund (IMF), World Bank, World Health Organization (WHO), or even the UN Security Council could contribute to greater regionalization. Trade barriers and restrictions on flows of people, capital, and intellectual property may lead multinationals to continue building regional supply chains that hedge against geopolitical risk, expanding on the trends begun during the COVID pandemic.[9]

8. Ability of China to create a semiconductor manufacturing firm that meets or surpasses TSMC's capabilities

Efforts by China's government to bolster semiconductor manufacturing capacity are expected to increase chip manufacturing market share in non-leading-edge semiconductors over the next decade. Far less certain, however, is whether China's Semiconductor Manufacturing International Corporation (SMIC) or another enterprise in China could catch up with or even surpass TSMC's dominance in making the most sophisticated chips (<7nm).[10]

9. Shifts in the Taiwanese populace's geopolitical stance

Polls show, and have shown for decades, that Taiwanese citizens prefer the status quo of de facto autonomy to either integrating with China or formally declaring independence, knowing the latter could trigger a PRC attack or invasion.[11] Polls also show that Taiwanese rate the United States more favorably than China by a two-to-one margin. That said, Taiwan's Democratic Progressive Party (DPP) has, since its founding in 1986, leaned more toward independence. The Kuomintang Party, which ruled mainland China from 1927 to 1949, then considered itself mainland China's government in exile until the early 1990s, has shown more interest over time in improving relations with the PRC, even exploring ways China and Taiwan might merge on terms in Taiwan's interests. Changes in the ruling party over time, or within party platforms, could yield unexpected consequences.

10. Degree of scientific literacy of US versus China population and leadership

Scientific literacy affects the quality of technology workforces as well as public attitudes toward policy. A Pew study suggests Americans' scientific literacy, while higher than China's, is not universal.[12] China's government is actively engaged in trying to increase scientific literacy among the general public.[13]

11. Quality of education and training in China to advance semiconductors and related technologies

Increasing innovation and technological advancement has been a high priority for Beijing for more than two decades. Semiconductors are a particular focus. China's government is investing heavily in education to expand its skilled workforce capable of advancing the semiconductor industry, a workforce that already increased from 512,000 employees in 2019 to 745,000 in 2022. See chapter 8 for more on China's semiconductor workforce.

12. Quality of education and training in the United States to advance semiconductors and related technologies

Expanding and improving the US STEM (science, technology, engineering, mathematics) workforce would enable the United States to more effectively compete globally in key technologies, including semiconductors. The CHIPS Act's provisions could help. See chapters 3 and 4 for additional discussion on US semiconductor workforce development.[14]

13. Degree of secular shift in semiconductor demand patterns

Semiconductor fabrication can boom or bust, prompting manufacturers to deploy capital conservatively even when faced with high levels of demand. Demand from new classes of technologies or consumer applications could change that pattern, mitigating risk.[15]

14. Degree of the United States' and its partners' reliance on China's supply chains for strategic "green" technologies

China has outsized influence over the global supply chain for green energy infrastructure such as electric vehicles and solar panels, as well as for rare earths and other critical minerals used in clean energy infrastructure, such as lithium for rechargeable batteries.[16] New dependence on China in one priority technology field may affect US leverage in another, such as semiconductors.

15. Level of and response to tariffs, sanctions, or export restrictions by Washington or Beijing

China's public diplomatic response to the US Department of Commerce's October 2022 semiconductor technology export controls—instituted during a sensitive time of domestic economic stagnation, brewing zero-COVID policy discontent, and the 20th National Congress of the Chinese Communist Party, during which General Secretary Xi was appointed to an unprecedented third term—was initially muted, with a focus on redoubled domestic semiconductor industry subsidy within China to accelerate efforts toward autonomy. It is possible, however, that future export controls could provoke broad retaliatory trade measures by Beijing against the United States, or punitive actions toward specific US firms.

16. Possibility of leadership change or struggles in China, causing a sudden change in direction of China's foreign policy

Some of China's biggest political changes were not ones outsiders, or even many Chinese citizens, saw coming. Among plausible futures are these:

- General Secretary Xi stays in power throughout the next decade and continues on the same course.

- Xi stays in power but changes course in ways that make potential global leadership from China more acceptable or even attractive to many countries.
- Xi is replaced by either a leader or group of leaders who want to return to the trajectory of the "reform opening-up" era, or by leaders as ambitious as, or more ambitious and aggressive than, Xi.

Our Scenarios

Our scenario planning yielded four plausible futures about how that challenge may play out over the next decade (figure 1.3). These four quadrants are formed by two axes, the vertical one representing technology and innovation and the horizontal one representing the global economy.

The right two quadrants—the "east," borrowing from the directions on a compass—are futures with a more open global economy and freer flows of trade and innovation. The left two quadrants—the "west"—are futures with blocs or networks largely trading with other participants within the same bloc. The western quadrants are more turbulent, the eastern ones more peaceful, though with different powers leading.

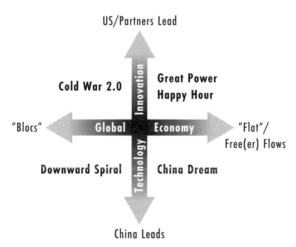

Figure 1.3. Our Scenarios Situated within Four Quadrants

The upper two quadrants—the "north"—are futures in which the United States and its allies lead in technology and innovation in strategically important spheres, including semiconductors. The lower two quadrants—the "south"—are futures in which China leads.

Again, the idea was not to make predictions, but to represent different plausible futures, recognizing that the actual future will likely be some mix of all of these scenarios, or may move from one of these scenarios to another.

Scenario No. 1 for 2032: "Cold War 2.0" (NW)

This is a future of trade blocs, perhaps dividing closed versus open societies, in which trading occurs especially within blocs. The two blocs here are led by the United States and China, though other networks may also emerge. Trade across blocs survives, but is more difficult and expensive. Nonaligned countries can trade with more than one network or shift among them, while protecting their own national interests as best they can.

The United States and its allies or close partners compete on their democratic and free-market values. China competes on its mercantilist willingness to trade with and invest in anyone, including via its Belt and Road Initiative (BRI) network. Neither China's leadership nor its approach has fundamentally changed from a decade earlier.

Geopolitical

US-China tensions increase as the two sides pull away from each other while maintaining a "war-readiness" footing. Fear of war in or around Taiwan or the South China Sea has risen, with US and regional concerns that China may try to take some islands or blockade Taiwan. China doesn't seize control of Taiwan, but does continue to act aggressively toward it. The United States, while still adhering to its "One China" policy, increasingly promotes Taiwan as a member of the international economic community.

Global institutions such as the United Nations and the World Trade Organization become sclerotic venues for episodic horse trading, after years of China increasing its influence in such organizations and insisting the now-China-dominated UN serve as a sort of "global government." In reaction, the United States and its allies rely increasingly on their own direct relationships with individual countries and with regional groupings, such as the Association of Southeast Asian Nations (ASEAN).

Global Trade/Investment

The United States and its allies continue rules-based trade, with economies that are "strong-ish"—healthy, but with increased defense spending. China doesn't accept many of those rules, and dueling standards and practices emerge. As the decade proceeds, nonaligned countries face growing pressure to choose sides.

China's economy is challenged, as some of its former top trading partners—the United States, the European Union, and Japan—have cut back their trade with China. China's trade with BRI partners does not make up the difference. China's digital RMB (renminbi/yuan) emerges as a clearing currency used within China's bloc, giving authoritarian governments a way to ease the bite of dollar-denominated sanctions imposed by the United States and its allies.

Technology and Semiconductors

The topography of the US and allied semiconductor industry has changed, with manufacturing and the supply chain more distributed and robust, as are the underlying applied R&D that sustains semiconductors' two- to three-year technology cycles. Taiwan remains important, but TSMC's semiconductor production is more geographically diversified.

The United States and its allies prioritize creating or enhancing industrial policies, STEM education from K–12 onward, and research and development. Immigration reform in the United States and among close partners welcomes students, researchers, engineers, scientists, and entrepreneurs from around the world to contribute to a strengthening international STEM ecosystem.

The United States and allies take steps to ensure access to raw materials and minerals needed for semiconductors and other critical technologies. China's state-led research and development efforts make some progress. But under increasingly centralized state control that squelches entrepreneurial energy and innovation, those efforts don't keep pace with the progress made by the United States and its partners. The United States and allies harden their defenses against intellectual property theft and espionage. China responds in kind, such as through international lawfare against US firms it accuses of incorporating China-origin technologies.

Scenario No. 2 for 2032: "Great-Power Happy Hour" (NE)

This future is a peaceful world marked by a return to a broadly integrated global economy and continued US and allied global leadership. That alliance is strengthened after the experience of coordinating sanctions against Russia in response to its invasion of Ukraine. Western liberal rules dominate, and the West keeps the tech lead—in part due to increased spending and focus on research and development and STEM education, especially related to semiconductors. The United States and its partners have created a robust semiconductor supply chain, and have an assured supply of semiconductors.

Geopolitical

The United States and its partners work well together, having overcome domestic divisions that had earlier impeded progress on policies. They now harmonize their individual national policies and share responsibilities on diplomatic, trade, and development policies. The United States listens more, is more involved, and is more inclusive. It still leads, but it wears its leadership mantle more lightly and acts like more of an equal partner. New partners, such as India, are integrated into this network, which is increasingly seen as more reliable and beneficial than any other.

Taiwan prospers, and its political status remains the same.

China stumbles. Global sentiment about China has turned more negative after years of its aggressive diplomacy and moves to support contentious territorial claims, and its approaches to trade and investment that prove to be far from the "win-win" that China promised. China may have new leadership, or Xi Jinping may have decided—or may have been forced—to curtail China's regional aggression and global ambitions.

US and allied defense spending remains robust, and extends to offering harder protections against espionage and intellectual property theft. But fewer military threats leads to funds being channeled into increased investment in education, industrial infrastructure, and the social safety net at home, as well as foreign investment and development aid abroad. These investments foster international goodwill and a desire to partner with the United States and its allies.

Global Trade/Investment

The United States and its allies' coordinated efforts reinvigorate a global investment and trading regime rooted in "Western" liberal values, and strengthen US and partner economies. These economies become a magnet for international investment and talented immigrants.

Taiwan prospers, enhancing its status as a globally important hub of innovation and leading-edge manufacturing.

China's economy is weaker. Its government's ambitions have been hampered at home by a slowing economy and an aging population that draws resources from a shrinking workforce. The Party's increased centralized control over the private sector has reduced innovation and entrepreneurial energy.

Internationally, China leads a bloc of lesser economies. Its Belt and Road Initiative network has shrunk in size and impact due to some countries deciding BRI membership in general, and certain investments by China in particular, are not in their national interests. Many such countries choose instead to "multialign," picking and choosing relationships that suit different aspects of those national interests. The United States and its partners show superior power to attract those making such choices. China continues to participate in this US-dominant system, as it still needs export earnings and a "seat" from which to try to game or change the system.

Technology and Semiconductors

Export controls remain in effect and are better coordinated by the United States and its partners, including in standards bodies that govern different technological domains. As parity grows, a "Semiconductor Coordinating Council" formalizes those export controls, subsidies, and tax policies around semiconductors among the United States and its partners. Such coordination makes advanced partner countries feel comfortable selling to China, which remains a significant market and a good source of legacy semiconductors.

China's decades of investment in research and development lead to technological advances that are useful and additive in this global system, including related to semiconductors, but do not put China in the lead and in a position to dominate it.

Scenario No. 3 for 2032: "Downward Spiral (in US-China Relations)" (SW)

This is a future in which China's belief that the East is rising and the West is declining is borne out, but with significant friction. Mercantilist China outcompetes the United States and its allies. The BRI is working well in terms of China's goal: creating a new network of global trade and power with China at the center, and assuring China's access to the resources it needs and the strategic positioning in the Indo-Pacific and around the world it wants, especially in ports along strategic waterways and their choke points. This positioning increasingly challenges and erodes the US military's counterbalancing role in the Indo-Pacific.

Geopolitical

The United States and its partners have responded to a rising and increasingly influential China by partially decoupling from it. They urge nonaligned countries to choose sides. Fewer and fewer do, resulting in a larger group of nonaligned states. ASEAN threatens to fracture under pressure from the United States and its partners on one side and from China on the other. For many ASEAN countries, arguments that the US side upholds superior values don't carry the same weight as the economic benefits from China's investments.

The United States arrived here through missteps. Internal political polarization, prejudice, violence, xenophobia, and the erosion of US democracy and rule of law have weakened American soft power. Greater polarization of US political parties leads to sclerotic responses to domestic and global challenges and opportunities. Increasingly, other countries decide that US partnership is unreliable, and they need to find their own way forward.

China got here with consistent, reliable, pragmatic economic policies, including investment in infrastructure at home and abroad, and in military modernization. China increasingly treats the Indo-Pacific as its "backyard," leading to widespread regional resentment. China has taken aggressive action to bring Taiwan under PRC control, but is not getting the benefit China's leaders thought it would from that action due to resistance on the ground in Taiwan, international sanctions, and a substantial hit to China's already-ropey global image. The United States may have lost soft power, but China hasn't gained it. Rather, China takes the lead globally through pragmatic, mercantilist deal making, and coercion when necessary.

Global institutions are reduced to arenas of rivalry and grievance.

Global Trade/Investment

The world is divided into two main blocs—the United States and its partners in one and China in another—and by many nonaligned nations who themselves may have left existing regional groupings to form new, smaller blocs. These smaller blocs do their own negotiating and deal making with other blocs. Trading and investment are increasingly done within the two blocs, though some commerce continues between them. The reach of China's BRI is vast, but because the relationship between China and member states is so transactional, with a hub-and-spokes system that mostly benefits China, member states still look for opportunities elsewhere.

China's economy has surpassed that of the United States. China outcompetes the United States and its partners, offering acceptable quality and much better price points on exports, including technological exports.

China's RMB-denominated economy becomes an attractive destination for capital and, increasingly, reserves. Its digital RMB currency has proven popular, especially among authoritarian governments looking to avoid the bite of sanctions from the United States and its partners. The power of the dollar as a reserve and clearing currency has declined.

A lack of US investment in education, innovation, R&D, and infrastructure has taken its toll. US economic growth slows down, as does US innovation. In a weaker economy, the United States and its partners try to compete by lowering prices, offering subsidies, and protecting intellectual property—all of which lower returns.

Technology and Semiconductors

China reaps the benefits of its decades-long investments in education, innovation, and research and development, as well as with canny acquisition of companies and intellectual property—both legal and extralegal.

China has become largely self-sufficient in many key technologies, and edges out the United States and its partners in exporting those technologies around the world, especially to BRI member states. China's self-sufficiency and dominance allow it to gather, analyze, and centralize ever more data from around the world, including data related to the movement of ships and cargo, thanks to China's presence in the dozens of seaports China's companies now own or manage, to better calibrate its strategic policies and political messaging.

Divergent standards arise for many technologies, as China develops and exports its own. China's voice in international standards-setting bodies has grown more prominent, even dominant.

China has attained the capability to make its own leading-edge semiconductors, so it doesn't need TSMC to get ahead. China's seizure of Taiwan has, in any case, diminished TSMC, with its workforce having scattered, some now working at other TSMC semiconductor foundries abroad and some at Samsung or Intel, which have stepped up as the new leading-edge semiconductor manufacturers.

China continues to dominate as a global source of legacy semiconductors, needed in everything from automobiles to military equipment.

China uses this leverage as a policy tool, often to the detriment of the United States and its allies.

China also maintains a near monopoly on rare earths and critical materials needed for semiconductors and other technologies. And China makes muscular use of this leverage, suspending or cutting off supply when aggrieved by a recipient country's actions.

Meanwhile, US internal political divisions make it hard for Congress to pass legislation on immigration reform or to increase spending on education and R&D, and private companies prefer to chase short-term gains rather than invest in R&D. Divergent standards, patchy access to raw materials, and a lack of foresight and investment in the future contribute to the United States falling behind China as technological leader.

Scenario No. 4 for 2032: The China Dream (SE)

In this future, China leads a free and more integrated international system where global stability is sustained with relatively few kinetic conflicts. Global institutions matter more, and China is at their helm. China has softened its positions on a variety of fronts, and changed its image enough that more people have made peace with being part of this system. China is now firmly in the lead in most technologies, including semiconductors. China has become the preferred destination for talented immigrants and investment. Trade is RMB-denominated. China is doing better than before at the soft-power game, having learned that reliable, beneficial partnership works better than "wolf warrior" diplomacy and coercion.

One possibility in this quadrant is that leadership in China has changed, and its new leaders are committed to making China a responsible stakeholder. Alternatively, China's current leadership may still be in power, and has found pragmatic ways to maintain a system that supports US and partner interests enough that they accept China's leading role, even as the United States and partners continue to protect and promote their interests.

The United States and its allies fail to outcompete China, economically or in terms of values, as US internal divisions and strife are out of sync with purported US democratic values. The US economy is in decent shape, but weaker than China's. The US dollar reserve status is effectively gone. The United States and its partners get a share of the pie, but not the biggest.

Geopolitical

This is a relatively peaceful world in which trade, not values, is the balm. Global institutions are more important, and China exercises significant influence over many of them. The United States and its allies resist, but those efforts are not particularly effective since the differences between their values and China's—as reflected by actions, not just words—are now less pronounced.

Taiwan has voluntarily become part of the People's Republic of China, after a Kuomintang Party victory leads to negotiations and an agreement with China that KMT leaders find to be in Taiwan's interests. Driving "unification" is a pragmatism that takes into account the powerful economic incentives offered by China and an acceptance of new realities—both China's dominance in the region and the lack of ability or willingness of the United States and its partners to protect Taiwan. Taiwan's population accepts this change as the best possible choice, and Taiwan's economy thrives.

Global Trade/Investment

China moves up the value chain, and is now a major global player in innovation, leading-edge technology, services, finance, and manufacturing. Global trade flows more freely, is quite transactional, and is RMB-denominated. Global standards and norms have been "harmonized" to predominantly reflect China's preferences. Some trade networks and bilateral trade agreements survive, but their rules are updated to reflect the new "language" of trade under China's leadership. China's stock exchanges are now where the action happens. China's financial firms are the leading deal makers, increasing China's global economic dominance.

The United States and its allies do comfortably well in this future economically, but they are passengers on the bus. They no longer lead in setting standards and norms, including trade rules, and they no longer benefit from the US dollar being the reserve currency and currency of record. Depending on whether prevailing domestic political winds at the time are isolationist or support a greater US role in the world, the United States and its partners may scheme to get back on top. Or—if led by a nationalistic, xenophobic, and protectionist government—the United States may decide that this is good enough, and in any case is better than spending time and money on improving America's place in the world, much less reclaiming a role of global leadership.

Technology and Semiconductors

China is firmly in the lead—with Taiwan and TSMC now working with it—in the design and manufacturing of most of the important technologies, including semiconductors. Global supply chains shift to reflect China's dominance. Meanwhile, China's famously efficient domestic supply chain networks feeding the tech sector become even more robust.

China is now fully in control of global technological standards bodies, including those related to semiconductors. Standards now more strongly benefit China's domestic capacities and support China's industrial and technological priorities.

The United States and its partners continue to fabricate semiconductors—perhaps now dependent on continued government subsidies, given the loss of technological edge to support profitability. But having lost their lead in innovation and design, they are increasingly dependent on China for advanced chips. China uses as leverage its near monopoly on critical minerals and raw materials essential for tech manufacturing, squeezing supply to reduce the chances that the United States and its partners can catch up. Having squandered the chance to invest in education, R&D, and immigration reform, the United States and its partners increasingly do what China did on its way up: reverse engineer designs and technologies and acquire companies and their IP, rather than create them.

The US and partner militaries are particularly challenged, not only in keeping up with China's high-tech weapons, surveillance, and cyber warfare systems, but also in having the legacy semiconductors they need for their existing weapons systems. US military positions and mandates need to be reconsidered, especially in the Indo-Pacific, where China makes it clear—through use of its economic, trade, and supply chain leverage—that a US military presence is no longer welcome.

Probable and Preferable Scenarios and Dynamics

Scenario planning encourages robust thinking about all plausible futures that matter to the group. In a ten-year time frame, elements of some or all of these scenarios may become reality, so action is needed now to prepare for any combination of them.

Having built a map of plausible futures, our scenarios team next began to speculate about which outcome seemed most likely, and which future would be most preferable for US interests.

We began work on our scenarios in early 2022. Since then, the forces that were leaning toward a more fragmented "bloc"-like future were amplified by Russia's invasion of Ukraine and by the coordinated US and allied response to it.

While the scenario team feels that all four scenarios are plausible in our ten-year time frame, the participants believe that it's all but certain that at least the early years of the decade will head west on our grid, toward Cold War 2.0 (NW) or Downward Spiral (SW)—a turbulent and confrontational future in which geopolitics may dominate (figure 1.4).

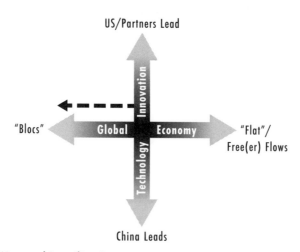

Figure 1.4. Westward Prevailing Current

The scenario subgroup also considered which "prevailing currents" could move us into particular quadrants. Among those they thought more likely than others are the following:

1. As shown in figure 1.5, the United States and its partners build on their cooperation in response to Russia's aggression, driving the world first into the northwest quadrant, then (via success in enlisting nonaligned countries, and the "benefit" of China's troubles) over to the northeast.

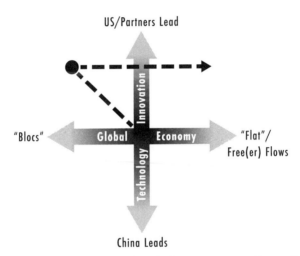

Figure 1.5. Flowing to Cold War 2.0 (NW), Then Great-Power Happy Hour (NE)

2. China succeeds in navigating the current politically fraught moment—which diverts US attention and assets away from the Indo-Pacific—and manages to move the world toward the Downward Spiral (SW). Then, confident enough in their position to begin to "liberalize with Chinese characteristics," they build on their trading and financial momentum to move the world to the China Dream (SE), as in figure 1.6.

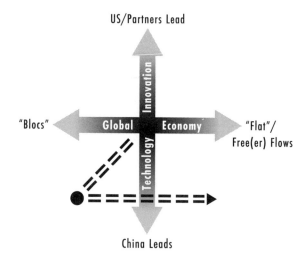

Figure 1.6. Flowing to Downward Spiral (SW), Then China Dream (SE)

3. As in figure 1.7, we "stall" in one of the western quadrants for the entire decade leading to 2032.

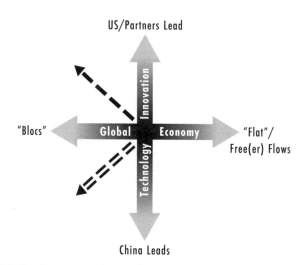

Figure 1.7. Flowing to West, Then Stalling

4. The United States and partners begin in a leadership role in Cold War 2.0 (NW), but falter for their own reasons, and/or are out-competed by China. The world slides into Downward Spiral (SW). Or, China is able to move the world to the southwest, but is either outcompeted or falters, and the world moves into Cold War 2.0 (NW), with the United States and its allies again in the lead, as in figure 1.8.

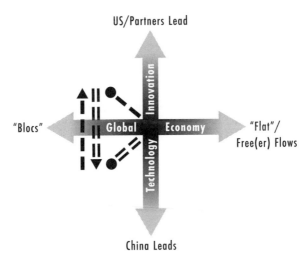

Figure 1.8. Flowing to West, Then Dynamic Struggle

Some in the group felt that the China Dream (SE) scenario, which is peaceful but with China leading, is the least preferable for US interests, since even the more turbulent Downward Spiral (SE) quadrant offered more possibilities for the United States to work its way back into a global leadership role. That said, many developing countries that simply want to prosper and protect their own interests may care more about whether the world as a whole is peaceful and stable, and less about who is leading the global system—so long as the leader doesn't try to impose its ideology or values, and isn't unduly coercive, predatory, or unfair.

A US failure to see this possibility—perhaps due to domestic political polarization and turbulence—is exactly what could lead to a China Dream (SE) future. Indeed, US polarization could lead many around the world to give up on US leadership, reasoning that it is effective only in episodic stretches, and ineffective and even destructive at other times.

Scenario Implications and Principles

Our scenarios team worked from scenario-specific implications ("if we knew for certain that this future was going to unfold over the next decade, we should do . . .") to create high-level recommendations for actions that are robust across all scenarios. These recommendations either make great sense in each scenario or are important in some but do no harm in the others, maximizing the possibility of desired outcomes for the United States and its partners. The team also identified actions in some scenarios that would be ineffectual at best or counterproductive or harmful at worst.

When scenario-planning exercises are done with governments, corporations, NGOs, and similar groups, much time is spent on contingent implications. The group then empanels early warning teams that spend the next several years watching for indicators that show contingent implications playing out, so the team can alert the organization to take appropriate action. Our working group, however, is a temporary convening of experts and specialists—meaning it won't be around to monitor emerging contingent implications. But we hope you, as a reader, do keep these in mind as the next decade unfolds, and that relevant US government departments, companies, and other potentially impacted organizations do the same.

What follows instead are "robust" implications and principles—the kind that make sense, or at least don't do harm, in each future the group imagined. These high-level implications reflect the group's thoughts on how the United States and its partners can continue to lead in a rules-based global order with a resilient supply chain for semiconductors and other critical technologies. They also include precautions to ensure the

United States and its partners are well positioned to respond to any of the scenarios—open to opportunities, hedged against risks.

Foreign Policy Principles

- Strengthen US relations with allies and friends. Listen well and pursue policies that work for them as well as for the United States.
- Communicate context. Explain where we are in these scenarios, and why the United States is acting, or proposing to act, as we are.
- Stay involved, and in some cases become more involved, in international organizations to better influence decisions. Continue to invest in leadership in organizations with global reach, such as the United Nations—but prioritize partner groupings and multilateral structures such as the G7 and ASEAN.
- Prioritize efforts to enlarge our circle of allies and friends:

  - Build on the Partnership for Global Infrastructure and Investment as an alternative to China's BRI offered by the United States and its allies.
  - Make judicious use of export controls, aimed almost exclusively at China and its authoritarian partners, while guarding against unintended consequences that may weaken US and partner technology leadership in the private sector.
  - Increase soft-power efforts to highlight our values, including the strength of democracy and resilient institutions. And then walk the talk.

- Promote Taiwan as a full member of the world economic community, stopping short of insisting on sovereignty. Support Taiwan's economy and its self-defense efforts and encourage people-to-people ties across business and civil society.
- Strengthen diplomatic ties with countries rich in key semiconductor raw materials.
- Rebuild the US Foreign Service by enhancing recruitment and training efforts, and by more quickly confirming ambassadors and other important foreign policy–related appointments.

Defense Policy Principles

- Increase investment in and licensing of advanced technologies in ways that benefit US and partners' militaries and economies.
- Broaden the array of semiconductor suppliers, shifting from a "trusted foundry" approach to "trusted assurance."
- Boost US naval presence in the Indo-Pacific. Prioritize deterrence.
- Actively help Taiwan build a "porcupine" posture to deter any attempted invasion, through these measures:

  - Selling arms and material, emphasizing coproduction of a "large number of small things"
  - Expanding joint training and planning
  - Hardening supply lines and stockpiles
  - Encouraging Taiwan to more rapidly pursue resilient energy supplies and infrastructure

Economic Policy Principles

- Play the long game: look for "win-win" policies and trade agreements, including through market access to allies and partners. Build those policies to be robust against possible decoupling from China.
- Strengthen the dollar as the clearing and reserve currency:

  - Create a fiat e-currency tied to the dollar.
  - Work actively to accommodate nonaligned countries.
  - Discourage, including by penalizing, shifts from the dollar to the RMB as a trading and reserve currency.

- Increase government investment in R&D, including applied research. Extend industrial policy to support critical industries and sectors, including semiconductors. Collaborate with partners in this effort.
- Encourage the US private sector to increase R&D spending, providing tax incentives and subsidies.
- Rethink our current antitrust approach. Allow semiconductor companies—and champions in other important tech sectors—to achieve the scale necessary to support R&D and competitiveness.

Technology Policy Principles

- Develop resilient supply chains for key technologies, including semiconductors. Source critical materials and other inputs from reliable suppliers.
- Actively participate in global deliberations on standards and rules.
- Increase the amount of engineering-based R&D spending. Use "moonshot challenges" to prioritize and create competition for key semiconductor and technology objectives.
- Increase investment in STEM education, including in K–12 as well as higher education, and workforce training.
- Encourage academic collaboration throughout US and partner trade and technology networks.
- Enact immigration policies that encourage talented students, scientists, and engineers to learn, research, and work in the United States. Ensure that the United States remains the most attractive global destination for such talent, alongside efforts to evaluate and improve the security of its research environment.
- Improve the manufacturing business environment within the United States and partner nations.
- Harden cyber defenses.
- Develop a safe and fair way to share US intellectual property with partners who can leverage it in our interests.

Semiconductor Supply Chain Priorities

- Emphasize resilience and robustness, stressing effectiveness and not just efficiency. Coordinate with partners to create policies, and make investments to encourage these outcomes:
  - Enhanced domestic manufacturing capacity
  - Extended commercial inventories of needed chip inputs, including legacy chips
  - A sufficiently skilled semiconductor workforce

- Build a semiconductor equivalent of the US Department of Energy's Energy Information Administration (EIA) to collect and

share information on the semiconductor global supply chain. Encourage participation from companies receiving government advantages such as orders, subsidies, or tax breaks.
• Work with US partners to implement the following:

  • Create a diverse network in the Global South for lower-margin parts of the supply chain.
  • Create incentives to encourage some refining and processing of critical materials within the United States or in trusted partner nations, and cultivate technologies and practices that minimize environmental impact.
  • Consider discouraging use of semiconductor inputs or services sourced from China.
  • Block advanced chips and chipmaking tools from going to China or its close partners.

• Recognize that domestic manufacturing has to be accompanied by simultaneous R&D investments to sustain production at the leading edge beyond a two- to three-year technology cycle.

The following chapters in this report unpack many of these general implications within the context of the "silicon triangle": reducing US vulnerabilities to semiconductor supply chain disruptions and increasing domestic competitiveness, all while enhancing Taiwan's stability and prosperity; and simultaneously guarding against vulnerabilities as China further develops its own semiconductor industry and other advanced technologies.

NOTES

1. A January 26, 2022, *New York Times* article (Julian E. Barnes, "How the Computer Chip Shortage Could Incite a US Conflict with China") and a December 27, 2021, Reuters investigation (Yimou Lee, Norihiko Shirouzu, and David Lague, "Taiwan Chip Industry Emerges as Battlefront in US-China Showdown") speculate how disruption of Taiwan's chip industry during a hostile conflict could disrupt the global chip supply chain and US economy.

2. A November 4, 2021, Voice of America article considered how B3W could interact with China's Belt and Road Initiative: Patsy Widakuswara, "'Build Back Better World': Biden's Counter to China's Belt and Road."

3. A February 2022 German Marshall Fund report considered a variety of avenues for EU-US cooperation on China: Andrew Small, Bonnie S. Glaser, and Garima Mohan, "US-European Cooperation on China and the Indo-Pacific."

4. US Department of State, "The Clean Network," 2021.

5. National Science and Technology Council, Fast Track Action Subcommittee on Critical and Emerging Technologies, "Critical and Emerging Technologies List Update," February 2022.

6. Yifan Yu and Cheng Ting-Fang, "TSMC in Arizona: Why Taiwan's Chip Titan Is Betting on the Desert," *Nikkei Asia*, June 3, 2021.

7. TSMC and Sony Semiconductor Solutions, "TSMC to Build Specialty Technology Fab in Japan with Sony Semiconductor Solutions as Minority Shareholder," press release, November 9, 2021.

8. For more information about ASML's dominant market position, see this February 9, 2020, *Economist* article: "How ASML Became Chipmaking's Biggest Monopoly."

9. For more information about how the COVID pandemic has accelerated regionalization, see this report from the Economist Intelligence Unit: "The Great Unwinding: COVID-19 and the Regionalisation of Global Supply Chains," 2020.

10. See this February 11, 2022, *South China Morning Post* article for more information about SMIC's efforts to close its gap with TSMC, including how SMIC plans to spend its record 2021 profit on capacity expansion: Che Pan, "US-China Tech War: Top Chinese Chip Maker SMIC to Invest Record US$5 billion in Capacity Expansion after Profits Doubled in 2021." See also Dan Wang, "The Quest for Semiconductor Sovereignty," *Gavekal Dragonomics*, April 20, 2021.

11. Kat Devlin and Christine Huang, "In Taiwan, Views of Mainland China Mostly Negative," Pew Research Center, May 12, 2020.

12. Brian Kennedy and Meg Hefferon, "What Americans Know about Science," Pew Research Center, March 28, 2019.

13. For more information about China's scientific literacy, see this *China Daily* article: Zhang Zhihao, "Scientific Literary Plan Announced," July 7, 2021. For more information about China's newest scientific literacy action plan, see this translation by the Center for Security and Emerging Technology (CSET): PRC State Council, "State Council Notice on the Publication of the Outline of the Nationwide Scientific Literacy Action Plan (2021–2035)," September 16, 2021.

14. For one perspective on the potential shortfall of semiconductor industry jobs in the United States, see this analysis from Eightfold AI: "How the US Can Reshore

the Semiconductor Industry," 2021. For another, see this February 2022 report from the CSET: Will Hunt, "Reshoring Chipmaking Capacity Requires High-Skilled Foreign Talent: Estimating the Labor Demand Generated by CHIPS Act Incentives."

15. As just one example, the global space industry is projected to grow to over $1 trillion by 2040, up from $350 billion in 2022. The most important short- and medium-term driver of this market growth is expected to be satellite broadband internet access provided by projects such as SpaceX's Starlink constellation or Amazon's Project Kuiper. See Morgan Stanley, "Space: Investing in the Final Frontier," July 24, 2020. Artificial intelligence compute is another.

16. A May 2021 International Energy Agency flagship report, as directed by IEA ministers, examined the role of critical materials in the clean energy supply chain. That issue was highlighted with a direction from ministers in the March 2022 meeting that IEA assume new responsibilities to consider the security of such minerals: "The Role of Critical Minerals in Clean Energy Transitions." Following the US Department of Commerce's October 2022 issuance of new export control and other rules targeting China's semiconductor industry, for example, China announced its own controls on the export of ingot and wafer production technologies used in the manufacture of solar photovoltaic panels. See Nadya Yeh, "China Drafts New Export Controls to Shore Up Solar Dominance," *China Project*, February 1, 2023.

CHAPTER TWO

Implications of Technology Trends in the Semiconductor Industry

H.-S. PHILIP WONG AND JIM PLUMMER

Today's semiconductor industry is not static—it undergoes constant reinvention, and it is built on mutual interdependencies. This chapter offers background on and discusses the implications of semiconductor technology and industry trends.

• • •

Chip Types and Uses

Semiconductor technology covers a very broad range of technologies, such as logic, memory, power electronics, sensors, actuators, analog, and high-frequency/radio frequency (RF), as shown in table 2.1. Crucially, in discussing semiconductor technology, one must be cognizant that the entire semiconductor space is much broader than advanced-node logic chips, which have been the focus of attention recently. Table 2.1 provides an overview of the structure of the global semiconductor market.

A word on logic chip nomenclature: Chips are often referred to on a "nanometer scale," which has become a proxy for complexity and computing power. While that nanometer measurement can be thought of as referring to the length of the smallest component on the chip, these nanometer-branded "process nodes" are now umbrella terms that manufacturers use to represent successive generations of upgraded

Table 2.1. Semiconductor Market Segmentation

TYPE	% OF 2022 INDUSTRY REVENUE	FUNCTION	EXAMPLES
Logic	44%	Digital processors that act as the "brain" of modern computing	CPU (central processing units) GPU (graphics processing units)
Memory	23%	Short- and long-term storage of digital information	DRAM (dynamic random access memory) acts as the computer's "working memory." NAND Flash memory acts as long-term storage for computers and devices.
Discrete, analog, and other (DAO)	33%	Interact with the physical world by generating or transforming signals from electricity to radio waves or light, for example	Chips that enable such functions as charging a battery, electric vehicle motors, and phone calls (by accessing radio waves)

Source: 2022 data from the World Semiconductor Trade Statistics (WSTS) global industry fore-cast for calendar year 2022, released November 2022; "logic" category includes WSTS "logic" and "micro" categories. See WSTS, "The Worldwide Semiconductor Market Is Expected to Slow to 4.4 Percent Growth in 2022, Followed by a Decline of 4.1 Percent in 2023," press release, November 29, 2022.

production processes. This disconnect between branding and measurements is particularly true as chips have increasingly become complex three-dimensional structures.[1] While the metric is still in common use (mainly for marketing purposes), the nanometer node designations from different companies cannot be directly compared—a snag that can complicate industry assessments. For example, US-based Intel's 10nm and 7nm nodes are said to be roughly equivalent to Taiwan's Taiwan Semiconductor Manufacturing Company's (TSMC) or Korea's Samsung's 7nm and 5nm technology, respectively, due to a similar basket of transistor specification metrics adopted by each.[2] Apart from logic chips, memory technologies also commonly adopt a nanometer-based nomenclature, while storage technologies can be referred to by the number of three-dimensionally stacked layers they have.

Generally speaking, the performance of logic and memory chips improves at smaller nanometer measurements: chips with a greater density of transistors have greater computational power and (to a lesser extent) memory capacity. The performance of analog and discrete chips, however, is not directly correlated with the nanometer scale. Their "performance" instead refers to the overall beneficial attributes of a chip technology, including speed, power and energy efficiency, and density (not just speed).

For advanced logic, the current state of the art in production is 3nm technology—TSMC introduced 3nm commercial-scaled production in early 2023. The most-advanced-logic chips are used in CPUs and GPUs as well as field-programmable gate arrays (FPGAs) and application-specific processors, such as those in cell phones.[3] Currently, the world's largest and most profitable chip manufacturer, TSMC, has focused its investments on fabrication of the most-advanced nodes, with its 7nm and 5nm production lines accounting for more than half its sales in 2022.[4]

Currently, only TSMC, Samsung, and Intel have logic fabs (chip fabrication facilities) capable of manufacturing chips below 10nm at commercial scale, while major foundries United Microelectronics Corporation (UMC; Taiwan) and GlobalFoundries (US/UAE) have chosen not to invest in competing at the leading edge. China's Semiconductor Manufacturing International Corporation (SMIC), as of 2022, has generally not commercially produced chips below 10nm, with the exception of a cryptocurrency-mining chip that is claimed by third parties to exhibit some features consistent with manufacturing below 10nm.[5]

While leading-edge logic chips are profitable and central to advancing the technology frontier, in 2019 less than 5 percent of global manufacturing capacity was actually for nodes below 10nm.[6] To build a complete electronic system, one needs more than the logic chips— at a minimum, memory and storage are required, and depending on applications a system might also require analog devices, sensors, high-frequency/radio frequency (RF) devices, and power devices. Leading-edge logic is important for peak-speed performance as well as overall industry revenue—but securing these chips is not sufficient for the totality of electronics end uses.

While emerging technologies and high-end consumer applications—e.g., supercomputers, gaming computers, cloud computing infrastructure, neural network accelerators for AI applications, and smartphones—require leading-edge chips, many parts of the economy operate on trailing-edge mature chips. Mature nodes are often defined as manufacturing processes at 28 or 40nm and above, used in the production of many automotive semiconductors, image signal processors for digital cameras, and other chips such as LCD (liquid crystal display) and LED (light-emitting diode) drivers and power-management controllers. A single car will use hundreds or even thousands of chips. A 40 or 65nm logic chip, for example, may be embedded within a larger assembly of sensors (i.e., discrete/analog/optoelectronic [DAO] devices) to allow the vehicle to function.[7]

It's a common misconception that such chips are simply older versions of the advanced nodes and the only difference is their lower cost. This misconception arises because the label "trailing-edge mature nodes" actually consists of two categories of chips: (a) digital logic chips of legacy nodes, and (b) specialty technologies.

Because that second category of specialty technologies is often derived from a digital logic platform, it is easy to conflate them with digital logic of mature nodes. These specialty technologies include, for example, sensors and actuators; power electronics; embedded memory; analog/mixed-signal and RF devices; power management integrated circuits (PMIC); and high-temperature/high-reliability and radiation-hardened technologies used in aerospace applications. While such specialty technologies use fabrication processes that derive from trailing-edge "mature" logic nodes, significant efforts must still be expended to develop and qualify them for these tailored applications. These technologies are a special category per se and should not simply be interpreted as cheaper products. For example, the claim that the US military's use of microelectronics often requires trailing-edge "mature" nodes typically refers to use of these specialty chip technologies and not necessarily (old) digital logic chips of mature or legacy nodes. The world's third-largest contract chip manufacturer, UMC, now focuses its investment on fabrication of these chip technologies at 28 or 40nm process nodes for a variety of these specialized applications.

Cost also matters. Today, as in the past, consumers of semiconductors must weigh the functional gains of more-advanced chips against the much greater costs. A product such as an iPhone 13, which is designed around a 5nm chip, simply could not exist without using that advanced technology. Others point to the popularity of chips produced using 28nm technologies as the "sweet spot" between cost and function. It is perhaps most accurate to say, however, that for each product segment, there is a suitable technology node given the cost and performance trade-off. One has to meet both the performance and the cost targets.

After logic chips, memory and storage chips are the second-largest category of semiconductors, representing 32 percent of global manufacturing capacity and 26 percent of revenue in 2019.[8] While memory chips often do not receive the same attention as logic chips, they are similarly ubiquitous in enabling the function of electronic devices. As such, they merit similar supply chain resilience attention. The dominant memory technology today is dynamic random access memory (DRAM). Samsung (Korea) is the dominant supplier of DRAM (44 percent market share) followed by Micron (US, though with most production overseas) and SK hynix (Korea), with about 22 to 27 percent each. Meanwhile, NAND Flash is the dominant storage technology. Samsung also dominates NAND storage (35 percent market share), followed by Kioxia (Japan, formerly Toshiba) and its joint venture partner Western Digital (US, though NAND is produced in Japan with Kioxia), SK hynix, and Micron sharing market shares in the teens. While significant innovation occurs in both fields—one may hear, for example, of NAND storage being progressively stacked in three-dimensional configurations of 176 or 232 "layers"—memory and storage chips are generally considered to be more commoditized than logic chips. They are often combined interchangeably from different vendors within a finished electronic system, given that these chips are more likely to be produced to industry-wide common specifications representing different device architectures and manufacturing methods.

This standards-based interchangeability is in part why China's emerging DRAM and NAND manufacturers have been able to make better progress than China's logic chip manufacturers.[9]

Defense Needs

Military chip needs are of particular interest. In addition to having corporate information technology (IT)–type chip and consumer electronic demands much like any other complex global organization, the US Department of Defense (DoD) is concerned with the procurement and maintenance of specialty transport, communications, and weapons platforms that have unique semiconductor capabilities and security requirements. Javelin missiles—sent by the thousands to Ukraine, for example—rely on over 250 chips to manufacture before reaching the shoulder of the warfighter.[10] A deployed soldier himself may carry upward of six Global Positioning System (GPS) chips for his radios, range finders, and other equipment, with each GPS chip relying on other semiconductors for specific capabilities.[11] Although many of the components in such systems are similar to semiconductors used in consumer electronics—a weapons system, much like an automobile, may rely on hundreds of distinct logic chips, memory chips, communication chips, and sensors—the US defense apparatus also requires chips with higher levels of reliability and performance for unpredictable environments of conflict.

DoD chip-security concerns are therefore broad. First, like other chip consumers, DoD is concerned with supply chain resilience. In other words, because it relies on foreign suppliers, its supply may be cut off through global disruptions, or the threat of intentional disruption could be used as strategic leverage against US interests.[12] Second is a more unusual information-security concern: the risk that its chip designs or specifications may be leaked to adversaries through the production process, or the risk that hidden vulnerabilities could be inserted into a chip through a foreign supply process. Finally, DoD has been concerned that semiconductor-related capabilities and know-how—which underpin much of the so-called third offset of the US military's comparative strength and which were largely invented in the United States—could fall into foreign hands. This last concern has largely already come to pass with the spread of leading-edge chip research and development (R&D) around the world and the migration of large portions of the semiconductor supply chain overseas; hence DoD is no longer always the first to capitalize on chip advances.

Because of these special performance requirements and security concerns, many military-grade microchips are subject to a higher level of production oversight, testing, and quality control than those used in consumer electronics. Even so, while the defense industry is reliant on chips, the chip industry as a whole is no longer reliant on the defense customers. In its infancy, the semiconductor industry got its start and was nurtured by US defense needs.[13] Today, US DoD and contractor chip needs are about two billion chips per year, estimated to be less than 2 percent of the market.[14] Reconciling these special needs with a relatively small purchasing power has led to a unique portfolio of supply streams. Those defense uses, in rough order of increasing specialization, include these:

- *Purchases of commercial off-the-shelf semiconductors*, including analog, memory chips, or GPUs, produced in the United States, Korea, or Taiwan. Such chips are subject to the same global supply chain resilience concerns as consumer products.
- *Field-programmable gate arrays (FPGAs)*, which are application-agnostic upon manufacture but can then be programmed or reprogrammed by the chip integrator to perform the functions needed for that application. FPGAs have large commercial market applications in data centers and communication switching networks. But the use of modular FPGAs is also attractive in the defense industry because of the small volume of chips often needed for specific use cases: using modular FPGAs, the customer is able to purchase relatively advanced–logic chips from a commercial fabricator without needing a high-volume, custom-designed production run; further, there are fewer security concerns with the supply chain, as the chip designer and fabricator do not need

to have full visibility on final circuit configurations (which could otherwise reveal characteristics of the weapons platform in which the chip is being used). The flexibility of FPGA chips does come at some cost: while easier to produce at small volumes, these chips are less dense (in terms of logic gates per square centimeter) and generally slower than the more optimized, application-specific chips described below. The US firm Xilinx—a pioneer in FPGAs, acquired by US chip design firm AMD in 2022—designs such chips and sells them to DoD users; Xilinx chips are fabricated at least in part by leading Taiwanese fabs UMC and TSMC.[15] Intel is another provider of FPGAs, through its 2015 acquisition of Altera (US); Intel/Altera has historically used both TSMC and Intel itself for fabrication of its FPGAs.

- *Application-specific integrated circuits (ASICs)* whose functions are optimized from the beginning for particular platform needs. Because ASICs are designed and produced to match specific end uses, there are more security concerns surrounding their production—those involved in their creation could gain information about the strengths and weaknesses of the weapons they enable. In part for this reason, twenty years ago DoD established its "Trusted Foundry" program to provide for domestic design, manufacturing, and assembly of very small volumes of classified or radiation-hardened chips meeting high security standards—and for a premium price.[16] The Trusted Foundry program certifies (and provides availability payments to) a constellation of suppliers—all of them currently US based. These suppliers range across the chip supply chain, from designers to IP block vendors to mask producers, fabricators, and testing; Trusted Foundry certifies each participant to be able to handle what DoD terms "Critical Program Information." The important downside of this approach to security is that the extra cost and overhead needed to maintain and certify such protections—which can affect things like staffing of facilities[17]—combined with the small volumes of chips that are needed from it (thought to be as little as 2 to 10 percent of DoD's own needs[18]) means that the most-advanced commercial chip firms choose not to participate in it. In turn, DoD is left with slower innovation cycles and older technologies underlying its most secure chips, including for chips that are meant to underpin next-generation weapons systems. Recent initiatives—including DoD's multibillion-dollar Rapid Assured Microelectronics Prototypes using Advanced Commercial Capabilities (RAMP) and State-of-the-Art Heterogeneous Integrated Packaging (SHIP) programs—are intended to more flexibly access commercial semiconductor capabilities, given DoD security needs.[19] While real technical hurdles still stand in the way of a complete transition from a "trusted" to a "zero trust" (quantifiable assurance) model for DoD chip buyers, that desired end goal is the correct one, and accelerated efforts toward quantifiable assurance would contribute to US national security.[20]

Two other specific classes of defense industry chips that are small in market volume but have important area applications are these:

- *Compound and wide-bandgap semiconductors*, which are ideal for high-power and high-frequency applications such as radios and microwaves used in defense and aerospace. Compound semiconductor chips are produced using gallium arsenide (GaAs), silicon carbide (SiC), and gallium nitride (GaN), in addition to the conventional silicon substrate of typical commercial semiconductors. Skyworks is one US-based producer and fabricator of such chips; Skyworks' chips are also manufactured on a contract foundry basis by WIN Semiconductors (Taiwan).[21]
- *Radiation-hardened (rad-hard) semiconductors*, meanwhile, are needed to perform reliably in high-radiation environments— including in outer space and in nuclear accident environments— and in strategic nuclear weapons systems.[22] Chips operating in such environments are subject to Single Event Effects (SEEs) stemming from the interaction of atmospheric neutrons produced from cosmic rays or alpha particles from radioactive decay of thorium and uranium.[23] While less likely, these sorts

of interactions also pose potential concern in high-reliability ground systems (e.g., autonomous vehicles, electric vehicles, unmanned aerial systems, or smart grid). Without hardening or other resilience to SEEs, affected chips can malfunction or return unexpected outputs.

Major rad-hard chip producers include Microchip Technology (US), BAE Systems (UK), Honeywell (US), Renesas (Japan), Crane Aerospace & Electronics (US), and Infineon (Germany). Such chips can be produced by device and technology design and with the use of physical hardening materials. Their production is small volume and expensive—and thus the use of semiconductors in these environments is often many generations behind the commercial state of the art. Alternately, they can be certified for rad-hard resilience through "serendipity"—that is, when a commercial off-the-shelf component, when tested in relevant environments, happens to have good radiation performance without the traditional physical hardening processes. For example, the 7nm Xilinx Versal FPGA-type chip, fabricated by TSMC, was not designed to be rad-hard but performs well in space and other high-radiation environments.[24] Rad-hard by serendipity—or the use of self-checking and redundant processing architectures—is of growing importance to the market because of the growing number of space systems being constructed and sent to orbit.[25] Even so, the overall radiation-hardened chip market remains small, expected to be worth only $1.8 billion by 2027.[26]

In short, the US defense industry wants to feel comfortable with the security of its chip supplies, but it also wants access to the latest chip technologies. Getting that balance right has been difficult. Many observers argue that the defense industry has gone too far in the direction of security. Having access to advanced domestically produced chips (subsidized by measures such as the CHIPS Act) would in a way be an "easy answer" to DoD's quandary, as opposed to more fully pursuing a more flexible "quantifiable assurance" model of chip procurement.

The Commercial Semiconductor Value Chain

The semiconductor industry demands high levels of both R&D and capital expenditure (capex). These demands have created commercial incentives for a globally distributed and highly specialized global supply chain. The value chain can be summarized as having four production steps, each with various inputs:

Production Steps

1. *Chip Design*: Semiconductor design firms use technology-proven units of intellectual property called "IP cores"—which are previously designed circuit blocks known to function correctly—and electronic design automation (EDA) software to design chips for specific end uses (e.g., AI accelerators or chips for smartphone memory). This stage involves close collaboration between the design firm and the end customer (such as a systems integrator or original equipment manufacturer [OEM]), and chip design firms compete to develop the highest-performance or most efficient chips, or desirable application-specialized chips. Large systems companies such as Apple, Alphabet, and Amazon have also started designing their own chips.

   - *Design stage software inputs*: EDA software is a collection of powerful computer-aided design tools to map out the components on an individual chip, simulate and verify designs, optimize chip layouts for performance, assess manufacturing margins, and create physical masks for the manufacturing process. Today's EDA tools allow chip designers to start from high-level descriptions of desired system behavior instead of designing every transistor circuit explicitly, thus allowing the design of chips with hundreds of billions of transistors.
   - *Design stage IP inputs*: The fundamental IP building blocks are used as starting points in the semiconductor design process. Key examples are the Advanced RISC Machine (ARM) architecture for mobile devices and the x86 processor architecture for CPUs. These specialized firms continuously invest in and upgrade their IP blocks to remain competitive.

2. *Production Technology Development*: Just as chips themselves
need to be designed, so do the manufacturing processes themselves. If a particular chip design is like a recipe for a dish, and
the fabrication step (below) is the cooking of that dish, then this
middle step can be thought of as the conceptualization of the
restaurant, the scope of its menu, and the design of its kitchen.
Often ignored in policy discussions, the manufacturing technology development step is difficult and expensive, often learned
over time and sustained though tacit knowledge—and therefore
poses high barriers to entry.

- *Customer service and business coordination*—that is, working with end-use system integrators (whether internal to the
firm or external, as in a contract foundry model) to identify
the technology specification and cost trade-offs for a commercially viable chip technology, given the application needs. This
close, trust-based process also involves working with semiconductor equipment manufacturers to road-map new tool
capabilities for fabricating the desired chip technology within
an overall production process.
- *In-house design of fabrication processes*: These production
protocols can run into hundreds or thousands of steps.
- *Simulation and experimental prototyping*: Combined device
and process technologies are tested at small scale to achieve
technology targets, followed by ramping up of those prototype
technologies deemed feasible into high-volume production
with high yield. Such prototyping capability is expensive to
set up. It is often done in the same physical location as the fabrication facility, and uses some of the same skilled workers, to
ensure a smooth handoff between R&D and manufacturing.

3. *Fabrication*: Chip designs are then manufactured at specialized
facilities called "fabs" or "foundries." The fabs use specialized
equipment to print the geometric circuit patterns onto silicon
wafers, which are then treated with chemicals to etch or deposit
the pattern onto the wafer.[27] The customer of a stand-alone fab

company will often be a chip design firm, which will then sell the finished chip on to the system integrator/OEM.

- *Fabrication stage equipment inputs*: Semiconductor manufacturing equipment (SME) is a category of tools required for manufacturing (such as lithography and etching tools, including stencil-like masks that are specific to a chip design) and for metrology (tools that allow high-precision monitoring and measurement of the manufacturing process).
- *Fabrication stage chemicals and material inputs*—that is, specialty chemicals, gases, and materials that are used in the manufacturing process
- *Fabrication stage wafer inputs*—that is, the silicon wafers onto which individual chips are etched and deposited

4. *Test and Assembly*: After fabrication, the printed wafer is tested to ensure function, cut into individual integrated circuits (die), and packaged alongside complementary chips into specific product applications, itself an increasingly complex process.

As the industry has developed, six regional hubs have emerged in the semiconductor value chain: the United States, South Korea, Japan, China, Taiwan, and Europe. Broadly speaking, the United States currently specializes in many of the less capital-intensive (and more profitable) parts of the value chain, such as EDA software, intellectual property (IP), chip design, and manufacturing equipment. The US advantage in these areas derives from a leading global talent pool, a hub of world-leading universities, and high levels of government investment in basic research. The countries of East Asia, meanwhile, lead in capex-intensive activities, such as production technology development and fabrication as well as packaging, assembly, and testing.[28] These countries tend to have strong government incentives to establish facilities, as well as a larger, cheaper pool of both low-skilled labor and high-skilled talent. In earlier decades, the United States also led in these activities, but over time it has outsourced them, largely to Asian economies.

The often used, somewhat simplified motif of design versus manufacturing belies the fact, however, that developing new generations of semiconductor technology (the technology development step outlined above) or developing increasingly related advanced packaging technology also requires very large, colocated R&D efforts. While the United States excels in basic science research, East Asian countries often do very well in translating such research into practical technologies, and their governments often have incentives and infrastructures that facilitate such technology translations. So, while upper echelons of these firms' engineering development teams are in fact often staffed at least in part by experts trained in the United States, they oversee the work of hundreds or thousands of local, highly skilled R&D staff who enable that continuous process of translation from basic science to applied commercial technology.

Industry Structure

The global chip industry structure now exhibits both specialization for efficiency among the different segments of the value chain described above and consolidation of players within each segment.

Today, we are down to three major players in leading-edge logic (Intel, Samsung, and TSMC), a second tier of perhaps three major players in mature logic (Taiwan's UMC, US/UAE's GlobalFoundries, and China's SMIC), and three to four major players in memory (Korea's Samsung and SK hynix, US-based Micron, and the Japanese-US Kioxia/Western Digital). The semiconductor equipment companies have also consolidated into five major players (US-based Applied Materials, Lam Research, and KLA; Japan's Tokyo Electron; and ASML in the Netherlands). The EDA software companies have also consolidated into three players (US-based Cadence and Synopsys, and German-US Siemens/Mentor Graphics). FPGAs—which as described above are used in data centers and many military applications—once designed by Altera and Xilinx and manufactured at foundries domestically or abroad, are now part of Intel and AMD (which uses TSMC as its foundry), respectively.

Because of the high cost of capital investment and the long time horizon for maturing the technology, startups in both semiconductor manufacturing equipment and chip production technologies or chip manufacturing itself (e.g., foundries) are almost nonexistent in the United States. And while there have been a number of US memory device startups, none has been successful. Rather, whatever companies are left are quickly consolidating. The few successful startups in the semiconductor manufacturing equipment space (e.g., US-based Cymer and Inpria) are all part of larger companies now (ASML and Japan's JSR, respectively). In software EDA, US startups with a key innovation (often in an algorithm) or a niche application often get acquired by one of the big three incumbent chip software companies (Cadence, Synopsys, or Siemens/Mentor Graphics). These startups in EDA software typically no longer organically grow into larger companies in the United States—it is often difficult to remain independent for long because their products need to be plugged into the larger, more comprehensive design infrastructure dominated by the large firms.

One exception to this trend is in so-called fabless chip design companies: instead of manufacturing its own chips, fabless firms produce their designs for sale to customers using a third-party foundry's production lines (e.g., TSMC or UMC) on a contract basis. The capital needs of fabless firms are lower, and there are many startups. In a way, foundries play the role of venture capitalists: foundries "invest" in the startups by offering wafer capacity, with the goal that those wafers that are used to prove out a product will eventually turn into larger wafer orders down the line. Fabless chip design firm US-based Nvidia's use of TSMC's manufacturing capacity for its groundbreaking GPU chips was a prime example of this symbiotic relationship.

Even here, however, there are emerging warning signs regarding the health of this startup ecosystem—namely, a primary bottleneck for fabless startups has become lack of access to foundry capacity to prove out their ideas in fabricated chips. In a tight supply-demand environment, leading logic fabs prefer to instead allocate access to prime wafer capacities to established customers (such as Qualcomm or Apple) with large wafer volumes that lead to surefire profits. Increasingly, whatever access smaller chip design startups then have is often a few technology generations (nodes) behind. This dynamic limits the pace of innovation in a segment of the chip supply chain where the United States has traditionally dominated.

Regional Value Chain Concentration

The small handful of countries and regions holding major concentrations in the chip supply chain (see table 2.2) has driven concerns about the resilience of supply to external shocks and geopolitical tensions. Chapter 6 in this report delves deeper into some of the regional specialties, and their future ambitions to extend or to diversify from current strengths.

Table 2.2. Countries with Leading Positions in Different Segments of the Semiconductor Supply Chain

CHOKE POINT	COUNTRY	COMPANIES	DESCRIPTION
Semiconductor design	US	Qualcomm, Nvidia, Broadcom (and systems companies such as Apple)[a]	The US is home to 10 out of 20 top global semiconductor design companies, which account for 50% of global revenue.[b] US firms account for >90% of market share for the design of advanced-logic products.
EDA software	US	Cadence, Siemens/ Mentor, Synopsys	The US is home to the three largest EDA firms, which account for 85% of global market. Near-term alternatives to these three firms are likely infeasible.[c] Mentor is now owned by Siemens (Germany), but its HQ remains in the US.
Manufacturing equipment (SME)	US, Japan, Netherlands	Applied Materials, Lam Research, KLA-Tencor, & others (US) Tokyo Electron (Japan) ASML (Netherlands)	US firms collectively account for >50% of global market share in 5 of the major manufacturing process equipment categories.[d] ASML has 100% global share in EUV lithography equipment, which conveys a major advantage in leading-edge manufacturing (at 5nm and below).
Technology development and fabrication of leading-edge logic chips	Taiwan	TSMC	TSMC has a lead of 2 to 3 years in leading-edge logic manufacturing technology over all other industry competitors.

Table 2.2. (*continued*)

CHOKE POINT	COUNTRY	COMPANIES	DESCRIPTION
Technology development and fabrication of memory (DRAM) and flash storage (NAND) chips	South Korea	Samsung, SK hynix	South Korean integrated device manufacturers are dominant in the design, fabrication, and assembly of memory chips. They have 75% of the global DRAM market and 45% of the global NAND market.[e] But China-based memory manufacturers have rapidly been gaining capabilities and market share.
Wide-bandgap and compound semiconductors	US, Europe, Japan	Wolfspeed/Cree, ON Semiconductor (US) Infineon, STMicroelectronics (EU) ROHM, Mitsubishi Electric (Japan)	A variety of products and applications across power electronics, RF, and LED lighting. There is no clear market leader among the major players in the US, Germany, Netherlands, and Japan. China has identified power electronics as a focus area to reduce reliance on Western producers.
Photoresist processing equipment	Japan	JSR, TOK, Sumitomo Chemical, Shin-Etsu	Japanese companies have ~90% share in the global photoresist processing market.[f]
IP cores	UK	ARM Holdings	ARM architecture and processor cores are dominant in the mobile and tablet market. A $40 billion acquisition of ARM by Nvidia was abandoned under regulatory pressure in early 2022.[g]

[a]Systems companies such as Google, Facebook, Amazon, and Microsoft have started designing their own chips.

[b]Antonio Varas, Raj Varadarajan, Jimmy Goodrich, and Falan Yinug, *Strengthening the Global Semiconductor Supply Chain in an Uncertain Era* (Boston, MA: Boston Consulting Group and Semiconductor Industry Association, April 2021).

[c]Nurzat Baisakova and Jan-Peter Kleinhans, "The Global Semiconductor Value Chain: A Technology Primer for Policy Makers," Stiftung Neue Verantwortung, October 2020.

[d]The five categories are deposition tools, dry/wet etch and cleaning, doping equipment, process control, and testers. Varas et al., *Strengthening the Global Semiconductor Supply Chain.*

[e]The White House, *Building Resilient Supply Chains, Revitalizing American Manufacturing, and Fostering Broad-Based Growth: 100-Day Reviews under Executive Order 14017*, June 2021.

[f]Baisakova and Kleinhans, "Global Semiconductor Value Chain."

[g]Nvidia, "NVIDIA and SoftBank Group Announce Termination of NVIDIA's Acquisition of Arm Limited," press release, February 7, 2022.

Chip manufacturing or fabrication capabilities in particular are at the center of geopolitical tensions over semiconductors, along with controlling access to the technology that enables design and manufacturing. The chip fabrication stage of the supply chain has the following key features:

- *Production is highly concentrated.* Enormous R&D and capex costs of leading-edge production have seen regional and industrial concentration. Leading-edge fabs cost up to $20 billion to build.[29]
- Leading-edge logic volumes are very low yet generate substantial portions of revenue and device integrator/OEM economic activity. One source shows that less than 5 percent of global volumes in 2019 were below 10nm (although precise measurements are not possible given the difficulty of directly comparing the process technology of different companies).[30]
- *At the leading edge for logic, Samsung and TSMC dominate.* Only TSMC and Samsung are producing commercial volumes of the leading-edge 3nm and 5nm chips. TSMC is one to two years ahead of Samsung and two to three years ahead of Intel.
- *Intel has fallen behind in leading-edge logic.* Intel encountered delays with its 14nm and 10nm technologies, and its 7nm (roughly equivalent to TSMC's 5nm) production has been further delayed. These cumulative delays partly explain TSMC's recent ascension to leadership alongside its business strategy to focus on these more profitable leading-edge logic chips since securing Apple as a key customer a decade ago.[31]
- *SMIC (China) is pursuing both leading-edge and mature-logic fabrication.* China's national chip manufacturing champion has achieved commercial production at 14nm, and it may have shipped small volumes of products with aspects of 7nm technology by early 2022.[32] It has also invested heavily in less-profitable mature-logic manufacturing capacity.
- *EUV equipment conveys a major advantage at the leading edge.* Commercial production at 5nm and below is greatly facilitated (and made profitable) by extreme ultraviolet (EUV) lithography

equipment, for which the Netherlands' ASML is the monopoly supplier.[33] China does not have access to this technology due to an export control agreement between the US and Netherlands governments.

The United States has never had a credible pure-play (contract) foundry company. The foundry concept was pioneered by TSMC in Taiwan in 1987, and today, essentially all pure-play foundries are in Asia. It is worth noting, however, that while TSMC is headquartered in Taiwan and manufactures most of its chips there, the firm is publicly traded: about 75 percent of its shares are foreign owned (with US entities as top shareholders), and half its board members are US citizens.[34] Meanwhile, US-headquartered (and majority foreign-owned[35]) GlobalFoundries is a much smaller player (6 percent of the global contract foundry market) than TSMC (56 percent) and Samsung (16 percent), and it does not compete in the latest technology nodes.[36] Despite some attempts, even during periods when Intel was successful in manufacturing chips for its own use, Intel was never successful in the contract foundry model—a failure that has been attributed to company cultural as opposed to technical barriers.

While Intel's capabilities as a traditional vertically integrated device manufacturer (IDM)—functioning across the value chain of both chip design and manufacturing—gave the United States a strong position in logic chip manufacturing for many years, it has repeatedly stumbled in the past five to ten years. Intel held a three-year lead (at least one node generation) until recently. But its 14nm node was one year late, its 10nm node was three years late, and now its 7nm node is expected be at least two years late. These delays are cumulative—so what was a three-year lead six years ago is now a three-year lag. TSMC (and, to a lesser degree, Samsung) has more advanced digital technology today than Intel does; even Intel now outsources the manufacture of its most advanced chips to TSMC since it cannot build them in-house.[37] It is the opinion of many US industry observers that this situation is unlikely to change in the near term despite Intel's stated plans to regain leadership. While Intel now claims to have fixed the internal problems that led to high defect rates and delays, the real test will be whether it ships its newest technologies.

Meanwhile, the vast majority of memory (and, more recently, storage) chip production has been in Asia for decades. In the chip manufacturing domain, Intel stopped making memory chips (DRAM) more than thirty years ago, and sold its NAND Flash business to SK hynix in 2012. While the jury is still out, memory and storage has emerged as an area of notable early success for China's chipmakers.

For example, the China-based storage (NAND Flash) company Yangtze Memory Technologies Co. (YMTC) started from a blank slate in Wuhan, China, in 2016. It pursued a technology that was rather new to the NAND Flash storage companies at the time—the use of copper-to-copper hybrid bonding to stack a conventional logic wafer on top of a flash storage array wafer. The mainstream storage chip companies generally ignored this approach. Today, however, all the flash storage companies are considering using the same approach. YMTC has traditionally offered low-end products (e.g., USB storage sticks), but more recently it gained attention when Apple considered using YMTC NAND Flash chips for China's domestic market iPhones (but dropped its plan due to US export controls imposed on YMTC).[38] Established global competitors are all watching how YMTC might grow and eat into the higher-end markets as well.

Similarly, the DRAM memory company ChangXin Memory Technologies (CXMT) was started in Hefei, China, in 2016—a surprising market to enter, as DRAM is considered a difficult segment in which to make money (hence the general absence of US firms). Today, CXMT offers DDR4 DRAM products. While its market share is small (a few percent), CXMT now has a strong plausible growth story: first, leading-edge DRAM technology development has significantly slowed down due to an inability to continue to miniaturize the memory cell (now progressing at just one or two nanometers of improvement per generation, while a paradigm shift from two- to three-dimensional memory architecture has not yet happened); and second, commodity DRAM memory products have standard interfaces, so there is little distinction among manufacturers as long as the products meet industry specification standards. As of mid-2022, company leadership was confident that CXMT, despite being a very late entry in the space, could catch up to the global leading edge within three to four product generations (from today's 14–15nm leading node for DRAM memory to a future 10nm leading node).

US firms (e.g., Texas Instruments, Analog Devices, and ON Semiconductor) competitively manufacture specialty products like analog chips or wide-bandgap power management devices. These are worldwide segments with production distributed among many more players than in other parts of the semiconductor supply chain. While these specialty products use lower-resolution lithography, the process technologies themselves are sophisticated and require substantial R&D efforts to sustain commercial development. Complex systems (e.g., vehicles or weapons systems) require these technologies, and the United States remains a world-class manufacturer of these products. Even so, despite the more distributed global production of these analog and power management chips, there are growing concerns that China's efforts at chip self-sufficiency—and associated subsidies of lower-margin or unprofitable domestic manufacturers—may one day flood the global market with these older-node and specialty products. Research and development of these specialty technologies does not require sophisticated (Western) equipment—just talented people. As a result, China's focused efforts in this area, intentionally or not, could kill off market-based Western or other Asian competition via consistent underpricing to gain a controlling advantage over what was once a distributed global supply chain.

It is also helpful for industry outsiders to appreciate the deep sense held by semiconductor manufacturers—especially when chip shortages are in the news and on the minds of customers—that the semiconductor industry has been a boom-and-bust industry. This mentality is borne out by the financial histories of even today's leading and very profitable manufacturing firms such as TSMC or Samsung. One driver of this boom-bust cycle is the fact that chip manufacturers cannot gradually add incremental capacity: a new fab costs around $20 billion and provides a huge increase in capacity; customer markets, meanwhile, tend to grow gradually, so bringing a new fab online almost guarantees that there will be overcapacity for some period of time.[39] Even with the broad growth in future demand for semiconductors from seemingly every sector of the economy and across countries, this underlying boom-and-bust dynamic isn't likely to change going forward—at least for leading-edge technology. This boom-bust phenomenon also is blamed for the resistance of manufacturing firms to invest in new capacity of more mature trailing-edge chips, which (given their ubiquity on final products) can be the source of many supply bottlenecks, but which (given their commodity nature) are generally even less profitable than leading-edge chips. In short, once there is a shortage, market conditions will change by the time a new fab can come online.

Beyond fabrication, as described in table 2.2 above, the United States has a strong position in semiconductor manufacturing equipment (with companies such as Applied Materials, Lam Research, KLA, and others). ASML is the only supplier of EUV lithography tools but also supplies manufacturing equipment for a variety of mature nodes, including widely sold deep ultraviolet (DUV) lithography machines.[40] And as for chip manufacturing inputs, the silicon wafers on which chip designs are fabricated are mostly manufactured in Asia, while Japan is a strong player in the variety of pure chemicals needed for semiconductor manufacturing steps.

The United States further has a strong position in electronic design automation software tools, with Synopsys and Cadence being the leading worldwide suppliers. But given the perceived possibility in recent years that the US government could declare these software tools to be "foundational technologies" and prevent their sale to companies in China, indigenous software tools and indigenous equipment manufacturers have become an attractive area of private sector commercial investment in China, driven by the assumption that such firms could effectively capture a hugely subsidized and rapidly growing domestic chip industry. Developing design software is easier—or at least cheaper—than building a fab, and all it takes is time and talented people who are not subject to export controls. Moreover, there are already competent electronic design automation software startups in China, and China-based companies will become competitive in tools sooner rather than later.

Trends in Commercial Technology

"Moore's Law"—named after Intel's Gordon Moore—observes a general trend in the semiconductor industry: the number of transistors on commercial microchips doubles every two years while costs fall. This is not a natural law, of course, but rather a self-fulfilling prophecy that has been borne out by R&D, continued investment by leading companies, and intense competition.

For the past fifty years, a primary enabler of such advancement has been the continued "two-dimensional" reduction in chip element sizes, from the larger to the smaller nanometer node sizes described earlier. Two-dimensional downscaling—that is, making devices (such as transistors, memory, and the wires) smaller and smaller—allows manufacturers to pack more components on the same chip area and thereby achieve lower cost per function. This pathway has given structure and predictability to the semiconductor industry, offering a clear road map of the state of the art year by year.

Recently, however, that pathway of two-dimensional scaling is reaching saturation, primarily driven by the escalating cost of pushing to ever-smaller process nodes. But there are many other avenues for chip technologies to progress. This diversification of chip technology pathways has led to discussion not of the death of Moore's Law but of the "post-Moore era," when innovation will be driven instead by the way chips are fabricated, stacked, and packaged, and by how networks of chips (sometimes called "chiplets") can be made to interact with each other or deployed for application-specific purposes.[41] For example, to provide more components on the same chip, one can go to three dimensions, like (analogously) building high-rises in Manhattan. As another example: instead of using silicon transistors to perform all the functions desired of a chip, one can use other materials and other devices that are fabricated specifically for a certain function, and then integrate these functions together on the same chip. It may take more or different kinds of innovation to build high-rises and to come up with new materials and devices, but there are no physical limits to doing so. In that sense, the future of chip technologies is full of possibilities. Certainly, three-dimensional chips, advanced packaging (chiplets), and application-tailored "heterogenous compute" device technology and chip architectures will play a role. But the path forward is more diversified than it used to be.[42] And in this new paradigm, it's not clear who has the technology advantage. Whoever figures out how to make progress will likely become the leader, which has implications for the use of any policy tool that seeks to encourage—or impede—technological progress.

That changing semiconductor technology landscape is likely to affect industry structure. For example, it used to be the case that the development of chip-level manufacturing technologies could be carried out somewhat independently from the design of the system where the chip would be used (e.g., a smartphone). The abstraction boundary has worked quite well in the past, in that these two activities could occur in parallel because the trajectories of the two activities were clear and predictable (due to the predictable trend of two-dimensional device miniaturization of approximately 0.7 times per generation). Now, because performance (broadly defined as not just the speed of computation but all aspects of performance, including energy efficiency and power consumption) gains are harder to achieve, firms increasingly need to codesign the system with the chip technology. Both sides need to optimize the engineering trade-offs together. The result is that chip design companies (such as Apple, Nvidia, AMD, and Qualcomm) are working even more closely with the foundries throughout the entire design cycle, from early conception to final product. Among other things, this collaboration requires a substantial degree of trust among leading designers, fabs, and system integrators: they need to share not only product road maps but also innovation ideas that are not yet proven.

What might this trend mean for the relative future competitiveness of today's national semiconductor manufacturing champions?

One possibility is that, as two-dimensional scaling slows down across the industry, progress is going to come from system-specific (or domain-specific) technologies. This possibility means that system companies—not chip manufacturers—are increasingly likely to steer technology directions. For example, companies like Apple may start to work with new companies that specialize in advanced packaging as a service, so that they can use chiplets from multiple suppliers and build their own "2.5"-dimensional and three-dimensional technologies. More focus on heterogenous—i.e., specialized—computing applications may even drive large customers to develop more specialized IP blocks such as AI accelerators, moving beyond, for example, general-purpose ARM or x86 architectures as the main compute core.

Another possibility is essentially the opposite—that due to the consolidation of fabricators (including advanced packaging), chip production technology developers and manufacturers may occupy a more commanding position in the value chain due to their integrations with both designers and systems integrators/OEMs. This outcome would further increase the capital-intensity and barriers to entry at the leading edge of the chip industry.

Still one more possibility is that an incumbent leader like TSMC may slow down through such a complex transition, which could make it easier for Intel or other challengers to catch up.

There may even be new business models due to the changing industry dynamics. For example, chip customers are coinvesting up front in building manufacturing capacity with the foundries to ensure adequate supply. Indeed, automobile manufacturers—which often obtain chips through chip design companies (e.g., Infineon, NXP, and Renesas) and thus are second-tier customers of foundries—are increasing interaction with foundries directly to take more control of the supply of this increasingly central component of their products.[43]

What about the implications for China's semiconductor technology competitiveness as it attempts to rapidly advance? Unlike in the past, there are now many possible paths for advancing chip technology—so it is certainly possible that China may pick the right path and pull ahead of the rest of the world. Still, China does not appear to be focusing on the development of particular technology pathways that are more promising than those other countries are pursuing. The semiconductor research community, much like the broader semiconductor supply chain itself, is global and is highly competitive.

Beyond this likely transition from single-minded two-dimensional miniaturization to a plethora of ways to advance chip technology, are there more fundamental technology "leapfrog" applications that could enable China's chip firms to seize a more commanding market position?

Recently, for example, the People's Republic of China's (PRC) government has trumpeted the arrival of "third-generation" semi-conductors.[44] These refer specifically to wide-bandgap semiconduc-tors, which use more exotic materials—for example, silicon carbide (SiC), gallium nitride (GaN), and diamonds. The term *wide-bandgap* derives from the closer spacing of the atoms in these materials, which results in stronger atomic bonds and wider electrical bandgaps. But while the term *third-generation* suggests an evolution or even an ad-vance from the first- and second-generation semiconductors, these wide-bandgap third-generation semiconductors are not a replace-ment for or successor to the foundational silicon-complementary, metal-oxide semiconductor (CMOS) material system, nor do they necessarily constitute a straight advancement of semiconductor tech-nology from first generation (silicon) to second generation ("III-V" materials used in optoelectronics and microwaves). Each of these so-called generations serves very different applications and markets, and they are under the big tent of semiconductor technology. The ap-plications of these wide-bandgap semiconductors, for example, are principally in high-voltage and high-power electronics. These are use/case-specific technologies that are also very important for electric ve-hicles, the electric power grid, and battery management—intrinsically very important, and likely increasingly so, but not replacements for other semiconductor applications.

Quantum computing is another emergent technology that is often mentioned in discussions of "leapfrog" potential. It is a very special-ized technique to solve a very limited—though very important—class of problems. An analogy for quantum computing might be along the lines of the use of lasers in light—extremely useful for certain applications and enabling of new technologies, but not a replacement for general lighting. Thus, in the foreseeable future, quantum computing should not be considered an alternative to semiconductor technology, and the use of quantum computing will not be as ubiquitous as conventional semiconductor chip technology; revenues from the quantum computing industry round to zero percent of the semiconductor market, and that will be true for some time. On the contrary, for quantum computing to become a practical technology, it would need very sophisticated semiconductor technology to serve the control and signal-processing functions required for a practical system, and it would likely use the same fabrication infrastructure as today's microelectronics.

In summary, the technology trends today and going forward suggest a closer coupling among various parts of the semiconductor value chain. The emergence of the foundry and fabless model heralded a decoupling of the various parts of the value chain. Now, we see the opposite. Fabless chip design companies have to work closely with chip manufacturing companies, and the chip manufacturing companies in turn have to work closely with materials and equipment suppliers. While we may not see the revival of firm-level integrated device manufacturers like Intel or Samsung due to the need for economy of scale and the high degree of specialization, technology trends will reward tighter integration overall. Tighter integration will change the dynamics and ecosystem of the entire industry. In short, we are still at the beginning of this evolution, and we do not know where it will take us.

Trends in Research and Development

The United States has enjoyed a leading position in university-based R&D in semiconductors for decades. Today, however, China has at least as broad a set of university programs as the United States does, and China likely has many more PhD students working on traditional semiconductor (silicon) technology and devices. The leading semiconductor R&D journals (published by the Institute of Electrical and Electronics Engineers, IEEE) are now dominated either by university-based submissions from China or by the Belgium-based R&D consortium imec, which represents the industrial R&D community.

This shift is arguably the result of a severe underfunding of academic research on semiconductors in the United States for over two decades. For example, after nurturing the early semiconductor industry through government procurement, and later funding major R&D efforts through the 1980s and again in the 1990s (through the industry consortium Semiconductor Manufacturing Technology [SEMATECH]), the DoD's semiconductor R&D funding focus diverged from that of the much larger commercial R&D market to more narrowly targeted, longer-term niche technologies with specific defense applications.[45] The Department of Energy, meanwhile, primarily funds fundamental, basic science and high-performance computing (i.e., building supercomputers), but it typically does not sponsor research between these two extremes. The National Science Foundation, meanwhile, institutionally focuses on "science" and "discovery" while generally undervaluing "engineering" and "technology" and the translation to industry, which is most important to semiconductors. Overall, as compared to the 1990s, semiconductor research in US academia has been stagnant: an analysis of the combined top paper presentations at the International Electron Devices Meeting (IEDM), the International Solid-State Circuits Conference (ISSCC), and the Symposia on VLSI Technology and Circuits (VLSI) shows that, between 1995 and 2020, US-authored papers sustained a roughly 40 percent share of the total, while combined papers from Taiwan and South Korea grew from just 6 percent to 26 percent, and those from China grew from nothing to 10 percent.[46]

Meanwhile, the same changes in technology development described in the commercial industry—slowing progress in two-dimensional lateral scaling (miniaturization) of device dimensions—will also affect R&D patterns now. This result was predictable, and the challenges were universally understood. In fact, for over a quarter century, an actual international road map (ITRS, the International Technology Roadmap for Semiconductors) guided chip R&D in industry and in universities. This road map coordinated R&D programs, including national programs such as the Semiconductor Research Corporation (SRC), because everyone had a common picture of where the industry was heading. The last edition of the ITRS was updated in 2013, and there is no equivalent industry road map today. As discussed above, with the slowing down of lateral scaling because of physical limits, the path forward is a lot less clear.

Many of the possible paths forward involve technologies that are difficult for universities to contribute to. For example, advanced packaging tools are not commonly found in university labs, and currently there is no national shared facility that researchers can access to work on these kinds of R&D problems. Furthermore, the solutions will likely be specific to particular systems. For example, getting better system performance in data centers is likely a different problem than getting better system performance in power management. Single-point solutions such as improving traditional silicon CMOS transistor density, which used to be the solution, are likely not the solutions of the future.

This all may require a rethinking of university R&D structures and approaches. In particular, academia should work even more closely with the chip industry; while industry by and large has known what needed to be done in the past five decades, today the future paths for advancing chip technology are more ambiguous. And industry may increasingly rely on academic and lab-based research to explore possible paths forward, because university research is more nimble and less costly.

R&D and manufacturing form a close symbiotic relationship. Manufacturing without R&D is not sustainable because a company must have a pipeline of future products. And R&D without manufacturing is like building a bridge to nowhere—research in isolation may lead to technologies that are not manufacturable.

In sum, despite the narratives of the past two decades, semiconductor knowledge and advancements today do in fact provide foreign countries a fair degree of asymmetric advantage over the United States—especially when combined with the ability to manufacture.

Trends in Workforce

While the challenges of STEM education in the United States in general are well documented, the semiconductor industry exhibits specific structural problems that more fellowships, internships, and stipends for STEM graduate students will not solve. Given current and expected needs, it is not accurate to say that the United States has a workforce shortage problem in semiconductors. Rather, there are structural and incentive problems in the industry.

The word *manufacturing* may conjure the image of traditional factory work that can be performed with skill levels at the technician level—but a majority of the work in modern microelectronics manufacturing requires a relatively high skill level. While TSMC is sometimes regarded in the industry as being particularly reliant on advanced-skill workers given its emphasis on the leading edge of logic chip innovation, it is nonetheless an important benchmark: as of 2022, 79 percent of TSMC employees had at least a bachelor's degree, (strikingly) 51 percent had at least a master's degree, and 4 percent had a PhD.[47] Going forward, advanced-semiconductor manufacturing will increasingly rely on automation, data analytics, and artificial intelligence (AI)—and the R&D for those next-generation technologies, for which the path forward is less clear (as discussed earlier), will increasingly require PhD-level engineers.

Given the foundational nature of semiconductors in the economy, without continued advancements in semiconductor technology, it will be difficult to fulfill the high expectations now placed on adjacent future technology applications, such as AI, 5G, quantum computing, or self-driving cars. The phrase *continued advancement* is therefore often used in industry because semiconductors must constantly improve to showcase their value to society. In other words, semiconductors are not a commodity like oil—the value of semiconductors is in their ability to do more year after year. Manufacturing and R&D are both needed to achieve these next generations. Thus, a highly skilled talent pool is required.

It is important to recognize that engineering graduates in the United States (including foreign graduates of US universities) are not decreasing—they are in fact increasing. So the semiconductor workforce issue is not so much the total number of technical graduates in the United States, but rather the choices those graduates are making about career paths they wish to follow—and in which countries they follow them.

Consider that in the US technology sector today (and even within the US semiconductor value chain itself), talent tends to be attracted to end-product consumer-facing companies, and not the companies that make the components (such as the chips themselves, or the tools and equipment that produce the chips). The skills of graduates are transferable across the value chain—for example, someone who is skilled in algorithms and consumer software is equally valuable for a chip electronic design automation software company as for a social media company. Algorithm and data science skills that are useful for developing next-generation AI-enabled chip manufacturing systems are similarly valuable to financial technology (fintech) companies. And someone who is skilled in manufacturing semiconductors is also valuable to companies that design consumer-facing electronics products using those same chips. To construct fabs, one needs a variety of both technicians with trade skills and highly educated engineers. To run a fab at the leading edge, technicians are still required, but firms mostly need engineers with the ability to understand and analyze data from the fabrication process, to report problems, and to make decisions on the fly. In Taiwan's experience, that means most fab engineers have at least a bachelor's or master's degree. And culturally, working for a fab in Taiwan today means good pay and high social cachet—TSMC is seen as one of Taiwan's most desirable employers, and new hiring windows make national news.[48]

Meanwhile, in the United States, highly skilled engineering and technology graduates tend instead to be consumed by companies that make the end products—such as Apple, Google, or even Nvidia—and many of them are software or systems applications companies. Students can imagine how, working at these companies, their engineering talents can lead to exciting products. Even though chips are at the heart of these products, they are nonetheless largely invisible. Perhaps more importantly, mirroring trends in service versus manufacturing sectors elsewhere, profits tend to accrue to these firms that produce differentiated customer-facing end products, not the companies that make the chips. As a crude illustration, consider that the price difference between an iPhone that has 256 GB versus one with 128 GB of storage is $100, but the price difference between the chips themselves is $8. Thus, it's easy to see why companies like Apple or Google or Facebook might have nicer cafeterias and higher compensation than semiconductor companies. The value capture and compensation differences are substantial. Indeed, a 2022 McKinsey analysis noted that US employees rank semiconductor firms lower than consumer technology or even automotive employers not just in compensation, but also in spillovers to work-life balance, perceived quality of senior management, firm culture, and overall perceived career opportunities.[49]

Assuming the demand side of semiconductor workforce development is eventually solved, and assuming there is a new interest from US students wanting to be trained in semiconductors, the best way to meet that demand will be to then increase R&D funding in semiconductors and to build up semiconductor research and teaching facilities on university campuses. This approach will grow the number and quality of professors and instructors in the field of semiconductors, making available both quality course offerings and hands-on training opportunities that are vital to excellence in technology development and manufacture. Quality professors and hands-on training experiences can also help today's technical graduates see how careers in the chip industry might let them apply their skills toward meaningful, global-scale societal problems such as the environment, human health, or AI that they consider more important than consumer electronics.

In sum, the semiconductor industry arguably has an unaddressed structural issue: even though developing semiconductor technology requires top talent, US chip companies are generally not able to offer the money or the excitement to acquire it. Improving this situation, as discussed further in chapter 4 of this report, should not be left to market dynamics—it should be an objective of policy.

NOTES

1. H.-S. Philip Wong, Kerem Akarvardar, Dimitri Antoniadis, Jeffrey Bokor, Chenming Hu, Tsu-Jae King-Liu, Subhasish Mitra, James D. Plummer, and Sayeef Salahuddin, "A Density Metric for Semiconductor Technology [Point of View]," *Proceedings of the IEEE* 108, no. 4 (April 2020): 478–82.

2. Given this, there have been proposals to replace the nanometer naming convention with a density metric instead, but this approach has yet to gain industry traction.

3. FPGAs are modular, multipurpose chips that can be flexibly programmed and reprogrammed by the end user for various tasks. They are commonly used today in data center applications; see below on FPGA defense sector applications as well.

4. TSMC, *2022 Second Quarter Earnings Conference*, July 14, 2022.

5. TechInsights (blog), "SMIC 7nm Technology Found in MinerVa Bitcoin Miner," accessed May 13, 2023.

6. Antonio Varas, Raj Varadarajan, Jimmy Goodrich, and Falan Yinug, *Strengthening the Global Semiconductor Supply Chain in an Uncertain Era* (Boston, MA: Boston Consulting Group and Semiconductor Industry Association, April 2021).

7. Cars with autonomous or driver-assistance capabilities also now increasingly require leading-edge logic chips, given the computational complexity of these real-time processes. For more on contemporary automotive chip needs, see Jack Ewing and Neal E. Boudette, "A Tiny Part's Big Ripple: Global Chip Shortage Hobbles the Auto Industry," *New York Times*, April 23, 2021.

8. Varas et al., *Strengthening the Global Semiconductor Supply Chain.*

9. Both DRAM chips and NAND Flash chips can be referred to as either memory or storage chips in that they both store digital information. The differences are in how fast they can be written and read, how long they can store information, the density of storage they provide, and the cost per bit of storage. Generally, DRAM (which is quite fast) is placed in close architectural proximity to a computer's CPU logic chip. NAND Flash chips are slower and are further away (architecturally speaking, not necessarily physically speaking). Generally, the slower a memory technology is, the higher the density of storage, and hence the lower cost per bit it provides.

10. Yuka Hayashi, "Chip Shortage Limits US's Ability to Supply Weapons to Ukraine, Commerce Secretary Says," *Wall Street Journal*, April 27, 2022.

11. Vikram Mittal, "US Soldiers' Burden of Power: More Electronics Means Lugging More Batteries," *Forbes*, October 26, 2020.

12. See, for example, comments in US Government Accountability Office, *Semiconductor Supply Chain: Policy Considerations from Selected Experts for Reducing Risks and Mitigating Shortages*, GAO-22-105923 (Washington, DC: US GAO, July 2022).

13. These beginnings are well documented by Chris Miller in his history of the industry, *Chip Wars* (New York: Scribner, 2022).

14. Jon Y, "The Government Semiconductor Chip Buying Problem," *The Asianometry Newsletter*, November 3, 2021.

15. Shujai Shivakumar and Charles Wessner, "Semi-Conductors and National Security: What Are the Stakes?," Center for Strategic and International Studies, June 8, 2022.

16. Representing eighty-one suppliers as of August 2022. For more details, see "DMEA Trusted IC Program," Defense Microelectronics Activity, accessed May 13, 2023.

17. Mark Lapedus, "A Crisis in DoD's Trusted Foundry Program?," Semiconductor Engineering, October 22, 2018.

18. Michaela D. Platzer, John F. Sargent Jr., and Karen M. Sutter, *Semiconductors: US Industry, Global Competition, and Federal Policy* (Washington, DC: Congressional Research Service, October 26, 2020).

19. See Brad R. Williams, "DoD Seeks $2.3B to Bolster US Chip Making," *Breaking Defense*, June 4, 2021.

20. A recent public review by the DoD Office of Inspector General reports some delays in this process; a provision of the 2023 National Defense Authorization Act mandates additional reviews to this end. See Department of Defense Office of Inspector General, "Evaluation of the Department of Defense's Transition from a Trusted Foundry Model to a Quantifiable Assurance Method for Procuring Custom Microelectronics (DODIG-2022-084)," May 4, 2022.

21. Eric Lee, "How Taiwan Underwrites the US Defense Industrial Complex," *The Diplomat*, November 9, 2021.

22. Keith Holbert and Lawrence Clark, "Radiation Hardened Electronics Destined for Severe Nuclear Reactor Environments," US Department of Energy, February 19, 2016.

23. Jonathan Pellish, "A New Market for Terrestrial Single-Event Effects: Autonomous Vehicles," NASA, May 2019.

24. Xilinx calls this chip an adaptive compute acceleration platform (ACAP).

25. Michael Johnson, ed., "A New Approach to Radiation Hardening Computers," NASA, last updated August 12, 2022.

26. "Radiation Hardened Electronics Market by Component," MarketsandMarkets, May 2022.

27. Examples include ultraviolet lithography tools, which use certain wavelengths of light to print the circuit pattern onto the silicon wafer.

28. Including South Korea, Japan, China, and Taiwan. Southeast Asian nations such as Singapore, Vietnam, Malaysia, and the Philippines are also starting to play larger roles, especially in outsourced assembly, packaging, and testing (OSAT). See chapter 6 for more detail.

29. Semiconductor Industry Association, "US Needs Greater Manufacturing Incentives," July 2020.

30. Varas et al., *Strengthening the Global Semiconductor Supply Chain*.

31. Pushkar Ranade, "The Apple-TSMC Partnership," Bits and Bytes, March 6, 2022.

32. Given that this SMIC 7nm chip lacks static random access memory (SRAM), which typically takes up half the area of a processor chip, it is probably inaccurate to describe this as a bona fide 7nm technology. Claims of 7nm originally reported in "SMIC 7nm Technology Found in MinerVa Bitcoin Miner," *TechInsights*, accessed May 13, 2023.

33. It is possible to produce 5nm technology without EUV, but not profitably at scale. The development of EUV by ASML was supported by investments from Intel, Samsung, and TSMC. Intel was the most visible early supporter.

34. TSMC, *Annual Report 2021(I)*, March 12, 2022, 66.

35. Wallace Witkowski, "GlobalFoundries IPO: 5 Things to Know about the Chip Company Going Public in a Semiconductor Shortage," *MarketWatch*, last updated October 23, 2021.

36. Foundry revenue figures as of the third quarter of 2022. See TrendForce, "Global Top 10 Foundries' Total Revenue Up 6% in 3Q 2022," *EE Times Asia*, December 16, 2022.

37. Industry trade press in 2021 reported that Intel had contracted with TSMC for a significant fraction of TSMC's 3nm production capacity. See, for example, Monica Chen and Jessie Shen, "TSMC to Make 3nm Chips for Intel, Sources Claim," *DIGITIMES Asia*, January 27, 2021.

38. Reuters, "Apple Freezes Plans to Use China's YMTC Chips—Nikkei," October 17, 2022.

39. Indeed, following the widely reported chip shortages of 2021 (and broad growth in semiconductor industry profits), financial results of Q2 2022 showed market softening. In fact, on the same day that the CHIPS and Science Act of 2022 passed the Senate, Intel announced its first net loss in thirty years and a reduction in expected capex on account of weaker demand. Global industry financial results were soft across Q4 2022 and into Q1 2023. See Dylan Patel, "Intel Cuts Fab Buildout by $4B to Pay Billions in Dividends," Semianalysis, July 28, 2022; and Nicholas Gordon, "Chip Glut Batters Semiconductor Industry as Intel Shares Lose Almost All Their 2023 Gains after Dismal Earnings," *Fortune*, January 27, 2023.

40. ASML has suggested that 90 percent of equipment it has ever sold is still in use on chip manufacturing lines.

41. Samuel K. Moore, "The Transistor of 2047: Expert Predictions," *IEEE Spectrum*, November 21, 2022.

42. Mark Liu, "TSMC Chairman Mark Liu Describes How the World's Largest Chipmaker Is Reimagining the Semiconductor Industry," *Fortune*, June 8, 2022.

43. See, for example, the Sony-TSMC joint ventures on research and fabrication in Japan, and the GM-GlobalFoundries joint investment. Masaharu Ban, "Sony Begins Funding TSMC's Japanese Chip Plant," *Nikkei Asia*, January 26, 2022; and Jane Lee, Joseph White, and Steven Nellis, "GM Inks Deal with GlobalFoundries to Secure US-Made Chips," Reuters, February 9, 2023.

44. Shiyin Chen, Yuan Gao, and Abhishek Vishnoi, "Xi Jinping Picks Top Lieutenant to Lead China's Chip Battle against US," *Bloomberg News*, June 16, 2021.

45. Marko M. G. Slusarczuk and Richard Van Atta, "The Tunnel at the End of the Light: The Future of the US Semiconductor Industry," *Issues in Science and Technology* 28, no. 3 (Spring 2012).

46. Japan saw a major decline during this period alongside its loss of global semiconductor manufacturing leadership, from 39 percent in 1995 to just 10 percent in 2020, equaling China. See Jan-Peter Kleinhans, Julia Hess, Pegah Maham, and Anna Semenova, "Who Is Developing the Chips of the Future?," Stiftung Neue Verantwortung, June 16, 2021.

47. TSMC, *Annual Report 2021(I)*.

48. Cheng Hung-ta and Frances Huang, "TSMC, Evergreen, Fubon Financial Dream Employers for Job Changers: Poll," *Focus Taiwan*, January 14, 2023.

49. Ondrej Burkacky, Marc de Jong, and Julia Dragon, "Strategies to Lead in the Semiconductor World," McKinsey & Company, April 15, 2022.

CHAPTER THREE

An Insurance Policy for Dependence of US Supply Chains on Foreign Providers

CHRISTOPHER FORD

The United States should adopt an "insurance policy" for its overseas semiconductor supply chain exposure through realistic onshoring and other measures that enhance independence and resilience.

Emergent security and geopolitical concerns that were less evident a decade ago now warrant additional policy attention in maintaining commercial semiconductor supply chain resilience in both leading-edge and mature chips; a variety of short- and long-term government policies and business sector options need to be considered to address this challenge.

A special subset of semiconductor supply chain disruptions could lead to the United States losing access—temporarily or for a protracted period—to advanced-semiconductor exports from trusted partners in Asia. For example, this inaccessibility could occur in the event of a People's Republic of China (PRC) blockade of Taiwan or some form of armed conflict on or around the island. A natural disaster could also severely disrupt access, at least temporarily. In view of these threats, the United States should invest in some degree of diversification, especially with regard to the manufacturing of chips, which would diminish short-term economic or strategic damage to the United States—and provide the nucleus of scalable supplementary capacities—in the event of supply chain

Any views expressed and characterizations made by Dr. Ford herein represent his personal perspective, and not necessarily that of anyone else in the US government or elsewhere. Dr. Ford is grateful for the contributions made by his coauthor on this chapter, but that coauthor has requested public anonymity.

disruptions. Implementation of the CHIPS and Science Act of 2022 should be evaluated by these imperatives.

Beyond the time-limited subsidies available through the CHIPS and Science Act, it is important to recognize the key role of private capital and commercial business decisions—including investment decisions made by US partner–domiciled firms in Taiwan, Japan, or Korea—in realizing US public interests in sustaining additional semiconductor activity over time. The main way to do this is by making this country an attractive place to do business from a cost and regulatory perspective. Both the federal and US state governments have responsibilities to this end. Otherwise, subsidies are a bridge to nowhere.

That said, ensuring access to Taiwan's semiconductor exports should not become a significant factor motivating US decisions to help defend Taiwan. Such a commitment should rest on broader principled and strategic grounds, including Taiwan's global importance to democracy and the world economy. After all, China's interests in Taiwan also rest on its broader political and strategic interests, and potential semiconductor-related benefits or implications will not weigh heavily in Beijing's calculus regarding the use of military force against Taiwan.

•   •   •

In early 2021, the lead times for the manufacture of semiconductor chips sharply spiked. A previous average lead time of twelve weeks reached fifteen weeks by January 2021, then stretched to seventeen weeks by March and April. These delays triggered an unprecedented global chip shortage and caused several downstream industries to warn of upcoming production deficits. Chip shortages led to major losses for systems integrators—for example, the global automotive industry was estimated to have lost $210 billion in sales in 2021.[1]

The chip shortage of 2021 and early 2022 can largely be attributed to market dynamics—namely, a demand shock resulting from poor industry planning and a subsequent surge in orders emerging from the COVID-19 pandemic. But one particularly stressed class of victims of this sharp swing in orders was carmakers, who were forced to review their practice of maintaining lean inventories as cost-savings strategies. The problem began when new vehicle sales essentially halted in spring of 2020 and the industry drastically cut orders for parts and materials, including the chips needed for a growing number of automotive applications such as touch screen displays and collision-avoidance systems.[2]

Meanwhile, the consumer electronics industry soaked up those unsold chips, as a surge in demand occurred from consumers working from home for personal computing products and more general technology. Then the problem was exacerbated when China's own electronics firms—including multinational champion Huawei—began stockpiling chip supplies in anticipation of further US sanctions.[3] By the time vehicle demand began to rebound in late 2020, chip manufacturers were already committed to supplying major customers in consumer electronics and could not meet resurgent demand.

More important than the 2021 shortage itself, however, may have been the significant media and policy attention it directed to the way that global supply chain fragilities, by creating alarm, ultimately worsened the crisis. This led to a close examination of the United States' dependence on the global chip supply chain.

Despite the well-documented weaknesses in the manufacturing and packaging of chips, the United States still holds the world's strongest position across the rest of the semiconductor supply chain—namely, in semiconductor manufacturing equipment, electronic design automation (EDA), chip design software, and high-end fabless chip design. Less appreciated is the fact that the United States is also home to many of the world's most important retailers and device integrators—that is, end customers of chips who integrate them into valuable consumer products. These systems integrators and original equipment manufacturers (OEMs), such as Apple and auto manufacturers such as GM, capture much of the value of a differentiated final consumer product and hold tremendous influence over the operating decisions of their suppliers, especially those in the chip sector.

Of the various concerns that have arisen about the robustness of the semiconductor supply chain, especially since the COVID-19 pandemic, the most elementary one is the risk that the US strengths in the semiconductor supply chain will be undermined by its domestic weaknesses in chip manufacturing. This chapter explores US semiconductor strengths and weaknesses and suggests short- to medium-term measures that could be taken to mitigate the risk of deep US reliance on overseas manufacturing. We will also suggest new domestic resiliency initiatives and manufacturing competitiveness reforms that will make US supply chains more dependable as the world becomes more fractious.

Before proceeding, we also issue a word of caution. Semiconductor shortages or surpluses from periodic mismatches in supply and demand are a normal feature of this capital-intensive and fast-moving industry, and managing them should remain largely a business matter rather than a responsibility of US government policy. Ford F-150 pickup trucks, for example, would likely still have been backlogged in 2021 for want of, say, window regulator control chips, even if the United States had an entirely autarkic semiconductor supply chain.

As we move increasingly toward a world of intensified trade among like-minded blocs of nations, moreover, the United States will continue to benefit from its reliance on friendly partners and their comparative contributions to a complex international chip supply chain. Thus the medium-term goal of US policy efforts on semiconductors should be to make our rapidly evolving network of trusted participants in the chip supply chain more reliable and attractive. A balanced policy will pursue efficiencies and growth through trade (with particular growth among partners) while assuming some new economic costs as a sort of insurance policy against catastrophic foreign supply chain disruption or manipulation.

To that end, as soon as possible the United States government should aim to do the following:

- Preserve the business competitiveness of its existing areas of innovation and strength in the semiconductor supply chain by maintaining an attractive global investment environment and by continuing to facilitate the availability of skilled workers, including immigrants.
- Subsidize investment in existing areas of weakness, such as advanced-semiconductor manufacturing and packaging, where

medium-term market-driven economics are likely to trail those of even friendly trading partners.

- Incentivize, or itself establish, novel supply chain resiliency mechanisms, including aggregating information, stockpiling, and practicing extended inventory management where the public interest requires more resiliency in light of risks of disruption or strategic manipulation.

In short, the United States should do what it takes to facilitate both domestic production capacity and closer reliance on Taiwan, South Korea, Japan, and other partners that provide key steps in today's semiconductor production supply chain. With such a successful insurance policy, the US commander in chief would not feel his or her national security decision making was constrained in a future Indo-Pacific crisis *due to domestic failures to mitigate supply chain risks alone*. A decision this weighty should be determined by values and strategic interests, not a shortage of microchips or commercial concerns.

US Semiconductor Strengths

The United States remains the world's leader in the design and marketing of advanced chips. Nvidia, Intel, AMD, Apple, and Qualcomm are all at the top of their industries and will remain there for a long time. The US chip ecosystem is built upon historical US leadership in research at universities and corporate research labs.

As described in the previous chapter, the United States is home to ten of the world's top twenty semiconductor design companies, including Qualcomm, Nvidia, and Broadcom. US firms collectively enjoy nearly 90 percent of global market share for the design of leading-edge logic chips, and over half of chip design revenue in general. Through firms such as Cadence, Synopsys, and Mentor Graphics (now part of Siemens), the United States dominates in EDA software tools; together, these three US firms account for 85 percent of the global market and represent an important choke point area for the industry, since there are no presently feasible alternatives to them.

The United States also has leading-edge semiconductor manufacturing equipment companies such as Applied Material, KLA, and Lam Research. Table 3.1 summarizes some of these key US firms across today's supply chain.

Table 3.1. Key US and Non-US Players by Semiconductor Value Chain Step

CATEGORY	VALUE CHAIN STEP	US COMPANIES	NON-US COMPANIES
Inputs	Semiconductor manufacturing equipment	Applied Materials Lam Research KLA-Tencor	ASML (Netherlands) Tokyo Electron (Japan)
	Specialized chemicals and materials	Dow Chemical, DuPont	Tokyo Ohka Kogyo (Japan) Showa Denko (Japan) SK Materials (Korea) Foosung (Korea)
	EDA software	Cadence Synopsys Mentor Graphics (US HQ, German ownership)[a]	Altium (Australia) *Huada Empyrean (China)*
Design and manufacture	Integrated device manufacturers (IDM)	Intel Micron Texas Instruments	Samsung (Korea) SK hynix (Korea)
	Semiconductor designers (fabless)	Broadcom Qualcomm Nvidia	MediaTek (Taiwan) Novatek (Taiwan) Realtek (Taiwan) *HiSilicon (China)*
	Foundries (contract fabs)	GlobalFoundries (US HQ, UAE ownership)	TSMC (Taiwan) UMC (Taiwan) *SMIC (China)*
Assembly, packaging, and test	Outsourced assembly packaging and test (OSAT)	Amkor	ASE (Taiwan) *JCET (China)* UTAC (Singapore)

[a]Owned by Siemens since 2017.

Note: Italics = China-based company

Source: Adapted from Randy Abrams, Tseng Chaolien, and John Pitzer, "Global Semiconductor Sector: The Uneven Rise of China's IC Industry," Credit Suisse, January 2021.

These firms all produce for the US domestic market as well as for customers abroad. For example, the United States in 2019 exported about $8 billion in chips annually to China chip designers, as well as around $4 billion in design tools and manufacturing equipment. The United States also exports around $400 million in raw materials to China, including photographic plates, wafers, and wafer material.[4]

Major US tech firms such as Google, Amazon, and Apple are also both chip designers and chip consumers. As the world's leaders in their respective ecosystems, they lead trends on design and implementation, which are hard to disrupt without the emergence of novel technologies. Their large revenue streams and longer investment time horizons also allow them to invest in new chip designs that may take years to bear fruit. Their order sizes and cofinancing of new production capacity often give them priority in manufacturers' outputs, offering them first access to new generations of technology and helping to insulate them from supply disruption during times of shortage. Their choice of suppliers for components in new products—e.g., for memory in a new iPhone, or a modem chipset—can make or break an upstart manufacturer. And their preferences on logistical arrangements, including location of manufacture, can be negotiated as part of their supply contracts. Thus their influence on an industry's direction should be utilized, not ignored, in considering how to fortify chip supply chains to align with national security issues.

US Semiconductor Supply Chain Weaknesses and Vulnerability

But the picture is not all rosy. The US share of global chip manufacturing has dropped from 37 percent in 1990 to 12 percent in 2020. Chip assembly and packaging—a critical link in the chip supply chain—is also relatively weak, with the United States having only about 15 percent of global market share.

The loss of leadership in leading-edge logic chip production was primarily due to private investment decisions, as US industry chose to concentrate investment on the higher–gross margin fabless design business and yielded the lower-grossing, capital-intensive manufacturing business to Asia. As described in chapter 2, leading companies such as Intel also made strategic errors that contributed to the loss of US leadership.

The decline in trailing-edge chip fabrication was driven by market forces—e.g., lower labor cost and more attractive capital structures in some Asian countries—as well as by better incentives offered by the governments of East Asian nations. As a result, the United States today has almost no commercial manufacturing capacity for legacy logic chips with the node sizes above 28nm.

Manufacturing costs remain much higher in the United States than in Asia. The Semiconductor Industry Association (SIA) estimates that the ten-year total cost of ownership of a new fab located in the United States is now 25–50 percent higher than in Asia, an estimate confirmed by Taiwan Semiconductor Manufacturing Company (TSMC) in connection with its current work to establish two new leading-edge logic fabs in Arizona. Overall, SIA assesses that only 6 percent of the new global capacity will be in the United States if present trends continue. By contrast, China is projected to add 40 percent of new global capacity over the next decade.[5]

Beyond manufacturing, there is also more recent industry concern about the strength of the US pipeline for innovation through new market entrants across other links of the semiconductor supply chain, even in current areas of strength such as semiconductor design and equipment. The perspectives of private investors are illuminating here.

Consider the example of venture capital (VC) as a development route for a prospective US semiconductor manufacturing equipment startup firm. In the 1990s, the semiconductor industry was one of the hottest sectors for US venture capital. Today, while overall US VC investment in semiconductors has grown, the sector has declined as a share of the US total VC investment. Some investors suggest that capital losses in the cleantech sector early in this century created distrust among US VC investors in the hardware industry, compared to software, which is less capital-intensive and offers quicker returns. Furthermore, advances in consumer internet technology also moved entrepreneurial interest away from semiconductors.

The success of a startup ecosystem relies in part on the number and variety of experiments that are attempted therein: the more experiments there are across a wider variety of areas, the better the chances for a breakout success. But for US semiconductor design and equipment startups in particular, two main issues now inhibit these experiments. First, as touched on in the previous chapter on industry and technology trends, it takes roughly $30 million of financing to even prove out the viability of a new prototype chip design, and another $100 million or more to get to volume production. Second, the potential universe of acquiring companies has become more limited because of public market consolidation; fewer buyers means smaller acquisition premiums and smaller exits for venture investors. Huge capital costs, combined with a small buyer universe and smaller and less profitable exits, do not make for an attractive area for investment. When combined with today's macroeconomic environment characterized by higher interest rates, this limitation risks creating a cycle of diminishing interest and funding in US semiconductor startups.

While US semiconductor VC investments easily constituted the majority of global semiconductor VC investments from 2000 to approximately 2017, the US portion has since declined significantly. VC semiconductor investments in China, however, have not lagged and have largely filled that gap.

Recent Policy and Industry Responses

A series of high-profile industry announcements have followed the pandemic-era chip shortages. Together, these new investments have the potential to form the core of a sort of insurance policy against catastrophic consequences for the United States if global chip supply chains were to be severed, particularly in manufacturing.

First, in 2020, Taiwan's TSMC announced that it would build a $12 billion fab in Arizona, scheduled to begin production in 2024. In late 2022, TSMC's founder indicated that a second, more advanced fab would be added to that same Arizona site.[6] Samsung and Intel have also announced $17 billion and $20 billion investments, respectively, to increase manufacturing capacity in Texas and in Ohio.[7] In addition, in mid-2022, Taiwan's GlobalWafers announced a $5 billion investment in a new silicon wafer manufacturing facility in Texas.[8] Qualcomm and GlobalFoundries also announced a $4.2 billion purchase agreement to fund expansion of GlobalFoundries' New York facility.[9] The US firm Micron, meanwhile, announced a $40 billion investment in domestic memory chip manufacturing through 2030, which it claimed would increase the US market share from 2 percent to 10 percent.[10] These announcements are motivated by a combination of commercial interests—that is, customer preferences—as well as by the raft of state and federal government subsidies proposed or enacted in response to the shortage of chips and fears of foreign supply chain disruption. Whatever the motivations, they represent the beginning of what could be a very significant shift in this sector.

In his December 2022 speech marking the "tool-in" of the company's first Arizona fab, TSMC founder Morris Chang described that stage in the construction process (and by extension the current state of geopolitically driven semiconductor supply chain reconfiguration) as "the end of the beginning."[11] The sections that follow describe which beginning policy steps are already being taken in the United States, and what more could be done to improve the resilience of the US sector.

Federal Spending

At the federal level, a consequential 2020 SIA and Boston Consulting Group (BCG) industry association report on global government incentives for chip manufacturing set off a flurry of executive and legislative activity.[12] The report modeled the impact of several potential US policy approaches—a baseline in which the US share of global manufacturing would further decline from 12 percent to 10 percent by 2030, a $20 billion federal subsidy program that would allow the United States to sustain its current 12 percent market share, and a $50 billion subsidy program would result in an increase to 14 percent. Implicitly, the report advocated for the highest tier of government involvement in order to reverse a decline in US semiconductor manufacturing—and assure at least a minimum (and thereafter potentially scalable) degree of domestic production capacity for critical needs should global chip supply chains be severely disrupted. These investment figures ultimately helped inform the proposed $52 billion "CHIPS for America" manufacturing grant program as part of the US Senate's US Innovation and Competition Act of 2021.

Elements of that bill were passed as the CHIPS and Science Act on a bipartisan basis in July 2022, after significant legislative wrangling between the two congressional chambers. Its goal is to boost American semiconductor research, development, and production. It contains the following provisions:

- $52.7 billion for manufacturing, workforce development, and research, including $28 billion in manufacturing incentives for leading-edge logic and memory chips (largely grants, but also $6 billion in loans and loan guarantees)
- Approximately $10 billion in grants and loan guarantees specifically for mature or current-generation chips and industry suppliers
- $11 billion for a National Semiconductor Technology Center and a National Advanced Packaging Manufacturing Program, as well as National Institute of Standards and Technology (NIST) metrology (chip measurement) R&D programs
- $2 billion for Department of Defense chip technology development and domestic prototyping needs
- $500 million focused on international semiconductor supply chain security

These funds are to be distributed over a period of five years, with about half of the total to be expended in 2023. The bill also includes a grant clawback "guardrail" clause, requiring that firms receiving grants will not significantly expand semiconductor manufacturing or joint technology development in China or other countries of concern (legacy chips, defined as 28nm or above, are excepted).[13]

This all represents a very important start. There are, however, areas for further improvement:

As the rules for these CHIPS Act subsidies are established by the US Department of Commerce and disbursement proceeds, the focus must turn to execution of these projects. And it is fair to regard this targeted subsidy of semiconductor manufacturing as a public experiment. If it fails, there will be little justification for similar efforts in other critical technology areas, and the US effort to develop what has been termed a "modern industrial and innovation strategy" might be regarded as having failed.[14] To preserve bipartisan support for effective competitive strategy in the technology arena, it will be essential to prevent cronyism and protectionism, or policy-maker capture by particular business, labor, or local political interests, from distorting and discrediting these efforts.

Given the primary goal of establishing at least minimal onshore manufacturing capabilities, *awards of funding should be made to the firms—whether headquartered domestically or in friendly jurisdictions abroad—that have the best chance of executing on this promise from a technology risk and operational efficiency perspective.* The CHIPS Act effort will be at risk and future efforts much less likely to win support if the United States does not at least manage to get two fabs up and running that are capable of producing commercially viable, leading-class logic chips at competitive yields within the program's five-year time frame.

Federal Tax Efficiency

Semiconductor manufacturing is a notably capital-intensive industry. Industry participants report that, given the level of private investment that goes into upgrading or expanding production facilities each year (many multiples of any public grants), tax efficiency on that capital investment is an even larger motivator than direct public spending. To that end, perhaps more impactful than the CHIPS and Science Act's direct expenditures was its 25 percent (Section 48D) investment tax credit for capital expenses for the manufacturing both of semiconductors themselves and of semiconductor manufacturing equipment over the period 2023–26, which is estimated to be worth as much as $24 billion (depending on private investment levels).[15] This sector-specific measure built upon the more general tax efficiency measures of the 2017 Tax Cuts and Jobs Act (TCJA), which included an overall corporate tax rate reduction from 35 percent to 21 percent (below that of many Organisation for Economic Co-operation and Development [OECD] nations), as well as a 100 percent bonus depreciation tax deduction for short-lived capital assets, such as equipment used in semiconductor manufacturing facilities (a depreciation currently set to phase out from 2023 to 2026). Both of these pieces of legislation represent important moves into tax-based investment incentivization.

But there are further areas for improvement here as well:

- Well over half of the cost of a new semiconductor fab derives from the equipment purchased by the manufacturer to build production lines. *Extending full tax depreciation for short-lived capital assets beyond 2022* could therefore improve the competitiveness of US semiconductor and semiconductor equipment manufacturers.
- Modern semiconductor and semiconductor equipment manufacturers reinvest significant portions of their revenue into research and development each year in order to sustain leading-edge capabilities. As part of TCJA negotiations, deductions of US firm R&D spending are now (since 2022) required to be taken over five years, instead of immediately in the year incurred. *Reverting to full tax deductions of R&D expenses on an annual basis* would benefit a broad swath of knowledge investments in this and other critical research-intensive industries.

Federal Regulatory Reform

The time-consuming and burdensome procedures mandated by the 1970 National Environmental Policy Act (NEPA) will impede the growth of the US semiconductor industry, despite the passage of the CHIPS Act. In the United States, a construction project classified as a "Major Federal Action," for instance, could be subjected to a lengthy review process, lasting 4.5 years on average.[16] In comparison, other advanced democracies such as Germany and Canada—neither of which is usually reticent about imposing regulatory burdens upon the private sector—have more efficient permitting processes than does the United States, and both generally conclude reviews within a mere two years.[17] Construction of fabs involving federal funding could trigger this level of heavy environmental regulation, with associated permitting delays.[18]

So far, only limited steps have been taken at the federal level to address this risk. For example, Title 41 of the Fixing America's Surface Transportation Act of 2015 (FAST-41)—made permanent in the 2021 Infrastructure Investment and Jobs Act—included provisions to hasten the federal permitting process by improving early consultation, interagency coordination, transparency, and accountability in specified sectors (e.g., highway construction).[19] In November 2021, Senators Portman, Hagerty, and King added an amendment to the Fiscal Year 2022 National Defense Authorization Act that incorporates sectors relevant to national security, including semiconductors, into the FAST-41 fast-track process.[20]

President Biden also announced the launch of a sector-specific interagency expert working group on permitting and permitting-related project delivery issues for high-tech manufacturing.[21] This group is to build on CHIPS Act provisions by boosting interagency coordination as well as federal-state coordination, consistent with the administration's general permitting plan launched in May of 2022.[22] Federal-state coordination to avoid redundancy in regulations and oversight has been identified by analysts as a particularly important area for improvement.[23]

Further areas for improvement are these:

- Despite efforts to categorically exempt semiconductor fabs from burdensome environmental reviews—the US Chamber of Commerce, for example, wrote to the secretary of commerce in the spring of 2022 urging the department to exempt semiconductor fabs from lengthy NEPA reviews[24]—facilities receiving CHIPS Act funds are expected to be subject to existing NEPA regulations.[25] Given that leading-edge logic technology cycles are themselves on the order of two years, this permitting process barrier, if applied to fabs, could prevent the United States from ever producing the world's most advanced chips. Indeed, since the NEPA process for "Major Federal Actions" takes more than *twice* as long as this cycle, applying NEPA rules to chip fab facilities would ensure that US-located manufacturing falls progressively further behind the state of the art. *Care should be taken to ensure that federal financing intended to speed the development of this sector does not inadvertently slow it.*

- While direct Environmental Protection Agency (EPA) permitting itself may account for only a small portion of regulatory requirements, a new project must manage many other federal and state regulations that often require EPA's input. For example, in Arizona, the Department of Environmental Quality (DEQ), a state agency, grants permits that are required under the federal Clean Air Act (CAA), the Resource Conservation and Recovery Act (RCRA), and the Clean Water Act (CWA), as well as other state-level regulations. These permit processes also receive input from the EPA. *A policy of timely EPA reviews for critical industries* such as chip fabs could therefore improve private investor confidence in project delivery schedules—which is particularly important given their large up-front capital outlays and the need to coordinate long-lead-time equipment orders from dozens of vendors.

Flexible air and water permits are another potential approach to allow companies to make changes to their plants without triggering new environmental reviews. Flexible permitting is a way to avoid EPA or other federal permitting delays within willing host communities while preserving environmental performance. For example, Oregon's Plant Site Emissions Limit (PSEL) program allows such flexibility as long as overall emission limits are met. Intel has cited this flexibility as the reason behind saving "hundreds of business days associated with making operational and process changes to ramp up production," and added that without it they would have had to move production away from Oregon.[26]

According to a 2017 McKinsey report, indirect "scope 2" emissions, largely from purchases of power generated off-site to run production facilities, are the largest contributors (45 percent of the industry's total) of greenhouse gases (GHG) from semiconductor companies.[27] Access to not just cheap power, but low-carbon power too, has become a major factor for companies to decide on fab locations. The United States in general is quite competitive in this regard, compared to the dirtier power grid mixes in China, South Korea, Taiwan, and Singapore. Direct "scope 1" emissions (35 percent) also contribute to sectoral GHG emissions. They are associated with high-global-warming-potential process gases in tasks such as wafer etching and chamber cleaning, as well as leakage of heat-transfer fluids into the atmosphere when used in chillers to control wafer temperature. Meanwhile, semiconductor "scope 3" emissions (roughly 20 percent) arise from suppliers, chemicals and raw materials, and transportation to customer facilities. Large chip buyers and OEMs themselves are increasingly pushing suppliers to improve the environmental performance of their operations as part of consumer-oriented efforts to green their own supply chains.

- Especially given the intense global competition for semiconductor manufacturing as well as government climate objectives, *care should be taken not to inadvertently introduce new chip regulatory barriers.* For example, the Inflation Reduction Act of 2022 subjects fabs to EPA oversight on GHG emissions.[28] While this oversight per se is a relatively modest action focused on reporting, it should be considered against the totality of compliance costs that this sector's investments face in the United States compared to attractive sites abroad. The EPA's March 2023 proposal to set strict "zero-level" per- and polyfluoroalkyl substance (PFAS) standards for drinking water, for example, was not aimed at the semiconductor industry, but fabs rely on these fluorinated chemicals for chip manufacturing.[29]

It is understood that reducing emissions and improving resilience of the semiconductor supply chain are both important government objectives, but without care in implementing such rules, issue fratricide could occur that betrays all such equities—such as if environmental regulations undermine semiconductor initiatives and imperil US job growth while leaving global chip manufacturing concentrated in foreign locales with dirtier energy grids and lower standards.

Federal Immigration Measures

The United States does not have a direct STEM (science, technology, engineering, mathematics) workforce shortage problem in semiconductor manufacturing today—there simply not being much demand for labor today at all, given low levels of manufacturing activity. But the industry does face structural workforce-related problems that the traditional solutions of more fellowships, internships, and stipends to improve the "pipeline" of STEM graduate students will not be able to solve as labor demand from new semiconductor investments does materialize.

Some US academics have pointed out that as the United States has foregone actual domestic production of the technologies it invents, the way that we educate students, particularly in electrical engineering, a core discipline of semiconductor development, has ossified. Rather than training their students as broad system designers—that is, people who can take ideas from disparate disciplines and create new systems by merging those ideas—most US electrical engineering departments now focus their teaching and research narrowly on computing and communications applications. This practice stands in contrast to, for example, US computer science programs, whose curricula and culture emphasize learning coding tools and principles to solve many different practical problems. The consequence is that electrical engineers see more limited applications for their knowledge—indeed, domestic enrollments in the field have plummeted, as prospective students see more interesting opportunities elsewhere. By contrast, US computer science graduates can enter a variety of compelling industries, and enrollments have grown steadily.

This issue is solvable. More domestic activity across the entirety of the semiconductor value chain, including manufacturing, will let students see new applications of their work and will motivate universities to adjust. New semiconductor manufacturers and suppliers will bring to the United States not just their production facilities, but also their supporting industrial R&D apparatus; these R&D ecosystems will facilitate today's missing demand signal and help translate university training to evolving commercial needs. (Given the fast pace of semiconductor manufacturing in particular today, commercial know-how far exceeds what is presently taught in universities.)

But it will take time. As the United States addresses these issues over the long term, labor markets will naturally adjust to actual needs. In the transition, we can look to high-skilled immigrants to function as a bridge to meet increased demand for labor in domestic semiconductor (or other advanced technology) manufacturing.

As the politics of broad-based immigration law reform continues to confound a US Congress long polarized and paralyzed on such topics despite widespread popular dissatisfaction with the immigration status quo,[30] the only recent reforms relevant to semiconductors have been narrow administrative efforts under executive purview. The Biden administration, for example, has been focused on increasing retention of international STEM students in the US workforce—that is, domestically employing a higher proportion of our relevant engineering graduates who come from abroad. (International students compose around two-thirds of graduates today in semiconductor-related fields.[31]) In January 2022, the Department of Homeland Security added twenty-two new STEM fields to the Optional Practical Training (OPT) program, allowing more STEM graduates on F-1 visas to work in the United States for a longer time after graduation.[32] Such measures, however, are inadequate to the need.

Further areas for improvement, therefore, include the following:

- *Additional legislative measures are needed to capture skilled immigrant talent for the US semiconductor industry*. Administrative tweaks to visas offer only minor help compared to larger and more substantive changes to programs such as the H-1B visa program or green card caps, either of which would require legislative action. While both US industry and the public appear to support increasing skilled immigration,[33] targeted bipartisan reforms have been held hostage in broader political debates on illegal immigration.

This legislative reticence to address immigration-related measures—however important—was reflected in the legislative history of various proposed semiconductor and competitiveness bills, elements of which were eventually passed in the CHIPS Act, which generally shunned immigration in favor of education and workforce-training provisions, which are less likely to have significant impact, especially in the short term. Representative Michael McCaul's (R-TX) and Senator John Cornyn's (R-TX) original Senate bill from June 2020, for example—the Creating Helpful Incentives to Produce Semiconductors (CHIPS) for America Act—did not contain any provisions for immigration reform or attracting STEM graduates to work in the semiconductor industry.[34] Similarly, while the related Restoring Critical Supply Chains and Intellectual Property Act of 2020 sponsored by Senator Lindsey Graham (R-SC) added further emphasis on domestic educational pipeline reforms, it also did not address skilled immigration.[35]

Reflecting the broader scope of contemporaneous proposals from the House of Representatives, the America COMPETES Act (HR 4521)—passed largely along party lines in February 2022—added a number of skilled immigration measures not found in the similar June 2021 Senate bill. That later bill included exemption from annual green card caps for international STEM PhDs and master's degree holders in "critical industries" such as semiconductors.[36] It also included measures from Representative Zoe Lofgren's (D-CA) proposed 2021 Let Immigrants Kickstart Employment (LIKE) Act, which would have created a new visa category for immigrants interested in establishing venture capital–backed startups. Moreover, HR 4521 would have established US STEM scholarships funded by a $1,000 supplemental surcharge for green card recipients. Perhaps reflecting the complicated bargaining and political valences involved in any immigration-related legislation, the House measure also included substantive pro-union proposals that could increase costs, including prevailing wage requirements on fab construction projects receiving federal funding, $4 billion to expand apprenticeship programs, and union neutrality requirements for employers receiving federal dollars under the Act.

Ultimately, these House immigration provisions proved politically unpalatable in the Senate—even many Senate Democrats opposed them in conference. Thus, they were dropped from the final stripped-down legislation package, even as some workforce development and union measures were retained.[37]

Given Congress's failure to pass any meaningful immigration reform, *legislative skilled immigration measures are urgently needed* to improve the impact of the CHIPS Act. Such measures would also be helpful in increasing private funding for domestic semiconductor manufacturing facilities in the near to medium term. These efforts should be paired with incentives to train Americans as both hardware and materials engineers, as well as the skilled tradesmen and technicians needed in constructing and operating semiconductor fabs or semiconductor equipment manufacturing and packaging facilities, as described in chapter 4 of this report.[38] Such initiatives would both help smooth a rapid labor market transition and improve the chances of success for timely construction and cost-effective operation of new manufacturing facilities.

- Toward these ends, the United States should consider *waiving numerical H-1B visa caps and making them available to all international students who complete a STEM graduate program at an accredited US university*. Until the United States can dramatically increase its domestic pool of relevant science and engineering talent (a task that will, at a minimum, take a decade), it will not be able to restore its international competitiveness in high-tech manufacturing.
- In parallel, community colleges and related industry apprenticeships located within the region of a semiconductor manufacturing cluster should be supported to provide the skilled trade and tool

operators that constitute the bulk of jobs in fabrication facilities. Given the efficiencies realized through geographic clustering of semiconductor production and the relative lack of US labor mobility for these trades as compared to engineers, *a regional focus for such technician-oriented programs is important.*

State Incentives

Mitigating the risk of reliance on foreign semiconductor manufacturing through increased domestic production will rely as much on the policies of individual US states working in their own economic self-interest to attract private investment as it will on the strategic actions taken by the federal government. To the extent that the cost of doing business is higher in the United States than in Asia, it is the US states that hold many of the policy levers that could help narrow that gap, including local income and property taxation policies, support for physical infrastructure, building permits, and access to high-quality electricity and water supplies. US states with existing semiconductor industry footprints have been the most proactive in trying to facilitate new investments. The following paragraphs survey illustrative examples of where state governments have, to date, stepped in to support various initiatives:

Arizona

Based on employment statistics, semiconductor manufacturing has consistently been among the three largest manufacturing sectors in Arizona, where the state's Qualified Facility Tax Credits (QFTC) and Quality Jobs Tax Credits (QJTC) are among the chief incentives for semiconductor companies.

The QFTC was established by the Arizona legislature in 2012, and subsequently amended in 2016, 2020, and 2021, to promote the location of new or expansion of existing headquarters and manufacturing or R&D facilities in the state.[39] In 2021, TSMC Arizona Corporation was given a preapproved tax credit in the amount of $30 million.[40] In the 2014 QFTC annual report, two facilities from Intel Corporation are also listed as having received such tax credits—the first received $10.9 million, and the second received $6.7 million. Three other pre-approved companies also received around $2 million in total. Table 3.2 lists companies involved in semiconductor manufacturing that received tax credits under this program, and illustrates the importance of tax credits not just for a single fab, but for the health of complementary suppliers and technology vendors.[41]

Table 3.2. Arizona Semiconductor Tax Credit Recipients

YEAR	COMPANY	AMOUNT GIVEN	NOTES
2014	Intel Facility 1	$10,860,000	
	Intel Facility 2	$6,680,000	
2015	Essai Inc.	$320,000	Essai, since acquired by Advantest; leading supplier of semiconductor final-test, system-level test sockets and thermal control units
	ASM America, Inc.	$1,280,000	ASM is a leading supplier of semiconductor process equipment for wafer processing.
	Intel (Chandler)	$10,860,000	The Chandler fab was designed to use larger equipment required for manufacturing wafers.[a]
	Intel (Ocotillo)	$6,680,000	
2016	Essai Inc.	$260,000	
2017	Infineon Technologies Americas Corp.	$600,000	Semiconductor manufacturer
	RJR Technologies	$398,500	Innovator in preapplied adhesive technology for semiconductor industry
2018	Fujifilm Electronic Materials USA Inc.	$1,020,000	Produces high-purity chemicals and materials for semiconductor manufacturers
	Texas Instruments Incorporated	$700,000	Semiconductor manufacturer
	Infineon Technology Americas Corp.	$500,000	

Table 3.2. (continued)

YEAR	COMPANY	AMOUNT GIVEN	NOTES
2019	Intel Corporation	$540,000	
	Intel Corporation	$11,600,000	
	Semiconductor Components Industries, LLC	$4,000,000	Designs and manufactures semiconductor components. Now known as ON Semiconductor or Onsemi.
	Fujifilm Electronic Materials USA Inc.	$1,020,000	
2020	Auer Precision Company LLC	$344,827	Leading contract manufacturer of precision metal and thin-film polymer parts for semiconductor markets
	Intel (Ocotillo)	$28,900,000	
2021	Advantest America Inc.	$4,200,000	Japanese manufacturer of automatic test equipment for semiconductor industry
	Essai, Inc.	$1,180,000	
	Intel Corporation	$420,000	
	Intel Corporation	$2,300,000	
	Intel Corporation	$21,600,000	
	Intel Corporation	$8,140,000	
	Microchip Technology Inc.	$1,200,000	Manufactures microcontroller, mixed-signal, analog, and flash-IP integrated circuits
	TSMC Arizona Corporation	$30,000,000	
	Foresight Technologies, Inc.	$242,895	Provides critical machine parts and subsystems for semiconductors

ᵃDon Clark, "Intel Arizona Plant to Remain Idle," *Wall Street Journal*, January 14, 2014.

In March 2021, Arizona's QFTC was expanded via HB 2321 to increase the cap from $70 million per year to $125 million per year.[42] The bill passed with strong bipartisan support.[43]

In addition, Arizona's Qualified Jobs Tax Credit provides nonrefundable income and premium tax credits to qualifying taxpayers—$3,000 per year for each continuously maintained job for up to three years.

Texas

In November 2021, South Korea's Samsung announced the construction of a new $17 billion fab in Taylor, Texas (about forty miles north of Austin), where Samsung has operated a separate fab since 2004.[44] This investment was expected to include $6 billion in property improvements and $11 billion in machinery and equipment. While Texas is attractive to employees because it levies no state income taxes, localities within the state do have high property taxes. Taylor, for example, has a total property tax rate of 2.54 percent.[45] To offset their high rates, state and local governments in Texas have reduced the cost of business for prospective semiconductor manufacturers through both tax relief and regulatory easing. Subsidies toward the Samsung fab in Taylor include these:

- A $27 million Texas Enterprise Fund grant[46]
- A $20,000-per-employee bonus from the state for hiring veterans[47]
- $67 million in road improvements at the state level, and $120 million in road improvements at the county level, plus bonds to pay for $18 million in water/sewer extensions
- 92.5 percent of city and county property taxes abated in the first ten years, 90 percent in the next ten years, and 85 percent in the following ten years—for a total estimated value of $467.8 million over 30 years
- Additional property tax abatements of $314 million over ten years from the local school district[48]
- Expedited permitting and reimbursement for city-level permitting development review costs
- A federal capital gains tax break (since the property is in a federal Opportunity Zone)

Additional commitments to Texas in the semiconductor manufacturing sector have followed. Texas Instruments (TI) announced a modern twelve-inch-wafer-based fab in Sherman (sixty-five miles north of Dallas) in November 2021, with potential for up to four fabs on the new site.[49] TI's investment level is expected to be around $30 billion. The city of Sherman has subsequently filed tax abatement proposals for each fab plant for 2025, 2032, 2037, and 2045, which would yield a total of $148 million in tax relief over ten years, a 90 percent abatement for TI.[50] Later, in June 2022, after GlobiTech, a subsidiary of Taiwan's GlobalWafers, announced an expansion of silicon wafer production in Sherman as well, it was set to receive a Texas Enterprise Fund grant of $15 million and a $10,000 bonus per hired veteran.

To be sure, these efforts have come under some criticism. The Texas Enterprise Fund, for example, has been called "crony corporate welfare"—in particular, some argue that cities will lose revenue and freedom of association by catering to Fund-preferred investments, or that innovation could ultimately be hampered due to a concentration of human capital in a small collection of large firms.[51] Criticism has also been directed toward recipient companies for exploiting their grants to mischaracterize the number of jobs required or actually created under the contract.

Ohio

A newer entrant to attracting semiconductor firms is Ohio. In June 2022, HB 687 became law. It provides $600 million for performance-based onshoring incentive grants aimed at making Ohio "more competitive with Asian markets"; $101 million for water and wastewater infrastructure improvement; $205 million for state and local roads; and $300 million for water reclamation facilities.[52] Notably, to qualify for these funds, companies must have their corporate headquarters in the United States, incur the majority of R&D expenses in the year preceding tax credit approval within the United States, and build and operate semiconductor wafer manufacturing factories in Ohio.[53] Accordingly, unlike the more broad-based competitiveness measures described in Arizona and Texas, the Ohio bill was seen as tailored specifically to Intel: a few months before, Intel had announced a $20 billion investment in the state, and was now being wooed to build two new fabs, supported by up to $2 billion in state incentives.[54]

There is no one ideal policy model that emerges from this interstate competition, but it is on the whole healthy that states see it as important to offer a hospitable location for semiconductor fabs, and such efforts are likely to redound to the United States' net benefit in reshoring a core manufacturing capability. Nevertheless, further areas for improvement include these:

- *Geographic clustering matters for semiconductor manufacturing.* TSMC's leadership expects that, compared to their fab and supplier clusters in Hsinchu, Taiwan, their upstart Arizona facilities will cost 50 percent more to operate. They estimate that perhaps half of that increase will be due to the lack of geographic clustering of the requisite spare parts, equipment, service firms, and workers that help improve factory uptime and yields. States are free to choose and compete with one another on regulatory and policy strategies, and it is to America's benefit that they do so because they can play a key role as "innovation laboratories" in devising better ways to catalyze a US semiconductor renaissance. *But it is also in the broader national interest that individual states with advanced manufacturing endowments remain attractive places to innovate and do business in order to promote such clustering.*

To that end, ease of doing business across US states remains a key consideration for semiconductor firms, which are weighing investment opportunities around the world. While no one state-level condition will dictate outcomes, indices of state-level economic freedom (such as those calculated regularly by the Cato Institute) provide a good list of possible inducements. These include both fiscal measures—such as state taxation, local taxation, government consumption, and investment—and government debt and regulatory policies, including land-use rules, health insurance markets, and labor-mobility restrictions such as occupational licensing.[55]

Among US states, Arizona ranks highly for its ease of new business entry, liberalized pricing, right-to-work laws, and its E-verify mandate. Texas, meanwhile, ranks the highest in the nation for the freedom of its labor market, including right-to-work laws, no additional state minimum wage, and optional workers' compensation coverage. Ohio, by contrast, without right-to-work laws, ranks lower even than other Rust Belt states such as Indiana, Michigan, and Wisconsin. New York, another potential locus for semiconductor manufacturing given GlobalFoundries' operations there, actually ranks last in Cato's economic freedom index, given its high state and local taxes, land-use regulations, and occupational licensing rules.

- *California merits special attention.* Although Silicon Valley has long lost much of the integrated circuit manufacturing for which it was once known, it remains an important locus for other links in the US semiconductor supply chain, including as the headquarters for globally dominant semiconductor equipment manufacturers (such as Lam Research, KLA, and Applied Materials), as well as powerful OEMs and device integrators (such as Apple or Google) and a host of chip design firms (from small to large players, including Qualcomm and Nvidia). California is also home to top engineering schools such as UC Berkeley, Stanford, and Caltech, whose graduates can help staff these, and prospective future, semiconductor firms.

California, however, has also come under scrutiny for its increasing cost of doing business—which has led some firms, including tech firms, to decamp.[56] Moreover, the state ranks poorly on national measures of economic freedom, and lacks a right-to-work rule; also, the legislature has continued to increase a statewide minimum wage of $15 per hour, which is already high by national standards. Perhaps more importantly, rent control rules in California discourage the construction of new rental housing, and local development policies, high construction labor costs, and clean energy–related building codes have all conspired to severely restrict housing supply in desirable coastal areas.[57] An additional issue is the use of the 1970 California Environmental Quality Act (CEQA), which not only requires environmental mitigations for major construction projects but also permits citizen and interest group lawsuits to force additional analysis and delays, increasing costs.[58] While the state has taken some steps to alleviate local building restrictions—such as by challenging single-family housing zoning—firms still report that wages for comparable employees in metropolitan areas of the state exceed those required to attract talent in other parts of the country.[59]

It is hard to imagine a semiconductor (or other critical-technology) renaissance in the United States in which California does not play an important role, but California's regulatory structure makes this more challenging. One hopes that California's own relatively weak competitive posture will not undermine chances for a broader American high-technology industrial renaissance, but problems with the ease of doing business in the state arguably have global implications that may not be fully appreciated in local or state politics.

Novel Public Measures to Improve US Chip Supply Chain Resiliency

Get Better Data

As embedded semiconductors move to the center of our economic vitality and lives, we find ourselves in much the same position on semiconductors today as during the early 1970s with energy. Up until that point, the US energy system was basically seen as the exclusive province and responsibility of major private sector consumers and producers. The federal government did not even collect proper supply-and-demand statistics. When the dual energy crises hit—and national security and social interests, built up around what had been seen as a purely commercial matter, began to reveal themselves—our adversaries abroad were the first to realize how to exploit them.

One result of the 1970s oil embargoes was the (somewhat controversial) creation of what would become the US Department of Energy. Less controversial was the establishment within it of a federal Energy Information Administration (EIA), to which Congress gave power to compel the provision of energy trade and pricing data across a variety of fuels and technologies from major US energy industry participants. That commercially sensitive data, in turn, would be professionally managed by an independent agency for the creation of publicly appropriate and comprehensive energy-statistics databases, forecasting models, and technical policy analyses.[60]

EIA's success in improving the transparency of the US energy market should be a model for our country's current information deficit on the strategically important semiconductor sector. If we are as a country to meet the competitive challenges presented by global supply chain risk and China's potential manipulation of such dependencies for strategic advantage, US policy makers in the executive branch and national legislature—and indeed in state governments as well, for the reasons outlined above—should be better equipped for the complex decisions involved in this arena.

Remarkably little is actually known in detail about the various streams that make up the semiconductor supply chain—especially the sourcing for raw materials and the types of semiconductors. The semiconductor sector has built exquisite mechanisms to take advantage of global variations in cost margin, economies of scale, labor, capital quality, pricing, technical comparative advantage, and logistics architectures. But most of this optimization has taken place on a disaggregated basis and in response to market forces. As a result, there is no good way for policy makers—or market participants themselves—to understand "who's who" across the complete supply chain or to easily perform analyses of supply chain risk with regard to questions of potential ownership or control by unfriendly entities. Better data could improve decision making around semiconductor technology export controls and in mitigating global supply chain disruptions in the near to medium term.

What have we already tried, and what are the options going forward that would help build better supply chain information capabilities?

Existing US government public trade databases—such as the International Trade Administration's modernized Exporter Database (EDB), which presents annual dashboards on US merchandise exporter characteristics, or the US Census Bureau's tracking of goods exports—do not disaggregate data into categories specific enough to be useful for the semiconductor sector. Nor do multilateral economic institution databases such as those of the International Monetary Fund (IMF) fare better in offering insight into the specifics of semiconductor supply chains.

In one effort to inform the planning and design of potential programs to incentivize investment in domestic semiconductor manufacturing facilities and to respond to the chip shortages of the time, the Department of Commerce launched a "voluntary" semiconductor RFI (request for information) in September 2021 that sought commercial data from both major global producers and consumers on a two-month timeline. The request included the following information:

- A description of the company's role in the supply chain
- Technology nodes, semiconductor material types, and device types the firm provided
- Estimates of annual sales for 2019 to 2021
- Products with the biggest backlog—including attributes, sales, location of fabrication, and packaging and assembly
- Each product's top three customers
- Estimated lead times for top products
- Bill-to-book ratio
- Inventory for inbound, in-progress, and outbound product
- Questions regarding firm strategy for allocating available chip supply
- Questions regarding what might be needed to increase production capacity[61]

Because this novel request met a cold reception among both domestic chip buyers and foreign partner suppliers,[62] it is unclear how successful the response rate was, and Commerce eventually published a very general public summary of findings from the request.[63]

One alternative pathway to getting more-detailed data would be through executive action to actually impose licensing requirements on semiconductor-related materials, equipment, and technology. Importantly, license requirements would be used not to impede supply chain transfers, but rather to provide visibility and data. Even where presumptively approved, the mere existence of licenses as records of transactions would offer valuable visibility into what is moving, where it is moving, and to whom.

Of course, industry may resist the paperwork burden of licensing the export of complex products that move at scale through global supply chains. And in the past, it may have been more worthwhile to forego the availability of such information in the name of market-transactional efficiency, especially where it was assumed that export controls had little purpose. But given the emerging national security stakes now—both the risks to Western semiconductor firms of being displaced by state-subsidized firms from China and the risks to Western governments of being manipulated by economic dependencies on those firms in China—the balance has shifted in favor of acquiring better information that can ground policy making on export control and supply chain resiliency questions.

Indeed, the Department of Commerce already obtains a great deal of information about semiconductor-related exports through its Bureau of Industry and Security (BIS). So even if it did not impose additional requirements on companies, it could do much more with the information it already has by sharing it more widely with interagency partners, including the intelligence community, and with Congress (albeit in a more summarized and less commercially sensitive form). Especially in the era of China's "military-civil fusion" policies, such export information is important in any analysis of the capabilities China is acquiring. We need to have a clearer understanding of how well China is doing in meeting its industrial policy targets, and what technologies are being made available to China's military or security services. Such information would also underpin efforts to conduct technology net assessments that compare Western and Chinese capabilities, assess trends of each, and chart relative rates of progress. In short, such information would help us draw out the economic, military, and strategic implications of this globalized, complex supply chain. In order to permit the government to benefit from such analyses, *Commerce should systematically share more of its information with other agencies.*

The sophistication of such analyses—either by Commerce or through another suitable US government interagency collaboration, or even a public-private partnership arrangement—deserves more attention. Licensing information represents merely the tip of the data iceberg, and globalized supply chains can impose risks beyond disruption, to include infiltration or corruption of supplied products as well. It is relatively easy, for instance, to obfuscate corporate ownership or control relationships—making the supply chain, from a risk-management perspective, opaque in its connective details, even where one has some basic information about the entities involved. Despite the remarkable amount of information available from commercial data aggregators who collect and trade in the so-called digital exhaust of the modern economy, effective analytical tools are not yet widely available, or at scale, to permit transactional linkages to be traced very far backward or forward through any given supply chain. Neither do the existing tools allow one to understand nonobvious relationships between and among entities therein.

Perhaps the most comprehensive private effort at collecting and disseminating global semiconductor supply chain data is by World Semiconductor Trade Statistics (WSTS), an independent body run by an executive committee composed of representatives from semiconductor industry member organizations. WSTS collects monthly data pooled from industry members, checks and aggregates it, and participates in industry conferences to share world industry forecasts. Products include a monthly Blue Book, covering worldwide semiconductor shipments,[64] as well as a Green Book, which aggregates visual representations of the Blue Book data. WSTS also releases an End Use report annually, as well as a biannual industry forecast for the current year and upcoming two years. This information is accessible only to subscribers.[65]

SIA, also in the private sector, has also developed multilevel chip supply chain analytical capabilities that are indispensable to national security, even though they are proprietary.

Some progress is being made on the data and analysis issue; namely, the CHIPS Act allocated $2.3 billion to the Department of Commerce to develop a comprehensive report on the global semiconductor supply chain, including exposure to firms in China as well as US domestic weaknesses. This generous level of funding—almost twenty times the EIA's annual budget for US energy data—should form the core of a US government data fusion and analysis center, operated either directly through an agency or supported by specialized contractors or federally funded research and development centers (FFRDCs). Such a data center should collect and digest the full breadth of relevant information that is now available from commercial data aggregators and market research firms. It would not only acquire such information but employ state-of-the-art data analytics, modeling, and decision-support tools in providing high-quality analysis to inform federal decisions. *The government needs to establish itself as a locus of analytical expertise and understanding on these complex issues*, and it needs to be capable of reaching independent conclusions that are in the public interest. Private sector analysis can then augment this public baseline.

Finally, learning from the resistance that Commerce encountered in its fall 2021 attempts to gather such sensitive commercial data from firms even in friendly nations, special consideration should be given to how such a data center can gain acceptance as mutually beneficial to the international partners on whom its success rests. In that sense, and with an eye toward the United States more effectively navigating what could be a jarring transition to a like-minded, bloc-based trading and technology-sharing pattern, a more appropriate energy data analog may in fact be the multilateral OECD's International Energy Agency (IEA). Similar to the DOE EIA's domestic role, the IEA collects, analyzes, and disseminates detailed energy supply-and-demand statistics from across OECD member nations and volunteering observer nations. Also founded in the throes of the 1970s energy crises to represent the interests of major oil-consuming nations—and with data that is used in service of a broader mission to coordinate oil stockpiles and joint drawdowns across member nations during times of geopolitical disruption—IEA's approach of drawing together like-minded nations around concrete tools to serve mutual interests should be a basis for chip comparison.

Chip Stockpiling and Extended Inventory Management

Could IEA's approach toward oil stockpiling and coordinated draw-down be applied to mitigate sharp dislocations in semiconductor sup-ply chains, too? A condition of membership in the IEA is that countries hold a strategic reserve of oil equivalent of ninety days of net imports, both to reduce actual economic and price impacts caused by supply disruption and to reduce the potential geopolitical leverage of suppliers or other actors who might wish to disrupt energy supply chains.

A combination of public and private chip stockpiles that could cre-ate a buffer against one of the most frightening and damaging supply chain risks conceivable—a blockade, war, or natural disaster disrupt-ing supply from a key US partner such as Taiwan—is a model that could improve global semiconductor supply chain resiliency. Even so, there are complicating considerations that suggest a more nuanced ap-proach may be needed.

The first complication is the practical challenge in stockpiling so-phisticated, high-end semiconductors in advance of a loss of access. To the degree that such cutting-edge chips come only from Taiwan's TSMC and would be rendered unavailable by conflict, such chips would in-deed disappear from the supply chain with the outbreak of hostilities or a natural disaster. But such chips would also be quite expensive to stockpile, given both their per-unit market price and the fact that their value reflects their novelty—stockpiling last year's best logic chips sim-ply ensures depreciation (and, at best, access to last year's technology during a time of conflict).

A more reasonable stockpiling goal, which could keep critical elec-tronic systems functioning in the event of severe supply chain disrup-tion, would therefore focus on more broadly commoditized legacy chip designs. Even this approach, however, has shortcomings. Strategic stockpiles for crude oil work well because the product has a long shelf life and is not very specialized. But the semiconductor industry is highly diverse. A single chip firm such as Texas Instruments alone produces as many as eighteen thousand types of chips, with upward of two hundred thousand to three hundred thousand product lines being produced at any one time across the industry. It is unclear (but deserving of further study) how useful even the inclusion of the top fifty types of chips within a strategic stockpile would be. Stockpiling may be more feasible for memory chips than for logic chips, since the memory chip industry is more organized around commodity chips from interchangeable suppliers all meeting standard specifications (see chapter 6). Of course, this reality also makes it less likely that the whole memory chip supply chain could be severed.

Moreover, these ideas say nothing of the logistical challenges of operating such a stockpile, particularly if it were managed by a nonexpert public sector entity. By comparison, consider how even the US stockpile for personal protective and common medical equipment—which Congress established near the end of the George W. Bush administration in preparation for pandemics—was poorly sustained and barely replenished over time as other political and budgetary priorities arose.

All these impediments, however, do not mean that buffering chip supply chains is impossible.

For example, *"lifetime buys" of commercial components in critical systems* have long been a facet of the aviation and aerospace industry, which faces problems of replacement part obsolescence and unavailability within the functional lifetime of an aircraft.[66] Typically, lifetime buys of replacement parts are a reactive step taken to stockpile parts once a particular component has already been slated to be discontinued. Doing so more proactively for semiconductor components, however, might be a prudent step given our reliance on complex global supply chains, despite the potential cost or performance trade-offs of doing so. For example, when the US Department of Defense (DoD) purchases weapons systems and other military electronics, it has begun to procure in advance some chipsets on a "lifetime of the system" basis. DoD planning in this regard is likely still incomplete, for it is generally based upon anticipated peacetime service life rather than surge demands that might be required in wartime (i.e., in repeatedly replenishing the US arsenal of precision-guided missiles or other munitions, existing peacetime-level stocks will very quickly be expended once the shooting starts, as in Ukraine). Nevertheless, proactive stockpiling is a principle that should be broadly applied for DoD weapons platforms. The feasibility of an up-front lifetime chip procurement approach should be investigated for other security and critical infrastructure needs as well, such as communications systems and the electric grid.

The second complication is the value of leveraging the latent knowledge of the private sector. While the US government has no experience in managing semiconductor or semiconductor input inventories, chip firms do, as part of their normal operations. Their incentives, of course, are to keep such inventories to a minimum to reduce carrying costs. The COVID-19 pandemic, however, revealed that inventory-light just-in-time manufacturing and distribution models can be quite fragile during times of systematic market disruption, with negative consequences for both the private and public sectors.[67] Recognizing the public interest in preventing such problems with semiconductors, *the US government should therefore encourage a private sector strategy of extended inventory management by creating a new tax credit on semiconductor inventories exceeding some normal duration of time*—e.g., a 25 percent credit on inventories exceeding forty-five days—for chip-consuming and -integrating firms in key sectors such as automotive, aerospace, defense, machinery, and electronics. This strategy is a way to progress toward the goal of creating a supply chain buffer that would increase decision time in the teeth of a severe global disruption, and that would do this in a scalable way, without having to develop new government capabilities or heavy-handed interventions.

Beyond purely private inventory management, we believe there are other novel ways to combine private sector supply chain expertise with a broader public resiliency purpose. While a government-only stockpile would likely fail, some have suggested instead *a limited "smart" buffer that would be run as a public-private partnership*. A private operator, independent or perhaps through an FFRDC under contract, would regularly buy and sell volumes of commonly traded chips under normal market conditions—that is, a chip exchange, whose inventory at the scale of a few hundred million dollars would remain property of the US government until sold. Day to day, such an exchange could provide some liquidity within a volatile private market and provide a return to the operator through arbitrage or management fees. But during severe supply chain crises, the inventory in place would flip to government needs such as defense or critical infrastructure. As this proposal would be much more sophisticated than the public stockpiles or exchanges that are operated for other commodities today, such as for oil or sugar, its dynamics within the evolving semiconductor market deserve further analysis.

A final consideration might be *preplanning for allocation and potential chip rationing during a significant supply chain upheaval.* On the one hand, the government could simply not assume such a responsibility on account of lack of knowledge and expertise. On the other hand, in past times of duress, US government bodies have invoked emergency authorities and become involved in the production and distribution of scarce goods that otherwise should remain the province of the private sector—with mixed results. With that history in mind, it would surely be better, in extremis, to turn to a plan carefully drawn up ahead of time on the basis of solid data, sophisticated modeling, and careful planning, than it would be to make such decisions on the fly in a crisis through ad hoc improvisation and guesswork under pressure. A basic prioritization framework should seek to be predictable, administrable, and defensible. Defense and national security applications (e.g., munition replenishment and the replacement of military and naval assets, sensors, and communications systems subject to combat attrition) would presumably be at the top of this chip-allocation priority list, followed by the needs of the civilian economy, such as civilian critical infrastructure systems, emergency and critical health care facilities, aviation safety, and cybersecurity functions. A directive to critical systems integrators to "know your supplier" (plus two or three levels of dependencies beyond) would be a place to start gathering data for such an effort, and would itself be a step of considerable value in light of the ways in which supply chain derisking has moved into the spotlight. It is also essential that our leaders begin a high-level national discussion of just what US national security chip-allocation priorities should actually be in a crisis: dialogue and stakeholder engagement on such topics is best begun before the need actually arises.

In sum, there are several medium-term ways in which the United States can increase the likelihood of commercial success of its current efforts to onshore an augmented share of its chip supply chain, while also taking other steps to mitigate the risk of what is sure to be a continued reliance on friendly partners abroad. Here, our specific relationships with Taiwan and China bear closer examination, as the chapters that follow show.

But with some key semiconductor-related funding and tax measures already in place in the United States, it should be possible to look back in ten years and see concrete progress along both dimensions of onshoring and supply chain risk mitigation, for it is against these two imperatives that today's major policy initiatives such as the CHIPS Act will be evaluated. Demonstrating success will be important not just for semiconductor security, but also as a responsibility to show American taxpayers what they have bought through these emergent yet unconventional public-private policy efforts undertaken in the name of national security. These efforts must be implemented with temperance and in faith in the intentions of the drafters. Securing semiconductor supply chains will not be achieved through one-off legislation. The intersection of the semiconductor business and national security interests is, as former secretary of state George Shultz would observe, not a solvable problem—but rather a "work-at" problem. And there are other critical technologies beyond semiconductors that may need to be worked at in the future, too. So much rests on the execution of today's first legislative steps.

NOTES

1. Hyunjoo Jin, "Automakers, Chip Firms Differ on When Semiconductor Shortage Will Abate," Reuters, February 4, 2022.
2. Bindiya Vakil and Tom Linton, "Why We're in the Midst of a Global Semiconductor Shortage," *Harvard Business Review*, February 26, 2021.
3. "China Stockpiles Chips and Chip-Making Machines to Resist US," *Bloomberg*, February 2, 2021.

4. Chip exports in this case comprise sales both from US integrated manufacturers (such as Intel) and from fabless chip designers (such as Qualcomm) whose chips would have actually been manufactured in third countries. US International Trade Commission (USITC) trade data as originally reported in Center for Security and Emerging Technology (CSET); see Saif M. Khan, "US Semiconductor Exports to China: Current Policies and Trends," CSET, October 2020.

5. Antonio Varas, Raj Varadarajan, Jimmy Goodrich, and Falan Yinug, *Government Incentives and US Competitiveness in Semiconductor Manufacturing* (Boston, MA: Boston Consulting Group and Semiconductor Industry Association, September 2020).

6. TSMC, "TSMC Announces Updates for TSMC Arizona," press release, December 6, 2022.

7. See Samsung, "Samsung Electronics Announces New Advanced Semiconductor Fab Site in Taylor, Texas," press release, November 24, 2021; and Intel, "Intel Announces Next US Site with Landmark Investment in Ohio," press release, January 21, 2022.

8. Lisa Wang, "GlobalWafers Plans US$5bn Texas Fab," *Taipei Times*, June 29, 2022.

9. GlobalFoundries, "GlobalFoundries and Qualcomm Announce Extension of Long-Term Agreement to Secure US Supply through 2028," CISION, August 8, 2022.

10. Micron, "Micron Announces $40 billion Investment in Leading-Edge Memory Manufacturing in the US," press release, August 9, 2022.

11. Kevin Xu, "Globalization Is Dead and No One Is Listening," *Interconnected* (blog), December 12, 2022.

12. Varas et al., *Government Incentives*, 2020.

13. NIST, *CHIPS for America: A Strategy for the CHIPS for America Fund* (Washington, DC: US Department of Commerce, September 6, 2022).

14. The White House, *National Security Strategy* (Washington, DC: The White House, October 12, 2022).

15. Patricia Zengerle and David Shepardson, "Factbox: US Congress Poised to Pass Long-Awaited China Semiconductor Bill," Reuters, July 28, 2022.

16. John VerWey, *No Permits, No Fabs: The Importance of Regulatory Reform for Semiconductor Manufacturing*, CSET Policy Brief, October 2021, 20.

17. Hideki Tomoshige and Benjamin Glanz, "What Environmental Regulations Mean for Fab Construction," CSIS, July 2022.

18. NEPA requires federal agencies to consider the environmental consequences of proposed actions and inform the public about their decision making. The three levels of environmental analysis possible under NEPA include (1) categorical exclusions (as proposed by individual agencies for routine actions, in

consultation with the White House Council on Environmental Quality; not currently applicable to semiconductor fabs); (2) an environmental assessment (requiring roughly eighteen months to consider an overview of potential environmental impacts, often resulting in some degree of required mitigation or monitoring); or (3) a full environmental impact statement (which includes a detail reporting and public review process and can take many years to complete along uncertain timelines).

19. US EPA, "FAST-41 Coordination—Fixing America's Surface Transportation (FAST) Act," last updated September 27, 2022.

20. US Department of Homeland Security, "Portman, Hagerty, King File Bipartisan Amendment to NDAA to Improve Permitting Process for Key Technologies Impacting National Security," November 2021.

21. The White House, "FACT SHEET: CHIPS and Science Act Will Lower Costs, Create Jobs, Strengthen Supply Chains, and Counter China," August 9, 2022.

22. The White House, "The Biden-Harris Permitting Action Plan to Rebuild America's Infrastructure, Accelerate the Clean Energy Transition, Revitalize Communities, and Create Jobs," accessed May 16, 2023.

23. VerWey, *No Permits, No Fabs*, 20.

24. US Chamber of Commerce, "US Chamber Comments on the Department of Commerce Strong Domestic Semiconductor Industry RFI," March 2022.

25. Phillip Singerman, Sujai Shivakumar, Gregory Arcuri, and Hideki Tomoshige, "Streamlining the Permitting Process for Fab Construction," CSIS, August 29, 2022.

26. VerWey, *No Permits, No Fabs*, 18.

27. McKinsey & Company, "Sustainability in Semiconductor Operations: Toward Net-Zero Production," May 17, 2022.

28. The Act appropriates $5 million to the EPA until September 30, 2031, "to support enhanced standardization and transparency of corporate climate action commitments and plans to reduce greenhouse gas emissions." Matt Hamblen, "Chips Fabs Face EPA Review of Their Emission Targets in Budget Bill," Fierce Electronics, August 11, 2022.

29. US EPA, "Per- and Polyfluoroalkyl Substances (PFAS): Proposed PFAS National Primary Drinking Water Regulation," last updated May 9, 2023.

30. In a November 2022 Economic Innovation Group survey of US voters, 66 percent of respondents said that the immigration system needs major changes or a complete overhaul (including 81 percent of Republicans and 57 percent of Democrats). Kenneth Megan and Adam Ozimek, "US Perspectives on Skilled Immigration: Results from EIG's National Voter Survey," Economic Innovation Group, November 14, 2022.

31. Will Hunt and Remco Zwetsloot, "The Chipmakers: US Strengths and Priorities for the High-End Semiconductor Workforce," CSET, September 2020.

32. These fields include bioenergy, human-centered technology design, cloud computing, climate and geoscience, earth systems science, and so forth.

33. The same 2022 Economic Innovation Group survey reported including 60 percent of Republicans, 72 percent of Independents, and 83 percent of Democrats favoring more skilled immigration.

34. The bill's only educational provision was listed as "Developing and deploying educational and skills training curricula needed to support the industry sector and ensure the US can build and maintain a trusted and predictable talent pipeline."

35. It directed, for example, the secretaries of interior and labor to conduct studies to design educational programs at the undergraduate and graduate levels to support critical mineral supply chains, including grants for faculty positions at institutes of higher learning.

36. US Congress, Space, Science and Technology Committee, *H.R. 4521, United States Innovation and Competition Act of 2021*, 117th Congress, 2021–2022.

37. Commerce Secretary Gina Raimondo suggested that implementation of CHIPS and Science Act of 2022 subsidies would come with "strings attached," and House Speaker Nancy Pelosi told reporters, "What's really important . . . is that there would be guardrails to ensure that chip investments benefit US workers, not foreign companies." For construction of manufacturing facilities themselves under the Act, Davis-Bacon prevailing wage requirements will apply. See Jeremy Dillon, "Congress Nears Passage of Innovation, Research Bill," E&E News, July 25, 2022.

38. As a point of reference on the relative compositions of needed workers, TSMC reported that of its fifty-seven thousand employees in 2020, about six thousand were "managers," twenty-eight thousand were "professionals," five thousand were "assistants," and eighteen thousand were "technicians." Professionals and managers generally hold master's degrees or above. See TSMC, *2020 Corporate Sustainability Report*, 2021.

39. Refundable income tax credits equal the lesser of 10 percent of a total qualified investment, $20,000 per net new job at a facility for investments less than $2 billion, $30,000 per net new job for investments over $2 billion, or $30 million per taxpaying firm per year. Arizona Commerce Authority, "Qualified Facility," accessed May 16, 2023.

40. Arizona Commerce Authority, *Qualified Facility Tax Credit Program: Calendar Year 2021 Annual Report*, April 29, 2022.

41. Compiled from Annual Reports from 2013 to 2021, as available here: Arizona Commerce Authority, "Qualified Facility," accessed May 16, 2023.

42. Arizona House Bill 2321, *Qualified Facilities*, Fifty-Fifth Legislature, 2021.

43. The expansion was backed by the Arizona Commerce Authority, with the president and CEO, Sandra Watson, testifying before the Senate Appropriations

Committee that HB 2321 would enhance the state's competitiveness. At the same time, the bill was criticized by the American Conservative Union (ACU). In the ACU Foundation's 2021 ratings of Arizona, QFTC, and in particular HB 2321, were criticized as providing "competitive advantage to select industries and businesses while shifting tax burdens to other taxpayers not favored by government." See the American Conservative Union Foundation Center for Legislative Accountability, *Ratings of Arizona 2021*, 13, 24.

44. Samsung, "Samsung's $17 Billion Investment in a New Facility Will Boost Production of Advanced Semiconductors," press release, November 24, 2021.

45. Austin Chamber, "Property Tax," 2023.

46. "The Texas Enterprise Fund (TEF) awards 'deal-closing' grants to companies considering a new project for which one Texas site is competing with other out-of-state sites. The fund serves as a performance-based financial incentive for those companies whose projects would contribute significant capital investment and new employment opportunities to the state's economy." Awards tend to be tied to expected job creation levels. See Texas Economic Development, "Texas Enterprise Fund," 2023.

47. Office of the Texas Governor, "Governor Abbott Announces New $17 Billion Samsung Manufacturing Facility in Taylor," press release, November 23, 2021.

48. "Incentive Package to Lure Samsung to Taylor Is the Biggest in Texas History," *The Dallas Morning News*, December 29, 2021.

49. Office of the Texas Governor, "Governor Abbott Announces Texas Instruments' Potential $30 Billion Investment in Sherman," press release, November 17, 2021.

50. Brad Johnson, "Texas Instruments Plans $30 Billion Investment in Sherman Semiconductor Facility," *The Texan*, November 17, 2021.

51. See, for example, Bethany Blankley, "Group Calls on Governor, Legislature to End Texas Enterprise Fund, Cut Taxes Instead," The Center Square: Texas, February 2, 2021.

52. Gov. DeWine's statement: Mike DeWine, Governor of Ohio, "Governor DeWine Highlights Historic Investments in Capital Budget Bill," June 14, 2022.

53. Ohio Legislative Commission, Ohio HB 687, *Ohio Revised Code—Grants to Foster Job Creation*, Section 122.17, div. (A)(11)(a)(ii), 2.

54. Intel, "Intel Announces Next US Site with Landmark Investment in Ohio," press release, January 21, 2022.

55. In Cato's 2021 ranking, the five states with the highest economic freedom scores were (from high to low) Florida, Tennessee, New Hampshire, South Dakota, and Idaho. The five states with the lowest economic freedom scores were (from low to high) New York, Hawaii, California, Oregon, and New Jersey. See William Ruger and Jason Sorens, *Freedom in the 50 States*, 6th ed. (Washington, DC: Cato Institute, 2021), 36.

56. Lee Ohanian and Joseph Vranich, "Why Company Headquarters Are Leaving California in Unprecedented Numbers," The Hoover Institution Economics Working Paper 21117, September 2022.

57. For example, annual average nonfarm employment has grown at a higher rate of increase than total housing units and permits in the San Francisco–Oakland–Berkeley metropolitan area. This problem persists in New York City too, where jobs grew much faster than housing stock over the same period after the Great Recession. See Eric Kober, "The Bay Area: The Land of Many Jobs and Too Few Homes," Manhattan Institute, March 25, 2022; and Emily Badger and Quoctrung Bui, "Cities Start to Question an American Ideal: A House with a Garden on Every Block," *New York Times*, June 18, 2019.

58. Ethan Varian, "Governor Newsom is Blasting CEQA: What Is It and Why Does It Matter?," *The Mercury News*, March 6, 2023.

59. San Jose, California, home to many leading US semiconductor firms, has 94 percent of its residential land zoned for detached single-family homes. This compares to Los Angeles at 75 percent and Seattle at 81 percent. The California legislature has passed a variety of bills to address this issue: SB 8 limits local authorities' abilities to block housing projects and limit housing density by downzoning; SB 9 allows construction of up to four units in single-family zones by right; and SB 10 eases upzoning near transit hubs and restricts cities' ability to use the California Environmental Quality Act to block projects.

60. The EIA today has a staff of approximately three hundred employees and a budget of approximately $125 million.

61. Bureau of Industry and Security, Office of Technology Evaluation, US Department of Commerce, "Notice of Request for Public Comments on Risks in the Semiconductor Supply Chain," September 24, 2021.

62. See, for example, Korean industry and government concerns on competitiveness implications as described here: Shin-Young Park, "US Pressures Samsung, Chipmakers to Disclose Key Internal Data," *The Korea Economic Daily*, September 26, 2021.

63. US Department of Commerce, "Results from Semiconductor Supply Chain Request for Information," January 25, 2022.

64. The Blue Book features 205 semiconductor product categories by revenue and 241 product categories by units, 57 categories thereof split by the regions Americas, Europe, Japan, China, and Asia Pacific/All Other. The data collected by WSTS includes but is not limited to total billing by geographic location, regional growth rate, and total growth rate for each product.

65. Beyond WSTS, private consulting firms and investment banks also publish regular statistical updates on the semiconductor industry for investors. Such analysis tends to focus on trends in gross margin and operating profit as opposed to

forecasts and transparency of the supply chain, though firms including Nathan Associates and Gartner do offer private analyses on semiconductor market share and demand and firm inventory levels.

66. See, for example, dynamics as described in Chris Wilkinson, *Obsolescence and Life Cycle Management for Avionics*, Federal Aviation Administration, DOT/FAA/TC-15/33, November 2015.

67. James Timbie, "National Security Supply Chain Resilience," Hoover Institution, National Security Task Force December 2020 Report.

CHAPTER FOUR

A Long-Term Competitiveness Strategy for US Domestic Semiconductor Technology

EDLYN V. LEVINE AND DON ROSENBERG

The United States has an overriding national interest not just in maintaining a secure semiconductor supply chain, but also in pursuing leading capabilities, including in design, software tools, manufacturing equipment, materials, manufacturing, and advanced packaging—as well as the advanced products in which chips are used.

The long-term economic dynamism of the United States, its global technological leadership, and its military deterrence capability require both pushing forward semiconductor—and other critical-technology—frontiers and translating those technology breakthroughs into commercial success. US success across both realms will also accrue to its global trade and technology partners, and benefit the broader human condition.

This chapter details the steps that the US government and its partners can take to foster overall technological progress on semiconductors and the ability of the United States to benefit from those inventions.

• • •

The best way to predict the future is to invent it.
—ALAN KAY

Technology is now the primary battleground of modern superpower competition. The ability of one nation to impose its will on another has expanded to include a nation's ability to wield technological assets, control access to high-tech supply chains, and develop novel innovations that drive economic growth and impact geopolitics.

In the twentieth century, a rich ecosystem for innovation was founded in the United States on the principle of translating fundamental scientific breakthroughs into solutions to engineering problems. Liberal capitalism produced a winning formula that combined scientific research, manufacturing, free enterprise, skilled workforce, and the rule of law (including effective legal protection for intellectual property). The exigencies of twentieth-century wars further catalyzed scientific innovation and demonstrated the importance of a robust research-industrial base. For instance, the manufacturing and research institutions composing the "Arsenal of Democracy" in the United States went head-to-head against the industrial conglomerates of IG Farben and Vereinigten Stahlwerke in Nazi Germany during World War II. The United Kingdom, by contrast, had a strained manufacturing sector and had to export new inventions such as the cavity magnetron (critical to radar) to the United States to exploit their full military potential for the war effort.

By the twenty-first century, this Arsenal of Democracy had faltered. The COVID-19 pandemic exposed a crisis in US science and technology industries: they were unable to provide the necessary surge in personal protection equipment, pharmaceuticals, and respirators.[1] This failure was a consequence of the decades-long erosion of the US industrial base. The commercial entities that supply advanced technologies have long taken advantage of market efficiencies by outsourcing manufacturing to low-cost locations, leading to complex and geographically dispersed supply chains. We see this phenomenon clearly with semiconductors, critical materials, photonics, aerospace, biotechnology, nuclear materials, energy production, energy storage, and more.

The contraction of the US manufacturing sector and dispersal of the US supplier networks are deeply concerning. Not only does the loss of these complementary assets diminish the capability of the US industrial base to provide surge capacity during a crisis, it also subjects the United States to an outright denial of critical technologies by other nations as a means of exerting influence. The most pressing concern resulting from the dispersal of high-tech manufacturing, however, is the loss of future technology superiority and technology-driven economic growth.

This concern is rooted in the principle that an innovative country's ability to *create* value in the form of new technology does not necessarily translate into that country's ability to *capture* value by scaling those inventions into meaningful, market-competitive products. Capturing value from innovation requires command of the "complementary assets" needed to scale innovations. These assets include capital, advanced manufacturing capabilities, supplier networks, and a highly skilled workforce. Additionally, value creation in certain advanced-technology sectors is possible only through the interplay between experimentation and manufacturing, giving an innovation edge to the countries that maintain robust manufacturing sectors.[2]

Today, no high-tech industry is as strategically important to US technology leadership as is the semiconductor industry. As described in chapter 2, semiconductors are produced using one of the most complex manufacturing processes ever conceived, consisting of thousands of steps to achieve near-atomic-level precision at high production volumes. The complexity of the involved physics, chemistry, and engineering epitomizes the virtuous cycle connecting inventive research to innovative manufacturing; that cycle is imperative for progress in semiconductors.

This chapter evaluates the longer-term policy options available to the United States to secure its strategic autonomy through control of critical technologies such as semiconductors in light of today's complex technological and geopolitical realities. In particular, how can we better capture the value of (i.e., commercialize) emerging technologies to ensure continued US technological superiority and economic competitiveness?

Defining a US Policy Objective: Strategic Autonomy via the Control of Critical Technologies

Technologically and economically derived power shifts occur over decades, and result from progrowth policies applied consistently over many political cycles to achieve a national purpose. China's rise is the most recent example of long-term coordination between political and industrial sectors to achieve economic and strategic aims consistent with the country's nationalistic objective of global leadership by 2049. In comparison, we have observed how US policy in recent decades has lacked purpose, instead focusing on the near-term political demands of election cycles.

For the United States to ensure that it controls its own destiny on semiconductors over the long term, a drastic pivot is required—away from short-term, reactive politics and toward an intentional, well-defined objective, accompanied by consistent policy measures sustained over a meaningful duration.

This chapter proposes that the objective of US policy over the next twenty-five years needs to be *strategic autonomy*: to protect and defend its sovereignty, liberty, and way of life—and those of its global partners—by means of technological superiority and economic leadership.

The ability of a country to control its destiny depends on its control of critical technologies. Advanced technologies are essential to life-supporting and economy-critical infrastructure (such as energy, food distribution, communications, health care, and life-support systems) and to national security and force projection (such as command and control, communications, surveillance, navigation and timing, advanced conventional weapons systems, electronic warfare, and space systems). Because semiconductors are a core enabling technology in all of these realms, controlling semiconductors is critical to achieving strategic autonomy.

Control of critical technologies implies four things. First, control requires guaranteed access to these technologies under all conditions, whether peace, international crisis, or war. No adversary should be able to impose its political will on the United States by denying or compromising access to a critical technology—either to the product itself or to its supply chain.

Second, control implies the option to deny an adversary access to the technology if that country threatens US or partner interests. Denial of access to US and partner technology, however, has costs for domestic tech industries—so it should be used sparingly. Importantly, the prospect of denied access must be sufficiently credible and impactful to a country to be a deterrent.

Third, control includes the ability to respond to a surge in demand for a technology in a time of crisis. This ability has implications for the location of manufacturing centers: geographic access to a manufacturing center that is not located domestically or in a partner country can be more easily denied in a time of crisis. Suppliers and skilled labor are also generally colocated with manufacturing centers, and knowledge spillovers are enabled by the technology ecosystems that grow up around manufacturing centers.

Fourth, control means having the ability to lead both the development (value creation) and commercialization (value capture) of future generations of a critical technology. Both are required to realize long-term domestic economic growth and to sustain asymmetric technology leadership. Doing so for semiconductors will require new policies to improve US weaknesses in manufacturing, economies of scale, and intellectual property (IP) that account for the following:

- Manufacturing and research are closely linked for semiconductors. Without research, manufacturing is a path to obsolescence; without manufacturing, research is a bridge to nowhere. Semiconductor technology requires continual research and development for new capabilities to be manufacturable, and continuous feedback from manufacturing to inform and scale research results.
- Economies of scale are critical for commercial success in semiconductors due to the high fixed cost and barriers to entry of advanced manufacturing. Countries that create favorable environments for large, capital-intensive semiconductor companies will more easily capture the value of new inventions due to the increased efficiency introduced by the capability to manufacture at scale.
- Semiconductor manufacturing technology is highly dependent on trade secret protection and may be especially vulnerable to trade secret theft or other IP misappropriation. Today's semiconductor

innovators—whether in the United States, Taiwan, Korea, Japan, or the Netherlands—are operating in a regime of weak appropriability due to actions taken by China and others to coercively or illicitly appropriate technologies invented in other nations.

In consideration of the policies needed to achieve strategic autonomy through the control of critical technologies, we cannot ignore the reality that the next twenty-five years may not be peaceful, but marred by warfare. Russia's invasion of Ukraine and China's repeated threat of military aggression to absorb Taiwan highlight this possibility. A technological advantage and a robust economy with a domestic manufacturing base are essential for any wartime effort. Thus, long-term policies undertaken today should better position the United States for any military conflict that may emerge.

Why Is the United States No Longer in a Position of Assured Technology Leadership?

The policies that should be adopted today should be informed by an understanding of industrial policies of the late twentieth and early twenty-first centuries: if we do not examine the policies responsible for the hollowing out of US semiconductor manufacturing and industry leadership, new efforts may simply perpetuate the policy failures of the past.

Recent US policy making has been dominated by near-termism. Even the novel and relatively ambitious Creating Helpful Incentives to Produce Semiconductors (CHIPS) and Science Act of 2022 is, in many respects, a victim of this malady: it provides tens of billions of dollars in government subsidies over just five years (which may be allocated as much by political motivations as by market-driven forces), as well as some time-bound tax credits—but it still does not address many of the root-cause factors, such as the overarching tax, trade, and regulatory environment that has driven the offshoring of manufacturing over decades. Reflecting the lack of long-term focus, the US Senate passed as part of the Inflation Reduction Act of 2022 (IRA) a punitive 15 percent tax on US corporations on the same day the CHIPS Act passed both chambers. History teaches that the CHIPS Act will be insufficient and inefficient, and portions of the IRA will be counterproductive to US interests.

Today, the United States accounts for only 12 percent of semiconductor manufacturing and a mere 2 percent of outsourced assembly and testing.[3] These figures represent a drastic decline from its former prominence as the leader of the semiconductor industry across the industry's value chain. During the 1950s and into the 1960s, the inception, growth, and early maturation of the semiconductor industry were solely a US affair. A naïve view toward comparative advantage would conclude that, with such strong domestic capabilities initially, the US semiconductor industry would remain dominant as a point of equilibrium. This view, however, neglects the fact that nation-scale industrial policies shape global markets: other countries, realizing the strategic importance of the semiconductor industry, adopted aggressive policies to shift the global distribution of the industry in their favor. The consequent loss of the US semiconductor manufacturing base, then, was a combined result of US policy failures and others' policy successes, including in Japan, Taiwan, South Korea, and China.

The free-market landscape in which multinational companies operate is actively shaped by the actions and policies of governments around the world. China's emerging strengths in today's market are particularly concerning in this light due to China's immense scale, key role in semiconductor-dependent global value chains, and market-distorting policies.

Companies evaluate and select new manufacturing sites primarily based on the availability of infrastructure (spanning power, water sources, and telecommunications), tax policies and incentives, regulatory hurdles and permitting timelines, proximity to customers, presence of adjacent industries, local workforce, and access to distribution channels.[4] Additional factors—access to capital (including debt financing and foreign investment), antitrust regulation, IP protection, and the impact of restrictive measures such as export controls, tariffs, sanctions, and visa limitations—have become increasingly important. These factors offer a rubric for policy makers as they seek to create environments favorable for manufacturers.

The reality today, however, is that the manufacture and packaging of semiconductors in the United States is economically noncompetitive—largely because US policy makers have inadvertently made the country unprofitable for such capital-intensive manufacturing. As a semiconductor industry executive stated:

> I'd love to make this product in America. But I'm afraid I won't be able to. . . . Wages have nothing to do with it. The total wage burden in a fab is 10 percent. When I move a fab to Asia, I might lose 10 percent of my product just in theft. . . . [The problem is] everything else. Taxes, infrastructure, workforce training, permits, health care. The last company that proposed a fab on Long Island went to Taiwan because they were told that in a drought their water supply would be in the queue after the golf courses.[5]

In short, the industrial policies of both competitor and partner nations in Asia, as well as US policy failings, have hollowed out the semiconductor manufacturing environment in the United States.

Policies to Achieve US Strategic Autonomy through Semiconductor Leadership

Given the above, we believe that US long-term semiconductor policy should include the following components:

- *Enhancing value capture* and commercialization of research through scaling innovation alongside the incubation of complementary domestic manufacturing activity
- *Strengthening national and economic security* by decreasing dependence on unreliable competitor nations and by diversifying geographic risk

- *Amplifying value creation* through investment in US research capacity for breakthrough technologies, which for semiconductors is strongly coupled to advanced manufacturing
- *Strengthening the global appropriability regime* by countering China's systematic theft of US and partner nation technologies

The core tenet of consistent policies across manufacturing, research, and appropriability is to ensure that the United States (together with its partners) leads in both value creation and value capture.[6] Success here over the next quarter century should be measured in terms of an increase in US semiconductor global market share in manufacturing and in assembly and testing; sustained market positions in design and manufacturing equipment; and the number of investments made in the United States in cooperation with partner-nation firms.

1. Policies to Enhance Value Capture

Capturing the value of new technologies is important for economic growth. The commercialization of new technologies leads to more domestic companies, domestic supplier and consumer networks, domestic jobs, and overall GDP growth. The United States has historically benefited from its ability to capture the value of its innovations: personal computers, cellular networks and devices, and social networks led to the creation of some of the world's largest and most valuable companies.

Recent US technology policy has focused almost exclusively, albeit parsimoniously, on value creation through research and development (R&D) funding. The resources and environment needed for breakthrough inventions, however, are very different from those needed to capture the market value of those breakthroughs—and a lack of policy focus has led to an atrophy of US ability to capture the value of new inventions.

Unsurprisingly, many US inventors lament that, although they were the first to invent a new technology, a competitor or imitator—for example, from China—has captured all of the profit. The photovoltaics industry and lithium-ion battery industry are two prominent examples of value capture by China; during the Eisenhower era, color TVs were an example of value capture by Japan. Andy Grove—the third employee and ultimately third CEO of Intel—aptly stated that to capture value, a new technology or tech industry "needs an effective ecosystem in which technology knowhow accumulates, experience builds on experience, and close relationships develop between supplier and customer."[7]

Creating these ecosystems should be the objective of policies focused on value capture. Value capture primarily depends on two factors: one, the ability to access the complimentary assets required to scale a new innovation, and two, the strength of the appropriability regime needed to protect the innovation.

Today, the semiconductor industry operates in a weak global appropriability regime, largely due to the actions of China and other countries to obtain strategic technologies. Although the United States has an imperative to counter the actions of China and other countries and strengthen appropriability as discussed below, the greatest opportunities to enhance US value capture from innovation—whether pioneered in the United States or elsewhere—come through augmenting domestic complementary assets.

Complementary assets for the semiconductor industry include advanced prototyping facilities, highly complex manufacturing facilities, packaging facilities, production and metrology equipment, digital design tools, access to electronics-grade materials, and downstream systems integrators. Without the domestic presence of these complimentary assets, US firms looking to scale production and capture the value of new innovations will increasingly be drawn abroad.[8] To tip the scale of value capture in favor of the United States, domestic policies favorable toward capital-intensive semiconductor manufacturing, packaging, equipment production, and materials processing are needed.

Several policy options exist to increase value capture through the augmentation of domestic complementary assets like manufacturing. These include taxes, regulation, antitrust, subsidization, immigration, and industrial commons. IP rights, which are also vitally important, are discussed in a subsequent section on global appropriability.

Taxes

Far from being globally competitive, the existing US tax code is structurally biased against capital-intensive businesses, especially manufacturers. The current tax code requires companies to spread deductions for capital investments over multiple years. For example, the capital expenditures associated with building a semiconductor foundry—which run in the billions—cannot be immediately deducted from taxable income, but instead must be spread over a thirty-nine-year period.[9] The reduction in the real value of deferred deductions over this time due to inflation and the time value of money causes an overstatement of taxable income for the manufacturer. The result is a tax bias in favor of service firms with high labor costs and low capital expenditures, and a tax penalty for firms requiring high capital expenditures and low labor costs. To that end, we recommend the following:

- US policy makers should eliminate the tax penalty against capital-intensive industries like semiconductor fabrication by allowing firms to deduct 100 percent of their capital expenditures in the first year of purchase.

Multinational semiconductor companies assess potential site locations for fabrication and packaging facilities based on national and local taxes. Foreign governments, including China, Vietnam, and Thailand, have offered generous income tax credits and even tax holidays to attract the high-capital-expenditure manufacturing projects of global semiconductor firms.[10] Tax and other incentives (land, grants, etc.) in China can account for up to 40 percent of the cost recovery of a new fab's total cost of ownership—well above that in other countries, including the United States.[11] We recommend the following:

- US policy makers should assess the effectiveness of the 25 percent tax credit passed in the CHIPS and Science Act of 2022 and consider extension or expansion of the tax credit to make the US a tax-competitive environment for semiconductor fabrication and packaging facilities. Such tax incentives should also be extended to cover the domestic manufacture of semiconductor equipment needed for nanofabrication, including etch, deposition, lithography, and metrology tools.

Semiconductors are a research-intensive technology, requiring companies to invest heavily in R&D spending every year to remain competitive. The US semiconductor industry reinvested 18.6 percent of its revenue into R&D activities in 2021.[12] The US tax code allows for R&D tax credits to incentivize corporations to undertake expenditures necessary to support R&D activities. Claiming the R&D tax credits is complicated for firms, and thus the tax credit is often inaccessible to small firms.[13] Overall, US R&D benefits are not as competitive as those of other Organisation for Economic Co-operation and Development (OECD) countries.[14] Further, under current law, companies will be required to amortize R&D costs over five years—thereby reducing the global competitiveness of the United States as an environment for corporate R&D. We thus recommend the following:

- US policy makers should permanently eliminate the tax code's five-year R&D cost amortization and simplify the R&D tax credit system.

Finally, the overall corporate tax rate in the United States will be the strongest determinant for attracting productivity growth investments of multinational firms. Without a globally competitive business tax system, eliminating the tax bias against manufacturing, providing tax credits for fabs, and making R&D credits more generous will not be effective in the long run. Before the Tax Cuts and Jobs Act (TCJA) was passed in 2017, the United States had a statutory corporate tax rate of 38.9 percent, the highest among OECD nations. The TCJA reduced the corporate tax rate to 21 percent and eliminated the alternative minimum tax (AMT) that has been shown to disproportionately affect mining, transportation, warehousing, and manufacturing.[15] Even so, less than five years after passing the TCJA, Congress passed the 2022 IRA, which reinstated the AMT and established other means such as a tax on US corporate book incomes. To raise government revenue, corporate taxes have historically proven to be the most economically deleterious, due to their chilling impact on corporate productivity-growth investments such as manufacturing and R&D.[16] We recommend the following:

- US policy makers should eliminate the alternative minimum tax and additional corporate tax hikes passed in the IRA because they have historically proven to disincentivize domestic manufacturing and other investments of multinational corporations. The US should create an internationally competitive corporate tax system by embracing lower statutory corporate taxes, such as the 21 percent rate introduced by the TCJA.

Regulations and Permitting

The ability of the United States to remain globally competitive in semiconductor technologies requires an ability to move quickly to build manufacturing capacity for legacy technologies, as well as to construct next-generation fabrication facilities. The CHIPS Act includes federal subsidies and tax credits for fabrication and packaging—but it does nothing to alleviate the regulatory burden on domestic semiconductor manufacturers.

Today's federal and state permitting requirements are unacceptably slow. Under the federal Clean Air Act (CAA), two permitting programs are primarily of concern to semiconductor manufacturing: preconstruction permits and operation permits. These permits are generally granted at the state and local levels but are subject to Environmental Protection Agency (EPA) review. The permitting process for new facilities can take upward of eighteen months, which is prohibitive for a competitive industry where time provides a decisive advantage.[17] A recent study analyzing the construction of greenfield fabrication facilities showed that the construction-to-production time of a new fab in the United States has increased by 38 percent over the last thirty years—significantly longer than in other regions, notably Taiwan and China.[18]

Expedited permitting and regulatory support is necessary for the United States to increase its domestic semiconductor manufacturing capacity. Doing so is especially important for attracting foreign companies to build outside of their headquartered countries where they often have ready access to policy makers to create favorable regulatory environments. And the need for reform is underscored by the fact that US firms are no longer at the leading edge of semiconductor manufacturing. We recommend the following:

- The EPA should create an expedited, simplified, and transparent permitting process for greenfield fabrication, packaging, and equipment manufacturing facilities to be constructed under the CHIPS Act, with a capped time for permitting decisions of three months. The permanent adoption of this expedited process should be considered for the construction of future facilities. Redundant federal, state, and local permitting requirements should be identified and removed.

A robust supply of chemicals, materials, and gases is essential both for domestic semiconductor fabrication and for ensuring US industry supply chain resiliency. Materials suppliers to the semiconductor industry often face even higher regulatory barriers than fabrication facilities. For example, raw materials suppliers face mining permits in addition to the construction permits faced by manufacturing facilities. A Taiwan-based supplier of specialty gases for fabrication estimated that building a factory in the United States is five to six times as expensive as in Taiwan, in part due to these regulatory barriers.[19] That appraisal was echoed on an earnings call in January 2023 by Taiwan Semiconductor Manufacturing Company (TSMC), whose CFO reported that their facility construction costs in Arizona exceeded those in Taiwan by four to five times.[20]

Additional EPA regulations may restrict the domestic production, supply, and use of certain chemicals necessary for semiconductor fabrication. Examples of chemicals subject to EPA regulations include N-methylpyrrolidone (NMP); octamethylcyclotetra-siloxane (D4); TBBPA; hydrofluorocarbons; and phenol, isopropylated, phosphate (3:1) (PIP (3:1))—all of which are important to aspects of semiconductor manufacturing, performance, and safety.[21] Recent EPA evaluations under the Toxic Substances Control Act (TSCA) may increase restrictions for US manufacturers to access these and other relevant semiconductor production materials, thereby increasing domestic supply chain uncertainty and disruption. This all was recently borne out with the EPA's restriction on usage of PIP (3:1), a common chemical in semiconductor equipment.[22]

These regulatory restrictions have contributed to zeroing out the domestic production of the chemicals, materials, and gases needed for semiconductor fabrication—today, the United States is almost entirely import dependent.[23] Many countries the United States depends on for these critical minerals do not have the same environmental protections and continue to damage the environment, albeit elsewhere on the globe. It would be environmentally advantageous and beneficial to US economic and supply chain resiliency to determine a means for producing and using these chemicals, minerals, and gases in an environmentally safe manner domestically, thereby reducing the geographic externality of outsourced environmentally damaging processes. We recommend the following:

- To address acute supply chain demands and strengthen the domestic availability of critical chemicals, materials, and gases, the EPA should provide near-term exclusions or exemptions for regulated substances. In parallel, funding and incentives for the discovery and development of alternative, environmentally friendly replacement materials and processes should be prioritized.

Antitrust Regulation

Size matters in the semiconductor industry. Capturing economies of scale is exceptionally important for managing the exorbitant costs of manufacturing semiconductors—which can include up-front capital commitments of $20 billion for a new fab. The distribution of production costs over a large number of manufactured devices is essential for driving down the cost per unit and making ownership and operation of a foundry economically viable.

Experience also matters in the semiconductor industry. The economic concept of "learning while doing" or the "learning curve" relates the reduction of unit costs to the accumulated learning needed to produce each successive unit.[24] This learning is particularly important for the complex high-tech manufacturing processes needed for semiconductor production. The rule of thumb is a 20 to 30 percent decline in unit cost for each doubling of experience or production volume.[25] The combination of size and experience can produce a decisive competitive advantage for a firm: a company with dominant market share can more rapidly accumulate experience and, consequently, perpetuate its cost advantage over rivals. Market power also enables firms to accrue the resources and capital necessary to fund their R&D.

Current antitrust regulation does not sufficiently account for the dynamic aspects of competition in evolving technology industries.[26] Nor does antitrust enforcement account for the importance of firms to advanced technology development, national security, and economic competitiveness.[27] The breakup of large technology companies leads, among other things, to the diminution of market power needed for research funding and related operational and capital expenses (e.g., owning, staffing, and operating R&D laboratories); a reduction in the learning efficiencies that benefit from economies of scale; and the loss of talent, capabilities, and assets that are often casualties of breakups. And once the scientific talent, institutional knowledge, and technology assets of a company are lost, they are virtually impossible to recover.

Antitrust enforcement against US technology companies over the latter half of the previous century and into the twenty-first century has led to a drastically reduced capacity for US firms to compete with the protected companies and industries of other countries. In no US tech sector is this more devastatingly apparent than in telecom equipment. For over a century, the United States led the world in telecom technology development, equipment manufacture, and hardware innovation. Companies like AT&T, Western Electric, ITT, and Lucent dominated the global market. But antitrust actions by the US Justice Department to weaken these companies led to a vitiation of the domestic industry to the point of nonexistence. Some conclude that "without the aggressive antitrust policies of the US government, America would still be the world leader in telecom equipment."[28] The loss of US telecom superiority has led to a loss of economic first-mover advantages in network infrastructure for 5G and 6G, and in turn has heightened the national security implications of the rise of China's Huawei and ZTE.

More of this antitrust enforcement could destroy both the capacity of US industry to innovate and the ability of the US economy to capture the value of those innovations. The US government's posturing to break up large Silicon Valley tech companies—some of which are at the cutting edge of semiconductor design and application—will have a similar deleterious impact on the US semiconductor industry's global competitiveness. Just as concerning is the recent approach by competition agencies toward acquisitions and mergers. Acquisitions often serve as the vehicle for moving the results of R&D to commercial practice. Indeed, a significant share of start-ups look forward to an established firm acquiring them for just that reason. We recommend the following:

- US antitrust policy should take into account a firm's impact on US economic competitiveness, national security, and innovation capacity by recognizing the importance of a firm's market power on its ability to invent and scale new technologies, as well as its ability to compete with the protected industries of other nations. Innovation-based antitrust evaluation requires improved methods and metrics for regulators to effectively assess global markets and downstream impacts on US technology leadership.

It is worth considering the chilling effect that antitrust enforcement can have on technology collaboration between firms. The National Cooperative Research Act (NCRA), passed by Congress in 1984, allowed companies within the same industry to form consortia to collaborate in precompetitive R&D. But the NCRA does not extend to the R&D required to scale differentiated products to the competitive market when in fact such collaboration may be necessary. In Japan, by contrast, liberal antitrust enforcement and the exemption of the computer and semiconductor industries contributed to the rise of Japan's industry in the 1970s and 1980s.[29] Ultimately, the United States passed its own antitrust exemption for the industry R&D consortium SEMATECH, which was formed in response to Japan's advances. We thus recommend the following:

- The US Congress should pass a similar antitrust exemption for semiconductor industry collaboration that may be undertaken in response to the CHIPS Act. This exemption should extend beyond the limiting scope of precompetitive R&D, and Congress should consider permanently adopting this exemption.

Subsidization

The provision of heavy government subsidies to preferred companies is a standard tactic of the mercantilist playbook to grow domestic champions, including in China. This approach has succeeded in creating Chinese technology juggernauts such as Huawei. Even so, it is massively inefficient and often corrupt, having led to a catastrophic waste of Chinese public funds—indeed, government subsidies are all too often distributed on the basis of political favoritism rather than market competition.[30] Historically, the United States' embrace of free-market competition has dampened the appetite for government subsidies to industry. Current budget considerations also contribute to a total lack of political will to compete with China on the magnitude of industrial subsidies—what might be termed a subsidy "race to the top."

Given this context, the US government must carefully consider the best means to provide taxpayer subsidies to the industry in a manner that avoids the market-distorting impacts of political favoritism and the artificial propping up of noncompetitive organizations at the expense of taxpayers.

Effective subsidies require assurance that taxpayer dollars are awarded in a market-competitive manner, which can be achieved by having the US government act as a customer. Creating market-competitive programs involves the US government buying down the demand risk for industry—enabling industry to focus on the technical risks needed to develop its desired services, infrastructure, or capabilities. In this way, subsidies can catalyze the building of complementary assets that are needed for future value capture of semiconductor innovation.

This demand-side method was used by NASA during the Commercial Orbital Transportation Services (COTS) program, which has encouraged the burgeoning of a globally competitive commercial space industry in the United States. COTS also made raising private financing a requirement for firms to receive NASA dollars—the understanding being that private capital would be loath to invest in a noncompetitive business.[31] Considering this, we recommend the following:

- Subsidies to incentivize onshoring of semiconductor manufacturing capabilities and other complementary assets—such as those of the CHIPS Act manufacturing incentives program—should be awarded on a market-competitive basis. This can be done by requiring firms competing for the subsidies to raise additional private capital to supplement taxpayer dollars. The US government can further reduce private investment risk by acting as a customer of some capabilities developed under the subsidy program, for example through commercial purchase agreements for chips needed in defense, energy, or other critical-infrastructure modernization needs.

The CHIPS Act subsidies also include a significant amount of funding for research infrastructure. Most proposals for the research-related CHIPS Act subsidies to date have focused on onshoring semiconductor fabrication facilities that already exist elsewhere in the world. Going forward, however, subsidies should also be directed toward building next-generation prototyping infrastructure that will be needed to overcome significant innovation barriers. Today, the cost and time associated with the invention and scaling of new semiconductor devices have drastically increased, and in many cases are prohibitive to innovators. The US government can use subsidies to derisk the development of novel, cutting-edge infrastructure that would give an asymmetric advantage to US innovators in capturing the value of their inventions domestically. We recommend the following:[32]

- Rather than invest taxpayer dollars in copying existing prototyping facilities that have proven to be cost-prohibitive for US innovators and startups, the US Department of Commerce should use CHIPS Act funding for the National Semiconductor Technology Center to build a next-generation network of digital and physical infrastructure needed to scale novel semiconductor devices. This new infrastructure should take the form of a network of new pathfinder fabs and facilities across the United States that leverage technical advances, such as cloud-native, full-chip simulation environments, AI-enabled design capabilities, and the digital twins of process flows with high-throughput experimentation. The goal of that spending should be to lower the cost of chip design and prototyping for US companies of all sizes.

Subsidies will have limited impact over time if the underlying industry economics remain uncompetitive. Beyond tax and regulatory issues, high labor costs in the United States are also particularly important for the competitiveness of the semiconductor packaging portion of the supply chain due to its high labor content. The United States is now home to only 5 percent of global semiconductor packaging compared to approximately 44 percent in China and 29 percent in Taiwan.[33] Funding the development of technologies to increase automation of packaging facilities is thus another effective use of CHIPS Act subsidies that have already been earmarked for packaging. Advanced packaging technologies will also be a key driver of semiconductor device performance enhancement over the next decade as two-dimensional scaling of transistors slows, as discussed in chapter 2. Making packaging an economically viable manufacturing activity in the United States is therefore a strategic imperative. We recommend the following:

- The Department of Commerce should use funding for the National Advanced Packaging Manufacturing Program of the CHIPS Act to fund the development of technologies that boost automation of manufacturing, effectively increasing the output efficiency per employee by one to two orders of magnitude. US packaging facilities built in response to the manufacturing incentives program should be incentivized to adopt these advances to ensure economically sustainable operation is achieved over the long term.

Skilled Labor

A skilled workforce is an essential complementary asset needed for effective value capture. And there is some concern that the United States currently suffers from a workforce shortage in the semiconductor industry.[34] In market economies like that of the United States, however, perceived workforce shortages are often a result of the compensation and perceived opportunities that an employer can offer.[35]

As noted in chapter 2, the US semiconductor industry competes with high-paying US internet technology hyperscalers (e.g., Amazon, Google, Meta), other tech firms, and Wall Street financial firms for engineering talent. This tough competition—combined with accessible and increasingly skilled low-cost labor in other countries—has led to the offshoring of US semiconductor jobs. A lack of demand for this type of employment domestically has led to a diminished workforce. Until the demand side for a domestic semiconductor workforce is addressed, putting more money into the supply side to increase the "pipeline"—for instance, more electrical engineers and materials scientists, the typical policy recommendation for workforce development— will not effectively build a domestic workforce, because these skilled workers will just migrate to higher-paying jobs.

Thus, if the United States wants to have a domestic industry with the requisite skilled labor force, it is going to have to pay for that labor force with higher wages. Expecting semiconductor companies to pay substantially higher salaries to US engineers is not a market-competitive option, given the availability of low-cost labor elsewhere in the world. Rather, the US government can provide direct means to boost remuneration in the form of individual tax incentives for workers in strategic industries. This approach is similar to the tax incentive provided by the government in the Netherlands, under their "knowledge migrant" visa program: highly skilled immigrants who emigrate with this visa are eligible to receive 30 percent of their income free of tax, allowing Netherlands technology companies to offer higher take-home pay.[36] We recommend the following:

- The US government should provide worker-oriented tax incentives for the semiconductor industry and other strategic sectors to boost take-home income.

That tax example highlights another aspect of the US labor market that needs to be fixed: high-skilled immigration. Today, the United States could do more to retain the talent that comes to our shores for education. US universities are among the best in the world and naturally attract the highest-achieving science and engineering students globally. Many of these international students seek advanced degrees with associated research training that is funded by government grants—in the field of electrical engineering in particular, 61 percent of graduate students studying in US universities are temporary visa holders.[37] Yet these students are all too often forced to return to their countries of origin after a brief postgraduation Optional Practical Training (OPT) work period if they cannot secure a long-term employer visa sponsorship. More of these skilled students want to stay in the United States than are able to.

The United States should provide pathways for these international students to stay after graduation, ensuring that US industry has access to the most innovative young technical talent in the world. Despite bipartisan support, the politics surrounding broader immigration policy continually sabotage efforts to pass legislation enabling such high-skilled immigration. For example, an amendment to exempt science and technology graduate degree holders from numerical visa caps was excluded from a revised version of the 2023 National Defense Authorization Act. We recommend the following:

- H1-B visas should be made available to all international students completing a graduate program in science or engineering at an accredited US university, and exempted from numerical visa caps.

Industrial Commons and Technology Hubs

The rise of Silicon Valley as a technology and innovation hub was serendipitous and unplanned by the US government. But Silicon Valley has served as a model for other nations to replicate through government planning and programming. Technology hubs consist of geographically concentrated tech companies that pursue cutting-edge innovation in close proximity to one another. These hubs have well-known benefits to enhancing a firm's productivity as well as the efficiency with which new technologies are invented and scaled.[38]

Hubs often benefit from favorable government policies, draw from leading R&D universities and trade schools, and attract upstream suppliers and downstream consumers to colocate. The result is a concentration of technical exchange, supplier linkages, skilled labor, and knowledge spillovers that turn technology hubs into powerful engines of wealth generation. For example, Taiwan's Hsinchu Science Park has evolved into one of the most productive hubs in the world: by one measure, firms located inside the hub are estimated to be 66 percent more productive than other Taiwanese firms operating outside of it.[39] Another successful example is the Saigon Hi-Tech Park in Vietnam, which succeeded in attracting an Intel packaging facility in 2006; fifty-eight other companies followed suit, bringing $2.03 billion in capitalization to the site.

Unsurprisingly, the creation of technology hubs is a result of a confluence of many value-capture policies. Most successful technology hub policies adopted by Taiwan, Singapore, South Korea, Vietnam, and China have focused on creating favorable business environments for large tech firms to move in, paving the way for smaller firms to relocate. These policies include favorable tax and regulatory environments, common infrastructure development, and public-private workforce development programs to train local talent.

The US federal government, by comparison, has adopted few policies focused on creating technology hubs. When such policies are considered, subsidization—rather than creating favorable business conditions—is often the method chosen by Congress. For example, the CHIPS Act authorized $10 billion in taxpayer dollars to create twenty technology hubs, but did not address creating the underlying business environments that would make those hubs more desirable. Targeted subsidies have not historically been successful in upgrading local economies and are subject to distribution based on political (rather than economic) factors.[40] Instead, the US government should adopt an approach that focuses on creating favorable business environments, including via accessible tax, regulatory, and legal reforms that reduce entrepreneurial barriers and increase commercial and manufacturing activity. Such an approach could be seen as analogous to the special economic zones that have been used to good effect in other parts of the world—including by China, whose government in the 1980s pragmatically and selectively compromised on its value of state control in order to achieve the broader goal of economic growth. To that end, we recommend the following:

- The US federal government should coordinate with state and local governments to create opt-in technology hubs through the implementation of policies that engender favorable business environments. These geographically limited hubs would adopt the beneficial tax and regulatory reforms needed for effective value capture that may not be possible to pass at the national level, such as expedited environmental review or permissible worker visas. Ongoing fine-tuning of legislation establishing such hubs should be encouraged through experimentation and pilot projects.

Global Technology Standards

Global standards organizations play a critical role in defining the evolution of certain technology industries that are downstream consumers of semiconductors. These organizations select amongst various technological choices and define paths for global interoperability. Because the selection of a particular technology can create favorable conditions for a supplier with existing market leadership, engagement in these standards-setting activities is thus commercially important for private firms.

Increasingly, coordinated engagement in global standards organizations is also becoming a national security matter—it is important that US and partner companies therefore maintain their participation in this process. In recent years, companies in China have been encouraged, and often directed, by their government to dramatically increase their participation in global standards setting. Using this coordinated approach, those companies and individuals can constitute the majority of standards body members and, as such, play an outsized role—often selecting technology paths that are favorable to China-based suppliers.

The telecommunications standards network 3rd Generation Partnership Project (3GPP) provides a notable example of China's heavy engagement in international standards setting. 3GPP has recently focused on 5G and 6G telecom standards, with implications for upstream semiconductor suppliers. The number of China-based companies participating in 3GPP as voting members, having more than doubled in recent years, is now twice that of US-based voting members.[41] This growing influence enables China to guide the direction of future technology development in the worldwide telecommunications industry. If the United States and partners do not respond, companies in open societies around the world will effectively have to comply with China's technology standards. Alternatively, as considered in the scenario work of chapter 1, two separate global technology ecosystems could develop, but that would eliminate the seamless interoperability that has been so critical to global communication and trade.

Multiple policy options exist to enhance coordinated US and partner participation in global standards setting. We recommend the following:

- Policy makers should consider incentivizing R&D investment to develop and patent next-generation technologies to incorporate in future standards; encouraging standards participation as a prerequisite to receiving subsidies and tax credits; eliminating or making exceptions to export controls that restrict US participation in standards bodies when China-based companies are active participants; providing antitrust exemption to US companies engaged in collaboration with other companies in recognized global standards bodies; and strengthening the rights of patent owners to demand a reasonable, market-based return on investment for contributions of essential technology to a global standard.

2. Policies to Strengthen National and Economic Security

Onshoring complementary assets to enhance US value capture and commercialization is important, but additional considerations are required to strengthen US national and economic security. In contrast to the minimal economic ties between the West and the Soviet bloc during the Cold War, today's liberal democracies are heavily intertwined with autocracies: one-third of democracies' imported goods originate in autocracies, democracies trade over $15 billion per day with autocracies, and autocracies account for 31 percent of global GDP, with 17 percent contributed by China alone.[42]

These numbers reflect significant economic dependencies on authoritarian nations that the United States and other open societies have developed. Further aggregation of critical supply chains by China has created choke points for which alternate suppliers are not available. For example, China is a near-monopoly producer of many chemicals, critical minerals, and metals—many of which are important for semiconductor devices and in other tech sectors such as aerospace, pharmaceuticals, and energy.[43] These dependencies strengthen China by exposing democracies to retaliation, in times of war as well as peace—as experienced by Japan during the 2010 Senkaku boat-collision incident and by Australia in 2020 over a request for an independent inquiry into the origin of COVID-19.

Ameliorating economic dependence on China will require skillful navigation. China has undertaken a program to asymmetrically decouple from the Western world, investing billions to achieve autonomy in semiconductors and other technologies. China's asymmetric decoupling is characterized by increasing Western and US dependency on China while simultaneously weaning China off economic dependencies on the West.[44] To achieve strategic autonomy, then, the United States must simultaneously reduce its critical economic dependencies on China while maximizing resilience in overall global trade. In addition to the value-capture policies of the previous section—which will reroute global supply chains to the United States in the long run—the United States must leverage additional policies of global trade, investments, economic access, and partnerships to strategically and selectively decouple from China on its own terms. In doing so, it is credible that such decoupling can be done in such a way as to reduce US critical dependencies on China, while maintaining some degree of trade (and codependence) with the West.

Incentivizing US Industrial Alignment

Actions of individual corporations can have significant impact on the competition between liberal democracies and authoritarian states. Companies benefit from the free-market environment, the rule of law, and the democratically accountable systems of government embraced by liberal democracies.[45] Firms in return comply with law and regulations and pay taxes on profits, but otherwise typically do not view themselves as being in service to the nation. The policies of democratic governments, meanwhile, have historically been ambivalent to encouraging globalization and offshoring of corporate assets to authoritarian nations, including to the People's Republic of China (PRC).

The enmeshing of the PRC and US economies was driven by years of aggressive PRC policies to attract foreign companies. To gain access to its large and lucrative economy, US corporations were more than willing to comply with China's policies of transferring intellectual property, relocating manufacturing, and forming joint ventures with PRC firms. Accessing the China market has made many US companies extremely prosperous while simultaneously making inexpensive technology products available to US consumers. As a result, China's economy has grown significantly in importance, further augmenting the incentives for US corporations to have a presence in China.

Throughout the 1980s, 1990s, and 2000s, the actions of US corporations to increase economic integration with China had the blessing of US policy makers. It was widely believed that Deng Xiaoping's market reforms were a harbinger of political reforms that would ultimately lead to China's liberalization. Thus, the financial interest of US firms to enter China's market aligned with overarching US policy objectives.

Only relatively recently has it become more widely accepted that free markets do not necessarily lead to free societies. Rising authoritarianism ushered in by Xi Jinping since 2012 has led to a drastic contraction of individual liberties, including enslavement of Uyghurs, suppression of democratic Hong Kong, brutal COVID-19 lockdowns, crackdowns on the Chinese tech sector, and threatening of Taiwan's self-determination. Rather than increase freedom, the West's fueling of China's economy has empowered China to emerge as the greatest existential threat to open societies around the world.

The rapid realization of the threat posed by China has led to a policy pivot by the US federal government. Now US priorities are to reduce economic exposure to the PRC market and halt the flow of US technology and industry to China. The rapidity of this policy shift—over the past six years—has left in its wake a misalignment of US policies with the financial interests of US companies. After decades of permissive US policies, it is not surprising that US businesses have built up extreme exposure to and dependency on China, and that China itself has now become a significant part of global market share. In semiconductors alone, China buys over 50 percent of the world's semiconductor components,[46] and fabs in China now constitute about one-third of total revenue of US semiconductor equipment manufacturers.[47] This exposure will take years to reduce and will require skillful crafting and handling of policies to move US business activity away from China in a way that does not cripple US corporations in the process.

Aligning US corporate financial interests with US policy objectives is paramount. In particular, conditions must be created such that to make the most money, US corporations will want to build capacity and business ties domestically rather than abroad. Policies should move assets that contribute to value capture (manufacturing) and value creation (research) out of China and back to the United States while simultaneously increasing market leadership of US companies. Global market leadership requires that policies enhance penetration of US technologies into China's market as well as the rest of the world. To be sure, China will still attempt to misappropriate and reverse engineer US technology—but their attempts to do so will be curbed by the fact that this type of activity is economically inefficient, and in any case should be deterred by active US trade and appropriability policies, as discussed later in this chapter.[48]

Today's US policies seem to be doing the exact opposite: cutting off the demand side from China via export controls while subsidizing capital-intensive building of overcapacity on the supply side is a dangerous policy mix that may overheat the US semiconductor industry and ultimately lead to its contraction. In 2022 alone, $1.5 trillion in market value of US semiconductor firms was wiped off the global markets due to a combination of slowing sales and tightened US export controls.[49] Additional antitrust sentiment by the Federal Trade Commission, the Department of Justice, and Congress against big US internet and consumer technology hyperscalers—some of which are the largest US consumers of US semiconductors—may further chill the demand for US semiconductor technologies.

Rather than antagonize US business interests, policy makers and industry in the United States should work together to incentivize the alignment of corporate activity with national security goals. Instead of threatening to break apart US hyperscalers, the US government should create a partnership with these companies, leveraging their significant market power to onshore manufacturing. This approach takes advantage of the priority placed on customers by semiconductor firms and the power large US customers have in shaping their supply chains. This was exemplified during a 2022 TSMC earnings call where its chairman, Mark Liu, stated that plans to build TSMC fabs in the United States and Japan were driven by demand from customers.[50] In light of these considerations, we recommend the following:

- Create incentives to align US corporate activity with US national security. For example, rather than threaten to break up big tech companies, the US government should partner with them, leveraging their market clout to encourage diversification of their supplier base.

Countering China's forced requirements for market entry is also an important measure. The US government should review and, if necessary, deem illegal the types of investments China demands from US firms, including forced joint ventures, financial commitments, and research and manufacturing commitments in China. US firms to date have evaluated the known loss of IP and technology to China in the context of near-term profits from operating in China—that is, whether the upside of doing business in China in the near term outweighs the significant and known downsides of forced technology transfer over the long term. By strictly regulating or making such activity illegal for US companies to engage in, the US government can prevent US firms from having to play by coercive rules set by Beijing in order to do business in China. The objective of such measures should be to ultimately force Beijing to allow commercial activity (e.g., the sale of US technology products in China) without requiring accompanied joint ventures, forced IP transfer, and buildup of complementary assets like manufacturing. We recommend the following:

- The interagency Committee on Foreign Investment in the United States (CFIUS) should review and restrict outbound investment—such as the building of manufacturing centers, research centers, joint ventures, and financial investment—in China and other authoritarian nations, especially when such outbound investments are required by those countries for entry into their domestic markets.

Finally, additional changes to the corporate tax system can be used to achieve better alignment between the long-term interests of the US government and the actions of US industry through incentives strong enough to encourage investment over the long durations needed for research and manufacturing activities at the leading edge of technology. To that end, we recommend the following:

- US policy makers should differentiate within the R&D tax credit those companies that are focused on critical and emerging technologies such as semiconductors versus technologies that lack a national security purpose. Additionally, US policy makers should differentiate the capital gains tax to provide better incentives for truly longer-term investment, for example over five or ten years versus simply the current single-year qualifier.

Export Controls

In this chapter, we make a countervailing argument to other voices in this volume: we believe that the use of export controls to restrict access to US technology should be applied sparingly. Recent use of export controls has been widely applied by the US government in an attempt to cut off China's access to critical technologies. These controls are often targeted at choke point technologies—that is, those technologies without which China cannot make progress on achieving specific, advanced capabilities. Extreme ultraviolet (EUV) lithography is one such choke point: EUV is needed to commercially fabricate semiconductors below 7nm at scale.[51] Controlling access to EUV has to date successfully prevented China from developing the capability to fabricate at the leading edge. However, there are very few technologies in the same class of uniqueness and complexity as EUV to justify application of export controls. Thus, although use of export controls to slow China has been widely lauded, it does not generally align US business interests with US policy objectives. And although it may create near-term strategic advantage for the US, this approach could ultimately weaken the United States' economic position over the long term—for three primary reasons.

First, the use of export controls today will weaken the effectiveness of any export controls or sanctions needed to counter PRC military action in the future. The United States does not have a monopoly on advanced technologies and savvy engineers. Parallel supply chains will grow in response to export controls—both within China and with its other trading partners—to replace technologies that were formerly sourced primarily from US firms. China's decoupling in response to US export controls is well under way: after being placed on the US Department of Commerce's Entity List in May of 2019, Huawei rapidly pivoted its supplier base, introducing a new cell phone with no US components by December of that year.[52]

It would be more advantageous for the United States to consider a strategy that maximizes penetration of US technologies into China's market while simultaneously taking measures to prevent the appropriation of that technology by PRC companies (discussed below). This approach would strengthen the position of the United States to impose export controls and sanctions as a means of last resort to deter belligerent PRC actions in the future. Some might argue that this future is now. The near-term strategic advantage from US export controls, however, is in conflict with long-term projection of US economic power. In contrast, China has been successful at building US dependency by penetrating its technology into US consumer, technology, energy, and defense markets, including for rare earths, batteries, magnets, and solar panels. The near-termism of export controls may very well accelerate an asymmetric decoupling scenario where China is less dependent on US technologies but the United States still heavily relies on Chinese exports.

Second, export controls could weaken the market position of US semiconductor firms and damage the United States' reputation as a reliable technology supplier. The size of China's market, discussed previously, is applicable here: by cutting off revenue from sales to China, the US government is curbing cash flow to US companies that is essential for maintaining competitive advantage in both technology development and economies of scale.

The unilateral nature of the current export control laws will also enable foreign suppliers to capture market share from US firms. Such capture occurred in the decade following the 1979 Export

Administration Act: in the wake of export control enforcement, the market position of US capital equipment suppliers dropped from 90 percent of global market share to only 50 percent by 1980, having lost 40 percent of the market to Japan-based suppliers.[53] The inefficient administration of export control laws in the United States exacerbated this market loss and led to a reputation that US technology was unreliably accessible and subject to lengthy, arbitrary licensing decisions.[54] History will repeat itself—unless countries such as Japan, South Korea, Taiwan, Singapore, and the Netherlands are willing to join the United States in locking China out of accessing the entire global semiconductor ecosystem.

Third, the concept of a choke point technology is ultimately an artificial one, bounded temporally by the evolving sophistication of a country's scientists, engineers, equipment, and technology ecosystem. This point is not to say that replication of existing complex technologies is easy—it is a prodigious task and exceedingly inefficient from an economic perspective. More than any other country, however, China has advantages that make it plausible that they will, eventually, be able to re-create technologies denied to them under export controls. One advantage is that re-creating existing technologies—no matter how complex—is easier than pioneering new capabilities. China has also benefited from tremendous technology transfer from the West and will continue to learn from Western technology, illegally if necessary. China is well known for cyber theft of intellectual property, reverse engineering hardware, and hiring Taiwan and Western talent. Finally, China is willing to stomach the heavy financial cost needed to gain technology independence—and with the imposition of export controls, China has ample motivation to do so.[55]

The use of export controls to restrict access to US technology should therefore only be applied as a last resort to impose political will. Economic analysis should be conducted to determine the long-term impact of export controls on a US technology sector before export controls are applied. In particular, if a technology is deemed to be easy to copy, it should *not* be controlled lest the targeted nation simply appropriate or otherwise rapidly indigenize the controlled technology, to the detriment of US industry's market share. In sum, we recommend the following:

- Use export controls sparingly. Rather, undertake policies recommended in this chapter that promote maximal penetration of US technologies into the global market and promote a strong appropriability regime to protect theft of those technologies. If export controls are used, apply them only to the most sensitive and difficult-to-appropriate technologies that directly pertain to security use.

Foreign Investment

As the scenario analysis in chapter 1 illustrated, the United States benefits from being a part of the larger global economy no matter what form global trade flows take in the future. Foreign direct investment (FDI) augments US economic activity through both greenfield investments—such as building facilities and operations from the ground up—and mergers and acquisitions (M&A). Through FDI, foreign companies contribute to creating domestic jobs, upskilling the labor force, funding R&D, and growing domestic industries and services sectors. Approximately 7.9 million Americans are employed by foreign companies that had invested $5 trillion cumulatively by the end of 2021—$405 billion of which was invested in 2021 alone.[56]

FDI in the form of greenfield investments has the potential additional benefit of increasing the resiliency of the global economy by onshoring critical nodes of the supply chain. A recent example is TSMC's construction of its 5nm Fab 21 in Arizona. This facility's projected capacity is comparatively small, at a planned twenty thousand wafer starts per month.[57] Its presence in North America, however, diversifies geographic access to leading-edge logic fabrication for the global economy. Such diversification is especially important given that, today, 92 percent of leading-edge (sub-10nm) capacity is located in Taiwan.[58] TSMC's FDI represents the surest near-term approach to advancing US domestic manufacturing capacity at the leading edge.

The United States should also collaborate with Taiwan's other semiconductor firms, such as United Microelectronics Corporation (UMC), Advanced Semiconductor Engineering (ASE Group), and MediaTek, to diversify their geographic holdings of fabrication and research facilities. This partnership starts, however, with providing a commercially attractive environment for investment in terms of capital efficiency and regulatory expediency. Today the opposite is more likely to be true. TSMC recently confirmed that "a range of construction costs and project uncertainty in Phoenix makes building the same advanced-logic wafer fab in Taiwan considerably less capital intensive." Some of those factors include "federal regulatory requirements that increase project scope and cost; . . . additional site prep and new infrastructure expense; and . . . state and local taxes on construction, facility, and utility use."[59] Unless these cost factors change, the United States will remain uncompetitive for FDI even as semiconductor firms may look to diversify their geographic holdings globally.

Attracting greenfield FDI from partner countries should, then, be a priority, especially for advanced technological and manufacturing capabilities that the US is lacking domestically.[60] And the many policies recommended elsewhere in this chapter also serve to attract greenfield FDI, including minimizing tax burdens for capital expenditures, implementing targeted fiscal incentives, improving domestic infrastructure, promoting skilled workforce development, and improving the regulatory environment. We recommend the following:

- Policy measures to enhance the fiscal environment, improve infrastructure, augment workforce development, and streamline the regulatory environment should be pursued to enhance greenfield foreign direct investment into the United States from partner countries. This is particularly necessary for attracting FDI from global semiconductor firms.

Through the Obama and Trump administrations, concerns grew about the security implications of FDI in the form of investments into and M&A of US companies. China in particular has invested in US companies to gain control of company boards, and has even outright acquired US companies to obtain a foothold in a new technology or to deepen strength and control of a strategic technology.[61] To counter these efforts, in 2018 Congress passed the Foreign Investment Risk Review Modernization Act (FIRRMA), which strengthens the process by which the interagency CFIUS process reviews FDI.[62] Although this legislation has led to a decrease in requests from China-based acquirers, its overall effectiveness in protecting US interests is, as yet, to be determined.[63]

Ultimately, the CFIUS review process has the difficult task of protecting US national security interests while simultaneously enabling the traditionally open US investment climate that leads to business opportunity for US companies and their employees. CFIUS' denial of foreign investment into US technology startups limits the capital available for those companies to scale and perhaps achieve successful exits in the form of acquisitions. Moreover, the CFIUS review process is opaque, leading to uncertainty when foreign companies from friendly jurisdictions—for example, Taiwan—seek to acquire a US company as part of broader US investment activity. Providing more transparency, increasing negotiation opportunities, and providing more certainty for foreign investors from partner nations would enhance the ability of US technology startups to attract the capital necessary to scale their innovations. We thus recommend the following:

- CFIUS inbound investment review should be a more transparent process with active engagement and negotiation with prospective foreign investors from partner nations. FDI into the United States from partner countries should be encouraged, whereas foreign investment from authoritarian countries that pose a national security risk should be strictly limited.

Armaments and Defense Acquisitions

All modern weapons systems contain semiconductor devices. Many defense programs of record develop complex and expensive platforms with long service lifetimes. While these platforms are often essential for modern warfighting capability, the Department of Defense (DoD) should complement them by acquiring large numbers of new classes of small, modular, inexpensive, and expendable systems that can be quickly and cheaply produced. Autonomous to semiautonomous drones for aerial or maritime operation or soldier-launched, sensor-equipped missiles are examples of modular, inexpensive systems that can be produced in large numbers. The acquisition and service lifetime of such systems would better match the rapid innovation cycles of the commercial semiconductor and consumer technology industries, allowing the DoD to benefit from economies of scale and cutting-edge innovation elsewhere in the economy.

The near-term focus should be to rapidly ramp up weapons production, especially in the wake of recent stockpile depletion needed to supply Ukraine's war effort—because currently, US arms makers are languishing.[64] Ukraine's war effort against Russia has further demonstrated the importance of semiconductor-enabled technologies to advanced warfighting capabilities and the effectiveness of adopting a strategy of deploying a large number of small, inexpensive weapons and precision guidance missiles. Ukrainian forces have depended on Switchblade drones, Stinger antiaircraft missiles, NLAWs (next-generation light anti-tank weapons), and Javelin missiles to fight Russia's forces. Each of these weapon systems contains a plethora of semiconductors.[65] Meanwhile, Russia has reportedly been struggling to equip its forces: without a domestic semiconductor manufacturing capability, Russia has been unable to gain access to semiconductors needed to replenish its precision-guided munitions due to export bans imposed by the United States and its partners.[66]

The lesson for the United States in the context of Taiwan is to take advantage of today's supply of semiconductors. Not only should the United States stockpile its own arsenal, Taiwan should also be equipped to defend itself with advanced capabilities today, in the manner that Ukraine has been only after invasion. Arming Taiwan with advanced, semiconductor-powered weaponry would be a true "silicon shield" for the Taiwanese people (in contrast to how the silicon shield is often described: the mere presence of the semiconductor industry in Taiwan, which will neither deter an invasion by Party General Secretary Xi Jinping nor be the decisive factor in a US defensive posture). Many in both the United States and Taiwan advocate for a "porcupine" strategy, which takes advantage of advanced, semiconductor-enabled weapons.[67] Crucially, given US supplier backlogs, doing so should include partnering with Taiwan's defense, electronics, and semiconductor firms to scale up advanced weapons coproduction, weapons codevelopment, and weapons deployment within Taiwan, as discussed in chapter 5. We recommend the following:

- Create a real "silicon shield" for Taiwan by partnering with its firms to scale up advanced weapons deployment, coproduction, and codevelopment on the island to make an invasion of Taiwan as costly as possible to potential aggressors. Partner with TSMC and Taiwan's significant semiconductor industry to supply state-of-the-art semiconductor devices for these new defense systems.

3. Policies to Amplify Value Creation

Value creation is the discovery of new scientific principles and the invention of new technologies that lay the foundation for future industries and enhanced human welfare. Policies to enhance value creation in semiconductors include increasing R&D funding in basic and applied sciences, building and maintaining R&D infrastructure, and educating the next generation of pioneering scientists and technologists. To improve return on investment to the taxpayer, this should be strongly coupled to the advanced-process and fabrication-oriented value-capture activities described above.

R&D Funding

Federal R&D funding as a percentage of GDP in the United States has been declining for several decades. The US government spent only 0.62 percent of GDP in 2017 on R&D (down from a peak of

1.86 percent of GDP in 1964), even as absolute federal funding has increased.[68] This diminution of the federal budget's R&D intensity has long been a point of concern, due to the recognition of the fundamental role that curiosity-driven R&D in basic and applied sciences has in value creation and future GDP growth.

In the context of the twenty-first-century great-power competition with China, the emphasis on funding value-generating R&D has never been more important. Yet the federal budget—of which more than 73 percent goes to various kinds of social insurance—does not reflect the importance of such a vitally important GDP-growing activity.[69] This neglect will ultimately lead to an economic and geostrategic death spiral: an ever-increasing portion of GDP allocated to social services, with ever-decreasing funding allocated toward value creation, will lead to economic stagnation and the demise of the innovation engine that has brought such vast prosperity to so many Americans. As one study put it, the US federal budget "is not the investment strategy of a focused superpower . . . competitor."[70] We recommend the following:

- The US Congress should increase and sustain federal R&D funding in basic and applied research, spanning established fields (e.g., conventional semiconductors) as well as frontier fields, such as beyond-CMOS (complementary metal-oxide semiconductor) devices that could someday complement today's predominant logic chips.

R&D Infrastructure

Increased funding for R&D in semiconductor devices is necessary but not sufficient for US value creation. Pure R&D programs will enable the US research community to explore trends in future computing, including the use of emerging devices that exploit physical phenomena such as spin, ferroelectricity, ferromagnetism, and phase transformations, as well as new materials such as oxides, nitrides, carbon, and chalcogenides for semiconductor transistor channels. Without access to fabrication facilities capable of integrating these emerging devices and materials with advanced CMOS architectures, however, US innovations will either fail to transition to commercial settings or be sent to offshore facilities for testing and scaling.

Today, the United States has no such facilities for exploratory research at foundry-relevant dimensions and scales. Previous US government–funded facilities have proven their importance, for example, in the Metal Oxide Semiconductor Implementation Service (MOSIS) program in the 1980s and the National Science Foundation's National Nanotechnology Coordinated Infrastructure (NNCI) in 2015, but they cannot address today's research needs in advanced and exploratory semiconductor technology.[71]

A national facility (or network of facilities) whose construction and operation are supported by the federal government is a key ingredient for US value creation and ultimately value capture.[72] Such facilities encompass capabilities at leading-edge fabrication, legacy nodes, and packaging capabilities, with the mission of enabling rapid, high-throughput experimentation. The construction of such facilities should be colocated with industry in technology hubs, and should leverage established infrastructure and methods, such as the use of a 300mm (i.e., modern commercial-scale wafer size) research pilot line, as well as advances that will drastically reduce cost and increase experimental learning cycles. Possible advances include simulating digital twins of process flows to create virtual environments for experimentation that are coupled to experimental facilities; using machine learning to identify novel experiments and process flows; and developing advanced, customizable tool sets with a wide range of operating conditions.[73]

This chapter has already recommended the use of CHIPS Act subsidy funds to build such infrastructure to enhance value capture. Even so, further R&D funding should be allocated to the building and operating of commonly available semiconductor research infrastructure—and not just specific research programs themselves—to ensure that the United States has indigenous research capabilities. We recommend the following:

- Allocate a portion of R&D budgets to the building and operating of new capabilities and research infrastructure rather than research programs alone.

Education

Training the next generations of scientists, engineers, and technicians will be vital to the United States' continued capacity to create value through new inventions.

Education in the quantitative sciences must start early. All too often, the US public education system fails to adequately prepare students in the K–12 system to be sufficiently competent in sciences and mathematics to seriously entertain pursuing careers in those fields at the collegiate level and beyond. Rectification of the dire state of scientific illiteracy and unpreparedness in the K–12 system should not be the responsibility of universities. Rather, solutions should be found to reform the US public education system and expose students in K–12 schools to high-tech industries that will drive the future economy and national security. Specific reforms are beyond the scope of this chapter, but acknowledging the importance of adequately preparing the next generation is not. We recommend the following:

- Enhance exposure to high-tech industries, including for semiconductors, in K–12 education and reform K–12 education to ensure students have sufficient training in mathematics and sciences to compete with global peers upon entry into universities or trade schools. For those pursuing collegiate degrees in semiconductor-relevant fields, increase the number of pathways to jobs as well as the industry's demand-side pull, for example, a semiconductor-focused version of the DoD SMART Scholarship program—which requires recipients upon graduation to work for a set number of years for the scholarship funder, and for whom a job is already in place upon graduation—financed in partnership with industry.

4. Policies to Strengthen the Global Appropriability Regime

Value capture is enhanced under a strong appropriability regime, defined as the efficacy by which knowledge and innovations can be protected from imitators.[74] The strength of appropriability is a function of the effectiveness of legal protections and the nature of the innovation (tacit or codified; easy or difficult to replicate). Today's global appropriability regime is weak, largely due to the unenforceable nature of legal protections for technology and innovation in the global setting. Transfer of US technologies to companies in other countries by both legal (but coercive) and illicit means has been rampant over the past few decades. China in particular has implemented an array of practices and policies that have resulted in a systematic transfer of US intellectual property to China. Beijing's support of IP theft by means of intrusions into US commercial networks is also well documented.

US innovation and value creation should not ultimately fuel China's economic growth and military-industrial complex. And yet, transitioning technologies to China (e.g., for production) is the paradigm under which US innovators operate today. Many US companies do not raise the issue of unfair trade practices for fear of retaliation and loss of business opportunities.[75] High-profile examples of technologies invented in the United States that are now produced by PRC firms include batteries, telecom equipment, photovoltaics, and, increasingly, semiconductors. China has repeatedly violated bilateral and multilateral trade agreements, and disputes brought by the United States and other countries via formal trade-resolution mechanisms have been slow and ineffectual.

Countering China's systematic theft of US technology and establishing a strong global appropriability regime is an imperative to ensure future technology leadership and strategic autonomy. The United States must also ensure that it does not continue to erode its domestic IP-rights strengths that incentivize innovators to undertake the risk and years of hard work needed to pioneer technologies.

Trade

The United States has increasingly taken unilateral action to counter technology theft by China. More often than not, unilateral action takes the form of restrictive measures, including export controls, the Department of Commerce's Entity List that restricts business with specific foreign firms, stricter CFIUS oversight of acquisitions, and expanded application of the International Emergency Economic Powers Act (IEEPA). For example, the Biden administration adopted sweeping export control measures to curb semiconductor technology and capability transfer to China.[76]

Ultimately, rectifying global trade will require bold action and determined leadership on the part of the United States. World Trade Organization (WTO) principles embrace free trade and disallow trade barriers that discriminate against countries of origin. The United States has no recourse to halt unfair PRC technology transfer practices under this system. The United States, therefore, must take action to build significant leverage over China, including a unified front of global partners, to force Beijing to change its behavior. Rather than act responsively and tactically, the United States should comprehensively reform global trade rules to respect and enforce strong appropriability, the rule of law, and other economic norms.

Once a clear objective for global trade is defined, the United States should act strategically, proactively, and persistently to reshape the international trading system as a whole, ensuring strong coordination with partner nations. We recommend the following:

- This and subsequent administrations should build a coalition of partners who share the US vision for a reformed global trade agenda; this coalition should then strategically shape international trade and counter China's market-distorting actions. As discussed in chapter 5, the United States should start by focusing on signing trade deals with partners—including Taiwan—to establish stronger trade relationships.

The United States has never put requirements on foreign firms for access to the US economy, yet this is routine practice in China: if a foreign company wants to sell a product in China, some fraction of that product must be manufactured in China, joint ventures must be established with China-based companies (often state-owned), and IP is forcibly transferred. The use of reciprocal policies by the United States would be counter to the free-market principles adopted after World War II, and serious economic analysis is necessary to evaluate what, if any, qualifications on access to the US economy should be enforced to protect US interests and to encourage foreign and domestic investment in the United States and like-minded partners. In the wake of recent PRC actions, however, there are several reasons to consider such policies.

The first concern is the predatory behavior of China to capture technology industries. For example, PRC government subsidies, its protected domestic market, and state-directed access to capital have directly contributed to China's domination of the photovoltaic industry. These policies allowed China's emerging photovoltaics manufacturers to sustain tremendous losses while contributing to a global supply glut and dumping product into export markets, crushing global competition. China's global share of photovoltaic cell production grew from 14 percent to 60 percent between 2006 and 2013 alone.[77] Sanctions imposed by the United States in response proved to be too late and rife with loopholes that rendered them useless.

The second concern is the national security implications of certain PRC products sold in the United States or in partner markets. This concern has led to banning Huawei and ZTE equipment in the United States and other countries. For example, the Secure Equipment Act, signed into law in November 2021, prohibited Huawei, ZTE, and any other company considered a national security threat from obtaining licenses for network equipment in the United States.[78] Even so, China is still allowed to export its illiberal vision to the rest of the world in the form of other products. National security experts and policy makers, for example, have raised concern over millions of US teenagers freely providing data to China-based social media platform TikTok.[79] The United States' ability to address these concerns can be described as muddled at best.

Tacit Knowledge

Although forced IP transfer and theft are of great concern, it is often the tacit knowledge of highly skilled scientists and engineers that is key to technology progress. The United States and other Western countries have trained Chinese students in STEM fields for decades. Originally, China was concerned that systematic brain drain would occur as the most talented Chinese youth would be lost to foreign countries.[80] But the lack of concerted effort by the United States to retain Chinese and other international students has quelled this fear.

The presence of foreign students from competitor nations studying critical technologies in US universities—or foreign nationals from competitor nations working for US critical-technology companies—is now viewed by some as a national security risk.[81] But crude steps (such as a ban on student visas for Chinese scholars and work visas for highly skilled Chinese scientists and engineers) will cut off the United States from a massive talent pool. Instead, the United States should consider how to accommodate those Chinese students and workers it accepts within its universities and companies, and give opportunities to those who wish to escape an increasingly authoritarian and illiberal regime under General Secretary Xi—as happened with scientists fleeing the Soviet Union.[82] We recommend the following:

- An evidence-based process should be adopted to screen for those with demonstrable ties to PRC military, security, or influence organizations. Otherwise, individuals permitted entry for studies or work should be allowed—and encouraged—to permanently relocate to the United States. Doing so will enable the United States to continue to be the greatest attractor of global and Chinese talent and fulfill Beijing's fears of brain drain to the West.

Meanwhile, China has established its Thousand Talents program to provide strong incentives to attract talented foreign nationals to its shores,[83] and it has aggressively recruited from international technology companies such as TSMC despite such recruitment being in violation of Taiwan's laws.[84] The tacit knowledge of US experts and leading researchers is of high value and is leveraged by Beijing and PRC firms for technology transfer—from high-profile cases of faculty members at leading US universities participating in the Thousand Talents program[85] to US corporations collaborating with universities in China that are closely tied to China's defense industrial base.[86] In consideration, we recommend the following:

- The United States should control the flow of tacit information to China by requiring a broader set of US citizens involved in critical technologies and sectors to obtain outbound visitation or training before travel to China. A similar measure was recently implemented in the new export controls implemented by the Bureau of Industry and Security: they require US citizens to obtain a license "to support the development, or production, of [integrated circuits] at certain PRC-located semiconductor fabrication facilities."[87]

Incentivizing US Innovators

A strong global appropriability regime will not be meaningful to US innovators if domestic intellectual property rights are eroded. The US government must therefore also ensure healthy and competitive domestic IP policies that incentivize US innovators to undertake the risky, difficult, and time-consuming work needed to invent new technologies.

The United States has been on a steady path for the past two decades to limit and devalue patents, progressively weakening US IP policies in almost all areas. Among the notable changes are limiting the availability of injunctive relief for infringement of IP rights, particularly by entities that are involved in licensing, not manufacturing; weakening IP rights in software-enabled inventions; and weakening the role of the US federal courts in patent cases through more extensive reviews of their decisions.

The Supreme Court decision in *eBay Inc. v. MercExchange, L.L.C.* and subsequent related rulings have all but eviscerated the foundational core of a patent right: the right to exclude. That line of cases now makes it almost impossible for a patent owner to enjoin the continued infringement of a patent by a proven infringer. These judicial rulings have encouraged what has been coined "efficient infringement" by companies that bet on the expense, disruption, resource drain, and uncertainty of outcome inherent in patent litigation and take the chance that if and when they are called to task, they will have to pay only the royalty that the noninfringers were willing to pay from the start.

The scope of patentable subject matter in the United States has also been limited to exclude abstract ideas by cases such as *Alice Corp. v. CLS Bank International*. This narrowing has made important inventions that previously would have been protected from theft or appropriation freely available. This limitation is in stark contrast to the situation in China, which issues patents for inventions that are far less novel and significant. China's approach to determine patent eligibility is much more pragmatic than the US approach: rather than test for abstractness (a vague concept), China's patent authority, the China National Intellectual Property Administration (CNIPA), encourages examiners to review a proposed invention as a whole and to focus on the technical solution. The result is a more favorable patent environment in China than in the United States: a recent study showed "more than 12,000 cases that had been granted in China and Europe but denied in the United States on statutory subject-matter grounds."[88]

Further erosion of IP protection in the United States has taken many forms. Antitrust law in the United States has been employed to preempt the legitimate statutory power granted to patents by treating them as monopolies, rather than as constitutionally mandated limited rights to exclude. The courts have further diminished patent rights by finding them exhausted by the sale of a product that embodies it, thereby restricting the patent owner's freedom to choose the means of recovering the expense of investment. Congress has spent years focusing on concerns about so-called patent litigation abuse, eventually passing amendments that favored infringers over inventors and placing even higher burdens on efforts to enforce patent rights. Of particular concern has been the trend to try to diminish the value and rights associated with standard essential patents, risking technological leadership in mobile communications and ceding control of standards to China. Congress also created a new patent review board that allows anyone to challenge a patent that is already issued, thereby prolonging the patent owner's effort to stop infringement. This body has overwhelmingly invalidated patents even when a district court has found them valid.

The weakening of US support for IP has only accelerated during the Biden administration, which supported waiving obligations under the WTO's Trade-Related Aspects of Intellectual Property Rights (TRIPS) during the COVID-19 pandemic, over the objection of our trading partners. This has sent a strong signal that US support for strong IP protections is on the decline.

Trade secret protection has also been diminished in the United States as an effective tool against misappropriation. This diminishing is of particular concern to companies that rely on trade secrets to protect against access to and use of their innovations. Semiconductor development and manufacturing is a prime example. The know-how and years of experience required to succeed in such a complex and capital-intensive field is not something one can describe in a patent application; this type of intellectual property is most appropriately treated as a trade secret. Yet, the law in the United States now favors very limited protection of trade secrets and largely prohibits such things as non-compete provisions previously employed to prevent employees from jumping ship and taking trade secrets to a competitor.

All of these changes and more have contributed to an attendant perception of instability and have had the effect of discouraging traditional investors from promoting new technology development—thereby stifling innovation in the United States. Many valuable innovations are simply no longer patentable in the United States but are patentable elsewhere in the world, including in China.[89]

Meanwhile, China has recognized that strengthening its patent system and the ability of its courts to enforce patent rights is essential to encouraging domestic innovation. Since 2000 alone, Beijing has also undergone massive reforms of its IP system, including four major revisions to its patent law and two major revisions to its trade secret law, as well as significant revisions to its technology transfer laws and contract laws. In contrast to the United States, PRC courts provide injunctive relief in nearly 100 percent of all successful cases; China has strengthened protections of software-enabled inventions, as well as in other fields; and China has established four national appellate IP courts and one national IP court of final instance. PRC companies are now among the top ten patent filers globally. China's patent office, CNIPA, has hired tens of thousands of examiners and has expedited time-to-grant for patent applications. Specialized IP courts in China provide rapid rulings and readily issue injunctions. In fact, US companies often now sue in PRC courts when they have a choice of jurisdictions in order to obtain the injunctive relief no longer available in the United States.

There is no lack of irony in the fact that IP rights have been weakened in the United States while being strengthened in China over the last two decades. The erosion of IP rights in the United States has contributed to the rise of economic and technological power in China and will continue to vitiate US capacity to develop new technologies. To reclaim leadership in technology innovation, the United States must embrace laws and policies that incentivize innovators by valuing and protecting IP rights, ultimately creating a more integrated and strategically focused approach to IP that better promotes US strategic interests. To that end, we recommend the following:

- The US IP regime should be modernized and made more efficient, competitive, and stable. This will require (a) clarifying and stabilizing patent eligibility criteria, to promote a range of high-tech industries and ensure that the United States is not placed at a competitive disadvantage; (b) making injunctive relief readily available in IP infringement cases of all types; (c) creating a team within the US Patent and Trademark Office to address the relationship between intellectual property and strategic competitiveness; (d) appointing US IP officials in a timely manner; and (e) ensuring that countries with which the United States forms deeper relationships through trade and "friend-shoring" have robust IP regimes, to avoid a repetition of the types of problems that US companies have faced in protecting IP in China.

Achieving Strategic Autonomy

Around the time of the founding of the United States, Alexander Hamilton stated that "it is impossible to foresee or define the extent and variety of national exigencies."[90] The United States is now facing an unprecedented challenge from a rising China that seeks to reshape the world order in its favor. China's vigorous pursuit of science and engineering—including a preeminent and self-sufficient semiconductor industry—exemplifies the tenet that technological superiority is the means of shifting the global balance of power. If the United States desires to ensure the continued liberty and prosperity of its people, it must continue to lead. To continue to lead globally, it must outcompete China, and thus it must augment its ability to predict the future—or, more precisely, to invent it and to own it.

In his book *On China*, Henry Kissinger presents an analogy to the differences between Western and Chinese strategic doctrine by comparison to the games of chess and *weiqi* (Go). Whereas chess values total victory, *weiqi* seeks to patiently accumulate strategic advantage. He writes:

> The players take turns placing stones at any point on the board, building up positions of strength while working to encircle and capture the opponent's stones. Multiple contests take place simultaneously in different regions of the board. The balance of forces shifts incrementally with each move as the players implement strategic plans and react to each other's initiatives. At the end of a well-played game, the board is filled by partially interlocking areas of strength. The margin of advantage is often slim and to the untrained eye, the identity of the winner is not always immediately obvious.[91]

Our future will be characterized by the evolving and interlocking strengths of the United States and China. Achieving strategic autonomy over the long term will require the United States and its partners to patiently accumulate relative advantage over China—in the manner of a *weiqi* player, rather than seeking decisive victory in the manner of a chess player. This is possible through the persistent application of policies consistent with the growth of the US economy, technology development, and enhancement of national security. The policies recommended in this chapter—spanning value capture, strengthening economic security, enhancing value creation, and strengthening appropriability—represent a set of moves all aligned with the objective of building the US position of strength well into future decades.

NOTES

1. Rowan Moore Gerety, "Unmade in America," MIT Technology Review, August 14, 2020.
2. Companies like Taiwan's Foxconn and TSMC demonstrate how manufacturing can be a key factor in driving innovations in design and manufacturing at scale. Foxconn has been ranked one of the fifty most innovative companies in the world, with a patent portfolio covering a wide range of technologies. TSMC has been granted over twenty-five thousand US patents, and it has a 98 percent patent grant rate for its applications by the US Patent and Trademark Office (USPTO). See TSMC, "Comment Regarding USPTO Request for Comments on Discretion to Institute Trials before the Patent Trial and Appeal Board, Docket No. PTO–C–2020–0055," US Patent and Trademark Office Comment, December 3, 2020.
3. Semiconductor Industry Association, *2021 State of the Industry Report*, September 2021.
4. Juan Alcacer and Kerry Herman, "Intel: Strategic Decisions in Locating a New Assembly and Test Plant (A)," Harvard Business School Case Study 713-406, September 2012 (revised December 2013).
5. Vaclav Smil, *Made in the USA: The Rise and Retreat of American Manufacturing* (Cambridge, MA: MIT Press, 2013).
6. David J. Teece, "Profiting from Technological Innovation: Implications for Integration, Collaboration, Licensing and Public Policy," *Research Policy* 15, no. 6 (1986): 285–305.
7. Andy Grove, "How to Make an American Job before It's Too Late," Research Gate, January 2010.
8. PIE Commission, *Report of the MIT Taskforce on Innovation and Production* (Cambridge, MA: MIT Press, 2013).
9. Erica York, Alex Muresiano, and Alex Durante, "Taxes, Tariffs, and Industrial Policy: How the US Tax Code Fails Manufacturing," Tax Foundation, March 17, 2022.
10. Alcacer and Herman, "Intel: Strategic Decisions."
11. Antonio Varas, Raj Varadarajan, Jimmy Goodrich, and Falan Yinug, *Government Incentives and US Competitiveness in Semiconductor Manufacturing* (Boston, MA: Boston Consulting Group and Semiconductor Industry Association, September 2020).

12. Semiconductor Industry Association, *2021 State of the US Semiconductor Industry*, September 2021.

13. US Government Accountability Office, *Tax Policy: The Research Tax Credit's Design and Administration Can Be Improved*, GAO-10-136 (Washington, DC: November 2009).

14. OECD, *Science, Technology and Innovation Outlook 2021: Times of Crisis and Opportunity* (Paris: OECD Publishing, 2021).

15. Curtis P. Carlson, "The Corporate Alternative Minimum Tax Aggregate Historical Trends," US Department of the Treasury Office of Tax Analysis, Working Paper no. 93 (Washington, DC: 2009).

16. Alex Durante and William McBride, "Reminder that Corporate Taxes Are the Most Economically Damaging Way to Raise Revenue," Tax Foundation, August 4, 2022.

17. President's Council of Advisors on Science and Technology (PCAST), *Report to the President: Ensuring Long-Term US Leadership in Semiconductors, Executive Office of the President*, January 2017.

18. John VerWey, "No Permits, No Fabs: The Importance of Regulatory Reform for Semiconductor Manufacturing," Center for Security and Emerging Technology, October 2021.

19. "Public Comment 12: Jing He Science Corporation," submitted to the Bureau of Industry and Security, April 2, 2021.

20. In response to an analyst's question, CFO Wendell Huang noted, "We're not able to share with you a specific cost gap number between Taiwan and [the] US, but we can share with you that the major reason for the cost gap is the construction cost of building and facilities, which can be four to five times greater for [a] US fab versus a fab in Taiwan. The high cost of construction includes labor cost, cost of permits, cost of occupational safety and health regulations, inflationary costs in recent years, and people and learning curve costs. Therefore, the initial costs of overseas fabs are higher than our fabs in Taiwan." Note that this does not represent overall cost differences, as most of a fab's capital cost is in equipment, not the building itself. See TSMC, "Q4 2022 Taiwan Semiconductor Manufacturing Co Ltd Earnings Call," January 12, 2023.

21. US Department of Commerce, Bureau of Industry and Security, "Risks in the Semiconductor Manufacturing and Advanced Packaging Supply Chain," Federal Register 86, no. 48, 14308–14309, March 15, 2021.

22. Semiconductor Industry Association, "Comments of the Semiconductor Industry Association (SIA) on Regulation of Persistent, Bioaccumulative, and Toxic Chemicals Under TSCA Section 6(h); Phenol, Isopropylated Phosphate (3:1); Further Compliance Date Extension," December 21, 2021.

23. Marc Humphries, "Critical Minerals and US Public Policy," Congressional Research Service, June 28, 2019.

24. Walden Rhines, *Predicting Semiconductor Business Trends after Moore's Law* (New York: Springer International Publishing, 2019).

25. Martin Reeves, George Stalk, and Filippo Scognamiglio, "BCG Classics Revisited: The Experience Curve," Boston Consulting Group, May 28, 2013.

26. David J. Teece, "Towards a Dynamic Competition Approach to Big Tech Merger Enforcement: The Facebook-Giphy Example," TechReg Chronicle, December 2021.

27. Aurelien Portuese, "Principles of Dynamic Antitrust: Competing through Innovation," Information Technology and Innovation Foundation, June 14, 2021.

28. Robert D. Atkinson, "Who Lost Lucent? The Decline of America's Telecom Equipment Industry," *American Affairs Journal* 4, no. 3 (Fall 2020).

29. David B. Yoffie, *Strategic Management in Information Technology* (Hoboken, NJ: Prentice Hall, 1994).

30. Michael C. Munger and Mario Villarreal-Diaz, "The Road to Crony Capitalism," *The Independent Review* 23, no. 3 (Winter 2018/19).

31. NASA's Commercial Crew & Cargo Program Office (C3PO), *NASA Systems Engineering Handbook*, SP-2016-6105 (Washington, DC: NASA Headquarters, 2016).

32. Richard A. Gottscho, Edlyn V. Levine, Tsu-Je King Liu, Paul McIntyre, Subhasish Mitra, Boris Murmann, J. M. Rabaey, Sayeef Salahuddin, Willy C. Shih, and H.-S. Philip Wong, "Innovating at Speed and at Scale: A Next Generation Infrastructure for Accelerating Semiconductor Technologies," ResearchGate, March 2022.

33. Varas et al., *Government Incentives*.

34. Will Hunt and Remco Zwetsloot, "The Chipmakers: US Strengths and Priorities for the High-End Semiconductor Workforce," Center for Security and Emerging Technology, September 2020.

35. David Leonhardt, "The Myth of Labor Shortages," *New York Times*, May 20, 2021.

36. Government of the Netherlands, Tax Department, "Knowledge Migrant Visa Program FAQs," accessed May 23, 2023.

37. National Center for Science and Engineering Statistics, "Survey of Graduate Students and Postdoctorates in Science and Engineering, Fall 2021," Table 4-20a, January 2023.

38. Gary P. Pisano and Willy Shih, "Restoring American Competitiveness," *Harvard Business Review*, July–August 2009.

39. National Research Council, *21st Century Manufacturing: The Role of the Manufacturing Extension Partnership Program* (Washington, DC: National Academies Press, 2013), 302.

40. Matthew D. Mitchell, Michael D. Farren, Jeremy Horpedahl, and Olivia Gonzalez, "The Economics of Targeted Economic Development Subsidy, Mercatus Center at George Mason University," November 21, 2019.

41. Yll Bajraktari et al., "Final Report: National Security Commission on Artificial Intelligence," National Security Commission on Artificial Intelligence, 2021.

42. *The Economist*, "Confronting Russia Shows the Tension between Free Trade and Freedom," March 19, 2022.

43. Congressional Research Service, "Critical Minerals and US Public Policy," June 28, 2019.

44. *The Economist*, "China Courts Global Capital on Its Own Terms," December 11, 2021.

45. David J. Teece and Bruce R. Guile, "Reinterpreting Adam Smith for Today's Economy," *California Management Review*, August 15, 2022.

46. Rhines, *Predicting Semiconductor Business Trends*, 86.

47. *The Economist*, "The American Chip Industry's $1.5trn Meltdown," October 17, 2022.

48. Ben Thompson, "Chips and China," Stratechery, October 17, 2022.

49. *The Economist*, "The American Chip Industry's $1.5trn Meltdown."

50. In response to an analyst's question on the Arizona Fab 21 project, TSMC chairman Mark Liu replied, "Our customer[s] in [the] US, they all want to load that fab. I mean, this is the need from our customers. And we also believe there is ample . . . business opportunity there." See TSMC, "Q2 2022 Taiwan Semiconductor Manufacturing Co Ltd Earnings Call," July 14, 2022.

51. Saif M. Khan, "Securing Semiconductor Supply Chains," Center for Security and Emerging Technology, January 2021.

52. Rhines, *Predicting Semiconductor Business Trends*, 86.

53. USITC, *Global Competitiveness of US Advanced-Technology Manufacturing Industries: Semiconductor Manufacturing and Testing Equipment*, Publication 2434, 1991.

54. USITC, *Global Competitiveness*.

55. Thompson, "Chips and China."

56. Global Business Alliance, "Foreign Direct Investment in the United States," 2022.

57. Anton Shilov, "TSMC Rumored to Increase Capacity of Arizona Fab," Tom's Hardware, March 4, 2021.

58. Varas et al., *Government Incentives*.

59. TSMC, "Comments in Response to the Commerce Department's Request for Information on the Implementation of the CHIPS Incentives Program, 87 FR 61570," Federal Register Number 2022-22158, 2022.

60. Other examples beyond advanced semiconductors might include rare earths processing, batteries, nuclear-related components, large electric transformers, and modern shipbuilding.

61. Michael Brown and Pavneet Singh, *China's Technology Transfer Strategy: How Chinese Investments in Emerging Technology Enable a Strategic Competitor*

    to Access the Crown Jewels of US Innovation, Defense Innovation Unit Experimental, January 2018.

62. Congressional Research Service, *CFIUS Reform under FIRRMA*, February 21, 2020.

63. Richard Vanderford, "Chinese Investors Still Leery of US Acquisitions after Oversight Changes," *Wall Street Journal*, April 14, 2022.

64. *The Economist*, "Despite Ukraine, These Aren't Boom Times for American Armsmakers," October 20, 2022.

65. William Inboden and Adam Klein, "A Lesson from the Ukraine War: Secure Our Semiconductor Supply Chains," The Hill, May 22, 2022.

66. Zoya Sheftalovich and Laurens Cerulus, "The Chips Are Down: Putin Scrambles for High-Tech Parts as His Arsenal Goes Up in Smoke," Politico, September 5, 2022.

67. James Timbie and James Ellis, "A Large Number of Small Things: A Porcupine Strategy for Taiwan," *The Strategist* 5, no. 1 (Winter 2021/2022): 83–93.

68. Mark Boroush, "Research and Development: US Trends and International Comparisons," NSB-2020-3, Science and Engineering Indicators, January 15, 2020.

69. Drew DeSilver, "What Does the Federal Government Spend Your Tax Dollars On? Social Insurance Programs, Mostly," Pew Research Center, April 4, 2017.

70. Michael Brown, Eric Chewning, and Pavneet Singh, "Preparing the United States for the Superpower Marathon with China," Brookings, April 2020.

71. Center for E3S, "2021 NSF Workshop on CMOS+X Technologies," accessed May 23, 2023.

72. Sankar Basu, Erik Brunvand, Subhasish Mitra, H.-S. Philip Wong, Sayeef Salahuddin, and Shimeng Yu, *A Report on Semiconductor Foundry Access by US Academics* (Washington, DC: National Science Foundation, 2020).

73. Gottscho et al., "Innovating at Speed and at Scale."

74. Teece, "Profiting from Technological Innovation."

75. Office of the United States Trade Representative, *Findings of the Investigation into China's Acts, Policies, and Practices Related to Technology Transfer, Intellectual Property, and Innovation under Section 301 of the Trade Act of 1974*, March 22, 2018.

76. US Department of Commerce, Bureau of Industry and Security, "Public Information on Export Controls Imposed on Advanced Computing and Semiconductor Manufacturing Items to the People's Republic of China (PRC)," October 2022.

77. David M. Hart, "The Impact of China's Production Surge on Innovation in the Global Solar Photovoltaics Industry," Information Technology & Innovation Foundation, October 2020.

78. Valerie Hernandez, "Have the Huawei Bans Achieved the US's Intended Goals?," International Banker, September 2022.

79. As discussed at length in Niall Ferguson, *Doom: The Politics of Catastrophe* (London: Penguin Press, 2021).

80. William Sweet, "Future of Chinese Students in US at Issue; CUSPEA Program Nears Its End," *Physics Today* 41, no. 6 (June 1988): 67–71.

81. White House Office of Trade and Manufacturing Policy, "How China's Economic Aggression Threatens the Technologies and Intellectual Property of the United States and the World," June 19, 2018.

82. Joyce Barnathan, "The Soviet Brain Drain Is the US Brain Gain," *Bloomberg*, November 3, 1991.

83. Brown et al., "Preparing the United States."

84. Matthew Strong, "Taiwan Finds More than 40 Cases of Illegal Recruitment by Chinese Companies," *Taiwan News*, September 16, 2016.

85. Bill Chappell, "Acclaimed Harvard Scientist Is Arrested, Accused of Lying about Ties to China," NPR, January 8, 2020.

86. Glenn Tiffert, ed., "Global Engagement: Rethinking Risk in the Research Enterprise," The Hoover Institution, July 2020.

87. US Department of Commerce, Bureau of Industry and Security, "Public Information on Export Controls."

88. Lia Zhu, "Experts: China Outpacing US on Patent Eligibility," China Daily, June 23, 2020.

89. Kevin Madigan and Adam Mossoff, "Turning Gold into Lead: How Patent Eligibility Doctrine Is Undermining US Leadership in Innovation," *George Mason Law Review* 24 (2016–2017): 939.

90. Alexander Hamilton, James Madison, and John Jay, "Federalist No. 23," in *The Federalist Papers*, edited by Jacob E. Cooke (Middletown, CT: Wesleyan University Press, 1961), 154.

91. Jeffrey Goldberg, "Henry Kissinger on the Assembly of a New World Order," *The Atlantic*, November 17, 2016.

CHAPTER FIVE

Deepening US-Taiwan Cooperation through Semiconductors

KHARIS TEMPLEMAN AND ORIANA SKYLAR MASTRO

Taiwan is a close, trusted partner in the global semiconductor supply chain. The United States and Taiwan should seek to use the semiconductor industry to promote Taiwan's prosperity and stability by creating an environment that fosters deeper business-to-business, research, academic, individual, and civil ties with Taiwan and other global partners in the semiconductor arena.

This strategy includes the active promotion of Taiwan semiconductor firm activities, including manufacturing, design, and joint research and development (R&D) in the United States; income tax abatement for cross-border workers; two-way semiconductor internship programs and academic exchange; semiconductor supply chain information sharing and resiliency planning; and defense industry coproduction in Taiwan.

With Taiwan's particular strengths in semiconductors, and continued long-term US interests there, this is an attractive foundation for broader shared civil and business ties that helps to deepen US commitments to Taiwan's democracy—and deters efforts to end it.

• • •

The fact that our partner Taiwan holds a key role in the global semiconductor industry should be seen as much as an opportunity for the United States as it is a risk. US interests in promoting Taiwan's stability and prosperity, and in preserving its way of life with values common to our own, long pre-date the rise of the island's chip champions. And those same interests will outlast any business cycle or supply chain configuration.

As this report argues, semiconductors are a matter of central concern for the future of relations among the United States, Taiwan, and China. More US op-eds and think pieces have likely been written on Taiwan in the past two years than in the previous ten; that interest is due to words and actions that the People's Republic of China (PRC) has shown toward Taiwan, but it is also animated by the heightened US public and political interest in semiconductors. At the same time, the US-Taiwan relationship is about more than chips. Americans should resist a transactional view of Taiwan's role in this realm. And they should appreciate that those in Taiwan hear, and react in strategic ways to, what Americans say.

Leaders in the United States and in Taiwan should be realistic about the real threat that the island faces, and their response to that should be to build the capabilities and the confidence of their people to weather coercion and deter attack. To that end, our shared interests in capabilities in semiconductors can help. We can learn from one another, collectively extending technological leadership that is attractive to partners globally. We can use this heightened mutual level of interest to grow substantive people-to-people, business, and even appropriate government ties at the working level. And we can use this momentum to break through long-standing bureaucratic frictions and improve interoperability in our economic and security relationships.

This chapter shows what the United States might learn from Taiwan's successful experience in building a leading global role in the semiconductor supply chain—which is much broader than Taiwan Semiconductor Manufacturing Company (TSMC) alone—and as the United States now wrestles with the tension of market integration with China alongside growing strategic concerns, it illustrates how Taiwan has attempted to navigate those straits for decades. Finally, it offers concrete opportunities for deeper collaboration on the back of our shared interests in chips, which could improve mutual prosperity and enhance deterrence.

Learning from the Rise of the Semiconductor Industry in Taiwan

How did Taiwan end up as the home of TSMC, the world's most strategically important company—and more than a dozen other major players in the semiconductor supply chain?[1] The answer is a mixture of nurture, culture, and luck. With the future of US leading-edge semiconductor manufacturing now running directly through TSMC's investments in Arizona, those in the United States who wish to see such endeavors succeed should understand what underpins Taiwan's own domestic strategy. And it should not be taken for granted that these new US fabrication facilities (fabs) will succeed simply because they are being built.

Nurture

The beginning of the semiconductor industry in Taiwan can be traced back to 1966, when US electronics firm General Instruments set up the first semiconductor plant in an export processing zone (EPZ) in Kaohsiung. It was followed by the Dutch manufacturer Phillips and several other foreign electronics companies. But these plants were focused on simple assembly rather than advanced manufacturing, and they had limited links to local suppliers in the broader economy.

The moment that set Taiwan's electronics industry on its current path occurred in 1973, when the Ministry of Economic Affairs (MOEA) founded the Industrial Technology Research Institute (ITRI). ITRI was a government-funded body set up to provide research and development and to contribute to Taiwan's industrial upgrading. In 1974, it established the Electronics Research and Service Organization (ERSO) to develop domestic expertise in electronics manufacturing. ERSO's first project was an integrated circuit (IC) demonstration factory, for which it partnered with the US manufacturer RCA. ERSO sent about forty engineers to the United States to be trained by RCA, and when they returned they put together Taiwan's first IC manufacturing facility, which opened in 1977. Many of those forty trainees became key figures in the semiconductor industry, or stayed with ITRI for their careers, and they played a fundamental role in developing Taiwan's electronics manufacturing capacity over the next several decades. The first domestic semiconductor company in Taiwan, United Microelectronics Corporation (UMC), was founded in 1980 when ERSO spun off the initial factory.

TSMC arrived on the scene in 1987 as the result of another ERSO project, this one focused on very-large-scale integration (VLSI) technology. Initial investment in TSMC was 48 percent from Taiwan's National Development Fund, 28 percent from Phillips, and 24 percent from other private sources. From the beginning, TSMC followed a pure contract foundry model: it focused exclusively on fabricating chips that met design specifications from its customers, and it eschewed any attempt to design its own. This pioneering decision freed electronics manufacturers from the need to build expensive factories themselves, and it led to a boom in chip design houses not only in Silicon Valley but also in Taiwan, which expanded from four in 1986 to forty by the end of 1987. The growth of these houses, in turn, led to rapid advancements in application-specific integrated circuits (ASICs), and the industry in Taiwan quickly attracted large investments from both foreign manufacturers (such as Sony and AMD) and domestic business groups.

In the 1990s, additional companies set up in Taiwan to fill other parts of the manufacturing process, and these clusters of companies built a more robust supply chain on the island. In 1994, ERSO spun off its submicron project to manufacture dynamic random access memory (DRAM) chips; the new company was called Vanguard International Semiconductor Corporation, or Vanguard for short. By 1995, six other companies manufacturing DRAM had also set up in Taiwan. By the end of the decade, Taiwan's semiconductor industry had many firms operating in at least one step of the chip-building process, including design, manufacturing, packaging, and testing.

In addition to public research and development funds and initial investment capital, government support has also come via subsidized land and infrastructure, preferential tax breaks, and investment in human capital. In 1980, the Taiwan central government created the Hsinchu Science-Based Industrial Park (now referred to as the Hsinchu

Science Park, or HSP) with the aim of re-creating some of the benefits of private sector clustering and interaction that had been so successful in Silicon Valley in California. HSP was created and has been run since its inception by the central government, which provides tax breaks for firms that locate there, as well as physical infrastructure for plants and parks and schools for the workforce. It is located near Taiwan's top two engineering universities, National Tsing Hua University and National Chiao Tung University, and it is also close to Taiwan's largest international airport, Taipei Taoyuan. ITRI's facilities are also located nearby. In 1999, three-quarters of the member firms of the Taiwan Semiconductor Industry Association (TSIA) were located in the park or nearby in Hsinchu or Taoyuan. Following the success of HSP, additional science parks have been established in Kaohsiung (Southern Taiwan Science Park, initially in 1994, then expanded to Tainan and renamed in 2003) and Taichung (Central Taiwan Science Park, in 2003). TSMC is building next-generation fabs in both parks.

The Taiwan government has also provided generous tax breaks for firms in the industry. From 1990 to 1994, for instance, the average effective tax rate for firms located in HSP was only 1.57 percent, as compared to 15.3 percent for the top one hundred manufacturing firms in Taiwan and 20 percent for the typical small and medium enterprises (SME).[2] Taiwan also does not have a capital gains tax. Semiconductor firms for many years exploited this feature by allowing employees to purchase a set number of shares at their nominal price and then immediately sell them at the much higher market price. This provided tax-free, risk-free bonuses to their employees. More recently, in January 2023, the government raised the tax credit firms will receive for R&D spending from 15 to 25 percent, capped at 50 percent of overall income.[3]

Taiwan has also invested in low-cost public higher education, which has provided a steady supply of engineering and managerial talent for the industry. The work of ITRI, especially in the industry's early years, also helped to develop an indigenous skilled workforce and to attract Taiwanese from abroad to return—including Morris Chang, the long-time leader of TSMC, who originally came back to Taiwan from the United States in 1985 to be the head of ITRI.

Culture

One hidden factor in the success of Taiwan's semiconductor industry is its culture of customer service. Unlike in Korea, where large *chaebol* (conglomerates) were the major exporters during the economic take-off there, in Taiwan, SMEs formed the backbone of economic growth. Taiwan's SMEs, many of them based on family or community networks, became especially good at contract manufacturing of consumer goods for buyers in advanced economies.[4] The best of these SMEs learned how to adapt to rapidly changing consumer preferences and to fill orders in a way that was cheap, fast, and reliable for the buyer. They also were entwined within a much larger network of subcontractors, which allowed them to quickly ramp production up or down based on the size of orders from US customers. This business culture of informal networks and complicated subcontracting relationships was eventually reproduced within the Taiwanese semiconductor industry. It also made TSMC's initial decision to strike out as a purely contract-based foundry company less of a leap than it might have appeared to outsiders; there was a precedent for this kind of business model in other parts of the Taiwan economy.

Taiwan's own work culture has contributed to the vitality of the industry in other ways, too. Workers in Taiwan log some of the longest hours in the world, and the country's labor rules remain relatively permissive. The chip manufacturing process requires a disciplined, knowledgeable, and reliable workforce, and firms in the industry have been able to require their employees to work regular overtime during particularly busy periods.[5] On a related note, semiconductor industry leaders in Taiwan have complained about American work culture as a formidable barrier to running manufacturing processes there.[6]

Taiwan's own quality of life, including its political transformation in the 1990s, has also made it a more attractive place for overseas Taiwanese to return to, and has helped with the talent-retention issues in the industry. The differences with the PRC mainland have been especially stark. As described in chapter 8, PRC efforts to poach semiconductor engineering talent and use Taiwanese expertise to jump-start its own domestic industry had some initial success. But in the last five years, this threat appears to have subsided. Many industry engineers who were initially attracted by offers of greater independence and responsibility and much higher salaries have returned to Taiwan.[7]

Luck

Taiwan's semiconductor industry leaders are modest, with even leader TSMC—now one of the ten largest firms by market cap globally—describing itself as being in a horse race with Intel and Samsung, where one wrong investment or technology decision could cause it to stumble and quickly fall behind. As chapter 2 describes, this view is borne out by the reality of TSMC's recent rise to dominance, which coincided with failures in execution and strategy by its rivals in both the United States and Korea following their own strings of success.[8] Taiwan's foundries chose to aggressively reinvest their capital into capacity expansion following the 2009 global financial crisis and economic downturn, which resulted in increased market share when smartphone demand took off. TSMC made breakthroughs in applications of Advanced Semiconductor Materials Lithography's (ASML) extreme ultraviolet (EUV) technology that other early R&D partners were not able to replicate.[9] And a protracted series of industrial design intellectual property (IP) lawsuits by Apple against Samsung in the early 2010s—Samsung had provided most of the advanced chips for early iPhones—led to a much closer relationship (and substantial coinvestment and risk sharing) between alternative supplier TSMC and Cupertino's burgeoning consumer electronics powerhouse.[10] Taiwan's deep-rooted contract outsourcing model, in which the supplier intentionally avoided competing with the client's business, had found new resonance at a critical moment in the industry.

Taiwan's Semiconductor Industry Today: Clustering and Limits to Growth

Today, the Taiwanese semiconductor industry occupies a central position in semiconductor manufacturing, especially in leading-edge logic chips. The economic ecosystem surrounding TSMC has also grown into concentrated business clusters, giving Taiwan one of the most diverse semiconductor supply chains in the world. This physical proximity of semiconductor and adjacent industries has led to significant economies of scale and tighter integration than that found elsewhere globally. Those in the United States may appreciate, for example, that one or two assembly plants do not make an auto industry—Taiwan's experience shows the need to similarly cultivate an industrial ecosystem will to reduce transactional costs and sustain global competitiveness beyond the limited window of government subsidies. And given that Taiwan has fast-growing firms in the semiconductor supply chains outside of manufacturing—such as in design, where US firms have significant strengths today—there is opportunity in both directions. US-Taiwan semiconductor collaboration is not a one-sided deal.

Taiwan Production and Consumption

TSMC is the largest semiconductor manufacturer in Taiwan and the largest pure-play semiconductor foundry in the world; it dominates the market for sub-10nm chip manufacturing and holds a virtual monopoly over logic chips at 5nm scale and below. Less appreciated is the strength of UMC, the world's second-largest pure-play semiconductor foundry (third in manufacturing volume overall); it focuses on specialized mature-node logic chips, such as for automotive and industrial applications. While both manufacturers have some operations in the PRC, the vast majority of their production takes place within Taiwan. In total, about one-third of global logic chip manufacturing capacity is physically located on the island.

Taiwan also has two major home-grown memory manufacturers—Nanya and Powerchip—and it has been quite successful in attracting foreign manufacturing investment. US-based Micron, the world's third-largest memory chip supplier, produces much of its leading-edge DRAM memory chips in Taiwan. As of 2020, 15 percent of global memory manufacturing capacity was located on the island.

Beyond front-end fabrication itself, Taiwan hosts more than half of global back-end outsourced semiconductor assembly and test (OSAT), which is required before a chip can be integrated into an end product. ASE Technologies, the largest OSAT firm in Taiwan and the world, alone holds 24 percent of the global market share.

As noted above, Taiwan's semiconductor contract manufacturing strengths have also contributed to a large and growing domestic fabless design industry. MediaTek, Novatek, Realtek, and Himax are the fourth-, sixth-, eighth-, and tenth-largest fabless design houses by revenue share in the world, respectively. MediaTek, in particular, has been a competitor to US-based Qualcomm in the mobile chip category, and it overtook Qualcomm in Android smartphone market share (by device) in 2022. In total, Taiwan holds 21 percent of the global fabless market share, second only to the United States.

For manufacturing inputs and materials, Taiwan's GlobalWafers is the third-largest supplier of silicon wafers in the world, with a market share of 18 percent in 2020. The four largest silicon wafer manufacturers in Taiwan—GlobalWafers, Sino-American Silicon Products (SAS), Formosa Sumco (a joint venture with Japan's SUMCO), and Wafer Works—account for one-third of the global market. This makes Taiwan the second-largest manufacturer of silicon wafers in the world after Japan.

Even with its considerable strengths, Taiwan still relies heavily on links to the semiconductor supply chain abroad. Taiwan's fabless semiconductor designers are dependent on the same US and European electronic design automation (EDA) software tools that all such firms use globally. Its manufacturing facilities rely on Japanese suppliers of specialty gases, chemicals, and lithography masks. Taiwan produces little indigenous semiconductor manufacturing equipment, leading its firms to spend tens of billions of dollars annually—$24 billion in 2021—on tool imports from the Netherlands, the United States, and Japan. This is a level on par with equipment purchases by Korea and by the PRC and, therefore, a major source of revenue for these suppliers.

Taiwan's contract foundry model also intrinsically links its firms very closely to its global customers. TSMC, for example, supplies mainly foreign clients. In 2021, Apple alone accounted for 26 percent of its revenue, and the US market as a whole was 64 percent. Domestic clients in Taiwan generated just 12.8 percent, while 10.3 percent of revenues came from firms in the PRC.[11]

In some senses, then, while policy makers in the United States may think mostly about US reliance on Taiwan, Taiwan is equally reliant on the United States. This reliance of course makes Taiwan a strong business partner for US-based firms, manifested by the typically conservative TSMC's willingness to invest in US-based manufacturing capacity—despite the significant cost premium and risk associated with that—to provide value to their key clients (read: Apple). In turn, TSMC likely expects that such added value to clients will be reflected in higher unit prices for its production in the United States.[12]

This closeness also makes Taiwan a necessary policy partner to US efforts to assert control over critical technologies. Taiwanese semiconductor firms' use of US technologies makes them vulnerable to US export controls or sanctions. For example, in 2020, TSMC terminated its relations with HiSilicon, Huawei's fabless semiconductor subsidiary, which was at the time its second-largest client. Given the intense global demand for its products at that time, however, the lost business was quickly absorbed elsewhere among the firm's nearly five hundred clients.

Domestic Issues

Taiwan's semiconductor industry leaders will regularly point to two looming domestic pain points: energy and worker availability.

As outlined earlier, Taiwan has long used a science park model to incentivize high-tech industrial operations, including through government support in the provision of land, electricity, and water. Rapid growth in the tech industry, including semiconductors, has nonetheless run up against constraints in these areas. For example, Taiwan recently experienced its worst drought in five decades (the drought ended in June 2021), which forced TSMC to tap groundwater from construction sites or to import supplies by truck from locations around the island.[13] While these periodic shortages can be disruptive, water is regarded as being a largely manageable proposition going forward due to continued advances in recycling and treatment technologies; it is worth it to invest in these capabilities, given the value of the chips these water inputs produce.

Of more concern is the availability and reliability of affordable and clean energy supplies. A particular concern is over electricity, which has seen rapid demand growth—power consumption from the information and communications technology (ICT) subsector alone in Taiwan has quadrupled since 2000 and now represents 21 percent of the island's total, more than that from the entire residential sector. TSMC itself is said to have used nearly 10 percent of Taiwan's electricity in 2022, and the government estimates that its consumption will rise threefold from 2020 to 2030; the industry has twenty new fabs recently completed or under construction, and it plans to build more than a dozen new fabs on the island in coming years.[14] This tech sector demand is also concentrated in Taiwan's north. Meanwhile, Taiwan's electricity supply growth, much of it in the south, has at times in recent years faltered; the island's zero-carbon nuclear plants are being shut down under central government policy decisions or by local pressure, and clean replacement generation has seen delays.[15] A result has been periodic blackouts—in August 2017, twice in May 2021, and again in March 2022.

Given the high capital intensity, a semiconductor fabricator's profitability is closely tied to its facility utilization rate. Moreover, the hundreds of manufacturing steps and precise equipment within a fab require high-quality electricity supplies. While fabs have backup generators, blackouts are costly propositions in the short term, and industry concerns over longer-term electrical resource adequacy can impede larger investment.

Then there is skilled labor—a concern shared by the semiconductor industry around the world, including in China and the United States. But it is particularly acute here, given the industry's outsized role in Taiwan's economy. A majority of Taiwan's engineering graduates already go into the semiconductor industry, which employs 290,000 people overall. TSMC alone, with its strategy on leading-edge capabilities and an R&D staff of over ten thousand, is estimated to already recruit four-fifths of Taiwan's eligible PhDs each year. A report in 2022 estimated that the industry had thirty-five thousand unfilled positions, a situation that could grow worse over time with Taiwan's poor demographics (low fertility and immigration rates) and declining number of students overall.[16]

The government has taken some steps to address this shortage, partnering with academic institutions and companies themselves to set up new "chip schools" to train the next generation of industry workers.[17] TSMC itself directly sponsors about two dozen PhD scholarships each year within Taiwan, its employees design and teach university courses, and it offers about 350 internships each year. As chapter 2 describes, working in the semiconductor industry in Taiwan is viewed with prestige; salaries and benefits are high by local standards, though low by US standards (an average starting salary, plus benefits, for an engineer with a master's degree at TSMC is about $65,000).[18] Yet, the industry could benefit from more women in the engineering workforce—US DRAM manufacturer Micron reports that while 44 percent of its new hires in Taiwan were women over the past three years, they represent only 22 percent of its total Taiwan workforce.[19] And as with other developed economies, additional targeted immigration measures from South and Southeast Asia are likely needed as well to span this gap. Chapter 6 describes, for example, the growing number of Indian-origin university students studying in Taiwanese engineering programs; even so, of TSMC's approximately eight thousand new hires in 2020, only 280 were from overseas.[20] These concerns about the local workforce may also have helped to encourage Taiwan's semiconductor manufacturers to make more investments and enter into joint ventures abroad (for example, the TSMC joint venture with Sony and automakers in Japan).

Taiwan's semiconductor sector does have a related concern about its workforce—that of talent poaching by PRC firms. This is perhaps less of a large-scale issue today than it was five to ten years ago, given the declining interest among Taiwanese youth in working and building careers in mainland China. But between 2014 and 2019, more than three thousand of Taiwan's high-level semiconductor workers reportedly moved to China, lured by large pay premiums.[21] It is still an area of considerable concern for leading industry talent, given China's industry ambitions and high levels of government support, so Taiwan has taken increasing steps over time to protect its industry.[22]

Taiwan's Investment Commission, for example, since the 1990s has required applications and screening for foreign direct investment (FDI), mergers, and acquisitions in high-tech areas; outbound investments into China over $50 million must also be registered, and Taiwan's government imposes limits on the level of production technology that can be used abroad (this affects TSMC's fab in Nanjing, for example).[23] Economic espionage is criminalized, with prison sentences of up to twelve years for those found guilty of transmitting "national core technology trade secrets."

In response to aggressive poaching of Taiwanese semiconductor talent, Taiwan has also begun cracking down on these recruitment efforts. This crackdown has included raids on PRC companies illegally operating in Taiwan's semiconductor science parks,[24] prosecutions of forty cases of illegal talent poaching by PRC firms,[25] limits on domestic advertising, and fines of 5 million New Taiwan (NT) dollars (roughly $170,000) for PRC semiconductor headhunters.[26] More recently, Taiwan's government has introduced a measure to require prior government permission for travel to China by chip company employees receiving some form of Taiwanese government support (most of them); this proposal, however, has received some pushback from Taiwan's semiconductor firms, which instead point to company internal trade secret protection protocols as a more important tool to prevent technology theft.

Notably, the US government now finds itself navigating similar concerns in balancing semiconductor sector economic freedoms alongside emerging national security dimensions—see, for example, the limits on US persons working in China's semiconductor firms unveiled in the October 2022 Bureau of Industry and Security export controls, as described in chapter 9. But Taiwan arguably has a much deeper experience to learn from here.

Postcards from the Future: For Taiwan, Economics and Security Have Always Been Linked

The scenario analysis of chapter 1 points to potential futures in which US international economic relationships become more oriented alongside shared values and security interests. If that came to pass, it would be a stark departure from a historical embrace of globalization; selective decoupling from China would imply new responsibilities for some of our leading enterprises and unfamiliar roles for US policy makers and regulators. Mistakes are likely and could be costly. Can we learn from Taiwan's heretofore unique experience in delicately managing a significant economic relationship with a country that is also its largest security threat—all under a democracy with the constant political undercurrents that entails?

For the Republic of China on Taiwan, economic development has always had fundamental security implications. In 1949, as the Chinese Nationalist Party's (Kuomintang or KMT) position on the Chinese mainland collapsed, the regime fled to Taiwan in disarray, bringing with it the institutions of the Republic of China (ROC) and over a million refugees from the mainland. From that point forward, it was caught in a relentless competition of political systems with the Communist Party–led People's Republic of China—one in which economic growth was a key part of political legitimacy.[27] In the early days of the Cold War, Taiwan was synonymous with "Free China": a beleaguered outpost of the capitalist West in imminent danger of an onslaught by the communists across the Taiwan Strait. Once the immediate danger of an invasion had been forestalled by US intervention at the beginning of the Korean War, stabilizing and revitalizing Taiwan's economy became the regime's foremost security imperative.

By the early 1960s, in an effort to wean itself off US aid, the KMT leadership switched to an export-oriented development strategy. It exploited the island's abundant labor and preferential access to Western markets to attract foreign direct investment, boosting economic growth rates and building a foreign currency reserve. The result was the vaunted "Taiwan miracle": for the next forty years, the island enjoyed almost uninterrupted rapid economic growth with low inequality. It also gradually moved up the export value chain: from textiles and toys in the 1960s to shoes and bicycles in the 1970s and finally electronics assembly and computer hardware manufacturing in the 1980s.

This rapid development lifted millions of Taiwanese out of poverty and turned the island into an industrial powerhouse. It also gave Taiwan's leaders an enhanced sense of security. By the 1980s, the regime's annual defense budget was fully half of the PRC's, for an island with a population of less than 2 percent of the mainland's. Its growth gave it the resources to invest in indigenous defense production of increasingly sophisticated weaponry, and to purchase from foreign suppliers the latest-generation platforms—F-16s from the United States, Mirage fighters and Lafayette-class frigates from France, and Zwaardvis-class submarines from the Netherlands. The gap in sophistication between Taiwan's military and the People's Liberation Army (PLA) became a chasm by the 1990s, with the ROC armed forces enjoying an enormous qualitative advantage across domains that more than offset the PRC's quantitative advantages.

It is easy to overlook now, but from the vantage point of the early 1990s, Taiwan was operating from a position of strength in the cross-strait relationship. Per capita income was twenty times that of the mainland. Taiwan's foreign currency reserves were the world's largest. Taiwan's political system was liberalizing, a process that culminated in the first free and fair direct election of the legislature in 1992, and of the president in 1996.

Most relevant for present purposes, Taiwanese companies were nimble competitors in the global economy, while PRC firms were still trying to adapt to market principles. Thus, when rising costs of inputs—chiefly labor and land—in Taiwan led many Taiwanese contract manufacturing firms to look around for cheaper alternatives, it made considerable economic sense for both sides that they relocate some of their activities to the Chinese mainland. It is well known that the capital and business acumen of "overseas Chinese" were instrumental in the PRC's early reform and opening-up period in linking mainland China into the global economy. It is less widely appreciated just how central Taiwanese businesspeople—*Taishang* in the local parlance—were in this process. They brought the advantages that Taiwan's SMEs had developed in contract manufacturing over the previous decades with them to mainland China as they moved production into special economic zones in coastal regions, especially the Pearl River Delta area and Fujian Province.[28]

Cross-Strait Ties and Partisan Politics

These deepening cross-strait economic ties took place in the face of a worsening political environment. Beijing viewed President Lee Teng-hui (1988–2000) with great suspicion, and government-to-government communication across the strait had ceased by 1999. Taiwan's regulatory frameworks continued to place burdensome limits on groups interested in traveling to, studying in, or holding cultural exchanges with the other side. The election in 2000 of Chen Shui-bian, the candidate of the China-skeptical Democratic Progressive Party (DPP), did not improve the political environment for cross-strait talks. Nevertheless, economic integration did *not* slow down but instead accelerated during his administration. Taiwan's investment in mainland China grew 50 percent per year during Chen Shui-bian's first term, and by the time he left office in 2008, cross-strait trade was nine times the volume of what it was in 2001.

These trends meant that when the KMT returned to power with the election of Ma Ying-jeou as president in 2008, Taiwan's economy had become deeply intertwined with the PRC's. At this point, the positions of the two main political parties on this economic integration began to diverge. The KMT's strategic approach under President Ma was to go "to the world through China." His government's central objective in cross-strait relations was to help the formal institutions "catch up" to economic reality by deepening the institutional and regulatory frameworks handling cross-strait relations. This, in Ma's telling, would eliminate the need for many of the costly workarounds in the economic relationship and further benefit Taiwan by hitching its economy more firmly to the Chinese growth engine across the strait.

A prominent example of this approach is the implementation of regular cross-strait commercial flights. Within days of taking office, Ma's representatives were in productive negotiations with their counterparts from the PRC, and by 2009 the two sides had established a regulatory framework to allow direct commercial flights for the first time between the mainland and Taiwanese cities; even today, one can get on a plane in downtown Taipei and be in Shanghai in less than two hours.

The DPP, in contrast, began to argue more and more loudly for balancing: seeking to mitigate the security vulnerabilities that came from overdependence on the mainland economy by diversifying Taiwanese firms' economic partners, customers, and manufacturing bases to other countries in the region. This position had limited appeal in the 2012 election, when Ma Ying-jeou was able to win reelection over the DPP's Tsai Ing-wen. But in Ma's second term, public opinion shifted in a more China-skeptical direction. This change came amid concerns about broader PRC influence over Taiwan's economy and the economic risk that even Taiwan's most advanced industries, such as semiconductor manufacturing, might be "hollowed out" by shifting production to the mainland. And more recently, the change in attitude has been furthered by Beijing's shift to a more aggressive and nationalist approach in foreign affairs, including the centralization of power under Party General Secretary Xi Jinping, the demise of Hong Kong's "one country, two systems" model, and growing bellicosity toward Taiwan.

With the election of Tsai Ing-wen in 2016, the DPP returned to power. The party also won a majority in the legislature for the first time, allowing it to pass laws without the approval of the KMT or other opposition parties. The party interpreted its victory as an electoral mandate to implement its alternative cross-strait economic strategy: balance against China. DPP leaders generally view Taiwan's heavy reliance on the PRC market, and the large number of Taiwanese firms that now carry out at least some of their production on the mainland, as a serious security vulnerability. From this perspective, continued economic integration gives Beijing additional economic leverage to use for coercive political purposes. It also facilitates Beijing's efforts to erode Taiwan's own long-standing economic advantages in the relationship by poaching talent and using Taiwanese personnel to build competitors to Taiwanese firms.

Taiwan Government Responses to the Rising Cross-Strait Threat

With this threat in mind, the Tsai administration has searched for ways to blunt these vulnerabilities without hurting Taiwan's own economic vitality. It has not unilaterally rolled back any of the Ma-era agreements, but it has sought to direct its new trade and diplomacy initiatives elsewhere, especially with its traditional democratic partners in the United States and Japan. For example, its "New Southbound Policy" provides incentives for firms to shift production out of the PRC to other destinations in Southeast and South Asia, and the Tsai administration has sought free trade agreements (FTAs) and other formal cooperation agreements with the United States and its allies and partners around the world. Despite these efforts, the PRC (including Hong Kong) continues to be the immediate destination for 39 percent of Taiwan's exports by value.[29]

One problem that the Tsai administration faces is that the Taiwanese state has only limited sway over the business decisions of large conglomerates such as TSMC but even less on those with major investments on the mainland, such as Foxconn (Hon Hai). It cannot force these companies to shift investment, personnel, and customer markets away from mainland China. It instead has to find policy carrots to encourage production shifts that may already be taking place for nonpolitical reasons.

In the DPP's favor, several factors are pushing in the same direction to make the PRC a less attractive place for Taiwan's manufacturing firms to locate their production. These include rapidly rising labor costs and a less favorable regulatory and tax environment; growing concerns about the loss of intellectual property, and the concurrent trend of China-based partners turning into direct competitors; and, above all, the rise of US-China trade tensions and concern in destination markets about the security and resilience of complicated supply chains.

Taiwan's semiconductor industry is at the center of these long-standing security concerns today. The emergence of TSMC, UMC, MediaTek, and other companies as critical players in this industry is a source of pride in Taiwan, but their continued success is also increasingly viewed as a vital national interest. The broader high-tech industry contributes an astounding 18 percent of Taiwan's gross domestic product.[30] Its economy boomed during the COVID-19 pandemic, despite near-total isolation for months from the rest of the world, because of the immense demand for semiconductors supplied by TSMC and others.

Many Taiwanese have also begun referring to TSMC in particular in starkly hard security terms, as a "silicon shield" (*huguo shenshan*) that protects Taiwan from a PLA invasion. The presence of such a strategically crucial company, the thinking goes, combined with the overwhelming reliance of industry in both the United States and the PRC on advanced semiconductors produced in Taiwan, gives both sides an incentive to preserve the status quo. The PRC would not dare to attack Taiwan and risk destroying such a crucial source of chips, and the United States would have to intervene in any conflict across the Taiwan Strait to defend Taiwan and protect its access to chips—regardless of any broader diplomatic or political calculations. From this perspective, Taiwanese public opinion is primed to resist the idea of TSMC diversifying its most advanced production away from Taiwan to other, less strategically vulnerable countries. Even putting aside the perceived economic downsides for Taiwan, doing so would conceivably go against the country's core security interests.

On the other hand, the DPP government remains eager to cooperate more closely with the United States, Japan, and other Western partners and allies to improve the security of semiconductor supply chains and limit PRC involvement in the industry. Foreign policy prioritization from the US government can be fickle, and the surging interest in semiconductors from policy makers and thought leaders in the United States has drawn broader attention to Taiwan generally from across Washington—more newspaper op-eds have probably been published about Taiwan in the past two years than in the previous ten combined. For a conservative US executive branch bureaucracy that has at times hesitated to engage more expansively with Taiwan, the sunlight brought by the semiconductor issue has been animating—even in areas that have little to do with semiconductors or critical supply chains.

And from Taipei's perspective, cross-national efforts to map out the next phases of chip development, to "friend-shore" production, and to keep advanced production sites away from mainland China are likely to be supported, particularly if a DPP government remains in power. As Taiwan's formal diplomatic space continues to be eroded by Beijing's economic clout, Taiwan has not shied away from acknowledging its strength in the semiconductor supply chain in its global interactions. Morris Chang, the charismatic founder and former chairman of TSMC, has repeatedly represented "Chinese Taipei" at the Asia-Pacific Economic Cooperation (APEC) forum (one of the handful of multilateral forums in which Taiwan has representation) starting in 2006 and then again since 2018. During the COVID-19 pandemic and amidst PRC pressures on Western firms to limit vaccine distribution in Taiwan, the idea was floated of a possible chips-for-vaccines deal; TSMC, Foxconn, and the civil society Tzu Chi Foundation later worked to purchase and donate fifteen million Pfizer-BioNTech vaccines.[31] And following China's blocking of imports from Lithuania after Vilnius permitted a "Taiwan" representative office to open in the country, Taiwan announced a $200 million investment plan in Lithuania, including partnerships around semiconductor R&D and manufacturing.[32]

US-Taiwan Cooperation on Semiconductors to Preserve Stability in the Taiwan Strait

How should one think about the links between Taiwan's semiconductor industry, US interests in this field, and implications for cross-strait deterrence—and what steps could policy makers in the United States and in Taiwan take to use our shared interest in semiconductors to substantively improve mutual capabilities and confidence in the face of a motivated rival? Importantly, such steps will be taken in an information environment in which malign interests may seek to exploit words or policy actions that could shape narratives otherwise.

The Silicon Triangle from Taipei

As discussed above, there is a long-standing argument in Taiwan that US reliance on Taiwan for advanced semiconductors makes US defense of Taiwan more likely. Proponents of this "silicon shield" theory argue that Taiwan's chip industry is an effective deterrent to invasion because attempting to take Taiwan by force would cause catastrophic damage to the PRC and the global economy.[33] There is some empirical basis for this idea. Taiwan accounts for 92 percent of the global production of advanced chips, and over 90 percent of semiconductors used by the PRC are either imported or produced by foreign companies. In Q1 2021, over 50 percent of Taiwan's exports to the PRC were semiconductors (largely for assembly and reexport, a key area of PRC employment and political sensitivity).[34] For these reasons, many have argued that the United States would use military force to protect its access to Taiwan's semiconductors as it has done in the past to ensure access to oil.[35] Indeed, TSMC's Morris Chang has referred to Taiwan's chip industry as "a holy mountain range protecting the country," a phrase popular in Taiwan.[36] This framing could therefore suggest that US moves toward securing its supply chains through onshoring would have the unintended consequence of signaling a disinterest in Taiwan's own safety—decreasing deterrence against the PRC.

On the other hand, some believe that Taiwan's leadership in semiconductors increases the probability of a PRC invasion instead of acting as a deterrent.[37] PRC writings are replete with arguments about the strategic nature of the semiconductor industry and its importance for national power and national security.[38] The critical nature of Taiwan's industry, and the PRC's inability to replicate it, only increases the attractiveness of the island to the PRC.[39] As chapter 8 describes in detail, the PRC has launched a herculean effort to build a domestic chip industry, with plans to invest over $150 billion in semiconductors from 2014 to 2030.[40] However, the results are mixed at best. Though the PRC has made inroads in importing large volumes of semiconductor manufacturing equipment and is quickly gaining market share in the production of some less-advanced chips as well as memory chips, its effort to build self-sufficiency in semiconductor manufacturing has faced numerous setbacks.[41] At least six new major PRC semiconductor manufacturing projects that collectively received over $2.3 billion in government funding have failed over the past three years.[42] Meanwhile, the PRC's semiconductor industry still relies on suppliers in the United States, Taiwan, South Korea, Japan, and Europe, and US and partner export controls increasingly deny the PRC access to key chip production equipment and software.[43] Given these punishing export restrictions and the PRC's failed chip investments, some analysts expect that the PRC's goal to achieve self-sufficiency in chips is unlikely to be successful, making Taiwan even more important to the PRC's technology ambitions.[44]

But it is important to recognize that having control over Taiwan does not necessarily mean having control of Taiwan's semiconductor industry. Semiconductor equipment must be operated by highly skilled engineers and maintained by service engineers from semiconductor equipment manufacturers (the majority of semiconductor equipment comes from the United States, Japan, and Europe). Even if China could continue to manage Taiwan's manufacturing plants, it would likely be impossible to maintain the plants' equipment without help from equipment vendors. Semiconductor technology must be constantly improved to maximize its value. The ability to deliver new generations of semiconductor technology rests on a highly skilled workforce capable of conducting advanced research and development. It is an open question whether high-level Taiwanese research engineers and semiconductor executives, many of whom were educated and trained in the United States, would remain in Taiwan under PRC rule. More importantly, as chapter 2 describes, the key to success for a semiconductor foundry is not only technological capability but also customer trust. A China-controlled TSMC may not earn the same level of trust from customers worldwide. At best, taking Taiwan by force would cause disruption worldwide, but the direct benefit to China in terms of advancing China's semiconductor leadership or chip independence is questionable.

The semiconductor industry also looms large within the broader bilateral great-power competition between the PRC and the United States. According to one Chinese scholar, Washington's anxiety in response to China's rise coinciding with the dawn of new, semiconductor-driven technologies such as 5G and artificial intelligence (AI) is precisely because technological revolutions are a key component of power transitions.[45] US attempts to consolidate the domestic semiconductor industry are seen in this light.[46] One researcher at the Chinese Academy of Social Sciences, Xu Qiyuan, even suggests that China can learn from the United States in terms of securing offshore supply chains through building relationships with other countries. Indeed, Xu notes specifically that his research found that "it is difficult [for a country] to maintain both competitiveness and influence *and* complete autonomy and supply chain independence when it comes to a globalized industry."[47]

PRC analysts and media outlets have also tried to take advantage of these dynamics to paint a transactional portrait of the US-Taiwan relationship, and to even sow distrust of the United States among the Taiwanese people. In this context, Chinese thinkers point to the US reliance on Taiwan for its semiconductors, speculating that this commercial concern may be a major motivator for US defense of the island.[48] And at least one Chinese writer has asserted that the United States plans to destroy TSMC equipment on the island in the event of invasion; coupled with US government encouragement for TSMC to build new factories on American soil, they suggest that the United States is not dedicated to the defense of Taiwan.[49] These narratives are corrosive and have troublingly found some resonance within Taiwan in the heated political environment of an election year—and among some ill-informed US commentators, too.

Consultations with Taiwan's Semiconductor Industry

US policies on its own semiconductor supply chain, on technological competition with China, and on Indo-Pacific security are followed closely in Taiwan. And economic interactions and coordination between the United States and Taiwan have generally been considered fair game diplomatically—see, for example, the US State Department's Economic Prosperity Partnership Dialogue with Taiwan, or the bilateral US-Taiwan Initiative on 21st-Century Trade, which was launched in 2022 given Taiwan's exclusion from the similar regional US-led Indo-Pacific Economic Framework for Prosperity (IPEF). Nonetheless, due in part to the island's continued formal international diplomatic isolation, Taiwan's businesses have long eschewed political engagement abroad and have been shy to acknowledge geopolitics at all.

Now the situation is changing, and Taiwan's companies have to change, too. Establishing a mechanism for collaboration between the semiconductor industries and academic research institutions of the United States and Taiwan on supply chain resilience, technology research and development, manufacturing capability, and workforce development could benefit both the United States and Taiwan.[50] TSMC has recently established a Washington office. Its chairman, Mark Liu, an engineer (US-trained) at heart, now regularly has to (perhaps grudgingly) deal with geopolitical issues. But the company has risen to the occasion, and so far navigated those challenges well. It would benefit our mutual interests if other companies in Taiwan could successfully navigate this dynamic geopolitical relationship, too.

Taiwan's ITRI—which has long acted as an interface between Western and Taiwanese technology firms—could be a conduit of this through an expanded mission. Since its establishment by Taiwan's government in 1973, ITRI has had an excellent track record of incubating new technologies and new companies (the most successful one being TSMC), and it carries out research on a broad array of topics, including semiconductors.[51] Notably, Taiwan's government in 2019 launched the Taiwan Semiconductor Research Institute (TSRI) under the Ministry of Science to conduct research in semiconductor manufacturing, design, and integration; to foster professional development; and to collaborate with industry and academia.[52] A key TSRI mission is to engage in cooperation with international partners, particularly the United States, including connecting with research communities, training workforce talent, and pursuing joint activities. ITRI and TSRI are logical Taiwanese partners for collaboration with the United States not just on technology research but on broader matters of supply chain resilience as well as geopolitical hopes and fears.

A potential American collaboration partner could be the American Semiconductor Academy (ASA) initiative, a proposed nationwide semiconductor education and training network of faculty at US universities and colleges engaged in semiconductor research and education.[53] Collaboration between TSRI and ASA could advance R&D and training programs in both the United States and Taiwan. As described earlier, in 2021, Taiwan established four "semiconductor colleges" within the top four universities in Taiwan; one of the goals of these semiconductor colleges is to raise the level of research in Taiwan and collaborate with US universities and semiconductor companies.[54] The United States could similarly establish mechanisms for US universities and companies to collaborate with Taiwan's semiconductor colleges and interested firms.

Another potential US collaboration partner would be the National Semiconductor Technology Center (NSTC), established by the CHIPS Act provisions of the fiscal year 2021 National Defense Authorization Act. With nearly $11 billion now appropriated for this purpose, the NSTC will be established by the secretary of commerce as a public-private consortium with participation of the private sector, the Department of Energy, and the National Science Foundation to conduct research and prototyping of advanced-semiconductor technology to strengthen the economic competitiveness and security of semiconductor supply chains.[55] The NSTC is intended to conduct research in manufacturing, design, packaging, and prototyping; strengthen the competitiveness and security of supply chains; and promote workforce training. There is considerable overlap between the missions of the TSRI and the NSTC, and these two government institutions could foster collaboration between the semiconductor industries and research universities of the United States and Taiwan.

Joint Workforce Development

As described above, talent is becoming a key choke point for sustaining leadership in semiconductor technology. Taiwan and the United States have joint concerns about the shortage of skilled labor.

Joint training programs, such as those undertaken by TSMC in Taiwan to train US staff for its new Arizona plant, offer one constructive way to deepen US-Taiwan ties and aid the development of the workforce in both countries.

The United States, meanwhile, has the best universities in the world, and these universities attract the best students from around the world for their education. There is a unique opportunity for the US government and US universities to partner with Taiwan on talent development with the goal of incentivizing chip manufacturers like TSMC or chip designers like MediaTek or others to grow their R&D efforts in the United States, and through US students. This could, in the long run, create the necessary conditions for TSMC and others to ramp up high-volume manufacturing of their most advanced technologies on US soil.

Partnering with US universities could also help these firms become more adept at working with foreign graduates, who represent only a small share of the semiconductor workforce in Taiwan today, but who could likely become more interested in the prospect of working in Taiwan, or with Taiwanese firms, through such early contact in their education and training.

A complementary strategic partnership opportunity is with the NSTC, which, if established properly (see chapter 4), will become a global center for semiconductor research. Encouraging global technology leaders such as GlobalWafers, MediaTek, TSMC, and UMC to join the NSTC as full-fledged members (along with semiconductor industry leaders outside of Taiwan, such as Samsung) would greatly accelerate the path from R&D to manufacturing.

Workforce and Cultural Exchange

While Taiwan's semiconductor industry already has a strong presence in and long-standing ties to Silicon Valley, more can be done on educational exchanges around the country. A potential model program is the initiative between the Taiwanese chip designer MediaTek and Purdue University to create a new chip design center.[56] Pairing Taiwanese chip designers and manufacturing firms with US engineering programs around the country could provide considerable benefits: industry experience and potential career opportunities for students, and access to engineering talent for firms. Less obviously, it could well have political and strategic benefits for Taiwan, bringing the island's semiconductor industry to the attention of politicians and educational leaders throughout the United States.

More attention should also be paid to reversing the decline in the number of Taiwanese students studying in US universities—a cohort that formed the original bedrock of Taiwan's chip industry. The number of Taiwanese students studying in US universities fell from approximately twenty-eight thousand in 2001 to twenty-four thousand just before the COVID-19 pandemic, and hit just twenty thousand in 2021—a declining trend that occurred alongside broadly rising international student enrollments in US schools.[57] Technology industry veterans in Taiwan will observe today that when they first entered their workplace after graduation decades ago, more than half of their colleagues would often have graduated from US universities; today the figure is much lower. There is no one magic bullet to address this, which is partly a reflection of attitudes among domestic Taiwanese students and their interest in engaging in the world, and partly a matter of competition within US graduate programs. One fruitful area for focus, however, would be on getting Taiwanese undergraduates into US master's degree programs, which are largely self-funded by the student and are a source of income for US university departments, so financial support would be needed from the Taiwan or US government to create such billets. But doing so at the master's level would, in turn, improve the pipeline of Taiwanese students to funded research PhD programs. Simultaneously, English coursework options should be expanded and encouraged within Taiwanese undergraduate programs.

In the other direction, Taiwan's appeal as a destination for Chinese-language study has been on a dramatic upswing over the past few years, as the PRC has become increasingly difficult for US students to enter. The US-Taiwan Education Initiative seeks to capitalize on this shift by encouraging American students to study Mandarin at Taiwanese universities.[58] This and other initiatives, such as summer internship programs for engineering, economics, and social science students, could be expanded.[59]

Finally, following the political crackdown in Hong Kong in 2020, Taiwan has become an increasingly attractive destination for nongovernmental organizations (NGOs) involved in social and political issues. Reporters Without Borders, Freedom House, the International

Republican Institute, the National Democratic Institute, and the Westminster Foundation for Democracy have all recently opened offices in Taipei, and the membership of the Taiwan Foreign Correspondents' Club has doubled as foreign reporters working the China beat who have been denied visas have relocated there. A US-led initiative to strengthen ties beyond the semiconductor industry should look to build on these trends and further institutionalize Taiwan's place as an alternative to mainland China.

Regular Evaluations of Shared Semiconductor Vulnerabilities

Periodic evaluations of both the United States' and Taiwan's semiconductor vulnerabilities to a range of natural and geopolitical disaster scenarios could reveal supply chain weaknesses that need to be addressed, and facilitate planning for recovery from potential incidents. These evaluations could include tabletop exercises of supply chain disruption and recovery, with US and Taiwan industry participation. A partnership between TSRI and NSTC would be a potential institutional structure for conducting such evaluations. TSRI would have access to sensitive information from the Taiwanese industry about vulnerabilities of semiconductor facilities in Taiwan (and facilities of Taiwanese firms in the United States and elsewhere) to earthquakes and other natural disasters, and about vulnerability to disruption of supplies of components, materials, and services. It would have access to contingency plans for recovery as well. The NSTC would have access to comparable information about vulnerabilities of US facilities and supply chains and access to the analytic capabilities of US industry and academia. Such supply chain disruption simulation and mapping exercises have already begun in earnest within the private sector; they would be made stronger with broader and shared participation.

Partnerships on Energy Supply Resilience

Any energy policy must balance the energy system's environmental impacts with its affordability and broader economic implications, and with the security and reliability of the architecture. This need is no different in Taiwan.

On the environment, Taiwan's people are as interested in climate issues as are those elsewhere in the world, and they also are very active regarding the local environmental impacts, for example, that of infrastructure development. As a democracy, Taiwan's civil society sector is extremely influential in the path of energy policy. Meanwhile, US chip buyers and other original equipment manufacturers (OEMs) are also increasingly concerned with the emissions profiles of their suppliers abroad, which impact the clean-energy purchase needs of producers in Taiwan.

On the economy, energy costs and the competitiveness of Taiwan's industries are major concerns—the electricity rate structure can be considered to be subsidizing the island's semiconductor sector today. Taiwan still has monopoly state ownership of its oil and gas and power sectors; as is common in such scenarios, each is generally loss-making given political concerns, and this can make sufficient capital inflows for new investment a concern, especially when attempting to transform the sector to a cleaner profile, as Taiwan wishes to do today.

Security, meanwhile, has emerged as an area of increasing importance for Taiwan—as it has in other parts of the Indo-Pacific (including the United States) and in Europe as well. The year 2022 and the Russian invasion of Ukraine have proved that the world is more dangerous than we had thought or hoped. Energy import–dependent Taiwan now faces three dimensions of energy security concern: (1) resource adequacy, and the balancing of energy supply with energy demand, such as in the power sector to meet demand growth (as this chapter has described, with rapid demand growth from the IT industry, blackouts can still be a problem despite somewhat improved adequacy margins)[60]; (2) traditional energy import security concerns, such as the reliability of one's suppliers abroad (mitigation of this risk generally involved diversification of global suppliers to avoid potential disruptions, and Taiwan has done well on this account over the past few decades, including through new liquefied natural gas [LNG] imports from the United States); and (3) special existential concerns, which add a whole new layer to Taiwan's other, more typical energy security problems (this has implications for electric grid robustness needs, resiliency planning and investment, distributed generation, contingency of operations or even planned rationing and selective service degradation under duress, hardening of supply lines, and energy storage capacity across fuels— according to Taiwan's Ministry of Economic Affairs' Bureau of Energy, while Taiwan maintains a roughly 130-day supply of oil and 40-day supply of coal, it mandates only an 8-day supply of natural gas).[61]

Taiwan is now making concerted efforts across each of these dimensions of its energy needs. But its policy has also been contradictory in places. For example, on the one hand, the current government has pledged to phase out both nuclear power and coal and to replace them with renewables and natural gas generation, while also aiming to reach net-zero carbon dioxide emissions by 2050. On the other hand, the government has failed to meet its renewables targets, and has been hamstrung even in its efforts to improve its LNG import infrastructure. Meanwhile, Taiwan's semiconductor industry is already consuming vast amounts of electricity, and consumption is set to rise dramatically over the next decade. The development of greater energy reserves, new electricity generation capacity, and greater grid resiliency is both an economic and security imperative. The choice to phase out nuclear power, for example, may have to be revisited (as it was in California), given evolving energy system dynamics.

Moreover, that challenge takes place against the injustice of Taiwan's isolation from what has elsewhere become an increasingly international energy and climate discussion. Taiwan lacks International Energy Agency (IEA) membership, which means that it is not well represented in international energy and emissions statistical sharing or policy modeling, and it has no United Nations Framework Convention on Climate Change (UNFCCC) membership, which means that it does not participate in global climate gatherings such as 2022's UNFCCC Conference of the Parties (COP 27). This exclusion points to great potential for increased bilateral as well as civil and academic US-Taiwan, Japan-Taiwan, or Australia-Taiwan cooperation on energy issues.

Climate, resource adequacy, and broader electric grid security issues are a fertile area for US-Taiwan technical collaboration in improving supply chain resiliency. The US Department of Energy and US national labs should increase their energy statistical and technical collaborations with Taiwan. Climate and energy also constitute a good area for subnational collaboration, for example with California, which already pursues such policy and technical memoranda of understanding with China; it should do so with Taiwan as well, given its jurisdictional freedoms for international collaboration in this sector.

Smoothing US-Taiwan Economic Frictions

Taiwan's government has made significant overtures to opening its domestic market to US exports; Taiwan is the sixth-largest US agricultural product export market, for example, with consumption levels of US agricultural products such as beef among the highest per capita globally. And Taiwan is a major US LNG export market. Overall, only Mexico and Canada have higher overall per capita trade relationships with the United States.

And as this and other chapters have discussed, Taiwan's firms have also made significant investments in the United States, including in different parts of the semiconductor supply chain.

But more can be done—specifically, to borrow the words of Taiwanese economic affairs minister Wang Mei-hua, the timely conclusion of a "real free-trade agreement" with Taiwan, something the island has sought for more than a decade.[62] Indeed, the Tsai administration has already spent considerable political capital reversing a ban on, and then campaigning against and winning a referendum on, the importation of US pork containing the feed additive ractopamine. That issue had been a long-running source of contention in the US-Taiwan economic relationship; Tsai's ability to face it down and resolve it is a strong indicator not just that her government is a willing partner in US economic initiatives, including semiconductor supply chain management, but also that the Taiwanese people perceive the broader security and stability benefits to Taiwan of deeper business and people-to-people ties with the United States.

Securing Taiwanese government and business cooperation on critical-technology supply chain management—a key US goal—is influenced by the political goals of the administration in power. Taiwan is, after all, a vibrant democracy. The KMT's previous approach, exemplified by the many cross-strait agreements signed by the Ma administration in the early 2010s, had been to seek economic prosperity by going to the world through China. This approach has now clearly become obsolete. Tsai's DPP has instead favored an alternative of economic agreements with other, friendly countries in the region to gradually rebalance Taiwan's economy away from the PRC. This strategy now looks increasingly appealing, and even urgent, to many Taiwanese. And with Taipei facing an implacably hostile regime in Beijing that has repeatedly sought to use economic leverage for political ends in the cross-strait relationship, President Tsai has signaled that she is eager to strike economic agreements with friendly countries that exclude the PRC. In the revived regional Comprehensive and Progressive Agreement for Trans-Pacific Partnership (CPTPP) trade mechanism, to which neither the United States nor China is a party (but to which Beijing has applied for membership), Beijing is nonetheless likely able to use its influence over some of that group's members to block Taiwan's accession. It will also be hard for Taiwan to negotiate trade deals with other countries that fear Beijing's reaction.

Thus, Taiwan's government, for the time being, will have to focus on bilateral partnerships, particularly with the United States. It is important that Tsai's counterparts in the United States also recognize, as she does, that free-trade negotiations are not just about lowering tariffs. They are strategic, and they are a deterrent to conflict. This should be evident in a US administration whose leader has at least four times offered his "commitment" to militarily defend the island from invasion. Why not a trade deal first? As of the spring of 2023, reports are that the US Trade Representative has concluded approximately one-third of the articles that would be necessary to complete such an agreement and is actively pursuing the rest. But it needs to move even faster.

In the meantime, the US Treasury can take a straightforward step that would remove another source of economic friction that will become more important as the items outlined here—including the success of TSMC's fab investments in Arizona—are pursued. Under current US law, Taiwanese nationals working in the United States—at TSMC's new plant or elsewhere—are going to face double income taxation, because Taiwan and the United States do not have a bilateral tax treaty.[63] Resolving this issue requires the United States to conclude an agreement with Taiwan, a jurisdiction that it does not recognize as a sovereign state. An agreement on taxation would require overcoming that diplomatic hurdle, and risk condemnation from the PRC, but it would improve one of the cost considerations for TSMC, GlobalWafers, MediaTek, and other Taiwanese semiconductor firms for doing more business in the United States. (The United States does have such an agreement with another likely CHIPS and Science Act beneficiary, Korea, and thirty-six other jurisdictions globally, including the Vatican.) The US Congress has offered bipartisan signals in support of the Biden administration taking such steps, including a July 2022 resolution by Senators Ben Sasse (R-NE) and Chris Van Hollen (D-MD) that stressed Taiwan's role as a crucial defense ally and key part of the global technology supply chain.[64] It encouraged the president to begin negotiations on an income tax agreement with Taiwan and encouraged further increased trade, technology, and investment ties with Taiwan.

Defense Industry Cooperation

While a treatment of US-Taiwan defense strategy and coordination is beyond the scope of this chapter, we generally endorse the writings elsewhere on the need for a "porcupine" strategy of both deterrence by denial and deterrence by resilience involving "a large number of small things" and the need for more concrete US-Taiwan cooperation on defense planning and large-scale training.[65] One specific defense opportunity does, however, relate more directly to Taiwan's electronics and advanced manufacturing sectors.

The war in Ukraine has exposed the fragility and limited capacity of the US defense industrial base. The invasion has contributed to multiyear backlogs in the delivery of US weapons systems to Taiwan that would materially improve its deterrence posture. At the same time, Taiwan's capabilities in precision manufacturing, electronics, and defense-grade semiconductors make it—if given a green light—a promising contributor to the manufacture of key weapons systems and munitions for both its own defense and even for export. This is a concept that has been endorsed by both the Taiwanese and US defense industries, and at least tacitly by the Taiwanese government. It is also important for US interlocutors to appreciate that, just as in the United States, Taiwanese leaders face political considerations in their defense budgeting systems, something that has led to some seemingly nonsensical domestic weapons program outcomes. It would be better to channel that political need into the most productive possible domestic weapons programs and, in doing so, help sustain Taiwanese public support for the recent substantial increases in defense spending—up to 2.1 percent of gross domestic product (GDP) in 2022, and likely heading higher.[66]

The best way to achieve that coproduction is not necessarily for members of Congress or prominent individuals to further debate the pros and cons of specific weapons. Rather, we need a process. The US government could materially improve regional deterrence by partnering with Taiwan's manufacturing firms to rapidly scale up local production of a large number of mobile, distributed, resilient weapons. Because these efforts will necessarily include the authorization of IP transfer and other use provisions of the US International Traffic in Arms Regulations (ITAR), bureaucratic inertia is the main enemy. To that end, the Biden administration should sponsor a joint industry task force of Taiwanese and US defense firms charged with identifying opportunities—and then working together to remove interagency barriers—for coproduction, followed by codevelopment, and possible later indigenization of US weapons systems within Taiwan, at scale. Doing so would most closely align the Taiwanese people's will to deter—and, if needed, win—a war with their own ability to deliver.

$$\bullet \quad \bullet \quad \bullet$$

The PRC threat to Taiwan is becoming more acute, and the challenge of deterring a PRC invasion is becoming more difficult. The existential nature of the threat to Taiwan's autonomy and security will continue to grow and must be addressed on an urgent basis. But the Taiwanese people are impressively resilient. They possess a vibrant democracy, and they are served by talented and dedicated individuals across the political spectrum, in both the private and public sectors. At the same time, Taiwan is increasingly isolated from the broader international community. Reversing this trend is critical to deterring the PRC from using force, and this requires both symbolic and substantive assistance on the part of the United States and other countries.

Taiwan's leaders are thoughtfully threading their way through a treacherous geopolitical situation. In fact, as this chapter argues, we can learn from their experiences in doing this. They now grasp the seriousness of the challenge Taiwan confronts, and they are trying to move the public toward a more robust and resilient response. What Taiwan most needs from the United States is a clear demonstration of commitment, independent of the rhetorical debate over strategic clarity or ambiguity. Other governments and opinion leaders in the region would likely appreciate this as well. And through semiconductors, the United States has an opportunity to demonstrate aspects of this commitment through the variety of deeper bilateral government, business, academic, and people-to-people interactions outlined here—while not formally announcing a shift to "strategic clarity." Words are important, but actions will speak louder than words.

NOTES

1. Much of this section draws from An-chi Tung, "Taiwan's Semiconductor Industry: What the State Did and Did Not," *Review of Development Economics* 5, no. 2 (2001): 266–88; and National Research Council, *Securing the Future: Regional and National Programs to Support the Semiconductor Industry* (Washington, DC: National Academies Press, 2003), chap. 3, "The Taiwanese Approach."
2. Chaun-wei Hsia, "Can Science Parks Be Duplicated?," *Commonwealth* 228 (2000): 102–10 (in Chinese).
3. Focus Taiwan, "Tax Breaks Insufficient to Cement Taiwan's Chipmaking Lead: Analysts," January 7, 2023.
4. See especially Gary Hamilton and Cheng-shu Kao, *Making Money: How Taiwanese Industrialists Embraced the Global Economy* (Stanford, CA: Stanford University Press, 2017).

5. Focus Taiwan, "Taiwan 'Work Culture' Keeps Chip Manufacturing Competitive: TSMC Founder," March 16, 2023.

6. *New York Times*, "Inside Taiwanese Chip Giant, a US Expansion Stokes Tensions," February 22, 2023; see also Dexter Murray, "TSMC Prepares American Engineers for Its First US Fab," *AmChan Taiwan*, August 31, 2022.

7. *New York Times*, "Engineers from Taiwan Bolstered China's Chip Industry: Now They're Leaving," November 16, 2022.

8. See, for example, on Intel: Mike Rogoway, "Intel's Manufacturing Crisis Puts Company at a Crossroads," OregonLive, August 16, 2020.

9. Liang-rong Chen and Hannah Chang, "Taiwan's Dominant Corporate Force: TSMC's Five Keys to Success," *Commonwealth Magazine*, November 24, 2019.

10. See, for example, comments in 2017 by Apple COO Jeff Williams and then-TSMC chair Morris Chang: Alan Patterson, "Apple Talks about Sole Sourcing from TSMC," October 24, 2017.

11. While far more than 10 percent of the value of TSMC's products are physically exported to the PRC for incorporation into consumer products (e.g., iPhones assembled by Taiwan-based contract assembly firms such as Foxconn and Quanta), the customer of a foundry is typically the chip designer—for example, Apple or Qualcomm. Approximately three-quarters of Taiwan's overall semiconductor exports to the PRC are for assembly by Taiwan-based assembly firms or systems OEMs, many of them for later reexport.

12. Dylan Patel and Gerald Wong, "TSMC's Heroic Assumption—Low Utilization Rates, Fab Cancellation, 3nm Volumes, Automotive Weakness, AI Advanced Packaging Demands, 2024 Capex Weakness," Semianalysis, April 20, 2023.

13. Nick Aspinwall, "As Drought Worsens Chip Shortage, Taiwan Fights Brain Drain to China," *The Diplomat*, May 1, 2021.

14. Hannah Chang and Liang-rong Chen, "Does Taiwan Have Enough Power for TSMC?," *Commonwealth Magazine*, July 28, 2020; Angelica Oung, "Net Zero, by . . . When?," *AmCham Taiwan*, November 11, 2017.

15. Evan A. Feigenbaum and Jen-Yi Hou, "Overcoming Taiwan's Energy Trilemma," Carnegie Endowment for Peace, April 27, 2020; National Development Council, "Taiwan's Path to Net-Zero Emissions in 2050," accessed May 28, 2023.

16. Judi Lin, "Fab Talent Crunch: Taiwan's Secret Sauce for Producing Excellent Semiconductor Engineers," DIGITIMES Asia, December 1, 2022; Liang-Rong Chen, "TSMC Fab in US Part of Second Wave of the Trade War: Industry Insiders," *Commonwealth Magazine*, May 21, 2020.

17. Sara Wu, "Slew of Chip Schools Race to Train New Talent," *Taipei Times*, March 14, 2022.

18. TSMC, *TSMC 2020 Corporate Social Responsibility Report*, 2021.

19. Crystal Hsu, "Semiconductor Hiring Slows Amid Labor Shortage," *Taipei Times*, August 16, 2022.

20. TSMC, *Corporate Social Responsibility Report*.

21. *The Economist*, "Taiwan Is Worried about the Security of Its Chip Industry," May 26, 2022.

22. Cheng Ting-Fang, "China Hires over 100 TSMC Engineers in Push for Chip Leadership," *Nikkei Asia*, August 12, 2020.

23. Chad P. Bown and YiLing Wang, "Episode 179: Why Taiwan Restricts High-Tech Investment into China," TradeTalks, February 23, 2023.

24. Reuters, "Taiwan Raids Chinese Firms in Latest Crackdown on Chip Engineer-Poaching," May 26, 2022.

25. Xiao Bowen, "中國企業在台高科技界挖角竊密 一年查獲40起不法行為 [Chinese Companies Poached and Stole Secrets in Taiwan's High-Tech Industry: 40 Illegal Acts Caught in One Year]," CNA, September 16, 2022.

26. *Taipei Times*, "Ministry Warns Job Sites on Chinese Job Ads," May 1, 2021.

27. Meredith Woo-Cumings, "National Security and the Rise of the Developmental State in South Korea and Taiwan," in *Behind East Asian Growth: The Political and Social Foundations of Prosperity*, edited by Henry S. Rowen (London: Routledge, 1997).

28. Hsing You-tien, *Making Capitalism in China: The Taiwan Connection* (Oxford: Oxford University Press, 1998); Shelley Rigger, *The Tiger Leading the Dragon: How Taiwan Propelled China's Economic Rise* (Lanham, MD: Rowman and Littlefield, 2021).

29. In 2022. Bureau of Foreign Trade, "Taiwan's Import and Export Statistic to Mainland China (including Hong Kong)," Ministry of Economic Affairs, May 2023.

30. Stephen Ezell, "The Evolution of Taiwan's Trade Linkages with the US and Global Economies," ITIF, October 25, 2021.

31. Raymond Zhong and Christopher F. Schuetze, "Taiwan Wants German Vaccines: China May Be Standing in Its Way," *New York Times*, June 16, 2021.

32. DW, "Taiwan to Invest $200 Million in Lithuania," January 5, 2022.

33. Craig Addison, "A 'Silicon Shield' Protects Taiwan from China," *New York Times*, September 29, 2000.

34. Antonio Varas, Raj Varadarajan, Jimmy Goodrich, and Falan Yinug, *Strengthening the Global Semiconductor Supply Chain in an Uncertain Era* (Boston, MA: Boston Consulting Group and Semiconductor Industry Association, April 2021); Michaela D. Platzer, John F. Sargent Jr., and Karen M. Sutter, *Semiconductors: US Industry, Global Competition, and Federal Policy*, RL34234 (Washington, DC: US Library of Congress, Congressional Research Service, 2020); Yimou Lee, Norihiko Shirouzu, and David Lague, "Special Report—Taiwan Chip Industry Emerges as Battlefront in US-China Showdown," Reuters, December 27, 2021.

35. Paul van Gerven, "Taiwan's Silicon Shield Is Strong as Ever," Bits&Chips, October 21, 2021; Becca Wasser, Martijn Rasser, and Hannah Kelley, *When*

the Chips Are Down: Gaming the Global Semiconductor Competition (Washington, DC: Center for a New American Security, 2022).

36. Lee et al., "Special Report—Taiwan Chip Industry Emerges As Battlefront In US-China Showdown."

37. Walter Lohman, "Taiwan's Semiconductor Dilemma," The Heritage Foundation, November 23, 2021.

38. See, for example, Ling Jiwei, "共赢'芯'机遇: 2021世界半导体大会观察 [A Win-Win 'Chip' Future: Observations from the World Semiconductor Conference 2021]," 新华网 [*Xinhuanet*], June 9, 2021; Xiao Hanping, "补齐半导体芯片产业链关键性短板, 应对全球供应链大变局 [Account for the Crucial Shortcomings in Semiconductor Supply Chains, Respond to the Huge Changes in Global Supply Chains]," 光明网 [*Guangming Daily*], May 20, 2021; Chai Yaxin, "美国把多家中国公司、机构及个人纳入"实体清单" 遏制中国注定徒劳 [The US Has Added Multiple Chinese Firms, Organizations, and Individuals to an 'Entity List': Its Effort to Contain China Will Be Futile]," 中央纪委国家监委网站, [The Central Commission for Discipline Inspection Website], January 9, 2022.

39. Wasser et al., *When the Chips Are Down*.

40. Semiconductor Industry Association (blog), "Taking Stock of China's Semiconductor Industry," July 13, 2021.

41. Jenny Leonard, Ian King, and Debby Wu, "China's Chipmaking Power Grows Despite US Effort to Counter It," *Bloomberg*, June 13, 2022; Arjun Kharpal, "China's Biggest Chipmaker SMIC Posts Record Revenue Despite US Sanctions," *CNBC*, February 12, 2022; Cheng Ting-Fang, "China's Yangtze Memory Takes on Rivals with New Chip Plant," *Nikkei Asia*, June 23, 2022.

42. Yoko Kubota, "Two Chinese Startups Tried to Catch Up to Makers of Advanced Computer Chips—and Failed," *Wall Street Journal*, January 10, 2022.

43. Jane Li and Tripti Lahiri, "The US Is Delaying China's Dreams of a Domestic Chip Supply Chain," *Quartz*, December 13, 2021.

44. Craig Addison, "China's Semiconductor Quest Is Likely to Fail, Leaving Rapprochement with US the Only Way Out," *South China Morning Post*, October 13, 2020.

45. Chai Yaxin, Its Effort to Contain China Will Be Futile.

46. Fu Suixin, "美日韩组建 '半导体联盟' 虚实, [The Realities of the US-Japan-South Korea 'Semiconductor Alliance']," *Huanqiu* [环球], August 25, 2021.

47. Xu Qiyuan, "[全球产业链重塑与中国的选择 [Reshaping of Global Industrial Chain and China's Choice]," 金融论坛 [*Financial Forum*] 8 (2021): 5–6.

48. Fu Suixin, "'Semiconductor Alliance'"; Sun Wenzhu, "美日鼓噪 '协防台湾' 背后算的几笔歪账 [The Ulterior Realities Behind the US and Japan Making Noise about 'Defending Taiwan']," 中国国际问题研究院 [China Institute of International Studies], January 10, 2022.

49. Wang Shushen, "'焦土拒统', 何其荒唐 [The Strategy of 'Scorched Earth to Prevent Reunification' Is Ludicrous]," 环球 [*Huanqiu*], December 25, 2021.

50. Jason Hsu, "Ensuring a Stronger US-Taiwan Tech Supply Chain Partnership," Brookings, April 12, 2022.

51. Taiwan Semiconductor Research Institute, "History and Introduction of the Institute," accessed July 30, 2022.

52. Taiwan Semiconductor Research Institute, "History and Introduction."

53. Hsu, "Ensuring a Stronger US-Taiwan Tech Supply Chain Partnership"; ASA Planning Team, "The American Semiconductor Academy Initiative," American Semiconductor Academy, February 1, 2022.

54. Sarah Wu, "Taiwan Invests in Next Generation of Talent with Slew of Chip Schools," Reuters, March 10, 2022.

55. US Congress, William M. (Mac) Thornberry National Defense Authorization Act for Fiscal Year 2021, Public Law 116-283, January 1, 2021.

56. Reuters, "Taiwan's MediaTek Pairs with Indiana's Purdue University for Chip Design Center," June 28, 2022.

57. Open Doors, "2022 Taiwan Fact Sheet," accessed May 29, 2023.

58. See the US-Taiwan education initiative webpage, at https://www.talent circulationalliance.org/us-taiwan-initiative.

59. See, for instance, Stanford's Global Studies internship programs; e.g., https:// sgs.stanford.edu/internships/taiwan-institute-economic-research-tier.

60. Taiwan Bureau of Energy, Ministry of Economic Affairs, "Energy Statistics Handbook: Energy Indicators," July 27, 2022.

61. Taiwan Bureau of Energy, Ministry of Economic Affairs, "Stable Supply of Natural Gas," November 7, 2022.

62. Rachel Oswald, "Path Uncertain for US-Taiwan Free Trade Deal despite Hill Support," *Roll Call*, October 3, 2022.

63. Lex, "TSMC: Double Taxation Puts US Expansion at Risk," *Financial Times*, Opinion, March 30, 2023.

64. US Senate, Resolution 175: Expressing the Sense of the Senate on the Value of a Tax Agreement with Taiwan, 117th Congress, July 21, 2022.

65. See James Timbie and James Ellis, "A Large Number of Small Things: A Porcupine Strategy for Taiwan," *The Strategist* 5, no. 1 (Winter 2021/2022): 83–93; and Michael Brown, "Taiwan's Urgent Task: A Radical New Strategy to Keep China Away," *Foreign Affairs*, January 25, 2023.

66. Taiwan's budget is quite fiscally conservative given its exclusion from international multilateral financial organizations, so even this somewhat modest spending amount represents a not-insignificant 22–25 percent of the central government budget.

CHAPTER SIX

US Allies, Partners, and Friends

DAVID J. TEECE AND GREG LINDEN

If the world shifts toward more balkanized flows of goods, investment, expertise, people, and ideas, the continued prosperity of liberal democracies will increasingly depend on their ability to collectively sustain technological superiority in fields such as semiconductors and other critical technologies. Meeting this challenge will require those who share common values and interests—as well as those with strong positions in the global semiconductor supply chain—to diminish their dependency on threatening authoritarian states and increase interdependence among themselves.

As the world continues to experience significant changes in global trade relations, the United States should aim not only to advance its position in the microprocessor supply chain but also to engender closer and more collaborative partnerships with like-minded countries—ones that, instead of threatening our supply chains with punitive economic actions or even war, can be relied on as trustworthy collaborators.

• • •

The United States is not alone in its renewed drive for near- to mid-term domestic supply chain resilience and longer-term global technological leadership in semiconductors. The shocks caused by the COVID-19 pandemic and increasingly fraught geopolitical relationships are context-agnostic "driving forces" (see chapter 1) that have changed the terms of the game for the United States and global partners. Using the parlance of the strategic scenario planning of chapter 1, our partners at least perceive the potential for a "westward" shift as flows of goods, capital, intellectual property (IP), and human talent become increasingly decoupled—and thus, they are pursuing self-reliance as a way to insulate against the uncertainty of a less-flat world. This concentration is already reflected in the impressive array of investments and policy instruments now being undertaken by the United States and its partners in the semiconductor sphere.

The lesson of our scenario-planning analysis, however, is more subtle than a simple reversion to self-reliance. The "context-dependent" business and policy responses of our partners illustrate how each country must use its starting position, historical strengths, and social priorities to filter those common driving forces. Purely domestic onshoring is economically inefficient: in a flat "eastern" world, economic growth comes from a focus on specialization and comparative advantage. And in a more balkanized "western" world, meanwhile, autarky is very costly. In a move toward a "western" world of more intensive trade among fewer partners, trade networks with the least friction among participants will be best able to prosper in a deglobalized environment. A shift "westward," then, would not call for further raising of barriers, but rather for selectively lowering them among those nations with shared values and interests.

Developing new strategies for economically and technologically repositioning ourselves to prosper in a deglobalized world is perhaps the key policy challenge of the coming decade. As one considers the pathways now being pursued by US partners in the semiconductor supply chain (partners other than Taiwan, which is the focus of the preceding chapter), our goal should be to identify opportunities to increase commerce and exchange as a way to offset the cost of potentially decoupling from China in the microchip field and other critical-technology fields. This selective opening is an underappreciated requirement for longer-term allied unity on, for example, semiconductor technology export controls; if cooperation on that front is just an ongoing cost to partner-country firms that do business with China, it will not be sustained. China, on its own, represents a substantial market with a skilled workforce and an impressive innovation infrastructure.

So how are our partners looking at and responding to this changing geopolitical landscape?

Japan

Key Laws and Policies

Japan is a good example of a country that, like the United States, has only recently begun to wake up to its semiconductor supply chain vulnerabilities.

According to Japan's Ministry of Economy, Trade, and Industry (METI), the country's automotive, electronics, and manufacturing technology sectors depend heavily on a reliable supply of semiconductors—the "rice of the industry."[1] Nevertheless, according to Yoichi Funabashi of Japan's Asia Pacific Initiative, before semiconductor shortages in early 2021 the Japanese government did not have sufficient understanding of supply chains, nor did it even have the authority to research them.[2] Disruptions in manufacturing due to COVID-19 not only helped upset US-China relations but also raised attention within Japan to the critical role semiconductors play in its broader economic and military security.

In June 2021, METI released a semiconductor strategy document suggesting that, if nothing was done, Japan's share of global production could fall from 10 percent to as low as zero by 2030. The main force driving toward this outcome was the resurgence of industrial policy in the United States. METI feared that the United States would not only rebuild its share of chip production, but in doing so also attract away Japan's prized chip manufacturing material supply firms.[3]

In October 2021, Japan's parliament elected Fumio Kishida, an experienced and moderate politician, as prime minister. His administration proposed a "new capitalism" policy framework, which included some major new growth strategies such as promoting science and technology and supporting startups, a field that has been a perennial weak spot in Japan's economy. Another element of the plan focused on "economic security," which included reducing Japan's dependence on China for strategic materials and parts as well as countering the misappropriation of IP used in the production of semiconductors.

In November 2021, the government approved a ¥774 billion ($6.8 billion) package for semiconductor investments in Japan. It was allocated as follows:[4]

- ¥47 billion for legacy production, such as analog and power management chips
- ¥110 billion for the research and development of next-generation chip technologies
- Up to ¥476 billion (50 percent of the projected capital cost) for a Sony–Taiwan Semiconductor Manufacturing Company (TSMC) manufacturing joint venture[5]
- At least ¥140 billion for other forms of advanced production, ¥92.9 billion of which was later allocated to a joint venture by memory producers Kioxia (Japan) and Western Digital (US).[6]

The government's aim was to increase the value of Japan's domestic chip production to match or exceed the growth of the global industry (i.e., remain near 10 percent of world output). To achieve that objective, the government seeks to triple its domestic semiconductor revenue to over ¥13 trillion ($114 billion) by 2030.[7] Later, in May 2022, the National Diet passed an economic security bill that was expected to designate semiconductors as a class of "specific important materials," making them eligible for further subsidies.[8]

The new TSMC joint venture factory in Japan's Kumamoto Prefecture is also a part of this package. That factory is expected to produce chips from 20nm to 10nm, making it Japan's most advanced-logic manufacturing facility ("fab"). (A fab belonging to US firm Micron and fabs belonging to Toshiba's Kioxia unit produce DRAM [dynamic random access memory] and NAND Flash memory chips, respectively, at similarly small nanometer ranges.) Construction began in April 2022, and shipments are likely to begin by 2025. TSMC is committed to producing chips in this new plant for at least ten years.[9]

Earlier in 2021, the Japanese government approved a ¥19 billion (about $140 million) subsidy for TSMC's new research and development (R&D) center focused on developing three-dimensional advanced semi-conductor packaging capabilities (referred to as "3D IC," or integrated circuits, as described in chapter 2). The Japanese government subsidy was about half the cost of the total facility, which is located inside the existing National Institute of Advanced Industrial Science and Technology (AIST), a large public Japanese research organization that collaborates with industry across a range of fields.[10]

In July 2022, just a few days shy of a "two-plus-two" dialogue with the United States involving both foreign and industry ministers, the government announced up to ¥92.9 billion ($678 million) to support Kioxia and Western Digital's new flash memory production facility in Mie Prefecture. The subsidy reportedly will cover a third of the project's capital expenditure.[11] The first phase of "Fab 7," intended to produce 162-layer NAND Flash memory, was opened in November 2022.[12]

With these and other new and expanding production facilities, Japan faces a problem shared with seemingly every other jurisdiction seeking to grow its activities: increased demand for talent met, at least in the short term, by meager supply. The number of Japanese twenty-five- to forty-year-olds working in electronic components and circuits manufacturing has decreased from 380,000 to 240,000 in the past ten years, while an industry association called for thirty-five thousand additional semiconductor workers needed by 2032.[13] In response, talent development programs, in partnership with universities and industries, are being formed by local governments in the Kyushu (Japan's "silicon island"), Tohoku, and Chugoku regions.[14]

Japan's Production and Consumption

Japan's share of world chip production, which reached 50 percent in 1990, has fallen steadily to about 10 percent currently.[15] Much of this decline is attributable to Japan's memory producers, which, apart from Toshiba, have been outcompeted by rivals in South Korea. Meanwhile, Japan's vertically integrated logic chip producers also proved less nimble than the US-based fabless startup ecosystem, which, like its

European counterparts, opted to focus on specialty processes instead of keeping up with the leading edge of technology.

In the late 1990s, the Japanese government helped bring about mergers of several producers' diminished chip divisions. Their record of success, however, is mixed. Elpida, which combined the memory business of NEC, Hitachi, and Mitsubishi, struggled for over a decade until it was bought out of bankruptcy by US-based Micron. Renesas, which combined the logic divisions of the same three companies that formed Elpida, fared better and is now a leading provider of microcontrollers to the automotive and industrial segments. Sony, which produces analog chips, is a major supplier of image sensors to the consumer, industrial, and automotive markets. But neither Renesas, Sony, nor Toshiba's memory division Kioxia currently ranks as a top-ten global chip firm overall.

US semiconductor producers are actually quite active in Japan.[16] US-based ON Semiconductor (onsemi) manufactures analog chips in Japan, as does Texas Instruments (in a 200mm wafer size fab it acquired in 2010). Micron, which has been making memory chips in Japan since acquiring Elpida in 2012, announced plans in 2021 for a new fab in Japan at a cost of up to $7 billion.

Whereas Japan's share of chip output has fallen, its role as a supplier of key inputs to chip manufacturing processes remains strong. In materials, for example, most of the world's supply of photoresist coatings, essential for photolithography, is made by Japan-based companies. And Japan's firms also have market shares of 60 percent or more of the global market for another seventy advanced materials used in semiconductor manufacturing.[17] Two Japanese companies, Shin-Etsu Chemical and SUMCO, together control roughly 60 percent of the global market for silicon wafers. In terms of overall materials used in manufacturing processes, Japan's market share is significant, about 30 percent.[18]

To secure necessary materials for semiconductor production (such as tantalum, germanium, and gallium), Japan's government works through the Japan Organization for Metals and Energy Security (JOGMEC), which was formerly known as Japan Oil, Gas and Metals National Corporation, to conduct overseas exploration projects. These efforts include joint ventures with businesses, aiding the Japanese company in acquiring buying rights that insulate them from market fluctuations.[19]

Japan also has significant strengths in semiconductor manufacturing equipment—a 32 percent market share in 2019.[20] Tokyo Electron, which makes machines for the deposition and etching process in chip fabrication, is the third-largest maker of fabrication equipment after Europe's ASML and US-based Applied Materials.[21]

Japan's position in other parts of the semiconductor value chain—including electronic design automation (EDA) software, chip assembly, and fabless chip design—is negligible. The lack of fabless chip companies of any significance—a long-standing point of strength in the United States' venture-backed landscape—is in large part a reflection of Japan's weak startup ecosystem.

On the consumption side, Japan's market for semiconductors was worth about $36.5 billion in 2021, or about 6 percent of the world's total demand.

Diplomatic Trends and Issues

On May 4, 2022, US Commerce Secretary Gina Raimondo met with Japan's minister of economy, trade, and industry, Koichi Hagiuda. This meeting followed Hagiuda's visit to IBM at the Albany NanoTech Complex, an advanced-semiconductor research facility involving Tokyo Electron, among other corporate partners, to discuss US-Japan semiconductor cooperation.[22] That meeting constituted "the first Cabinet-level meeting of the Japan-US Commercial and Industrial Partnership (JUCIP) . . . since its launch in November 2021."[23]

In June 2022, the United States and Japan agreed to jointly pursue 2nm production, aiming to start prototype production between 2025 and 2027.[24] This announcement came a year after AIST also began a research consortium for advanced-semiconductor manufacturing, including 2nm, with external support from Intel and IBM, plus an additional ¥42 billion ($319 million) in funding from METI.[25]

When President Biden met Prime Minister Kishida later that month, the press in Japan reported that they agreed to launch a joint task force to explore the development of next-generation computer chips.[26] And in late July, the two countries held a "two-plus-two" dialogue, in which they reaffirmed the commitment to the task force and promised broader supply chain partnerships under the new JUCIP. They also announced the creation of a new research facility in Japan with talent and equipment from the US National Semiconductor Technology Center to research 2nm, 5G, and quantum computing.[27] From these discussions, along with Japan's recent emphasis on economic security, it appears that Japan's government is eager to partner with the United States on semiconductors and supply chains at large, and this should serve as a good model for other future transnational collaborations.

It is also important to note that Japan, like Taiwan, has historically made extensive investments in chip manufacturing in China. In the 1980s, for example, Japan's chipmakers transferred technology to China for some of its first fabrication efforts. Direct investments in the semiconductor sector, however, were limited, and several unwound as Japan's chip firms reorganized. According to the Organisation for Economic Co-operation and Development (OECD), Japan's reliance on China for its final demand hovered around 10 percent for sectors encompassing semiconductor inputs in 2015 and higher than 3.6 percent for all industries.[28] Japan's current footprint in China appears to consist of one or two assembly plants belonging to Renesas and a handful of chip design centers.

Although Japan doesn't appear to be ready to burn its bridges with China, it has recently shown a greater willingness to resist Chinese pressure. For example, its latest defense white paper treats Taiwan separately from China, triggering China to register a formal objection. Japan, along with Taiwan, was also quick to accept the United States' proposed "Chip 4" alliance in March 2022—compared to initial hesitancy from South Korea in light of its own substantial commercial interests in China.[29]

US observers are aware of tensions between Japan and South Korea that date to Japan's colonial rule during the first half of the twentieth century. For example, in 2019 the Japanese government expressed displeasure over a South Korean court decision about forced labor during

World War II and placed restrictions on exports to South Korea of photoresist, hydrogen fluoride, and fluorine polyimide—all essential to the manufacture of chips and displays. Even so, some Japanese firms— such as Tokyo Ohka Kogyo (photoresist), Daikin (specialty gases), and Showa Denko (wafer polishers)—have nonetheless subsequently invested in new plants inside South Korea to circumvent the restrictions.[30] South Korea also responded by encouraging local firms to displace the need for Japan-based supply, an initiative that is apparently making some progress.[31] In March 2023, Japan announced its intention to lift the export curbs (but with no end date given) as part of a rapprochement with South Korea over historical differences.[32]

Chip Industry Trends

Japan companies are being compelled to recognize "decoupling" pressures with respect to US and China supply chains. In a survey of one hundred companies critical to Japan's economic security, the majority saw China as a significant medium- to long-term risk due to government sanctions by China, rising competition, and talent and knowledge outflow. And yet, none planned to reduce their share of overall sales to China. Rather, US trade barriers were a more immediate concern to them, as many companies were feeling the impact of US-China tensions. Of the Japanese companies, 59.5 percent reported cost increases from US quotas, as opposed to 33.8 percent from China. Some commentators in Japan argue that, sandwiched between US and China sanctions (and the Japanese government's evolving national security policies), they find it difficult to know which way to run.[33]

There have also been some instances of Japan's semiconductor companies expressing caution about US partnerships. In the same survey, referring to the US Department of Commerce's fall 2021 semiconductor supply chain request for information, one industry leader expressed frustration with the US government for asking for what he felt to be his company's trade secrets. He blamed Japan's government for not taking a clearer stance.[34] There are also hints in this survey that the trade tensions with the United States in the 1980s are still seen as the cause of Japan's semiconductor industry downfall. One business leader commented, "The United States always comes knocking politically when a foreign company exceeds a certain size."[35] Another said, "As the United States strengthens its economic security, Japan is likely to become its target. There's a need to revisit the lessons from the 1980s."[36]

Japan's industries seem to respond to geopolitical tensions by reshoring or relocating factories; 14.2 percent of firms responded that they would like to receive government subsidies for shifting existing production within China back to Japan or to other countries.[37] For overseas factories, Japanese companies have increased their presence in the United States, South Korea, and Southeast Asian countries such as Vietnam and Malaysia. Indeed, since the anti-Japanese movement in China in the early 2010s and production disruptions due to COVID-19, Japan's government has been intent on broadly reducing reliance on China through its "China Plus One" diversification strategy.[38] In 2020, METI began implementing the Overseas Supply Chain Diversification Support Program, which finalized its fifth application process in June 2022. The project grants subsidies to Japanese companies for projects in Southeast Asia, and of the 103 successful grantees, 6 were explicitly related to semiconductors[39]—which implies that Japan's government is deeply concerned about its chip supply chains.

South Korea

Key Laws and Policies

Chip-related government policies in South Korea have been relatively modest compared with industry-driven business strategies led by the powerful Korean conglomerates, namely Samsung and SK hynix.

Korea is a powerhouse in memory chip production, accounting for 59 percent of global industry value added.[40] But the story is not the same in logic chips, which involve a different set of design and marketing skills. In April 2019, the government launched the System Semiconductor Vision and Strategy, the latest in a series of (so far unsuccessful) public and private efforts to boost logic chip design. This initiative aims to boost the fabless-foundry ecosystem through skills training and investment, and is backed by an investment of ₩1 trillion (about $830 million) over ten years.[41]

Later in 2019, following a dispute with Japan that led to a cutoff of several of Japan's chip-related exports to Korea, the government announced several measures to improve Korea's chip supply base for materials and equipment. These measures included funds of at least ₩2.5 trillion in grants and tax deductions to support mergers and acquisitions (M&A) of foreign suppliers. Meanwhile, foreign suppliers of targeted technologies that invest in manufacturing in Korea were offered cost-sharing grants equal to 40 percent of total investment, and a program for the fast-tracking of applications and infrastructure provision was implemented.[42]

In May 2021, following similar responses by the United States, Europe, and China, Korea's government also announced a "K-Semiconductor Strategy." This strategy consisted of investment commitments by Korea's chipmakers totaling more than ₩500 trillion (about $450 billion) before 2030 to stimulate domestic semiconductor production, with promises by the government for tax incentives and infrastructure, including assured access to water and power. Leading the group of 153 companies, Samsung said it would increase previous investment plans by ₩38 trillion ($33.6 billion) to ₩171 trillion ($151 billion) through 2030 in both its system large-scale integration (LSI; Samsung's fabless division) and foundry businesses. At the same time, SK hynix pledged it would spend ₩125 trillion ($97 billion) on expanding existing foundry facilities, in addition to a previously pledged ₩140 trillion ($106 billion) on four new plants.[43] The plan envisioned a "K-Chip Belt" that sought to connect a group of cities involved in the semiconductor value chain more closely. The government also established a "semiconductor facility investment special fund"— worth over ₩1 trillion—to support facility investment through favorable interest rates. The government also promised to fund the training of thirty-six thousand semiconductor experts and said it would spend ₩1.5 trillion ($1.3 billion) on semiconductor R&D.[44]

In January 2022, Korea's Chips Act advanced in the legislature, with the final version passing easily in March 2023.[45] While the initial language of the Act was less ambitious than that of its US counterpart, some of its measures were strengthened in response to industry feedback. In particular, large firms (such as Samsung and SK hynix) that invested in "core strategy technology" would qualify for tax breaks of 30 to 40 percent on R&D expenses and 15 to 25 percent for facility investment. Small firms would qualify for a deduction of up to 25 percent for investments in facilities (up from 16 percent) and 50 percent for research.[46] The first major investment announcement under the Act came in March 2023: Samsung committed to building five fabs at a cost of roughly $228 billion through 2042 in a new industrial complex near Seoul; the government hoped these Samsung fabs would bring on as many as 150 materials, component, and chip design firms.[47]

While there were some concerns about whether the originally proposed Act would survive the change in presidential administrations, President Yoon Suk-yeol has only doubled down on President Moon Jae-in's semiconductor ambitions. In fact, in late July 2022 the Yoon administration announced plans to make Korea a semiconductor superpower by locally sourcing 50 percent of its semiconductor materials, components, and equipment by 2030—up from 30 percent today. Among other regulatory relaxations and incentives, Korea's road map includes expected industry-related infrastructure investments of ₩340 trillion by 2026; increased tax incentives for equipment and research investments; and a public-private investment of ₩300 billion for small-business innovation and M&A of chip design firms. It also renewed focus on "system semiconductors"—a Korean term for non–memory chip production—with a goal of increasing its current market share of 3 percent to 10 percent by 2030. From 2024 to 2030, the government will also invest ₩950 billion in feasibility studies on semiconductors used in the electrical power and automobile sectors; ₩1.25 trillion in artificial intelligence (AI) semiconductors; and ₩1.5 trillion to support thirty new fabless companies.[48]

The strategy also sought to address Korea's anxieties—shared with other countries—around building its own talent pool. Indeed, an industry organization had forecast that Korea's chip workforce needs would grow from 177,000 in 2021 to 304,000 by 2031. Accordingly, the government detailed plans to train over 150,000 engineers over the coming ten years through university programs and private-led "semiconductor academies." The government will also establish a public-private R&D consortium modeled on the US Semiconductor Research Corporation (dubbed the "Korean SRC") with ₩350 billion appropriated over the next ten years to train talented master's and PhD students in the field.[49]

In August 2022, Yoon pardoned Samsung vice chairman Jay Y. Lee—the de facto head of the Samsung group who had been convicted in early 2017 for bribery—to help overcome a "national economic crisis." So concerned was Korea with its chip supply chains that while on parole, Lee had been allowed to be present in a May 2022 meeting between Yoon and President Biden on Samsung's Pyeongtaek campus and to meet the Netherlands' powerful ASML CEO, Peter Wennink, regarding chip manufacturing equipment.[50]

Korea's Production and Consumption

Semiconductors are a major industry in Korea, accounting for 9.6 percent of manufacturing in the country and 17.3 percent of Korean exports in 2019.[51] In total, Korea's firms now produce 18.4 percent of global chips, which are being manufactured in some of the world's most advanced fabs.

In particular, Korea's firms were able to bootstrap themselves into the memory chip industry, starting in the 1980s with the help of short-term Japanese business partnerships. Because large Korean conglomerates, such as Samsung, had the financial resources to undertake the necessary investments, they became industry leaders. SK hynix, for example, was created in 2012 when the SK conglomerate invested in Hyundai's memory business, which had been struggling since the 2008 financial crisis.[52] By 2019, Korea's two largest chip producers, Samsung and SK hynix, accounted for nearly 60 percent of global memory chip production.[53]

Memory production features strong economies of scale because one chip design that meets industry standards can be replicated over and over. Because similar parts from different producers are nearly interchangeable, memory chips are considered a near commodity, with commodity-like rises and declines in profitability as the global economy fluctuates.

Logic chips, on the other hand, require a more application-specific approach, often customized to each particular end product. This specialization requires a very different set of skills compared to those for memory, ranging from design to marketing. Despite numerous attempts over the years to cultivate the logic business, however, Korea's firms have remained relatively minor players, with only about 3 percent of the global market for digital logic chips in 2019. Even Korea's auto sector relies mostly on imported chips—Korea's chip imports in 2020 were worth about $50 billion, roughly 11 percent of global chip production.[54]

Samsung is, of course, an exception. It began offering foundry services using its advanced processes in 2005, and has attracted major customers such as Apple and Qualcomm. Korea is the world's second-largest foundry provider, with a roughly 20 percent market share.[55] Even so, Samsung has struggled in recent years to keep pace with TSMC in advanced-logic chips: low yields at Samsung's 3nm and 4nm foundries have driven chip designer Qualcomm to shift production of its leading-edge chips entirely to TSMC, which now commands around a 50 percent market share.[56]

As in Japan, Korea's chip sector is dominated by large commercial groups, with fewer new startups. One consequence is a near absence of fabless chip design firms (apart from a recent spin-off firm called LX Semicon). One purpose of the country's "K-Chip Belt" strategy, mentioned above, is therefore to create a more supportive ecosystem for startups.

Finally, while Korea has hundreds of firms in its semiconductor supply chain, it is still dependent on imports for many chip manufacturing inputs. For example, its only wafer supplier, SK Siltron, accounts for only about 10 percent of the world's supply. And for materials overall, the market share of Korea suppliers was 16 percent as of 2019, while Korea firms accounted for only 4 percent of chipmaking equipment, 11 percent of chip assembly activity, and a negligible portion of chip design software (EDA).[57]

Diplomatic Trends and Issues

Unlike Japan, which has been more amenable to embracing the opportunities to partner with the United States, Korea has been more wary of teaming up with the United States, especially given concerns over competition for market share. In memory chips, Micron arguably overtook Samsung and SK hynix in technology (with its 176-layer NAND and 1-alpha DRAM chips) and in profit margins in 2021. And since Intel is now attempting to catch up to Samsung in chip manufacturing, there are some competitive issues that make collaboration more difficult.[58] As noted in the discussion in chapter 3 on improving global supply chain information, the United States triggered controversy when it requested supply chain data from Korea's chipmakers, who feared that such data could be used for commercial advantage.[59]

Korea has also been unwilling to fully endorse various US efforts to counter China because the latter absorbs about a third of Korea's exports.[60] Korea's chip firms have also invested billions of dollars in China-based manufacturing, which accounts for a substantial share of their output. For example, SK hynix opened a major DRAM fab in Wuxi in 2006 (initially a joint venture with Europe's STMicroelectronics, which SK hynix later bought out) that now produces 47 percent of SK hynix's DRAM memory chips. At the same time, Samsung has a flash memory fab in Xi'an that produces 42 percent of Samsung's total NAND Flash output.

Making the US-Korea chips ecology even more complex, in November 2021 the United States prevented SK hynix from importing ASML's extreme ultraviolet (EUV) machines to upgrade its Wuxi plant because of concerns that the technology could be used to benefit China's military.[61] Although the companies have not made official statements, SK hynix and Samsung officials are worried that further export controls by the Biden administration could hurt their operations in China while effectively advantaging their American memory chip rival, Micron, whose only manufacturing in China is for module assembly.[62] To ease this concern, the Biden administration's October 2022 export controls included preemptive one-year licenses for Samsung's and SK hynix's memory operations in China. After one year, however, both firms will need a "plan B" unless further exemptions are forthcoming.[63]

To be sure, some progress has been made between the United States and Korea. In December 2021, the two nations held the first (virtual) meeting of a new Semiconductor Partnership Dialogue to deepen ties in technology development, personnel exchanges, and investment.[64] And President Yoon has been in favor of a broader "technological alliance" with the United States, including in the semiconductor sector. Unlike his predecessor Moon Jae-in, Yoon has been much more closely aligned with the United States on security issues: he abandoned Moon's "three noes" policy with China, became the first South Korean president to attend a NATO summit, embraced the Indo-Pacific Economic Framework for Prosperity (IPEF),[65] and has even expressed interest in joining the "Quad" of the United States, Australia, India, and Japan. Just after taking office, he met President Biden at the Samsung Pyeongtaek semiconductor complex, where they pledged the continuation of the Semiconductor Partnership Dialogue and a "global comprehensive strategic alliance."[66]

Korea's large semiconductor firms have largely followed Yoon's footsteps in partnering with the United States. As described in chapter 3, in November 2021 Samsung announced a $17 billion fab in Taylor, Texas, near its existing US manufacturing facility in Austin. In July, Samsung followed up with plans to build as many as ten more fabs between Taylor and Austin over the next twenty years, for a total of $200 billion in investments.[67] In the same month, SK hynix committed $15 billion from its next round of investment in the United States to benefit its semiconductor ecosystem, including R&D collaboration with universities, investment in materials, and "restoration" of advanced-chip packaging.[68]

Even so, Korea has been more wary in committing to the March 2022 US proposal for a "Chip 4" alliance that would bring together the United States, Japan, Korea, and Taiwan. The issue, of course, has attracted the attention of China, which still needs its fabs from Korea to pursue self-sufficiency.[69] And, when editorials in China's *Global Times* warned of unspecified "countermeasures against South Korea" if Korea sides with the United States, Seoul was listening. In early August, Korea finally agreed to participate in the preliminary US meeting, but insisted that the group be called a "consultative body" not aimed at excluding China.[70] Other suggested regional foreign policy moves by Korea included Foreign Minister Park Jin's meeting with Chinese foreign minister Wang Yi in August of that same year (amid China's live-fire drills in the Taiwan Strait), as well as the snubbing of US House Speaker Nancy Pelosi when President Yoon failed to meet with her during her visit to Korea earlier that month.[71]

For Korea, the trade-off between cooperating with the United States or with China appears to be, as one semiconductor official put it, a competition between technology versus markets.[72] A researcher at the Korea Institute of Industrial Economics and Trade (KIET), a government-funded research operation, said that "receiving US support is very important [for Korea] in terms of building a high-level chip ecosystem from wafer fabrication to software and semiconductor equipment," and "it's very possible for the United States to grant access for the use of US technologies exclusively to its allies."[73] On the other hand, Korea has fabs in China, even though it has to be careful to monitor for technology leaks by tracking its chip engineers' travels as part of its intellectual property protection strategy.[74]

Potential technology benefits for Korea also extend to partnerships with Japan and the Netherlands. Top semiconductor equipment companies from those countries have set up or recently expanded R&D centers in Gyeonggi province.[75] A KIET report warns, however, that Western partnership upsides for Korea could be short-lived. Written in July 2022, it alleges that the United States and European Union (EU) are using Korea as crutches to increase domestic production and fade out reliance on Taiwan (and Asia at large) in the long run. And unlike the United States and Japan—which maintain advantages in fabless design and chip materials, respectively—Korea's industry profitability, which is based on commodity memory production, is expected to deteriorate around 2025 due to an oversupply of chips.[76]

Finally, President Yoon's administration has emphasized rekindling better relations with Japan, which could aid a strong trilateral partnership with the United States. Japanese and Korean foreign ministers met often throughout 2022, while Biden, Yoon, and Kishida also held a trilateral meeting at the NATO summit in late June of 2022. And in a March 2023 Korean independence day speech, Yoon declared, "Japan has transformed from a militaristic aggressor of the past into a partner that shares the same universal values with us."[77] To be sure, President Yoon will have to balance his desire to improve relations with Japan with his low domestic approval ratings and the opposition-led National Assembly.[78]

Europe

Key Laws and Policies

Commercial activities of the semiconductor industry in Europe and the EU, much like those in the United States, were not a policy priority until the pandemic-era chip shortage. Before then, government support in Europe had been directed primarily toward research projects.

In 2014, for example, the European Commission (EC)—the executive body of the EU—launched the research-oriented Electronic Components and Systems for European Leadership (ECSEL) initiative. From 2014 to 2020, €2.4 billion (roughly $2.7 billion at 2020 exchange rates) in public spending was split equally between the Commission itself and EU member states. Funding was matched by industry, research organizations, and universities to support research in areas such as CMOS (complementary metal-oxide semiconductor) technology, digital-analog mixed-signal and sensor technologies, power technologies, and fully depleted silicon-on-insulator (FDSOI) process technology that could be an alternative to conventional CMOS chip architectures for low-power devices.[79]

The ECSEL was renewed in 2021 for another six years under the auspices of the Key Digital Technologies Joint Undertaking (KDTJU), with €1.8 billion in additional funding from the EU's Horizon Europe research program and comparable amounts from member states and private industry.[80] And if the EU Chips Act (discussed below) is also enacted as originally proposed in February 2022, the KDTJU will become the Chips Joint Undertaking.

In 2018 came the start of a program called the Important Projects of Common European Interest (IPCEI) on microelectronics, another part of the European Union's push for greater "component sovereignty" in key domains such as defense, aerospace, and critical infrastructure.[81] The program involves thirty-two companies and research organizations from France, Germany, Italy, Austria, and the United Kingdom working across five technology fields: energy-efficient chips, power semiconductors, sensors, advanced optical equipment, and compound materials.[82] But IPCEI funding can finance only pilot production lines, not high-volume fabs. Moreover, its funding stems from the participating countries themselves, not the EU budget. Despite these program limitations, however, IPCEI supported the development of Bosch's 300mm fab, inaugurated in June 2021 in Germany, providing €200 million of an initial €1 billion investment.[83]

But while the EU has supported research, it has done less to stimulate high-volume production. Political attitudes are now shifting. In particular, technological "sovereignty" has become an issue. In recognition of the changing global landscape, the Commission has set an ambitious goal of accounting for 20 percent of global chip production by 2030, double its current level.[84]

Europe has work to do to attract foreign commercial interest. In 2021, Thierry Breton, the European Commissioner for the Internal Market, met with Intel, TSMC, and Samsung to discuss possible fab investments.[85] While Intel was clearly interested, Samsung made no public announcement, and TSMC let it be known it was not planning any Europe investment.[86]

In early 2022 the Commission proposed a European Chips Act, featuring €43 billion (about $45.2 billion) in spending. The European Parliament and member states, following extensive debate, provisionally agreed to the Act in April 2023.[87] The compromise agreement is split across three "pillars," and expected sources of funding are mixed: the Paris-based Institut Montaigne estimates that roughly €7 billion may come from existing EU semiconductor-related R&D funds such as Horizon Europe.[88] The remainder, including any money for building fabs, will have to come from national governments and private investment.

While the EU Chips Act aims to facilitate funding for large-scale manufacturing, fabs must still qualify as a "first-of-a-kind" facility in the EU in some product dimension (such as technology node or substrate material) and have a "funding gap" such that they would not be commercially viable without state aid.[89] But at least two projects appear likely to benefit if a package of state aid can be put together by Germany and approved by the Commission: an expansion by GlobalFoundries in Dresden and two new factories from Intel in Magdeburg. In September 2021, the German economy minister announced a €3 billion plan to stimulate production all along the microelectronics value chain.[90] Intel, meanwhile, was hoping for subsidies of €8 billion for its new investment plan, and it is reportedly asking for billions more by 2023, noting that its costs of doing business in Europe are rising.[91]

The Act also introduces tools for anticipating and responding to semiconductor shortages. These include a European Semiconductor Board with member-state representatives engaging in information sharing on interlocking supply chains. In addition, the Act empowers the Commission to impose "priority-rated orders" on facilities that benefit from subsidies and to act as a "central purchasing body" for "public procurement" on behalf of member states when crises arise.[92]

Europe's Production and Consumption

Since the late 1990s, Europe has been home to three large chip producers— STMicroelectronics, Infineon, and NXP—all of which were spun off from diversified electronics producers in France, Germany, and the Netherlands. They all produce chips primarily with specialty processes that give them some differentiation, and they are leaders in the fields of microcontrollers, sensors, and power electronics; they work closely with EU industrial firms, especially in the automotive sector. None of their fabs, however, are at the cutting edge of chip manufacturing technology. Since roughly 2015, the value of their production has rested at less than 10 percent of global chip output.[93]

Europe is also home to smaller specialty chip producers, such as Germany's Bosch (an auto industry supplier) and at least one contract foundry (meaning it produces chips for chip design specialists). The foundry, X-FAB, has plants in France, Germany, Malaysia, and the United States. Other fabs in Europe are foreign owned, including the Germany-based foundry fabs of GlobalFoundries and an Italian foundry fab known as LFoundry that, since 2019, has belonged to a China-based company, Wuxi Xichanweixin Semiconductor. Its most advanced production process is 110nm, suitable for analog applications.[94]

The most advanced chip production in the EU takes place at Intel's fab in Ireland, where Intel has invested more than €30 billion since 1989. The fab currently produces 14nm semiconductors. In March 2022, Intel announced that it would invest an additional $36 billion in Europe, including a major expansion of its Ireland fab and two new fabs in Germany.[95]

Europe accounts for about 20 percent of global sales of semiconductor manufacturing equipment. Its crown jewel is the Netherlands' ASML, which makes deep ultraviolet (DUV) and extreme ultraviolet (EUV) chip lithography equipment. Because ASML is the only producer in the world that can produce EUV lithography machines able to make chips at the smallest dimensions (5nm or below), cooperation by the Netherlands with the US embargo on exporting dual-use technology to China has been critical in preventing China chip producers from upgrading to the latest manufacturing processes. Today, ASML's only customers for EUV machines are Samsung and SK hynix in Korea, Intel in the United States, and TSMC in Taiwan. The first commercial application of ASML's EUV technology in the European Union will be at the fab Intel is expanding in Ireland.

European companies produce about 30 percent of nonwafer manufacturing supplies and inputs worldwide. Germany's BASF, the world's largest chemicals producer, is among the top five suppliers of materials to the chip industry.

Europe has recently taken an important place in chip design software. With its 2017 acquisition of the US firm Mentor Graphics, Germany's industrial giant Siemens became one of the top three providers of EDA (chip design) software, accounting for about 25 percent of global sales in this category.

Europe is also home to three leading research centers for nanoelectronics: imec (Belgium), CEA-Leti (France), and Fraunhofer (Germany). Each of these works extensively with international partners from industry and academia—including partners from China.

Europe has relatively few fabless (design-only) chip firms—accounting for only about 3 percent of the global total. For example, ARM (United Kingdom) is the developer of the processor IP core at the heart of most smartphones worldwide. As described in the discussion of industry and technology trends in chapter 2, ARM's IP core is a proprietary chip architecture that ARM licenses to other firms to speed their chip design process, provide access to the ARM ecosystem, and ensure product compatibility. ARM was a listed British company until Japan's SoftBank acquired it in 2016. SoftBank had sought to sell ARM to US-based Nvidia, but regulatory hurdles have complicated that effort, and in March 2023 Softbank announced its intention to relist ARM, this time in New York.

Notably, Europe has no significant chip assembly, test, and packaging sector, so complete chip supply chains invariably flow outside the continent.

On the consumption side, the greater Europe region (Europe, Middle East, and Africa, or EMEA) accounts for roughly 10 percent of global chip demand by systems integrators/original equipment manufacturers (OEMs). The largest sector by value is automobiles, and EMEA accounts for nearly a third of the world's auto chip demand. EMEA demand for general computing chips is nearly as large in value, but its demand is only about 6 percent of the world's total. Next-largest is EMEA chip demand for military and industrial uses; Europe accounts for about 20 percent of world demand. The EMEA region does not account for significant shares of the chip industry's other main markets in the consumer and communications sectors.

Diplomatic Trends and Issues

The European Union has become increasingly aware of China as a potential national security threat. A 2019 report by the European Parliament noted "the need for a common multi-pronged policy response to the systemic competition between the EU's market-based and China's state-capitalist economic models."[96] At the same time, that document forecasted the inevitability of continued engagement, calling China "a cooperation partner, a negotiating partner, an economic competitor, and a systemic rival." There is, of course, an unresolved contradiction implicit in this formulation.

The European Union has so far maintained a high-level dialogue with China on cooperation in the sciences and technology.[97] Even so, a high-level diplomatic summit between China and the EU in April 2022 brought out more areas of disagreement than cooperation.[98]

China's diplomatic support for Russia despite the latter's invasion of Ukraine has put new strain on the relationship. In a March 2023 speech, European Commission President Ursula von der Leyen characterized China as seeking "systemic change of the international order with China at its center."[99] She indicated that the EU is no longer trying to revive its Comprehensive Agreement on Investment with China, and that any military support for Russia would further degrade the relationship.

While the European Union once sought to avoid appearing to be too close to the United States in its efforts to counter China's expansion, it has since demonstrated a growing desire to cooperate. In December 2020, the EU proposed an EU-US Trade and Technology Council (TTC) as part of a revitalized transatlantic partnership,[100] and in June 2021 the US and EU announced the formation of that council, consisting of ten working groups, including ones for technology standards, secure supply chains, and ICT competitiveness.[101] A second Ministerial Meeting was held in May 2022, after which Thierry Breton, EU commissioner for internal markets, referred to "a joint ambition to strengthen supply chain resilience in other areas, from raw materials to semiconductors."[102] It will be important to watch for concrete follow-on coordination from this body given its rhetorical ambitions, especially after French president Macron and EC president von der Leyen's trip to China in April 2023.

Notably, the European Union and its member states, while having no formal relations with Taiwan (except for the Vatican), have recently stepped up their support through parliamentarian visits and by adding Taiwan to their Indo-Pacific strategy as an economic and political partner. In December 2021, the European Parliament adopted its first-ever stand-alone report on expanding EU-Taiwan relations. Lithuania opened a de facto Taiwan embassy in November 2021; Taiwan reciprocated by setting up a $200 million investment fund for semiconductors and biotechnology in Lithuania, as well as a $1 billion credit fund.[103] And in early June of 2022, Taiwan and the European Union strengthened ties by elevating talks on semiconductor collaboration in research and supply chain monitoring from the deputy ministerial level.

Although TSMC in 2022 denied it had plans for a fab in the EU, Taiwan nonetheless was still eager to develop an institutionalized partnership that could promote future investments in Europe.[104] One ongoing challenge to Europe's advanced-semiconductor manufacturing ambitions may be a lack of anchor customers—such as a major integrated smartphone OEM like Apple or a major chip designer like Qualcomm—that would motivate suppliers to colocate in the region.

Europe think tanks have recommended that the EU forge similar bilateral partnerships with other partners such as Japan, South Korea, and Singapore. Institut Montaigne, a think tank in France with large corporate sponsorship, observed that semiconductor alliances are important for early warnings of supply chain problems and can serve as part of a "Western counteroffensive playbook" against aggression.[105]

Southeast Asia

Southeast Asia has an important role in the semiconductor industry: it is the main destination for assembly, testing, and packaging (ATP) by multinational chip firms as well as outsourced semiconductor assembly and test (OSAT) firms. ATP, which makes up 13 percent of total global semiconductor industry capital expenditures and 6 percent of value added, is less capital-intensive than fabrication. OSAT capital expenditures are typically around 15 percent of their total revenues, compared to foundry companies' 35 percent capital expenditure share. Here, the region's cheaper labor costs (up to 80 percent below US levels) create a competitive advantage.[106] More advanced packaging processes—often colocated with chip fabbing itself—have become a critical part of overall chip performance and energy efficiency. Meanwhile, the traditional OSAT markets in Singapore and Malaysia have declined in the past ten years, with foreign investments and domestic firms diversifying into other parts of the value chain.[107]

With overseas firms looking to diversify their manufacturing bases outside of China, Southeast Asia nations have experienced tremendous growth in foreign investments. Although the region offers possible incentives to bypass Western export controls to China while also remaining close to Chinese customers, so far there has been little formal presence of outbound semiconductor investment from China in the region.[108] The development of multilateral trade agreements—such as the China-driven Regional Comprehensive Economic Partnership (RCEP), Japan-driven Comprehensive and Progressive Agreement for Trans-Pacific Partnership (CPTPP), and US-driven Indo-Pacific Economic Framework for Prosperity (IPEF)—may further stimulate investment and the region's involvement in semiconductor supply chains.

Although attitudes across the region are varied, a common refrain heard in the capitals of Southeast Asia countries is: "Don't make us choose between the United States and China." For example, in a recent survey of government, business, and academic leaders in the region, the majority of respondents from Malaysia (57 percent), Singapore (78 percent), and Vietnam (74 percent) believed that Southeast Asia should align with the United States if it had to choose between it and China (with 54 percent overall).[109] At the same time, however, in the same survey China was voted as the most influential economic, political, and strategic power in the region.[110] Interestingly, views in Malaysia and Singapore today favoring alignment with the United States have risen around 20 percentage points from 2020, with Malaysia virtually flipping sides.[111] Commentators in Malaysia, Singapore, and Vietnam believe that the US-China trade war will promote investment and growth in their semiconductor industries, with Malaysia (and possibly Singapore) indicating a growing interest in collaborating with the United States on semiconductors.

Malaysia

Industry and Policy

Although Malaysia has some fabs, its semiconductor activity has been dominated by assembly and testing. A foundry fab opened on the island of Borneo in the late 1990s, but since 2006 it has been owned by Europe-based X-FAB. It currently employs mature node processes down to 130nm.[112] SilTerra, an independent foundry that opened around the same time in a high-tech zone near Penang, was owned by a state-affiliated fund but was sold in 2021 to private Malaysian and Chinese capital; its most advanced node is at 110nm.[113] In 2006, Germany's Infineon opened a fab in Malaysia for power management chip production; and in 2022, Infineon announced an additional €2 billion for its third manufacturing line in wide-bandgap (silicon carbide and gallium nitride) semiconductors.[114]

Malaysia accounts for over 13 percent of the global OSAT market, with approximately 7 percent of the total global semiconductor trade flowing through the country.[115] Eighty percent of Malaysia's back-end output is concentrated in the island state of Penang, dubbed "the Silicon Valley of the East," which has been active in the industry for over fifty years.[116] While the industry has largely been dominated by the "big four" OSAT firms (Amkor Technology, STATS ChipPAC, Siliconware Precision Industries, and ASE Global), domestic automated test manufacturing (ATE) firms have grown rapidly and are catching up in terms of combined market capitalization.[117]

Many multinational electronics firms that consume semiconductors are also present. Over just the past two years, Malaysia has approved a record amount of foreign direct investment (FDI), mainly led by the electrical and electronics sector. In 2021, the country approved ninety-four such projects worth 148 billion Malaysian ringgit (RM)

($35.7 billion) and associated with over twenty-eight thousand jobs.[118] Sectoral exports rose by 18 percent to reach RM 456 billion in 2021, generating 56 percent of Malaysia's trade surplus.[119]

FDI projects include Intel's investment of RM 30 billion ($7.1 billion) over the next ten years into a new packaging and test facility, which is set to create over four thousand jobs at an Intel subsidiary that operates in Penang and in Kedah state. Nexperia, a Netherlands-based firm now owned by China's Wingtech, is investing RM 1.6 billion by 2026 to build automated production facilities for power-management semiconductors used in cars. Other recent investments are wide-ranging, including materials and components, front- and back-end manufacturing, and contract manufacturing from firms based in Austria, Germany, Japan, Taiwan, the United States, and China. Multinational corporations receive tax breaks and are perceived favorably by local enterprises.[120]

With investments pouring in, one concern in Malaysia is its tightening labor market. The Malaysia Semiconductor Industry Association (MSIA) reported that, with plants operating below capacity and threatening the country's competitiveness, its members need thirty thousand new trained workers immediately. To ease the labor shortage, the government lifted its freeze on foreign workers in August of 2022 and deferred a condition that at least 80 percent of electronics sector company workers must be Malaysian.[121]

Relations with the United States

Given Malaysia's key role in the back end of the chip manufacturing chain, the United States relies on Malaysia for a stable semiconductor supply.[122] While Malaysia's top import and export partner is China, the United States was Malaysia's number-three destination for exports, and in 2021 it accounted for the highest level of FDI at RM 15.6 billion, compared to China's RM 1.8 billion.[123]

In May 2022, US Secretary of Commerce Gina Raimondo and Malaysia's Senior Minister for International Trade and Industry Mohamed Azmin Ali signed the US-Malaysia Memorandum of Cooperation on Semiconductor Supply Chain Resilience. The memorandum included "guiding principles" to strengthen government-industry partnerships and to promote investments in the supply chain. No monetary commitments were made.[124]

Malaysia's industry views itself as well positioned in the current geopolitical arena. Malaysia Semiconductor Industry Association president Dato' Seri Wong Siew Hai sees China-Taiwan tensions benefiting Malaysia as countries look to manufacture more in Southeast Asia countries to mitigate risks.[125] He also believes that new leading-edge fabs operating in the United States following CHIPS Act funding will stimulate assembly investments in Malaysia, although he also expressed concern that the 15 percent global minimum tax reforms slated for 2023 may dampen such incentives. Malaysia's economists also fear that supply chain disruptions—which may occur given deeper US export controls or sanctions on People's Republic of China (PRC)-based firms, or direct conflict in the Pacific—could slow down growth and outweigh such benefits.[126]

Singapore

Industry and Policies

Singapore accounts for 11 percent of the global semiconductor market and 5 percent of global wafer fabrication capacity. It also holds a 19 percent share of semiconductor manufacturing equipment, including some lithography systems.[127] Since the 1990s, the country has developed four wafer fab parks via the JTC Corporation, a government agency employing over 13,500 people. Its twenty-one wafer plants represent Southeast Asia's most important semiconductor manufacturing base, with fourteen global semiconductor firms employing 18,600 workers.[128] Notably, they are home to Micron's new 176-layer NAND memory chip production, with Micron having invested a total of $15 billion in the country.[129] Other US firms, such as GlobalFoundries (which acquired a Singapore-owned foundry in 2009), also operate in the parks; together they compose Singapore's 18.3 percent share of US-headquartered firms' chip manufacturing capacity in 2021, which was the largest overseas share—even higher than Taiwan's 9.7 percent.[130]

Semiconductor manufacturing has a large presence in Singapore's economy, accounting for 80 percent of electronics sector output and 7 percent of Singapore's gross domestic product (GDP).[131] Singapore's appeal to overseas firms has been its high-skilled workers, modern infrastructure, and favorable tax and regulation policies. Currently, the Singapore government's semiconductor strategy is under its "Manufacturing 2030" vision, which includes a target to grow the country's overall manufacturing industry by 50 percent by 2030.[132] Both Singapore's Ministry of Trade and Industry and the Singapore Semiconductor Industry Association have launched various initiatives to attract and train talent, and two thousand new semiconductor jobs are expected in the next three to five years.[133]

Much of that manufacturing growth is expected to come from foreign investments, in which China is anticipated to have little direct presence. Of the $8.77 billion in manufacturing investments in 2021—42.3 percent of which was for the electronics sector overall—US firms contributed 67.1 percent, compared to China's 1.1 percent. In semiconductors, US/UAE GlobalFoundries announced a $4 billion investment to raise their Singapore production capacity to 1.5 million 300mm wafers annually by early 2024.[134] Other investments include plans by Germany's Infineon to make Singapore its AI innovation hub, Taiwan UMC's $5 billion fab for 22nm and 28nm logic chips, and a joint venture by Germany's Siltronic AG and South Korea's Samsung to build a €2 billion 300mm wafer plant.[135]

Singapore's success in luring foreign investment comes in part from cheap fab operating costs. According to a 2020 Boston Consulting Group report, when estimating ten-year total costs of operation of advanced-memory fabs, with the United States indexed to 100, Singapore came in at a score of 79—higher than China's 73 but lower than Japan's 99 and South Korea's 81.[136] In addition to tax breaks and subsidies for development and land procurement, infrastructure investments into centralized parks and economic zones have lowered the cost of business and shortened construction timelines. Such incentives arguably prompted GlobalFoundries to direct its 2021 investment to Singapore rather than its home, New York. The CHIPS Act, however, may shift the tide back toward reshoring.[137]

Singapore has also historically invested in R&D. The Agency for Science, Technology and Research (A*STAR), established in 1991, conducts joint research programs that include microelectronics with global companies. A*STAR's R&D budget has steadily increased: in 2020 it was allocated $25 billion, a 30 percent increase from the previous iteration.[138] And in December 2021, Applied Materials and A*STAR's Institute of Microelectronics announced a $210 million investment to extend joint research on 3D chip packaging.[139]

Relations with the United States

Singapore has been not only a vital economic partner to the United States but also a security partner—buying US weapons systems and participating in joint training exercises. Even so, Singapore has also had close economic and cultural ties to China and has seen itself at the intersection of these two contending powers. Recently, for example, although Singapore condemned Russia's invasion of Ukraine and imposed sanctions on Moscow, Prime Minister Lee Hsien Loong made explicit that the country was not aligning itself with US stances per se. While visiting the United States in March of 2022 and encouraging US engagement in Southeast Asia, Lee also emphasized that the United States should "give [China] some space to influence the global system" and build trust for cooperation.[140]

So, while Singapore is an important home to US firms' semiconductor manufacturing (especially with Micron's Singapore production base there), China is still its biggest import and export destination (the United States ranks fourth and third, respectively), making Singapore loath to overtly offend China.[141]

Vietnam

Industry and Policies

Compared to Malaysia and Singapore, Vietnam is a relative newcomer to the semiconductor industry. In 2009, the government began investing in semiconductors and set up research and education centers, semiconductor development programs, and labs at its new high-tech parks, catalyzing rapid growth.[142] In fact, between 2000 and 2019 Vietnam had the fastest growth in electric component exports in Southeast Asia, with a compound annual growth rate of 25.5 percent (followed by the Philippines at 7.4 percent and Malaysia at 5.9 percent).[143]

Because of its lower labor costs, Vietnam has attracted substantial foreign investment in back-end ATP. For example, Intel currently houses its largest assembly and testing plant in the country: it invested $1 billion in 2006 and another $475 million in 2021. Other firms with research centers and factories in Vietnam include Qualcomm, Texas Instruments, SK hynix, and NXP Semiconductors.[144]

While further investments in education and infrastructure will still be necessary for Vietnam to move up the value chain, firms have already begun expanding investments in semiconductor materials and components. Samsung, Vietnam's largest single foreign direct investor, announced a $3.3 billion investment to expand its "flip-chip ball grid array" packaging facility by July 2023. South Korea's Amkor plans to invest $1.6 billion for advanced packaging technology. And US OEM supplier Hayward Quartz announced plans to produce chip materials in a new $110 million factory.[145] While Vietnam's indigenous chip industry remains relatively immature, it hosts a growing ecosystem of around twenty domestic chip design firms.[146] Moreover, investment in the semiconductor industry is being incentivized by a zero percent corporate income tax for the first four years, followed by a 5 percent rate during the next nine years and a 10 percent rate over the following fifteen years—as opposed to a standard rate of 20 percent. In addition, semiconductor industrial parks fund 10 to 15 percent of training costs for companies operating within them.[147]

Unlike in other Southeast Asia countries, however, there is notably little US investment in Vietnam. In both 2020 and 2021, Singapore and South Korea topped the list, followed by China, Japan, and Taiwan.[148] Vietnam's biggest export destination overall is the United States (China is second)—though China is Vietnam's largest import partner by far, reflecting its current role as a supply chain intermediary between the two superpowers.[149]

India

Key Laws and Policies

For decades, India's chip sector was treated clumsily by government policy. India's underdeveloped infrastructure poses significant hurdles for fabrication facilities, which need reliable water, electricity, and transportation—services that Delhi has primarily left to state-level governments. Moreover, historical efforts (including import bans) to ensure that India's electronics OEMs would use only India-produced chips essentially resulted in the development of neither electronics firms nor chip producers.[150] Several private fab projects were floated during the 2000s, with support offered by the states involved—but none made it anywhere near production.[151] Similarly, when the central government announced a fab subsidy program in 2007, only one proposal was submitted, and the project stalled within a year. A renewed government effort in 2011 generated a round of nearly a dozen proposals, of which two were selected for support; both of those plans also failed.[152]

In 2020, alongside a suite of manufacturing-oriented production-linked incentives (PLIs) from the government of Prime Minister Narendra Modi, the central government announced the Scheme for Promotion of Manufacturing of Electronic Components and Semiconductors (SPECS).[153] SPECS offers a 25 percent subsidy on capital costs (excluding building construction).

In December 2021, the Indian cabinet approved a budget of ₹760 billion (about $9 billion) over six years in an ambitious effort to support semiconductor fabrication and assembly (as well as flat-panel display manufacturing).[154] Fabs targeting 28nm-or-less process nodes can receive grants for up to 50 percent of their total capital cost, with support sliding to 30 percent if the targeted process is 45nm to 65nm.[155] Fabs for sensors and other specialty products, as well as chip assembly plants, can also receive a 30 percent subsidy. A separate "design-linked incentive" offered up to 50 percent of covered expenses for the development of new chip designs. These incentives—part of the Program for Development of Semiconductor and Display Manufacturing Ecosystem—are administered by a newly created India Semiconductor Mission.[156]

India's Production and Consumption

India has one integrated circuit fab: the Semi-Conductor Laboratory, a 150mm-wafer fab started in the 1980s that designs and manufactures application-specific chips for India's telecom and space sectors.[157] Its most recent process upgrade was to a 180nm process node. Formerly attached to the Department of Space and the Ministry of Electronics and Information Technology (MeitY), the lab is being converted to a research institute under the India Semiconductor Mission.

Given this shallow base of experience, India's semiconductor manufacturing plans must rely on firms moving into the semiconductor space; industry investment grant proposals are evaluated by a bureaucracy that has similarly limited sectoral experience. Perhaps the most ambitious applicant for a subsidy to build a fab under the government's new scheme was a business group called Vedanta Resources, in partnership with Foxconn (Hon Hai), the Taiwan firm best known in India for its iPhone assembly facilities. A minority partner in the venture, Foxconn is seeking to diversify into chip production for the first time, including through the acquisition of intellectual property for 65nm-to-28nm logic chip production that could be used for domestic market smartphones, consumer electronics, and the auto sector.[158] In September 2022, Vedanta and Foxconn announced a planned investment of ₹1.54 trillion ($20 billion) in the state of Gujarat, pending award of government incentives, declaring that the deal would further India's goals to build a domestic, self-reliant "Silicon Valley" that would be less dependent on China.[159] In part, Gujarat was likely chosen instead of the more likely Maharashtra because of valuable land-related incentives, which beat out Maharashtra's offer of a 30 percent capital subsidy and a power tariff subsidy.[160]

Another applicant for the semiconductor fabrication incentives was ISMC, a joint venture between an Abu Dhabi–based venture fund and

Israel's Tower Semiconductor, which is in the process of being purchased by Intel. Tower has indicated that its role is limited to providing technology and know-how.[161] The proposed 65nm analog chip fab, in line with Tower's commercial experience, was expected to cost $3 billion—and as of mid-2022, the venture had signed a memorandum of understanding with Karnataka state.[162] Pratap Simha, a member of parliament from Mysuru state, which has also courted the investment, described his interest in terms of the local spillover benefits of infrastructure upgrades required for the plant, as well as the clustering effect from colocation of related electronics sector firms.[163]

In 2022, Sahasra—an Indian company that has historically imported and distributed memory modules—announced its intentions to move upstream and open India's first back-end memory chip ATP facility in Rajasthan, with a total planned investment of $94 million.[164] The plant was to receive support under the government's PLI and SPECS schemes, together with a "customized incentive package approval from [the] state government of Rajasthan."[165]

Despite so much focus on manufacturing, India's real chip strength to date actually lies in chip design, with more than one hundred chip design organizations. Most chip design activity takes place within foreign subsidiaries, including those of the top US and European chip companies. In Bangalore, where the majority of India's design centers are located, about two-thirds of the engineers work in these multinational subsidiaries. The first Indian chip subsidiary was opened by Texas Instruments in 1985, followed by others in the 1990s. While these subsidiaries initially focused only on implementing "back office" aspects of the design process (other aspects were then handed off to workers abroad), over time these domestic contributors have taken on more comprehensive responsibilities.

Many of India's large IT services companies—including Wipro, Tata, and Sasken—have also developed sophisticated chip design capabilities, but their focus remains on the low-margin, design-for-hire services rather than the riskier but potentially lucrative own-product business. Surprisingly, given this degree of human capital, there have been relatively few local spin-offs from multinational chip design activities, and chip design startups in India are still uncommon.

India's business conglomerates are generally respected for their quality of execution in a variety of other industrial and consumer-facing sectors, and they are now attempting to make inroads into the semiconductor industry. In 2021, Tata Sons acquired a majority stake in Tejas Networks, a telecom gear maker.[166] This acquisition was followed by the launch of an automotive-oriented chip design collaboration with the Japan-based firm Renesas, which receives about half of its revenue from carmakers (Tata Motors is the largest manufacturer of electric cars in India, and Japan's government owns 20 percent of Renesas's shares).[167] As of late 2022, Reliance Industries was also reported to be evaluating an investment in one of the three PLI applicant firms.[168]

Human Capital

Indians are now the fastest-growing student group in Taiwan, doubling over the last five years, with a majority pursuing postgraduate degrees. The Taiwan government in turn has offered programs to attract Indian students, including paid internships, scholarships for PhD students, language training, and research fellowships. The Indian and Taiwanese governments have jointly sponsored ten engineering projects since 2008, with each receiving up to $40,000 of funding.[169] And when, in April 2022, the All India Council for Technical Education (AICTE) approved the introduction of two semiconductor-related educational programs in integrated circuit manufacturing and in "electronics engineering for very large scale integration design and technology,"[170] they were paired with the introduction of optional East Asian language courses intended to better equip Indian students to pursue internships in the semiconductor industry in Taiwan and South Korea.[171] Such people-to-people programs have become a foundation for collaboration between India and Taiwan, amidst concurrent shared security concerns—tensions on the India-China border and PRC military exercises around Taiwan.

In August of 2022, the India Electronics and Semiconductor Association also announced a "Semiconductor Nation—Campus Connect" initiative to increase awareness of the semiconductor industry among college students. Targeting both undergraduate and postgraduate students in engineering fields, the program aims to increase the number of electronics students in India entering semiconductor-related industries.[172]

Diplomatic Trends and Issues

India is historically a member of the Non-Aligned Movement (NAM), which was established by a group of developing economies in the 1950s and 1960s when tensions were rising between Russia and the United States. Despite being "non-aligned," India turned to the Soviet Union for military support during its 1971 war with Pakistan. More recently, however, India joined the Quad, a partnership with Australia, Japan, and the United States created in 2007 in response to China's rising power. Even so, India, like many NAM members, abstained from the UN vote to condemn Russia's invasion of Ukraine.

Indians are painfully aware of the tech shadow cast by China, and under Prime Minister Modi, Delhi is pursuing a more aggressive policy of technology self-reliance under the moniker "Make in India," which extends from chips to electronic systems.[173] There is inherent tension in the Self-Reliant India (Atmanirbhar Bharat) policy between isolationism and a recognition of the need to engage with the world economy for needed new technologies and markets. Indeed, India has had a fraught relationship with China since the two fought a war in 1962. China's growing support for Pakistan is unwelcome in India, and tensions over disputed border areas in Ladakh, Bhutan, and Arunachal Pradesh have periodically broken into military conflict. The push by India's government for local production has given further reason to scrutinize dependencies on goods or technologies from China. In particular, India began to pressure China's firms after more than a dozen Indian soldiers died in a clash with Chinese forces at a disputed Himalayan border in 2020. India has, for example, banned hundreds of smartphone apps from China, used unofficial means to effectively bar technology firms

Huawei Technologies and ZTE from selling telecom equipment to its wireless carriers, and investigated the financial reporting of China-based smartphone firms Xiaomi and OPPO. Nevertheless, India's government has not completely written off all investment from China—so long as an investment is seen as enabling India-based value chains.[174]

In contrast, the United States is India's largest trading partner and most important export market.[175] The United States hosts the largest Indian diaspora, numbering over four million people; and roughly one-third of all immigrant-founded startups in the United States have Indian founders. The two governments maintain high-level ties on issues of common interest, including security, energy and climate, and finance. India was one of twelve countries to partner with the United States on IPEF, and both countries recently heralded the launch of a bilateral initiative on Critical and Emerging Technology (iCET), which was focused on long-term cooperation across a variety of technology areas, including semiconductors.[176]

In April 2022, the semiconductor trade associations of the United States and India—SIA and India Electronics and Semiconductor Association (IESA), respectively—signed a memorandum of understanding to identify potential opportunities in the semiconductor sector.[177] Dozens of US chip companies, including Intel and Qualcomm, have long-established design subsidiaries in India, centered in the city of Bangalore.

In April 2022, India and the EU also launched the EU-India Trade and Technology Council to address issues of technology, trade, and security as possible areas of cooperation, including a free-trade agreement and cooperation on 5G wireless and artificial intelligence.[178] This additional collaboration would create a more complete technology ecology with Europe's main chip companies (STMicroelectronics, NXP, and Infineon) that have had chip design and software development subsidiaries in India for over twenty years.

Summarizing India's current strategy, Delhi's envoy to Taiwan, Gourangalal Das, has emphasized the need to solidify India's semiconductor supply chain, noting that India's chip demand is growing at twice the global rate and is projected to reach 10 percent of global demand by 2030. The most credible results of India's efforts are likely to be in production of trailing-edge chips ranging from 65nm to 28nm as well as in back-end ATP. To that end, India's current overall subsidy scheme targets not just chipmaking plants but also the electronic systems industry—firms such as phone assembler Foxconn—and adjacent technology supply chains such as telecom, solar photovoltaics, and batteries.[179] As in the United States, execution and longer-term commercial sustainability in these efforts will be led by the private sector and ultimately depend less on government subsidies than on the competitiveness of the overall business and regulatory environment.

Israel

Key Laws and Policies

While relatively small, Israel's position as a US partner and global technology leader deserves special mention. Since the 1960s, Israel has pursued an industrial policy favoring science-based industry and has incubated an industrial structure composed of small- and medium-sized firms.[180] Israel's military also conducts advanced R&D, which has helped Israel establish a strong talent pipeline to the private sector.

Israel's government has also adopted incentives to persuade multinational technology companies to conduct manufacturing or research in the semiconductor sector—a tradition dating back to Intel's initial research investment in the 1970s. As Intel has invested more, Israel's government has provided tax rebates, grants, and flexibility in planning permissions—and over time, engineers from Intel and other multinationals have spawned a vibrant domestic semiconductor startup sector.

Israel's Production and Consumption

In the 1980s, Intel chose Israel for its first offshore fab. Today, it employs roughly ten thousand employees who work on microprocessor manufacturing and R&D—making Israel Intel's biggest offshore location, and making Intel Israel's largest private employer.[181]

Intel's Fab 28 began operations in the early 2000s and has since been upgraded with the aid of grants and tax breaks from Israel's government. More recently, Intel announced plans to build Fab 38—a 4nm EUV-node production site—in Israel, with operations beginning in 2024.[182] Total investment is expected to be about $10 billion, including as much as $4 billion in grants from Israel's government.[183]

In February 2022, Intel announced that it was acquiring Israel-based Tower Semiconductor for $5.4 billion. Tower provides foundry services for making analog chips and has fabs in Israel, California, Texas, and Japan. In 2017, Tower set up a partnership to build a fab in China, but its partner Tacoma (Nanjing) Semiconductor later went bankrupt, and the project appears to have ended. More recently, Tower has been part of a joint venture proposal to produce analog chips in India.

Israel also has a small but healthy fabless chip design startup ecosystem. Before the COVID-19 pandemic it was adding about a dozen firms a year, with half of their funding coming from Israel sources and about a quarter from US sources.[184] Exit for successful startup firms is often through acquisition by larger multinational firms. Intel, for example, has bought multiple chip startups in Israel. One of its recent acquisitions was Habana Labs, an AI chip designer, which Intel acquired for about $2 billion in December 2019. In 2017, Intel acquired Mobileye, which develops chips and other devices for autonomous driving, for $15.3 billion, the most ever paid for a company based in Israel.

Numerous other technology companies have opened or acquired chip design centers in Israel, including Amazon, Apple, ARM, Microsoft, Nvidia, NXP, Qualcomm, and Samsung. Google opened a design center in 2021, and Facebook is reportedly following suit.[185]

Diplomatic Trends and Issues

Israel has maintained an evolving posture of US strategic alignment, but alongside commercial relationships with China that often include high-tech areas. The degree of technology cooperation with China, however, has been adjusted based upon security considerations. China has reportedly been looking recently to Israel as a potential source of advanced chip design and integration technologies, with Huawei and Xiaomi investing in chip design there.[186] Meanwhile, in the spring of 2023, it was reported that China's financial regulators were slowing their review of

Intel's acquisition of Israel's Tower—a move interpreted to be taken in retaliation for US semiconductor technology export controls on China.[187]

The United States is by far Israel's largest export market (27.7 percent of the total in 2020), with China and Hong Kong a distant second (at 9.1 percent of export value).[188] Nonetheless, semiconductors compose a large part of Israel's exports to China: Israel-based firms sell inspection equipment for chip manufacturing to China-based firms,[189] and Israel's chip exports to China—largely from the Intel subsidiary— rose by 80 percent in 2018 to $2.6 billion.[190]

Under the Trump administration, the United States pressed Israel to further curb China's access to its advanced technologies, as Israel had agreed to do regarding military dual-use technologies during the Clinton administration. In 2019, Israel established a mechanism to vet foreign investment into potentially sensitive industries. Even so, in May 2020, Secretary of State Mike Pompeo warned that engaging with China in sensitive areas such as communications could threaten "the capacity for America to work alongside Israel on important projects."[191]

In this sense, Israel is a symbol of the complex set of conflicting interests that many other American allies, partners, and friends profiled in this chapter are also trying to reconcile. Given every country's increasingly contradictory commercial and strategic imperatives, their abilities to align with the United States in our rapidly changing world will rest not just on the force of arguments on security grounds, but on our ability to offer market and investment alternatives. In that sense, our own economic performance and our openness to business with like-minded partners is key to sustaining our collective national security too.

NOTES

1. Ministry of Economy, Trade, and Industry [経済産業省], "半導体・デジタル産業戦略検討会議 [Semiconductor and Digital Industry Strategy Conference]," August 2, 2022, https://www.meti.go.jp/policy/mono_info_service/joho/conference/semicon_digital.html.

2. Yoichi Funabashi, "地経学時代の経済安全保障論 [Economic Security Theory in the Age of Geoeconomics]," Asia Pacific Initiative, March 9, 2022, https://apinitiative.org/2022/03/09/34746/.

3. Tim Kelly, "Japan Sees Peril in US Chip Hub to Counter China," Reuters, August 17, 2021.

4. Yuki Furukawa and Takashi Mochizuki, "Japan Approves $6.8 Billion Boost for Domestic Chip Industry," *Bloomberg*, November 26, 2021.

5. Sony's share will be less than 20 percent. Another Japanese firm, Denso, has also committed funds and will become a partner at a lower level than Sony.

6. Kioxia, "Kioxia and Western Digital Jointly Invest in New Flash Memory Manufacturing Facility in Yokkaichi Plant," press release, July 26, 2022.

7. Takashi Mochizuki, "Japan Sets Goal of Tripling Domestic Chip Revenue by 2030," *Bloomberg*, November 15, 2021.

8. *Sankei News*, "経済安保推進法が成立　半導体などの供給網強化図る [Economic Security Promotion Law Passed to Strengthen Supply Networks for Semiconductors]," May 11, 2022, https://www.sankei.com/article/20220511 -SH2HDEMUM5NBZKTTZ55TBP5UDQ.

9. *Nikkei Asia*, "Japan to Subsidize TSMC's Kumamoto Plant by up to $3.5bn," June 17, 2022.

10. Ayumi Shintaku, "TSMC to Open Semiconductor R&D Facility in Tsukuba," *Asahi Shimbun*, June 1, 2021.

11. Takumi Wakai and Shimpei Doi, "Japan Set to Offer 92.9 Billion Yen to Kioxia's Joint Chip Plant Project," *Asahi Shimbun*, July 27, 2022.

12. Kioxia Corporation, "Kioxia and Western Digital Celebrate the Opening of Fab7 at Yokkaichi, Japan," press release, October 26, 2022.

13. *Nikkei*, "半導体人材、「厚み」課題 [Semiconductor Human Resources, 'Depth' Issue]," July 22, 2022, https://www.nikkei.com/article/DGKKZO62842330S 2A720C2TB0000.

14. Reuters, "半導体人材、産学官で育成強化 [Strengthening Semiconductor Human Resource Development through Industry-Academia-Government Collaboration]," June 28, 2022, https://www.reuters.com/article/idJP202205 0101000750.

15. Mathieu Duchâtel, "Racing for the New Rice—Japan's Plans for Its Semiconductor Industry," Institut Montaigne, April 8, 2021.

16. Semiconductor Industry Association, *2021 SIA Factbook*.

17. Julian Ryall, "Japan Strengthens Hold on Semiconductor Raw Materials amid Global Chip Shortage," *South China Morning Post*, 2021.

18. Kearney, *Europe's Urgent Need to Invest in a Leading-Edge Semiconductor Ecosystem*, fig. 9, p. 18, 2021.

19. JOGMEC, "ビジネスツールリスト 金属部門の各種支援ツールの紹介 [Business Tool List Introduction to Various Support Tools for the Metals Sector]," June 30, 2020, https://www.jogmec.go.jp/content/300369091.pdf.

20. Asian Development Bank, "Asian Economic Integration Report 2022," p. 27, 2022; also used for other market share statistics in this section.

21. Robert Castellano, "Applied Materials Will Regain Semiconductor Equipment Lead from ASML in 2020," Information Network, SemiWiki, November 29, 2020.

22. Ministry of Economy, Trade, and Industry, "Minister Hagiuda Visits the United States of America," May 6, 2022.

23. US Department of Commerce, "Readout of Secretary Raimondo's Meeting with Minister of Economy, Trade, and Industry Hagiuda Koichi of Japan," May 4, 2022.

24. Ko Fujioka, "Japan Seeks to Produce Cutting-Edge 2-nm Chips as Soon as 2025," *Nikkei Asia*, June 15, 2022.

25. *Nikkei*, "キヤノンなど先端半導体で連携　経産省、420億円支援 [Canon and Others Collaborate on Cutting-Edge Semiconductors; METI Provides ¥42 billion in Support]," March 23, 2021, https://www.nikkei.com/article/DGXZQOD F231RP0T20C21A3000000/.

26. *Kyodo News*, "Japan, US to Deepen Economic Security Ties amid Supply Disruptions," May 23, 2022.

27. *Nikkei*, "日米、経済版2プラス2初開催　半導体量産で協力 [Japan and the US to Hold First Economic Version of 2 Plus 2, Cooperating in Semiconductor Mass Production]," July 29, 2022, https://www.nikkei.com/article/DGXZQOUA 26C540W2A720C2000000.

28. Tomoya Suzuki, "米中・経済安全保障の総点検―規制に挟撃される半導体産業 [US-China Economic Security Review: Semiconductor Industry Pinched by Regulations]," NLI Research Institute, July 16, 2021, https://www.nli -research.co.jp/report/detail/id=68296?pno=2&site=nli.

29. Changwoon Cho, "日米が最先端半導体で協力、韓国の対応は？　米大統領訪韓に注目 [Japan and the US Cooperate in Cutting-Edge Semiconductors; How Will South Korea Respond? Focus on US President's Visit to Korea]," *Nikkei XTech*, May 10, 2022, https://xtech.nikkei.com/atcl/nxt /column/18/01231/00059.

30. Kim Eun-jin, "Japanese Semiconductor Material Companies Increasing Production in South Korea," BusinessKorea, May 4, 2021.

31. Sarah Kim, "Moon Says Japan's Export Curbs Led to Higher Self-Sufficiency," *Korea JoongAng Daily*, July 2, 2021.

32. Jeong-Ho Lee and Yuki Furukawa, "Japan to Lift Restrictions on Chip Material Exports to South Korea," *Bloomberg*, March 15, 2023.

33. Yoichi Funabashi, "地経学時代の経済安全保障論 [Economic Security Theory in the Age of Geoeconomics]," Asia Pacific Initiative, March 9, 2022, https://apinitiative.org/2022/03/09/34746.

34. Funabashi, "地経学時代の経済安全保障論 [Economic Security Theory].

35. Makoto Shiono, "中国ファーウェイ問題を「米国の立場」から見てみるべき理由 [Why We Should Look at the China Huawei Issue from the US Perspective],"

Diamond Online, September 4, 2019, https://diamond.jp/articles/-/213748?page=2.

36. Yoichi Funabashi, "地経学時代の経済安全保障論 [Economic Security Theory in the Age of Geoeconomics]," Asia Pacific Initiative, March 22, 2022, https://apinitiative.org/2022/03/09/34746.

37. Funabashi, "地経学時代の経済安全保障論 [Economic Security Theory]."

38. Natsuki Kamakura, "From Globalising to Regionalising to Reshoring Value Chains? The Case of Japan's Semiconductor Industry," *Cambridge Journal of Regions, Economy and Society* 15, no. 2 (May 2022): 261–77.

39. JETRO, "海外サプライチェーン多元化等支援事業のサービス [Overseas Supply Chain Diversification Support Project]," September 29, 2022.

40. Antonio Varas, Raj Varadarajan, Jimmy Goodrich, and Falan Yinug, *Strengthening the Global Semiconductor Supply Chain in an Uncertain Era* (Boston, MA: Boston Consulting Group and Semiconductor Industry Association, April 2021).

41. InvestKorea, "Semiconductor Industry Driving Korea's Economic Growth," September 8, 2021.

42. InvestKorea, "Semiconductor Industry Driving Korea's Economic Growth."

43. Sohee Kim and Sam Kim, "Korea Unveils $450 Billion Push for Global Chipmaking Crown," *Bloomberg*, May 13, 2021.

44. KBS World, "'K-Semiconductor Belt Strategy' to Establish the World's Largest Supply Network by 2030," May 17, 2021.

45. Jeong-Ho Lee and Sohee Kim, "South Korea Passes Its 'Chips Act' amid US-China Friction," *Bloomberg*, March 29, 2023.

46. Son Ji-hyoung, "Korea Sets Out Own Chips Act, in Less Ambitious Fashion," *Korea Herald*, January 24, 2022.

47. Jiyoung Sohn, "South Korea Plans Mega Chip-Making Base to Stay Ahead," *Wall Street Journal*, March 15, 2023.

48. *JoongAng Ilbo*, "尹錫悦政権「半導体超強大国達成戦略」を発表 [Yoon Administration Announces 'Strategy to Become a Semiconductor Superpower']," July 21, 2022, https://s.japanese.joins.com/JArticle/293441?servcode=200§code=200. See also Lee Ho-jeong, "Korea's Chip Industrial Policy Takes Shape with Road Map," *Korea Joong-An Daily*, July 21, 2022.

49. *JoongAng Ilbo*, "Yoon Administration Announces 'Strategy to Become a Semiconductor Superpower.'"

50. Edward White, "US Companies Lobby South Korea to Free Jailed Samsung Boss," *Financial Times*, May 20, 2021; Joyce Lee, Soo-Hyang Choi, and Heekyong Yang, "South Korea's Yoon Pardons Samsung's Jay Y. Lee to Counter 'Economic Crisis,'" Reuters, August 12, 2022.

51. InvestKorea, "Semiconductor Industry Driving Korea's Economic Growth."

52. Hyundai's nonmemory operations were spun off in 2004 as a company called MagnaChip, which made display drivers, sensors, and power integrated circuits. Efforts in 2020 by investors from China to buy part of the firm were blocked by US intervention, despite the fact that MagnaChip had little exposure to the US market. See George Leopold, "US Blocks Chinese Deal for Magnachip," *EE Times*, June 21, 2021.

53. Asian Development Bank, "Asian Economic Integration Report 2022," p. 27.

54. Jang Seob Yoon, "Import Volume of Semiconductors to South Korea from 2006 to 2020," Statista, September 2022.

55. Eun-jin Kim, "TSMC Widens Its Gap with Samsung in Foundry Business," *Businesskorea*, June 21, 2022.

56. Lee Shoo-hwan, "Qualcomm's 3nm AP Foundry Leaves the Whole to TSMC Instead of Samsung," *The Elec* (in Korean), February 22, 2022, https://www.thelec.kr/news/articleView.html?idxno=16130.

57. Asian Development Bank, "Asian Economic Integration Report 2022," p. 27.

58. Bo-eun Kim, "Micron Challenges Rivals in Memory Chip Market," *The Korea Times*, June 13, 2021; Katie Schoolov, "How Intel Plans to Catch Samsung and TSMC and Regain Its Dominance in the Chip Market," CNBC, November 6, 2021.

59. Debby Wu, "World's Top Chipmakers Provide Data to US as Deadline Arrives," *Bloomberg*, November 7, 2021.

60. Jeong-Ho Lee and Sohee Kim, "Biden Finds a Key Ally Wary of His Bid to Outpace China on Chips," *Bloomberg*, March 25, 2021.

61. Stephen Nellis, Joyce Lee, and Toby Sterling, "Exclusive: US-China Tech War Clouds SK Hynix's Plans for a Key Chip Factory," Reuters, November 18, 2021.

62. Karen Freifeld and Alexandra Alper, "US Considers Crackdown on Memory Chip Makers in China," Reuters, August 2, 2022.

63. Kim Jaewon and Cheng Ting-Fang, "Samsung and SK Hynix Face China Dilemma from US Export Controls," *Nikkei*, October 25, 2022.

64. *Korea JoongAng Daily*, "Korea, US Launch New Dialogue on Semiconductor Partnership," December 9, 2021.

65. Sue Mi Terry, "Yoon's Strong Start in Foreign Policy," *Foreign Policy*, August 18, 2022.

66. Mi-na Kim, "Yoon, Biden Come Together over Semiconductors," *The Hankyoreh*, May 21, 2022.

67. Bob Sechler and Kara Carlson, "Samsung Weighs Huge Austin-Area Growth: $200 Billion Investment, 11 New Fabs, 10,000 New Jobs," *Austin American-Statesman*, July 20, 2022.

68. Dashveenjit Kaur, "Here's What South Korean Giant SK Group Is Doing with Its US$22b Investment in the US," *TechWire Asia*, July 29, 2022.

69. Jiaxing Li, "Why Is China So Concerned at the Prospect of South Korea Joining a US-Led Chip Alliance?," *South China Morning Post*, July 23, 2022.

70. Chan-kyong Park, "South Korea Plays Down Concerns over Move to Join US-Led Chip Alliance," *South China Morning Post*, August 8, 2022.

71. Terry, "Yoon's Strong Start in Foreign Policy."

72. Young-bae Kim, "Chip 4 Is about More than Korea—It's about Breaking Up Taiwan's Monopoly," *The Hankyoreh*, August 9, 2022.

73. Yoo-chul Kim, "Seoul Expected to Join Washington-Led 'Chip 4' Alliance," *The Korea Times*, July 19, 2022.

74. Kotaro Hosokawa, "South Korea to Track Travel by Chip Engineers as Tech Leaks Grow," *Nikkei Asia*, February 5, 2022.

75. Eun-jin Kim, "Applied Materials to Run R&D Center in South Korea," *Businesskorea*, July 7, 2022.

76. Kim, "Chip 4 Is about More than Korea."

77. Choi Si-young, "Yoon, Calling Japan a Partner, Offers New Vision to Reboot Sour Relations," *The Korea Herald*, March 10, 2023.

78. Hyun-kyung Kang, "Domestic Politics Presents Major Stumbling Block to Korea-Japan Relations," *The Korea Times*, July 25, 2022.

79. European Commission, "A Chips Act for Europe," Commission Staff Working Document SWD(2022) 147 Final, 2022.

80. Key Digital Technologies Joint Undertaking, "KDT JU to Become Chips Joint Undertaking," press release, February 8, 2022.

81. European Commission, *Boosting Electronics Value Chains in Europe*, June 19, 2018.

82. IPCEI, "About the IPCEI," accessed June 21, 2022.

83. Mathieu Duchâtel, "Semiconductors in Europe: The Return of Industrial Policy," Paris: Institut Montaigne Policy Paper, 2022, p. 23.

84. The alternative to headquarters location is factory location, but those data are not publicly available. For the EU's digital sovereignty objective, see Ursula von der Leyen, "2021 State of the Union Address by President von der Leyen," European Commission, September 15, 2021.

85. Nick Flaherty, "Intel, Samsung and TSMC Are Expected to Be Part of European Commission Discussions Today over a 2nm Chip Fab," *EEnews*, April 30, 2021.

86. Sarah Wu and Yimou Lee, "Taiwan's TSMC Says No Plans for Now to Build Factories in Europe," Reuters, June 7, 2022.

87. Council of the European Union, "Chips Act: Council and European Parliament Strike Provisional Deal," press release, April 18, 2023.

88. Duchâtel, "Semiconductors in Europe."

89. Duchâtel, "Semiconductors in Europe," 28–29.

90. Oliver Noyan, "Germany to Invest Billions to Bring Semiconductor Production Back to Europe," Euractiv, September 3, 2021.

91. Reuters, "Intel Seeks $10B in Subsidies for European Chip Plant," Automotive News Europe, April 30, 2021; Dan Robinson, "Intel Rattles the Tin for Another €5B in Subsidies to Build German Fab," *The Register*, March 8, 2023.

92. Duchâtel, "Semiconductors in Europe," 30.

93. European Commission, "A Chips Act for Europe," 22.

94. LFoundry, "Technology to Enable Innovation Worldwide," accessed March 30, 2023.

95. Jeanne Whalen, "Intel to Invest $36 Billion in New Computer Chip Factories in Europe," *Washington Post*, March 15, 2022.

96. European Parliament, "Towards a New EU Policy Approach to China: 21st EU-China Summit–April 2019," 2019.

97. European Commission, "EU-China High Level Dialogue on Research and Innovation," January 25, 2021.

98. Shannon Tiezzi, "China-EU Summit Highlights Diverging Paths," *The Diplomat*, April 1, 2022.

99. Laurence Norman and Kim Mackrael, "China Wants to Be at Center of New World Order, Top EU Official Says," *Wall Street Journal*, March 30, 2023.

100. European Commission, "EU-US: A New Transatlantic Agenda for Global Change," press release, December 2, 2020.

101. European Commission, "EU-US Launch Trade and Technology Council to Lead Values-based Global Digital Transformation," press release, June 15, 2021.

102. European Commission, "EU-US Trade and Technology Council: Strengthening Our Renewed Partnership in Turbulent Times," press release, May 16, 2022.

103. Grzegorz Stec and Zsuzsa Anna Ferenczy, "EU-Taiwan Ties: Between Expectations and Reality," MERICS, January 17, 2022.

104. Ben Blanchard and Jeanny Kao, "Taiwan 'Happy' to See Chip Investment in EU, Wants Deeper Ties," Reuters July 12, 2022. TSMC in early 2023, however, did revive consideration of new facility in Germany.

105. Mathieu Duchâtel, "Semiconductors in Europe," 42.

106. Varas et al., *Strengthening the Global Semiconductor Supply Chain*, 35.

107. John Lee and Jan-Peter Kleinhans, *Mapping China's Semiconductor Ecosystem in Global Context*, MERICS, June 2021, p. 52.

108. Dan Wang, "The Quest for Semiconductor Sovereignty," Gavekal-Dragonomics, April 20, 2021, 20.

109. Sharon Seah, Joanne Lin, Sithanonxay Suvannaphakdy, Melinda Martinus, Pham Thi Phuong, Thao Farah, Nadine Seth, and Hoang Thi Ha, *The State of Southeast Asia: 2022* (Singapore: ISEAS-Yusof Ishak Institute, 2022), 32.

110. Seah et al., *The State of Southeast Asia: 2022*, 20–23.

111. Siew Mun Tang, Hoang T. Tha, Ho, Anuthida Selaow Qian, Glenn Ong, and Pham Thi Phuong Thao, *The State of Southeast Asia: 2020* (Singapore: ISEAS-Yusof Ishak Institute, 2020), 29.

112. X-FAB, "Our Fabs," accessed March 30, 2023.

113. SilTerra, "Technology Overview," accessed March 30, 2022.

114. Dashveenjit Kaur, "Semicon SEA 2022: Malaysia Seeks to Attract Semiconductor Giants like TSMC," *Tech Wire Asia*, June 22, 2022.

115. *The Star*, "Malaysia's Semiconductor Industry to Benefit from Chips and Science Act," August 15, 2022; John Neuffer, Letter to Mohamed Azmin bin Ali, May 28, 2021.

116. Dashveenjit Kaur, "Semicon SEA 2022: Malaysia Seeks to Attract Semiconductor Giants like TSMC," *Tech Wire Asia*, June 22, 2022.

117. Malaysian Investment Development Authority, "The Rise of Test Equipment Giants amid Tech Boom," September 23, 2021.

118. Malaysian Investment Development Authority, "Malaysia Attracted Record Approved Investment of RM306.5B in 2021, Driven by E&E Boom," March 8, 2022.

119. Nazatul Izma, "Labour Crisis Pushes Malaysia's Billion Ringgit E&E Sector to Breaking Point," *Free Malaysia Today*, August 22, 2022.

120. Scott Foster, "Big Chip and Tech Investment Pouring into Malaysia," *Asia Times*, December 23, 2021. Since 2021, other recent investments or announced plans include those in semiconductor materials and components (Austria's AT&S; Japan's Taiyo Yuden, Fuji Electric, Kaga, and ROHM), in assembly, test, and packaging (US's Micron, Germany's Bosch, Chinese and American joint venture TF-AMD), in front-end manufacturing (Taiwan's Foxconn; Japan's Denso and, again, Fuji Electric), and in contract manufacturing (US's Applied Engineering).

121. Malaysia Semiconductor Industry Association, "MSIA Is Fully Supportive of the Decision by the Government to Defer the Condition That at Least 80% of Companies Workforce Must Be Malaysian," press release, July 17, 2022.

122. In a May 2021 letter to the Malaysian government, the US Semiconductor Industry Association (SIA) asked for an exemption of the electronics/semiconductor sector from a two-week pandemic lockdown, stating that "US trade with Malaysia accounts for 24 percent of all US semiconductor global trade," and that "the United States imports more semiconductors directly from Malaysia than from any other country." This referred to the fact that semiconductors manufactured elsewhere pass through Malaysia for ATP before being received by US firms. See John Neuffer, Letter to Mohamed Azmin bin Ali, May 28, 2021.

123. OEC, "Malaysia (MYS) Exports, Imports, and Trade Partners," September 2020; R. Hirschmann, "Net Foreign Direct Investment (FDI) Flows to Malaysia in 2021, by Country," *Statista*, August 10, 2022.

124. US Department of Commerce, "Joint Press Release: US Department of Commerce and Malaysian Ministry of International Trade and Industry Sign Memorandum of Cooperation to Strengthen Semiconductor Supply Chain Resiliency and Promote Sustainable Growth," May 11, 2022.

125. Gloria Harry Beatty, "Malaysia Can Benefit from Semiconductor Supply Chain Disruption," *The Sun*, August 22, 2022.

126. Weng Khuen Lee, "Malaysia to Benefit from Trade Diversion amid Heightened Geopolitical Tensions," The Edge Malaysia, August 16, 2022.

127. Ang Wee Seng, "Speech by MOS Alvin Tan at the SSIA Semiconductor Business Connect 2022," Ministry of Trade and Industry (Singapore), May 19, 2022; Dylan Loh, "Singapore Plays Catch-up with Taiwan as Chip Investments Soar," *Nikkei Asia*, August 11, 2021.

128. Seng, "Speech by MOS Alvin Tan."

129. Hideaki Ryugen, "Micron Taps Singapore as Launch Pad for NAND Offensive," *Nikkei Asia*, February 3, 2021.

130. Over half of US firm front-end wafer capacity is actually produced outside the United States. See "2021 State of the US Semiconductor Industry," SIA, accessed September 7, 2022.

131. Seng, "Speech by MOS Alvin Tan."

132. Gayle Goh, "Singapore Seeking Frontier Firms for Manufacturing 2030," EDB, February 2, 2021.

133. Seng, "Speech by MOS Alvin Tan."

134. Dylan Loh, "Singapore Investment Inflows Show US Chip Hunger amid Overall Dip," *Nikkei Asia*, January 26, 2022.

135. Sharon See, "Global Chipmakers' Investments in Singapore," *The Business Times*, July 22, 2022.

136. Antonio Varas, Raj Varadarajan, Jimmy Goodrich, and Falan Yinug, *Government Incentives and US Competitiveness in Semiconductor Manufacturing* (Boston, MA: Boston Consulting Group and Semiconductor Industry Association, September 2020).

137. John VerWey, "No Permits, No Fabs: The Importance of Regulatory Reform for Semiconductor Manufacturing," CSET Policy Brief, October 2021.

138. NRF Singapore, "RIE2025 Plan," February 20, 2021.

139. Choo Yun Ting, "Applied Materials and A*Star Extend R&D Collaboration with New $286m Investment," *The Straits Times*, December 23, 2021.

140. William Chong, "Singapore and the United States: Speaking Hard Truths as a Zhengyou," *Fulcrum*, April 7, 2022.

141. China trade statistics including Hong Kong. OEC, "Singapore (SGP) Exports, Imports, and Trade Partners," June 2022.

142. Thanh Van, "Vietnam's Semiconductor Market to Grow by $6.16 Billion," *Vietnam Investment Review*, August 3, 2021.

143. Tieying Ma, "ASEAN's Potential in Semiconductor Manufacturing," DBS, September 23, 2021.

144. Filippo Bortoletti and Thu Nguyen, "Vietnam's Semiconductor Industry: Samsung Makes Further Inroads," *Vietnam Briefing*, August 30, 2022.

145. Bortoletti and Nguyen, "Vietnam's Semiconductor Industry"; Nhu Phu, "S. Korea's Amkor Technology to Build US$1.6-Billion Semiconductor Plant in Vietnam," *The Saigon Times*, December 16, 2021.

146. Dezan Shira & Associates, "Q&A: Electronics and Semiconductor Industry in Vietnam," *Vietnam Briefing*, July 2, 2021.

147. Shira & Associates, "Q&A."

148. Atharva Deshmukh, "FDI in Vietnam: A Year in Review and Outlook for 2021," *Vietnam Briefing*, February 17, 2021; Pritesh Samuel, "Vietnam's FDI Drops Slightly, but Reopening Measures Boosting Economy," *Vietnam Briefing*, January 27, 2022.

149. OEC, "Vietnam (VNM) Exports, Imports, and Trade Partners," 2022.

150. Dinsha Mistree, "From Produce and Protect to Promoting Private Industry: The Indian State's Role in Creating a Domestic Software Industry," Stanford Law School Working Paper 07-2018, June 2019.

151. Russ Arensman, "Move Over, China," *Electronic Business*, 2006.

152. Peter Clarke, "Report: 11 Firms Pitch Indian Wafer Fabs," *EE Times*, September 14, 2011; Sufia Tippu, "2 Fabs Get the Final Approval in India," *EE Times India*, September 13, 2013.

153. Ministry of Information and Electronics Technology (India), "Scheme for Promotion of Manufacturing of Electronic Components and Semiconductors (SPECS)," accessed August 12, 2022.

154. *The New Indian Express*, "Rs 76,000 Crore Budget to Design, Make Semiconductor Chips in India Gets Cabinet Nod," December 15, 2021.

155. PIB India, "India Domestic Electronics Production Reached $74.7B in FY2020-2021," *EE Times India*, July 22, 2022.

156. India Semiconductor Mission, "About Us," accessed June 5, 2023.

157. India also has at least one producer of discrete semiconductors (individual transistors, diodes, etc.), Continental Device India, which was established in 1964. See https://www.cdil.com.

158. Prasanth Aby Thomas, "India's Vedanta to Make 28-65nm Semiconductor Chips for Local Demand," *DigiTimes*, January 20, 2022.

159. *The Economic Times*, "Vedanta, Foxconn to Set Up Fab & Chip Facility in Gujarat," September 14, 2022.

160. Alok Deshpande, "How Gujarat Pipped Maharashtra to Win Vedanta-Foxconn's $22 Billion Project," *The Indian Express*, September 15, 2022.

161. Alan Patterson, "India Prepares to Build Nation's First Chip Fab," *EE Times*, May 10, 2022.

162. Next Orbit Ventures, "ISMC to Invest $3B in India's First Semiconductor Fab in Karnataka," *EE Times India*, May 6, 2022.

163. *The Hindu*, "How $3 Billion Semiconductor Plant Is Expected to Transform Mysuru," May 3, 2022.

164. Jingyue Hsiao, "India's First Memory Chip ATMP Plant Reportedly to Mass Produce by December," *DigiTimes*, July 25, 2022.

165. Sahasra Semiconductor, "About Us," accessed August 10, 2022.

166. Mint, "Tatas Just Came a Bit Closer to Being India's First Semiconductor Powerhouse," July 1, 2022.

167. Mint, "Tatas Just Came a Bit Closer."

168. Surajeet Das Gupta, "Two Indian Companies to Pick Up over 26% but Less than 51% Stake in ISMC," *The Business Standard*, November 8, 2022.

169. Mumin Chen, "Among International Students Studying in Taiwan, Indians Are the Fastest-Growing Group," *The Week*, February 22, 2022.

170. All India Council for Technical Education, "Circular," April 21, 2022.

171. ANI, "India Has a Lot of Interest in Boosting Semiconductor Industry: AICTE Chairperson," June 19, 2022.

172. FE Education, "IESA to Launch 'Semiconductor Nation–Campus Connect' Initiative," *Financial Express*, August 18, 2022.

173. Mint, "PM Modi Makes Strong Pitch for Self-Reliance in Technology Sector," March 2, 2022; ETAuto, "PM Modi Pitches for Self-Reliance in Semiconductor, Make in India," March 3, 2022.

174. Sankalp Phartiyal, "India Seeks to Oust China Firms from Sub-$150 Phone Market," *Bloomberg*, August 8, 2022.

175. US Department of State, "US Relations with India," July 18, 2022.

176. The White House, "FACT SHEET: United States and India Elevate Strategic Partnership with the Initiative on Critical and Emerging Technology (iCET)," January 31, 2023.

177. Abhilasha Singh, "India, US to Work Together to Beat Semiconductor Shortage," *Times of India*, April 12, 2022.

178. European Commission, "EU-India: Joint Press Release on Launching the Trade and Technology Council," April 25, 2022.

179. *Fortune India*, "India to Invest $30bn into Semiconductor Supply Chain, Tech Sector," June 16, 2022.

180. Dan Breznitz, "Innovation-Based Industrial Policy in Emerging Economies? The Case of Israel's IT Industry," *Business and Politics* 8, no. 3 (2006): 1–35.

181. Intel, "Intel in Israel," accessed June 5, 2023.

182. Scotten Jones, "The EUV Divide and Intel Foundry Services," SemiWiki, March 23, 2022.
183. Assaf Gilead, "Israel Has Major Role to Play in Intel Revival," *Globes*, October 3, 2021.
184. Gonzalo Martínez de Azagra, Noa Shamay, Ben Gilbert, and Jaime Deleito, "2022 Israel Semiconductor Landscape," Cardumen Capital, June 6, 2022.
185. Shoshanna Solomon, "Amid Battle for Workers, Multinationals Scale Up Chipmaking Plans in Israel," *Times of Israel*, April 4, 2021.
186. Dale Aluf, "Israeli Semiconductors and the US-China Tech War," *The Diplomat*, November 14, 2020.
187. Lingling Wei and Asa Fitch, "China's New Tech Weapon: Dragging Its Feet on Global Merger Approvals," *Wall Street Journal*, April 4, 2023.
188. OEC, "Israel," accessed June 5, 2023.
189. Aluf, "Israeli Semiconductors."
190. Jia Shaoxuan, "Israel: The Next Strategic Point for Sino-US Semiconductor Competition?," *iNews*, June 6, 2022.
191. US Department of State, "Secretary Michael R. Pompeo with Gili Cohen of Kan 11," May 13, 2020.

CHAPTER SEVEN

Jointly Deterring Beijing through Semiconductors

MATTHEW POTTINGER

China's current dependence on US and partner semiconductor technologies offers options and trade-offs for economically deterring China's regional military or other coercive aims.

What could puncture the confidence of China's leadership that using force against Taiwan would be easier than alternatives? Largely independent of the semiconductor supply chain security-, competitiveness-, and innovation-related points above, the United States faces deep questions today regarding the tools it has available—or does not have available—to deter unwanted military or other coercive global actions by China's leaders. Aggression toward Taiwan is a key example but not the only one.

Military strength, coupled with a will to use it, is a core component of such deterrence. There are also clear steps that Taiwan, the United States, and partners could take to improve military deterrence—not through a policy of strategic clarity, but rather through planning and coordination that could preserve the credibility of options within strategic ambiguity.

Moreover, a strategy to deter China's leadership from conventional combat in the western Pacific through military strength has arguably become necessary but insufficient, given China's improving military capabilities. Going forward, this dynamic points to the need for a more deliberate economic deterrence strategy, given China's particular reliance on the United States and its allies as trading partners.

Here, semiconductors offer a unique but difficult economic deterrence choice: should the United States work with Japan, Korea, Taiwan, and the

Netherlands to further restrict the export of semiconductor technologies, manufacturing equipment, and design tools to China—and not just at the leading edge—in order to extend China's current reliance on chip imports and partner technologies? Or do the downsides of those export controls outweigh the benefits? Indeed, this "jet-engine strategy," affecting tools and subsystems rather than the final product, could entail significant costs for US and partner firms—even slowing the overall global semiconductor technological frontier. But if successful, it could serve as a major tool for economic deterrence against future military conflicts with China with potentially unbounded costs.

The United States lacks comprehensive interagency institutional mechanisms and expertise (or multilateral fora) to fully weigh and consult with industry on the dynamics of such options, whether in semiconductors or other emerging intersections of economics and technology with national security interests.

• • •

This chapter recommends ways that Washington can mobilize its allies, and in the process inoculate itself and them against overdependence on China for semiconductors. Success in this effort would deprive China's leaders in Beijing of a key means of the coercive leverage that they seek. It might also erode Beijing's confidence in its ability to weather supply shocks in the event it attacks Taiwan.

These recommendations build upon the semiconductor export controls unveiled by the Biden administration on October 7, 2022— one of the most significant economic measures to date by the administration for improving the United States' competitive footing vis-à-vis China. As described in chapter 6, US partners have key strengths in different parts of the global semiconductor supply chain and are each pursuing further advances through different strategies. The United States should do more to align itself to be a part of their successes. The following recommendations seek to further expand upon the role of partners in supporting Washington's policy toward China—and they seek to tighten loopholes in *enforcement*, a perennial weakness of US export controls in recent decades.

First, it is important to appreciate how resolute China's leader, Party General Secretary Xi Jinping, is in his aim of making China into the world's chipmaking superpower. Dominance in semiconductor manufacturing has been his explicit goal for years. In 2014, China's State Council put forward "Guidelines to Promote the National Integrated Circuit Industry Development," which highlighted Xi's objective of achieving the world's dominant semiconductor industry by 2030 in terms of production, design, packaging, testing, materials, and equipment.[1] The guidelines included the objective of satisfying 70 percent of China's semiconductor demand using indigenous production by 2025. The State Council went further in 2019 when it stated that 80 percent of China's demand should be produced indigenously by 2030. And in a 2018 address to the Chinese Academy of Sciences and the Chinese Academy of Engineering, Xi declared that China must overcome "shortcomings" in its mission to seize the "high ground" of pivotal technologies, including "high-end microchips." "Our situation, in which key and core technologies are controlled by others, has not fundamentally changed," he warned.[2]

As detailed in this report's chapter 8 on China's semiconductor ambitions, Xi is putting big money where his mouth is. In 2017, the Washington, DC–based Information Technology and Innovation Foundation estimated that China had earmarked $160 billion in subsidies for the sector.[3] In December 2022, Reuters reported that Beijing was preparing a new round of subsidies and tax credits equivalent to about $150 billion.[4] Combined, the two figures are six times the $52 billion the US Congress allotted to support semiconductor manufacturing through the landmark CHIPS and Science Act of 2022. Suffice it to say, Xi has shown little sign of wavering from his semiconductor goals since beginning his second decade as paramount leader following the 20th Party Congress in October 2022.

It is also important to appreciate *why* Xi is pursuing this goal. Through his dual-circulation strategy, he has stated explicitly his objective of decreasing China's dependence on high-tech imports while also making the world's technology supply chains increasingly dependent on China. Further, he has stated a goal of ensuring that China can easily substitute imports from one country with those from at least one other country.

Xi characterizes these moves as defensive. "We must sustain and enhance our superiority across the entire production chain . . . and we must tighten international production chains' dependence on China, forming a powerful countermeasure and deterrent capability against foreigners who would artificially cut supply [to China]," he said in a major 2020 address.[5] In practice, however, leaders in Beijing also weaponize foreigners' economic dependence on China as *offensive* leverage to advance Xi's political objectives overseas.[6] Indeed, in recent years Beijing has restricted trade with Australia, Canada, Japan, Mongolia, Norway, the Philippines, South Korea, Pacific Island nations, and other countries in sometimes successful attempts to coerce changes in a targeted country's laws, policies, or judicial processes. Semiconductors are essential to Xi's strategy because they are integral to so many of the other technologies Beijing is vying to control over the next decade—from biotechnology and space exploration to autonomous vehicles and military systems.

Constraining Beijing's Ambitions

As I have argued elsewhere, the United States and its allies should pursue a policy of "constrainment" to foil Beijing's ambition of technological self-sufficiency, including in semiconductors.[7] The idea here isn't so much to cut off the flow of chips to China (though we should do what we can to keep chips out of China's hypersonic missiles, supercomputers, and other advanced military and surveillance systems), but to prevent China from accumulating the means to capture a large market share and then cut off the flow of chips to democracies. To put it in twentieth-century terms: our goal is not to cut off the flow of oil to China, but to prevent China from becoming OPEC. Permitting China to achieve a dominant OPEC-like status in chipmaking would hand Xi the means to cripple US and allied economies, blunt our technological edge, and compromise our military prowess.

The Biden administration's October 2022 export rules, if assiduously enforced, offer a good starting point for constraining Beijing's semiconductor ambitions.

One aspect of the rules builds upon the Trump administration's use of the once-obscure Foreign Direct Product Rule (FDPR). That rule forbids US or third-country companies from selling products made with US tooling, software, or design to blacklisted companies in China. Whereas the Trump administration used this approach against the telecommunications equipment maker Huawei, the Biden administration's new rules have expanded the blacklist to include companies in China involved in supercomputing or other military or surveillance uses. So far, the administration has put forty-nine companies on the blacklist in addition to Huawei.[8]

But the more significant part of the Biden administration rules targets China's *production* of chips by restricting the export of essential US software, equipment, and skilled labor. These rules include license requirements (with presumption of denial) for export of US products to fabs in China producing logic chips at 16nm or below, license requirements for semiconductor tooling components, and limits on US persons working at People's Republic of China (PRC) semiconductor firms that produce advanced chips.[9] Those restrictions mark an evolution in US strategy. Previously, US policy emphasized the promotion of domestic industry—and its short-term pursuit of revenue—rather than the restriction of China's technological progress toward its industrial goals. The combination of the new export controls with the subsidies contained in the 2022 CHIPS and Science Act means Washington is finally attempting to pursue both objectives simultaneously.

US National Security Advisor Jake Sullivan signaled the shift in a September 2022 speech:

> On export controls, we have to revisit the long-standing premise of maintaining "relative" advantages over competitors in certain key technologies. We previously maintained a "sliding scale" approach that said we need to stay only a couple of generations

ahead. This is not the strategic environment we are in today. Given the foundational nature of certain technologies, such as advanced logic and memory chips, we must maintain as large of a lead as possible.[10]

The new export controls indicate Washington is willing to take steps even when they are costly to US industry; the controls, at first announced unilaterally, serve as a sort of "down payment" before multilateralizing the effort in ways that would also require US allies to make commercial sacrifices. Washington knows that if the desired effects of the new policy are to be achieved and sustained, essential allies will need to be brought into the act, and soon.

An Example: Semiconductor Manufacturing Equipment Subsystems

Leading Dutch semiconductor equipment manufacturer ASML describes its role as one of an "integrator" that draws on a global supply chain of over one hundred thousand components, often from sole suppliers, to make the complex machines that produce the most complex chips.

Similarly, as China's emerging indigenous semiconductor equipment manufacturers seek to match the capabilities of Western vendors on whom China's chip manufacturers currently rely, they regularly buy subsystem components from a variety of suppliers in the United States, Japan, and Europe. Leading semiconductor manufacturing equipment firms in China include NAURA, Mattson, ACM Research, KingSemi, Piotech, ZKX, Hwatsing, and Raintree Scientific Instruments. In recent years, these firms have bought subsystems—including power supplies, fluid delivery systems, electrostatic chucks, vacuum systems, and magnets—from US and partner suppliers. Meanwhile, they have also recruited overseas engineers using significant compensation, bonuses, and equity stakes.

Constraining the shipment of certain types of subsystems that China uses to build its wafer fab equipment could be one option to slow down China's ability to build advanced semiconductor manufacturing equipment. Indeed, the leading equipment manufacturers in China rely on a host of subsystem suppliers based in the United States, Europe, Japan, or Korea:[11]

- *NAURA* is China's largest semiconductor equipment manufacturer, with $1.2 billion in sales in 2021 and a 53 percent (two-year) compound annual growth rate. It supplies equipment for physical vapor deposition (PVD), chemical vapor deposition (CVD), epitaxy (the growth of one thin film in a chip over another), and atomic layer deposition (ALD) processes, and for plasma etchers, tooling thermal management systems, and cleaning tools. US-based subsystem suppliers to NAURA include MKS Instruments, CoorsTek, Edwards Vacuum, and Advanced Energy. NAURA has also been supplied by Comet (Europe), and from Japan-based firms (or their Korean subsidiaries) including Kyocera, DAIHEN, Sumitomo, and Kyosan.
- *Mattson Technology* was founded in the United States and retains a headquarters in Fremont, California—but in 2016 it was purchased by an organ of the Beijing municipal government, Beijing E-Town. It booked $374 million in sales in 2021, representing a 47 percent annual growth rate, supplying manufacturing capabilities including thermal systems, plasma etching and dry stripping of photoresists, and epitaxy processes. Similar to NAURA, its US and partner-based subsystem suppliers include CoorsTek, Edwards Vacuum, Advanced Energy, Comet, DAIHEN, Sumitomo, and Kyosan.
- *AMEC* (Advanced Micro-Fabrication Equipment), similar in size to Mattson, had $388 million in 2021 sales, representing a 31 percent annual growth rate. AMEC supplies plasma etchers and CVD equipment that are enabled by foreign subsystems from CoorsTek, Edwards Vacuum, Advanced Energy, Comet, DAIHEN, Sumitomo, and Kyosan.
- *Piotech*, based in Shenyang, with $48 million in sales in 2021 and a 30 percent annual growth rate, supplies CVD and ALD equipment to chip manufacturers. US firms that supply subsystem components

to Piotech include XP Power/Comdel, MKS Instruments, and Advanced Energy; partner-country suppliers include Comet; Japan's Horiba, LINTEC, and DAIHEN; and Korea's KoMiCo and New Power Plasma (NPP).

- *ZKX* (Beijing Zhongkexin Electronics), with just $15 million in 2021 sales, supplies ion implant equipment. In turn, it purchases from US-based Entegris, New Zealand's Buckley Systems, and Japan's Kyocera and Matsusada Precision.

The point is not to emphasize particular firms or suppliers as problematic. Rather, it is to illustrate how a large constellation of players within the United States and our partner countries—some of them small- or medium-sized businesses—continue to make seemingly rational commercial decisions to supply to willing buyers in China. At the same time, those buyers are operating within a policy framework that explicitly seeks first to internalize these overseas technologies and then to displace them, both domestically and eventually globally through trade. We have seen this pattern play out over a host of other technology-driven industries as well, from high-speed rail to power plant components to telecom.

Limiting the shipments of these critical semiconductor subsystems to China, therefore, could sustain China's dependence on Western equipment and limit its ability to build advanced semiconductors. The willingness of US partners to cooperate in such a strategy would hinge on various government views toward the security versus commercial implications of China gaining indigenous capabilities in this area, as well as on the process and framework for arriving at such multilateral engagements.

"COCOM" 2.0

Export controls are not a silver bullet—they tend to delay, rather than deny, an adversary's acquisition of sensitive technology. Export controls are also more effective when combined with other measures, which is why they are only one of the approaches advocated in this chapter.

But export controls are nonetheless an important tool that the United States and its partners have had ample experience wielding effectively since the 1940s. And delaying Beijing's technology ambitions is a worthy goal in its own right, according to the logic embedded in Jake Sullivan's quotation above. Moreover, export controls are remarkably well suited to constraining Beijing's chip manufacturing ambitions, given how heavily concentrated the choke point technologies are in the hands of corporate actors domiciled in the United States and in a handful of partner countries—the Netherlands and Japan in particular. In other words, conditions favor the effective employment of export controls against China if the United States marshals its partners to the cause and follows through with strict enforcement.

It will come down to a question of US leadership. It always has been so. In 1949 the US Congress passed the Export Control Act, giving President Harry Truman something highly unusual: peacetime authority to restrict US technology exports. Such authority was normally conferred only during wartime. But as Washington's World War II alliance with Josef Stalin transformed into Cold War rivalry, the Truman administration created lists of controlled items that were either prohibited from export or that required State Department or Commerce Department licenses. Soon after, Washington multilateralized the effort by setting up an export control regime with its allies called the Coordinating Committee for Multilateral Export Controls, or COCOM for short. Formed at the start of the Cold War, the group of seventeen member states agreed to restrict the sale of sensitive technology to the Soviet bloc.

"The United States and its allies were relatively successful at the outset in controlling the export of items on the COCOM lists to the Soviet Union and Eastern Europe," wrote John H. Henshaw in his Stimson Center history of the network.[12] "In short, the effectiveness of COCOM has been tied to the quality of US leadership." The Achilles' heel of any export control regime is alternative sources of supply, which is what makes an allied—not just unilateral—approach so essential. By bringing along the Netherlands and Japan in particular, but also South Korea, Taiwan, Germany, Israel, and others, the United States can preempt loopholes before China has a chance to exploit them.

Restricting China's, as well as Russia's, Iran's, and North Korea's, production of microchips could serve as the kernel around which a revived COCOM structure could sprout. Such a renewal is needed in part because after the Cold War, Russia was brought into the Wassenaar Arrangement, the successor to the original COCOM. With Russia now waging war in Europe, a new body that excludes that authoritarian aggressor state is overdue.

Here are eight steps the US government could take to marshal its partners and amplify the impact of the recent export control rules.

1. *Elevate and expand.* Elevate trilateral talks on *semiconductor controls* to the national security advisors and select cabinet officials of the United States, the Netherlands, and Japan. In parallel, build a larger grouping that includes South Korea, Germany, Israel, Taiwan, the United Kingdom, and India to discuss *supply chain resiliency* for semiconductors specifically. The group should commission studies of existing and planned fab capacity at advanced and legacy nodes, as well as related segments of the semiconductor industry, such as chip packaging and testing.

2. *Remember that "legacy" matters.* I recommend Washington and its allies expand the scope of regulations to prohibit the export of equipment that China could use to make logic chips from 16nm to 28nm. Given the strength that China has already attained in 28nm fab capacity, trade tools such as tariffs should be considered to incentivize American and allied chipmakers to continue making these legacy chips. To be sure, the Biden administration rules restrict US exports that would help China make advanced-logic chips—that is, circuits etched below 16nm. But older generations of chips—referred to as mature or "legacy" nodes—are generally excluded from the regulations, even though, as described in chapter 2 of this report, they have many specialized commercial and military uses and still constitute a massive part of the global market. Chips of 28nm and older still power consumer electronics, vehicles and transportation equipment, high-capacity energy storage systems, and our

most advanced weapons systems. In particular, allowing China to dominate the market for logic chips in the range of 28nm or other specialized analog, sensor, and radio frequency (RF) chips, could be highly disruptive to this existing and more globally distributed production base. Locked out of advanced nodes, continued semiconductor subsidies in China could flood the global market with cheaply priced legacy chips, driving today's free-market chip manufacturers out of the space and eventually generating new US or partner dependency on China's supply. US and allied chipmakers could further be deprived of the revenue these legacy chips generate for research and development.

3. *Restrict deep ultraviolet (DUV).* The most effective way of hobbling China's ambitions to build the world's largest base for 28nm logic chips would be for the Netherlands to restrict ASML from selling DUV lithography tools used to etch such chips. The Dutch will argue that Beijing already has many of these machines. True enough—but scale matters. Many fabs in Taiwan and elsewhere outside China are on a waiting list to receive ASML DUV machines. The Netherlands could effectuate a "soft ban" on China by simply reprioritizing sales of DUV machines to non-China companies. Japanese and US companies, too, should be restricted from exporting tools and skilled labor for making 28nm chips in China.

4. *Expand the blacklist.* The Foreign Direct Product Rule blacklist should be expanded to include the subsidiaries and affiliates of listed Chinese companies, given the ease with which targeted China-based companies can evade export controls via affiliates. The blacklist should also incorporate China's machine tool firms to constrain Beijing's bid for self-reliance in this segment.

5. *Go beyond chips.* For the United States and its allies to build resilient microchip supply chains and reduce the potential for coercive leverage, it is important to incentivize the allied manufacture of not only memory and logic chips, but also the printed circuit boards, ingots, and assembly packaging and testing that accompany them. While not there today, according to Rick

Switzer of the Special Competitive Studies Project, China is currently on course to control over 80 percent of some of these market segments. Policy makers should dig deep into their tool kits to mobilize private capital (such as through investment partnerships with the US International Development Finance Corp.) to actively push more of these production lines to Southeast Asia, India, and Mexico.

6. *Restrict US government exposure to China's chips.* A provision of the 2023 National Defense Authorization Act passed by the US Congress strengthens the security of defense systems by prohibiting US government procurement of products that contain semiconductor chips from China's chipmakers with ties to the Chinese Communist Party, including Semiconductor Manufacturing International Corp. (SMIC), Yangtze Memory Technologies Co. (YMTC), and ChangXin Memory Technologies (CXMT). The legislation also requires the US government and its suppliers to understand their supply chains. Congress should close several loopholes in this important bill by expanding its scope beyond "national security systems"—an outdated construct limited to weapons and certain equipment required for defense and intelligence activities—to include "critical infrastructure." As evidenced by China's 2015 hack of the US government's most sensitive personnel records at the Office of Personnel Management, our national security relies heavily on "commercial" infrastructure. The updated provision should also be expanded from covering procurement of goods to also covering services. The public and private sectors typically spend more annually on services than on goods. Disruption to or compromise through a service, such as cloud computing, can have more profound effects than a single piece of equipment. For that reason, the bill should prohibit the government from buying not only goods but also *services* that depend on China's chips.

7. *Make Taiwan and South Korea into force multipliers.* The world's top chipmaker, Taiwan Semiconductor Manufacturing Company (TSMC), should be encouraged to further diversify its

production base beyond China or Taiwan to hedge its exposure to the risk of economic or military coercion by China, among other potential commercial benefits. Likewise, South Korean firms are currently producing in China about 12 percent of the world's total dynamic random-access memory (DRAM) chips and 19 percent of global NAND Flash chips;[13] they, too, should be incentivized to shift more of their production to places other than China. The executive branch should also align Taiwan and South Korea, both of which rely heavily on the United States for their defense, to the objectives of the Foreign Direct Product Rule. This alignment would preempt a longer-term risk that non-US-designed chips made in Taiwan and South Korea could flow to China's military-industrial complex.

8. *Enact a litmus test for the European Union.* The Biden administration has invested significant time and resources into coordinating with the European Union through the US-EU Trade and Technology Council (TTC). The TTC should be a venue for Europe to demonstrate its seriousness about strategic technologies by working with the Biden administration on joint export controls or trade actions to constrain China's semiconductor ambitions. Failure on the part of Europe to do so will cast doubt on the TTC's strategic relevance.

Enforcement

Washington's export control regime is only as good as its enforcement—and enforcement has been a perennial struggle.

China is a dictatorship in which a Leninist party overrules the rule of law. The Party can and does direct corporate behavior through a variety of methods, irrespective of the ownership structure of a particular company. These features make the system well suited to exploiting loopholes in US export controls: where there are gaps, entities will circumvent them by acquiring prohibited goods, technologies, and software through in-country intermediaries exempt from the scope of US rules.

It was reported in 2021, for example, that China's acquisition of nominally controlled US integrated circuit design and technology enabled it to leapfrog the United States in hypersonic weapons development.[14] Some China-based fabs, having successfully acquired and adapted Western technology, have manufactured more-advanced chips than are currently produced in the United States.[15] China also diverts "controlled" US integrated circuits to assist Washington's adversaries, including two sanctioned states, the Russian Federation and the Islamic Republic of Iran, whose weapons have been found to contain American chips and other components.[16]

The official body charged with conducting and enforcing US export controls is the Commerce Department's Bureau of Industry and Security (BIS). BIS is understaffed, short on China expertise, and traditionally oriented toward favoring export revenues over national security concerns. In turn, US and partner companies that stand to make money selling software, equipment, and services to China's heavily subsidized chip industry unsurprisingly lobby their governments for "nuanced" regulations that won't foreclose business opportunities in China. To address these split incentives, Congress should allocate BIS more funding (beyond adjustment for inflation) to handle its growing plate of responsibilities. Its fiscal year (FY) 2022 budget was $133 million, and it requested nearly $200 million for FY 2023. A study from the Center for Strategic and International Studies (CSIS) found that BIS's export controls budget has failed to keep pace with inflation since FY 2020 and that almost 90 percent of its $66 million requested budget increase would be absorbed by rampant inflation and other expenses unrelated to export controls.[17]

Among other things, BIS simply needs more staff. The bureau reportedly has at times had only two officers to conduct end-use export checks in China.

And BIS needs to upgrade its technical systems to private sector standards. BIS's internal database "is so unreliable that an identical data search query executed twice in a row will not necessarily retrieve identical records, as various parts of the system are often crashing or otherwise non-responsive," according to CSIS. Officers often "only have access to outdated versions of Microsoft Excel." BIS officers can't be reasonably expected to properly enforce these controls when they still work in the twentieth century.

BIS should also make better use of private providers of market intelligence and abandon the flawed "end-use" paradigm when it comes to China. China's military-civil fusion policy means that Beijing can require companies—irrespective of pedigree—to serve China's military modernization and to do so in secrecy. A small number of US officials, much less only two of them, can't be expected to reasonably determine the ultimate "end user" of US chips under such a large and complex system. US officers should assume that if Beijing can violate end-use agreements, it will.

Finally, permitting US persons to work in China's chip plants and directly transfer expertise and know-how for even legacy chips may also indirectly, but substantially, impact China's chipmaking capabilities at leading-edge nodes, the level where the technology-transfer restrictions apply. BIS should strongly encourage US talent to leave China's semiconductor industry and work elsewhere, including the United States, where numerous fabs are under construction.

One of the main opportunities provided by the CHIPS and Science Act is to smooth such US or partner transitions away from China—whether for personnel, production capacity, or equipment sales—alongside otherwise commercially costly restrictions.[18]

Eroding Beijing's Confidence in War

There is a popular idea in Taiwan that the island's dominance in chipmaking confers a "silicon shield"—that is, a deterrent against war since any wartime damage to Taiwan's fabs could create supply shocks that would hurt China's economy as much as anyone else's.[19]

As discussed in other chapters in this report, the degree to which Beijing perceives and respects a "silicon shield" over Taiwan is debatable, and perhaps even dubious. Some nationalistic commentators in China have asserted that Taiwan's fabs are a point *in favor* of Beijing's invading Taiwan, based on the (faulty) assumption that the fabs could be nationalized and easily put to work producing chips as part of China's industrial juggernaut.[20] In fact, Taiwan's fabs would struggle to produce much of anything in the aftermath of even a quickly successful invasion by China. Fabs unscathed by bombs would still find it difficult to maintain operations without the support of Taiwanese workers—let alone the equipment, engineering, consumables, software, and equipment upgrades provided daily by companies domiciled in the United States, Japan, and other democracies. Washington and its allies would be as loath to support Beijing's industry as they are loath to support the Russian economy following its February 2022 reinvasion of Ukraine. And Taiwan's contract foundry business model—which relies on close collaboration and deep trust between chip designer clients and the manufacturer—would be shattered. If there is a "silicon shield" over Taiwan, Beijing does not yet fear it.

Even so, there can be little doubt Beijing is weighing the effects of a potential war on its supply chains. While semiconductors are unlikely to be a primary factor for or against Beijing's decision to invade Taiwan, Washington should still do what it can to help Beijing ponder wartime scenarios and their likely impact on China's semiconductor supplies. Any realistic appraisal by Beijing would have to view the supply shocks—both to semiconductors and a broad range of other Western goods, services, and infrastructure on which China relies—resulting from any hostile acts, including invasion, as less of a "pro" and much more of a "con."

A decision by Beijing to commit aggression against Taiwan would ultimately be an act of *optimism* by Xi Jinping—optimism that he can achieve more through war than through peaceful means, and optimism that the costs of a war would be manageable. Depriving Xi of his path toward making China the OPEC of microchips, a journey described in the chapters that follow, might gnaw at his optimism about how well China could manage the economic shocks stemming from an invasion of Taiwan. Therefore, enlisting US partners into a coordinated strategy on semiconductors—both in shouldering shared costs and in mutually opening our markets to new shared opportunities—is an approach worth undertaking.

NOTES

1. Robert D. Atkinson, Nigel Cory, and Stephen Ezell, "Stopping China's Mercantilism: A Doctrine of Constructive, Alliance-Backed Confrontation," ITIF, March 16, 2017.

2. Ben Murphy, Rogier Creemers, Elsa Kania, Paul Triolo, and Kevin Neville, trans., "Xi-Jinping: 'Strive to Become the World's Primary Center for Science and High Ground for Innovation,'" DigiChina, March 18, 2021; see also Chinese original: "努力成为世界主要科学中心和创新高地," Qiushi, March 15, 2021 (speech given May 28, 2018), https://archive.vn/pC0k7.

3. Robert D. Atkinson, Nigel Cory, and Stephen J. Ezell, "Stopping China's Mercantilism: A Doctrine of Constructive, Alliance-Backed Confrontation," ITIF, March 2017.

4. Julie Zhu, "Exclusive: China Readying $143 Billion Package for Its Chip Firms in Face of US Curbs," Reuters, December 13, 2022.

5. Matt Pottinger, "Beijing's American Hustle: How Chinese Grand Strategy Exploits US Power," *Foreign Affairs*, August 23, 2021.

6. Pottinger, "Beijing's American Hustle."

7. Matt Pottinger, Matthew Johnson, and David Feith, "What China's Leader Wants—and How to Stop Him from Getting It," *Foreign Affairs*, November 30, 2022.

8. Originally used with Huawei and affiliates in 2020, the FDPR was again employed in October 2022 to include twenty-eight firms supporting supercomputing applications in China, and then expanded once more in December 2022 to cover twenty-one additional firms involved in computing for China's military. See Ellen Nakashima, Jeanne Whalen, and Cate Cadell, "US Widens Ban on Military and Surveillance Tech to China," *Washington Post*, December 15, 2022.

9. Bureau of Industry and Security, "Commerce Implements New Export Controls on Advanced Computing and Semiconductor Manufacturing Items to the People's Republic of China (PRC)," US Department of Commerce, press release, October 7, 2002.

10. The White House, "Remarks by National Security Advisor Jake Sullivan at the Special Competitive Studies Project Global Emerging Technologies Summit," September 16, 2022.

11. I am grateful to the Stanford University Gordian Knot Center's Steve Blank for this accounting of subsystem buyers and sellers.

12. John H. Henshaw, "The Origins of COCOM: Lessons for Contemporary Proliferation Control Regimes," Henry L. Stimson Center, Report No. 7, May 1993.

13. Son Ji-hyoung, "Is US Export Ban Forcing Korean Chipmakers to Exit from China?," *Korea Herald*, October 18, 2022.

14. China-based military supercomputing and simulation firm Phytium Information Technology was able to acquire advanced-logic chips of its own design but fabricated through Taiwan's TSMC using capabilities controlled inside China, before being added to a US blacklist. See Coco Feng and Che Pan, "US-China Tech War: Supercomputer Sanctions on China Begin to Bite as Taiwan's TSMC Said to Suspend Chip Orders," *South China Morning Post*, April 13, 2021.

15. As described earlier in this report and as originally reported by TechInsights, SMIC's 2022 MinerVa Bitcoin Miner was manufactured without the use of export-controlled extreme ultraviolet (EUV) etching technology (potentially DUV) to produce a 7nm application-specific integrated circuit (ASIC) sold commercially. See TechInsights, "SMIC 7nm Technology Found in MinerVa Bitcoin Miner," accessed June 6, 2023.

16. Ian Talley, "US Export Limits Target 28 Chinese Entities, Citing Alleged Ties to Iranian Military," *Wall Street Journal*, March 2, 2023; see also Dorsey & Whitney LLP, "United States Continues Expansion of Export Control Sanctions on Chinese Companies," JDSupra, February 17, 2023.

17. Gregory C. Allen, Emily Benson, and William Alan Reinsch, "Improved Export Controls Enforcement Technology Needed for US National Security," CSIS, November 30, 2022.

18. This 2022 Rhodium Group analysis offers estimates of ranges of costs to Western semiconductor firms resulting from different degrees of export controls and notes the potential for costs to be offset by new supply chain investment outside of China: Reva Goujon, Lauren Dudley, Jan-Peter Kleinhans, and Agatha Kratz, "Freeze-in-Place: The Impact of US Tech Controls on China," Rhodium Group, October 21, 2022.

19. Another formulation of the "silicon shield" concept is that Taiwan's role in the global semiconductor supply chain makes it so important that global powers will not abide its assault by China.

20. Jianrong Cai, "Ten Benefits of Taking Back Taiwan: We Can Nationalize TSMC Immediately," YouTube, September 23, 2021, translated and re-uploaded October 11, 2021.

CHAPTER EIGHT

China's Lagging Techno-Nationalism

GLENN TIFFERT

What tools has China historically employed to improve its semiconductor supply chain competitiveness and self-sufficiency—and what are the prospects for its future success? So far, China has a mixed record on policy design and execution. But, as in other sectors, it can be expected to sustain great losses over time as it continues adjusting its approach.

• • •

In 2021, China's national market for semiconductors was the largest in the world at $192.5 billion in sales or nearly 35 percent of the global total.[1] After decades of generous state support, capital stock in China's semiconductor industry has mushroomed, but the value of production by companies headquartered there is still only about 6.6 percent of consumption, and indigenous firms lag in many key segments of the market.[2] China's dependence on imported semiconductors, and the technologies and inputs to manufacture them, therefore, remains acute.[3] In addition, profitability has been elusive because of inefficiency, corruption, predatory pricing, and the cost of foreign licenses. While China's policy makers have redoubled their efforts to modernize the country's technology base, cultivate self-sufficiency, and improve the security of its supply chains, intensifying US countermeasures cloud their prospects for success and may thwart their plans for years to come.

Industry Origins in Techno-Nationalism

A defiant strain of techno-nationalism animates China's industrial policy on semiconductors.[4] Across the nineteenth and twentieth centuries, technological inferiority left China prone to repeated foreign aggression and invasion. Some in China draw parallels between that "century of humiliation" and the frustrated ambitions that their country purportedly suffers today at the hands of US power. Under General Secretary Xi Jinping, a "never again" mentality has grown more prominent, and those who share it dream of turning the tables on any who would try— for example, through export controls—to contain China, keep it down, or "strangle" (卡脖子) it. For Xi, the stakes are high. He has personally cited China's ostensible capacity to innovate, achieve technological breakthroughs, and recenter the world economy around itself as proof that his signature "new type whole-nation" (新型举国体制) socialism is superior to competing ideological systems.[5]

China's government first incorporated semiconductors into state planning and industrial policy in 1956, and for a short while, China counted itself at the forefront of East Asia in this emerging technology. It created its first integrated circuit in 1965, seven years after the United States. By the 1970s, however, China had fallen far behind some of its neighbors, and it has struggled to catch up ever since.

From 1990 to 2014, China's government undertook a succession of state-led development projects that fell far short of their goals but nonetheless laid the foundations for today's achievements.[6] Step-by-step, it imported machinery, established joint ventures with foreign partners, sent students abroad to study and acquire industry experience, hired expatriate talent, courted foreign capital, and pursued foreign intellectual property (IP) and trade secrets both legally and illicitly—all to facilitate technology transfer and build national champions. China's accession to the World Trade Organization (WTO) in 2001, its enormous and increasingly affluent consumer base, its centrality as a manufacturing hub for the global electronics industry, expanding state incentives, and protectionist local procurement policies all accelerated its progress. Some of today's leading firms—such as Huahong Group (comprising Hua Hong Semiconductor, HH Grace, and Shanghai

Huali) and Semiconductor Manufacturing International Corporation (SMIC)—were among the principal beneficiaries.[7]

But while China's semiconductor industry advanced quickly in these decades, it failed to catch up to its foreign competitors—they moved faster, and each successive generation of technology involved higher barriers to entry. Apart from Huawei's HiSilicon subsidiary, no domestic firms achieved breakthrough success as designers or manufacturers for the commercial market. Similarly, China's trade deficit in semiconductors widened because growing demand outpaced gains in domestic output. Frustrated, China's government responded not by changing course but by intensifying its mercantilist promotion of import substitution and national champions, as well as by its pursuit of foreign technology and know-how.

Doubling Down after 2014

In 2014, the State Council released a Guideline for the Promotion of the Development of the National Integrated Circuit Industry, one of sixteen megaprojects envisioned by an earlier Medium- and Long-Term Plan for Science and Technology (2006–2020; see table 8.1 for a timeline of the Guideline and other key national policies since 2014).[8] Like many industrial policy initiatives launched under Xi Jinping, the Guideline was a bold, campaign-style plan that mobilized resources on a grand scale and framed success as a test of discipline and will. Its goals included mastery of process nodes down to 16–14nm and the development of advanced indigenous players in assembly, packaging and testing, equipment, materials, and design segments. It proposed a national investment fund ("Big Fund") to finance these plans, as well as favorable tax treatment and complementary venture capital, equity investment, and debt-financing tools. To accelerate the transfer of technology and skills, it recommended strengthening cooperation with foreign R&D institutions and "vigorously promoting" recruitment of overseas technical, managerial, and entrepreneurial teams, including via the Thousand Talents program.[9] Fractal measures at the local and provincial levels followed.[10]

Table 8.1. Timeline of Major National-Level Semiconductor Policies in China

YEAR	POLICY	DETAIL
2014	Guideline for the Promotion of the Development of the National Integrated Circuit Industry (the 2014 Guideline), State Council	Marked the start of the current phase of semiconductor policy.
		Set initial targets, tax relief, direct financing, and equity capital through state-linked central and regional investment funds.
		Established the National Integrated Circuit Industry Investment Fund I (Big Fund I), raising a total of ~$20 billion.
		In 2019, Big Fund was recapitalized as Big Fund II with ~$32 billion of registered capital.
2015	Made in China 2025 (MiC 2025), State Council	Focused attention on China's goals for self-sufficiency.
		Set specific targets for attaining 40% self-sufficiency in China's semiconductor consumption by 2020 and 70% by 2025.
		Directed that China's enterprises reach the "international first grade" by 2030 in process equipment at nodes of 90nm and below and in lithography equipment, including extreme ultraviolet (EUV).[a]
		Targets proved unrealistic—has since exited official discourse.
2015	Digital Silk Road (DSR)	Entered official discourse as an extension of the Belt and Road Initiative (BRI).
		Likely goals: expand end markets for China's technology companies, serve a set of strategic goals, and increase adoption of China's digital standards.
2016	13th Five-Year Plan for Science and Technology Innovation 2016–2020 (13th FYPSTI), State Council	Semiconductor goals included 14nm etching equipment and 28nm immersion lithography machines.
2020	Several Policies to Stimulate a New Era of High-Quality Integrated Circuit and Software Development (Several Policies), State Council	Offered conditional tax breaks to leading-edge manufacturing (<28nm), design, and software companies; improved import tariff exemptions for materials and equipment.
		Offered an accelerated IPO review process for companies to list on relevant exchanges.

Table 8.1. (continued)

YEAR	POLICY	DETAIL
2021	14th Five-Year Plan 2021–2025 (14th FYP), State Council	Treated semiconductors as an independent category (unlike the 13th FYP), one of seven frontier technologies prioritized for national breakthroughs.
		Specifically aims for breakthroughs in integrated circuit design tools, key semiconductor equipment and materials, advanced-memory technology, and third-generation wide-bandgap semiconductors.[b]

[a]John Lee and Jan-Peter Kleinhans, *Mapping China's Semiconductor Ecosystem in Global Context: Strategic Dimensions and Conclusions*, Stiftung Neue Verantwortung and MERICS, June 2021.
[b]Xinhua News Agency, "中华人民共和国国民经济和社会发展第十四个五年规划和2035年远景目标纲," March 13, 2021, http://www.gov.cn/xinwen/2021-03/13/content_5592681.htm (CN).

The Made in China 2025 plan and the 14th Five-Year Plan (2021–2025; 14th FYP) reaffirmed this framework. The 14th FYP lists semiconductors among seven frontier fields to "attack" (攻关), calling specifically for research and development in design tools, key equipment, and high-purity materials; breakthroughs in insulated-gate bipolar transistors and microelectromechanical systems; advances in memory technology; and the development of wide-bandgap semiconductors (silicon carbide, gallium nitride, and other varieties).[11] In support of these priorities, national ministries, provinces, and localities again issued a cascade of complementary policies.[12]

State support for China's semiconductor industry is growing. According to one assessment, by 2021 the state controlled or owned 43 percent of the industry's registered capital.[13] The Organisation for Economic Co-operation and Development (OECD) calculated the share of state subsidies in total firm revenues for three of China's largest indigenous semiconductor manufacturers from 2014 to 2018; the results were SMIC, 40 percent; Tsinghua Unigroup, 30 percent; and Hua Hong, 22 percent. The comparable figure for three leading foreign firms—Taiwan Semiconductor Manufacturing Company (TSMC), Samsung, and Intel—was approximately 3 percent.[14] Likewise, a 2019 estimate valued China's total assistance to its semiconductor industry at 137 percent of global sales—compared to 11 percent for Japan, 3.8 percent for Taiwan, 2.3 percent for the European Union (EU), and 0.01 percent for each South Korea and the United States.[15] By one calculation, the ten-year total cost of ownership for a new manufacturing facility ("fab") in the United States is 37 to 50 percent higher than in China, and as much as 40 to 70 percent of that difference is directly attributable to People's Republic of China (PRC) government incentives.[16] These incentives include $73 billion in state-linked semiconductor investment funds at the national and local levels, as well as an unspecified quantity of government grants, reduced utility rates, free or discounted land, and concessional loans, the last of which may exceed $50 billion.[17] But even this accounting likely omits other forms of support. For instance, in 2021 the Shanghai municipal government alone set aside $50 billion in financing for a Shanghai integrated circuit cluster backed by the Ministry of Industry and Information Technology.[18]

These sums and the political signaling behind them sparked a gold rush. Between 2014 and 2020, the quantity of venture capital flowing into China's semiconductor industry grew more than tenfold.[19] Between 2014 and 2021, more than 110 new fabs were announced in China, with a total committed investment of $196 billion.[20] Entire production teams were recruited from Taiwan and Korea to staff these facilities and train local personnel. A 2019 report estimated that more than three thousand engineers—equivalent to nearly 10 percent of Taiwan's R&D workforce in semiconductors at the time—moved to China, lured by salaries double to triple what they could earn at home.[21] The transplants included luminaries such as former TSMC chief operating officer Chiang Shang-yi, former TSMC and Samsung senior executive Liang Mong-song, Inotera Memories chairman Charles Kao, and former United Microelectronics Corporation (UMC) vice chair Sun Shih-wei.

Today's Mixed Results

This combination of state support, technology transfer, and protectionism has yielded mixed results. On the one hand, in 2021 China ranked sixth in global semiconductor sales, according to estimates from the

Semiconductor Industry Association (SIA) and IC Insights, a market research firm. (See figure 8.1: note that "sales" refers to the final purchase of chips, which often goes through a chip designer independent of manufacturing location; for example, a US sale for 2023 would include US fabless chip design firm Qualcomm contracting with TSMC fabs in Taiwan to produce its latest Snapdragon 8 Gen 2 chips in order to be sold to PRC smartphone producer Xiaomi.)

Likewise, China has a 46 percent share of the global market in assembly, packaging, and testing, and it produces around one-quarter of the world's NAND Flash memory (including through Korea-based firms manufacturing in China). Overall, China has approximately one-quarter of the world's installed chip (wafer) manufacturing capacity—nearly all of it in high-volume, trailing-edge products (again, including fabs in China owned by foreign firms).[22] China's share of this segment is expected to grow rapidly as new fabs come online.

China-based firms have built notable positions in some segments of the global chip supply chain (table 8.2). For example, boosted by local procurement policies, China's largest indigenous pure-play foundries—SMIC, Hua Hong Semiconductor, and Nexchip—are ranked fourth, fifth, and ninth by worldwide chip manufacturing revenue in 2021, with 5.1 percent, 2.7 percent, and 1.1 percent global market shares, respectively. By comparison, industry leaders TSMC and Samsung accounted

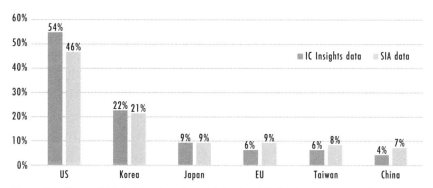

Figure 8.1. Share of Global Semiconductor Sales in 2021, by Corporate Headquarters Location

Source: Research Bulletin, *IC Insights*, April 5, 2022, Semiconductor Industry Association, 2022 Factbook, April 21, 2022, 3.

Table 8.2. Rankings of Leading PRC Semiconductor Manufacturing Firms by Category (2021)

MANUFACTURING SEGMENT	COMPANY	GLOBAL MARKET RANK WITHIN SEGMENT	GLOBAL MARKET SHARE WITHIN SEGMENT
Pure-play foundry[a]	SMIC	4	5.1%
	Hua Hong	5	2.7%
	Nexchip	9	1.1%
DRAM[b]	ChangXin Memory Technologies (CXMT)	5	1.4%
NAND[c]	YMTC	6	4.4%

[a]Thomas Alsop, "Leading Semiconductor Foundries Revenue Share Worldwide from 2019 to 2022, by Quarter," Statista, June 20, 2022.

[b]Horizon Advisory, "Project 506: CXMT and China's Semiconductor Industrial Policy," December 2022; Tom Coughlin, "ChangXin Memory Technologies Supplies Chinese Consumer DRAM Market," Forbes, June 9, 2021.

[c]Kim Eun-jin, "US Moving to Limit NAND Production Equipment Exports to China," BusinessKorea, August 3, 2022.

for 53.2 percent and 17.5 percent of manufacturing revenue.[23] In 2022, SMIC began mass production at the 14nm node and, as described earlier in this report, surprised the world with a rudimentary 7nm application-specific integrated circuit (ASIC). Also in that year, Yangtze Memory Technology Corporation (YMTC) leapfrogged the competition by releasing the world's first NAND Flash memory chips with more than two hundred layers.[24] YMTC's share of global NAND production grew from 1 percent in 2020 to around 5 percent in 2021, reportedly assisted by $24 billion in subsidies.[25]

GigaDevice, a fabless designer of NOR Flash memory (used in applications such as medical devices that require high reliability), ranked third in the world by sales in 2021, with a 23.2 percent share in that specialized market.[26] Startup NETINT's video processing units (VPUs), while still a small and specialized market, are widely used by content-delivery networks, social media platforms, and data centers in

China.[27] Finally, Quectel, Fibocom, and Sunsea captured half of the global market for the cellular internet-of-things (IoT) modules embedded in smart meters, point-of-sale terminals, health care devices, autos, and industrial systems. Use of PRC vendors in these technologies that interface with the physical environment has drawn concerns about data security and privacy.[28]

On the other hand, critical gaps remain in China's domestic semiconductor supply chain.[29] For instance, China has no major analog mixed-signal microprocessor, microcontroller, or specialty logic manufacturers in the global market, and its industry remains dependent on essential intellectual property from abroad—in particular, the electronic design automation (EDA) software used to design chips and the instruction set architectures (ISA) and IP cores that define them.[30] (As described in chapter 2 of this report, an ISA describes the interface between a device's processor and the software that runs on it. A well-known example is the x86 standard pioneered by Intel. IP cores, such as those offered by the UK-based company ARM, provide discrete blocks of functional logic that designers can license for incorporation into their chips.[31]) Additionally, China's equipment manufacturers trail the market leaders.[32] China is self-sufficient only as far as the 90nm process node because of the limitations of its indigenous semiconductor manufacturing equipment suite—indeed, its most advanced indigenous equipment, in areas of etching and thermal processing, reaches no further than the 28nm node.[33] Recent US export controls target those bottlenecks by blocking access to more-advanced foreign technologies— a move that will pressure China to devise circumvention strategies and alternatives.[34]

Despite hundreds of billions of dollars in state support, output has fallen far short of policy goals. While the value of semiconductor production by foreign and domestic firms in China greatly expanded in absolute terms, as a share of domestic consumption, it rose by less than two percentage points between 2014 and 2021, from 15.1 percent to 17 percent.[35] Foreign firms operating within China outproduced indigenous firms by a factor of two in 2020 and will continue to lead through at least 2025. According to official PRC customs statistics, in

Table 8.3. Made in China 2025 Performance Report

YEAR	TARGET	ACTUAL PRODUCTION	BY INDIGENOUS FIRMS
2020	40%	15.9%	5.9%
2025	70%	19.4%*	7.5%*

(*) = Forecasts

Source: IC Insights, "China Forecast to Fall Far Short of Its 'Made in China 2025' Goals for ICs," January 6, 2021.

2021 the dollar value of China's semiconductor imports was approximately twenty-eight times higher than that of its semiconductor exports.[36] The scale of this imbalance is due to China's dual status as the producer of 36 percent of the world's electronics and the second-largest final consumer market for electronics with semiconductors.[37]

The share of consumption produced by indigenous firms paints an especially unflattering picture. The Made in China 2025 plan boldly set self-sufficiency targets of 40 percent for 2020 and 70 percent for 2025. An industry publication estimates that China achieved just 5.9 percent self-sufficiency in 2020 and forecasts 7.5 percent in 2025 (table 8.3).[38]

What Held China Back?

The limits on China's past performance were attributable mostly to local factors, of which four were central: human capital, economics, fraud, and clientelism.

First, China's semiconductor industry has struggled to source qualified talent at home and has relied heavily on recruitment from abroad for its senior managers, engineers, and developers. Workforce development remains a severe bottleneck. In 2020, China graduated 210,000 college students with semiconductor-related majors, but many of them reportedly had weak skills, and despite high youth unemployment, just 13.77 percent of them entered the semiconductor industry. And trends remain unfavorable. China's labor pool is shrinking, only 12.5 percent of it has graduated from college, and those with technology majors have many career options in China and beyond.

Furthermore, turnover within the industry is high because of a demanding work culture, fierce competition, and the lure of other high-tech professions. Foundries, in particular, struggle to retain talent because the government entities and state-owned enterprises that invest in them are oriented toward output maximization rather than staff development, and high capital costs constrain operating budgets. In 2020, 17 percent of SMIC's employees left the firm, compared to a 12.5 percent turnover rate in the industry at large. Industry watchers report that engineers who staff production lines are leaving for design work, which offers higher pay and shorter, more predictable hours—the relative attractiveness of working in software-oriented rather than manufacturing roles is a phenomenon also observed in the United States, as described in chapter 2. Firms are scrambling to replace them and keep pace with ambitious expansion plans. Analysts predict more than two hundred thousand unfilled positions in China by 2023, though slumping demand for semiconductors may reduce that shortfall.[39]

Second, market forces militated against leadership and self-sufficiency. In general, China's semiconductor policy has pursued a two-track approach: one, cultivating a secure domestic production base of national champions through local procurement policies, state-assisted technology transfer, and preferential access to incentives; and two, fostering a vibrant ecosystem of other firms connected to the global marketplace and compelled to compete in it. The hope was to create a virtuous cycle in which the latter would power domestic innovation and elevate the former. But the contradictions between the mercantilist and market principles underlying each pole in that relationship have proved difficult to bridge.

By insulating a subset of firms from foreign competition and market discipline—as well as taking a firmer hand in their management—the central government has impeded efficiency and innovation where it needs them most. Seeking lower investment risk and higher returns on capital, provincial and local governments commonly passed over indigenous firms in favor of prestigious foreign rivals with superior technology and proven capabilities. Global leaders such as Intel, SK hynix, Samsung, TSMC, and UMC capitalized on this preference, feasting on state incentives to shift manufacturing to China. To this day, these foreign outposts dominate China's output. They have brought sought-after technology, trained local personnel, and stimulated an ecosystem of secondary suppliers—all of which, over time, may yet lift the competitiveness of China's national champions. But until the indigenous firms are more exposed to market discipline, their potential to lead in technology—let alone in volume or price—remains an open question.

Venture capital has also followed the market, further suppressing local self-sufficiency in favor of the distributed division of labor that is typical of other global supply chains. Hence, in 2020, 67.2 percent of venture capital deals in China's semiconductor industry involved design firms, drawn by comparatively low startup costs. This investment catapulted China to third place among the world's fabless design centers. By one estimate, as of 2022 about a dozen firms in China were producing 5nm designs, and some were on the cusp of advancing to 3nm.[40] To realize their creations, these designers used the most-advanced tools and partners available to them—US software and Taiwan's foundries—and irrespective of export controls, the knock-on effects of design firms doing so left China lagging in many key segments, including EDA tools, manufacturing equipment, supporting software architectures, and high-end materials, particularly wafers and chemicals.[41] So long as indigenous firms could tap the best of what the world had to offer, local investors had low economic incentives to reinvent the wheel (see figure 8.2).

Third, the state consequently had to shoulder much of the capital-intensive burden of self-sufficiency by itself—and, as with past "great leaps forward," hyperbole, waste, and corruption flourished. Drawn by official largesse, a tidal wave of firms registered as integrated circuit–related enterprises—fifty-eight thousand during the first ten months of 2020 alone. A great many hastily rebranded themselves from other lines of business, reportedly squandering state assets as "three no" (三无) enterprises: no experience, no talent, and no technology.[42]

Dozens of promised fabs were never delivered, and some of the most high-profile projects and firms collapsed amid lurid scandals and allegations of fraud. The case of Wuhan Hongxin was notorious. In

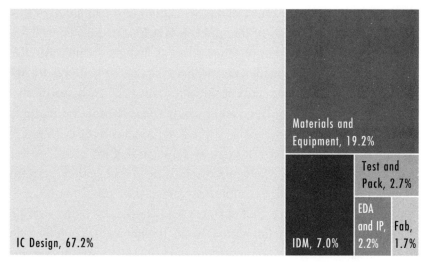

Figure 8.2. China Semiconductor Venture Capital Investment by Sector (2020)
Note: IDM = integrated device manufacturer; IC = integrated circuit
Source: Jane Zhang, "China's Semiconductors: How Wuhan's Challenger to Chinese Chip Champion Turned from Dream to Nightmare," *South China Morning Post,* March 20, 2021. Investment data from Winsoul Capital.

early 2018, officials in the city of Wuhan broke ground on a site that was billed to include China's first 7nm production line as well as a companion 14nm line, each to have an output of thirty thousand wafers per month. The project recruited Chiang Shang-yi, former chief operating officer of TSMC, to serve as chief executive of a team that comprised more than one hundred engineers from TSMC. According to municipal authorities, it would ultimately involve $18.5 billion in investment, of which more than $2 billion had been delivered by the end of 2019. But when the project collapsed the following year, no buildings were complete, and today the site lies derelict. Among its cofounders, one had no more than an elementary school education and was operating under a false identity; another was known as a vendor of traditional herbal medicine and tobacco rather than high-tech goods. Both vanished.[43] Between 2019 and 2021, at least five other major chip ventures also failed, including a $100 million joint venture between US-based GlobalFoundries and the Chengdu city government that was touted as a "miracle"—but never started production. Projects by

Tacoma Semiconductor and Dehuai Semiconductor met similar fates, but after securing billions of renminbi (RMB) in state financing.[44]

No firm soared as high or fell as hard as Tsinghua Unigroup. Led by a real estate mogul with extraordinary access to state credit, the firm entered the semiconductor business just ahead of the opportunities created by the 2014 Guideline and quickly spent its way to the top of China's semiconductor industry. Over a five-year period, it sought to invest $47 billion in Western companies, including a $23 billion bid for Micron that jolted US regulators into heightening their scrutiny of PRC investments and was ultimately blocked by the Committee on Foreign Investment in the United States (CFIUS) process. After defaulting under a $30 billion mountain of debt, Tsinghua Unigroup filed for bankruptcy in 2021 and reemerged after a court-led restructuring and ownership change the following year.[45]

Fourth, beyond straightforward fraud, the marriage of state power and capital behind such deals also reinforced more subtle existing pathologies of governance in China by creating rich opportunities for intra-elite competition, clientelism, and rent seeking. For instance, Jiang Mianheng, son of late Party General Secretary Jiang Zemin, personally presided over Shanghai's emergence as China's semiconductor capital via a network of investment vehicles through which he channeled immense quantities of state and foreign capital.[46] In Beijing, Tsinghua Unigroup's meteoric (if fraudulent) rise actually began when Hu Haifeng, son of Party General Secretary Hu Jintao, served as its corporate party chairman. In a 2020 article since deleted, state media explored shadowy connections between the Wuhan Hongxin debacle and senior military figures, including air force general Liu Yazhou and his younger brother, PLA intelligence department major general Liu Yasu, who were quietly arrested in December 2021. The older Liu is the son-in-law of the late PRC state chairman Li Xiannian, who had once served as mayor of Wuhan.[47]

In the summer of 2022, the state tacitly acknowledged the depth of clientelism and high-level corruption when it arrested or placed under investigation several officials who had long guided the implementation of its semiconductors policy, including Xiao Yaqing, former head of the Ministry of Industry and Information Technology (MIIT); Ding Wenwu, former president of the Big Fund and chief of the semiconductors policy department at MIIT; Lu Jun, former chief of Sino IC Capital, which manages the Big Fund; Ren Kai, a vice president of Sino IC Capital and a director of SMIC; Zhao Weiguo, former chairman of Tsinghua Unigroup and YMTC; and Diao Shijing, a former Tsinghua Unigroup copresident.[48] The details of each case may never fully emerge—but even beyond any personal culpability in the disappointing performance and scandals detailed above, their downfall and the patronage networks of senior political and military figures they were quietly connected to set off speculation about intrigue at the highest levels of power.[49]

Looking Ahead

The intensification of US export controls since 2018 has laid bare the gaps and vulnerabilities in China's semiconductor industry. If enforced strictly, US restrictions on lithography tools, EDA software, high-performance chips, and components will not only block the industry's ascent up the value chain but also degrade its current capabilities by hampering the performance, maintenance, and replacement of equipment already in the field. Employment restrictions on US citizens and green card holders—coupled with parallel measures by Taiwan and growing unease in Japan and Korea—promise to choke off imported talent where local capabilities are weakest: upper management, manufacturing, and R&D. The expanding roster of semiconductor companies on the Department of Commerce's Entity List, including SMIC (logic), YMTC (NAND), and Cambricon (artificial intelligence [AI] chips), will impair operations at some of China's flagship firms. The short- to medium-term impact of these measures will be devastating.

Nevertheless, Xi appears undaunted, and foreign pressure plays to his techno-nationalist instincts. As an illustration: Xi selected Jin Zhuanglong as the minister of industry and information technology in July 2022. Before assuming this post, Jin served as chairman of the Commercial Aircraft Corporation of China (COMAC), China's homegrown contender in the commercial aviation market against Airbus and Boeing, and as executive deputy director of the Office of the Central Military-Civilian Integration Development Commission, the body charged with coordinating China's policy of military-civil fusion. Jin's appointment, then, suggests that the state will take a more active role in the management of the semiconductor industry. It also implies that China may adopt a posture oriented toward national security considerations and great-power competition, not globalized cooperation.

The state continues to funnel copious resources into the semiconductor industry, and it is introducing new policies and refining old ones to manage present challenges. For example, up until now, PRC-based firms have been reluctant to settle for domestic semiconductor manufacturing equipment when superior foreign alternatives were available. In principle, recent US export controls hand much of the market back to indigenous suppliers, and the PRC government is reportedly preparing to subsidize this transition. China's equipment manufacturers will need to rise to this opportunity by developing the products their captive market demands.[50] Similarly, Shenzhen has drafted a plan to subsidize a move to domestic EDA tools, which trail their foreign competitors by a wide margin. The plan also funds the use of advanced IP cores in domestic chip designs, promotes R&D on advanced packaging techniques (such as chiplets), and subsidizes development on RISC-V (reduced instruction set computer "five"), a free and open instruction-set architecture that has attracted strong interest from PRC firms.[51] The promotion of domestic equipment and RISC-V reflects a broad effort to mitigate the risk of exposure to US technology by designing it out of supply chains. To the extent that foreign firms perceive a commercial advantage in facilitating that abatement, their interests may coincide with China's, eroding the effectiveness of US export controls and the position of US technology in the marketplace.

A suite of other initiatives is under way. PRC universities are at the forefront of fundamental research in semiconductor-related fields.[52] In 2022, the government began underwriting the costs of specialized schools for integrated circuits at Tsinghua University, Peking

University, and Huazhong University of Science and Technology; in cooperation with industry partners, these schools hope to foster the commercialization of basic research and teach practical skills. They aim to create pipelines for better-trained engineers and technicians to enter the industry and improve job placement and retention.

To bridge the gap between startups and national champions, the government has breathed new life into a program to support ten thousand "little giants" (小巨人) from among China's small and medium enterprises in strategically important sectors. Chastened by recent experience, this program seeks to prevent fraud by carefully screening applicants and tracking performance.[53] Regulators have also approved a surge of domestic initial public offerings (IPOs) that could improve the access of local firms in critical segments to capital. During the first eleven months of 2022, forty-six design, fabrication, components, and materials firms went public—compared to nineteen during the same period the year before.[54] Exchange-traded funds from firms such as ICBC Credit Suisse Asset Management and ChinaAMC allow international investors to participate in this market.

PRC-based firms are adapting creatively to the obstacles in their path. Some, for example, are concealing their successes to avoid unwanted scrutiny. Neither SMIC nor YMTC publicly announced their respective breakthroughs at the 7nm and 232-layer scales in 2022, feats that would have been celebrated loudly in years past. Instead, industry watchers discovered and analyzed the chips after they had entered the supply chain. Other firms, such as Alibaba and Biren, are throttling back the performance of their latest designs so that TSMC can continue to manufacture them without running afoul of US restrictions.[55]

Blocked from pursuing high-end manufacturing, the industry is shifting investment to trailing-edge logic and memory, which still account for the lion's share of global sales. Following the examples of solar panels, batteries, and telecommunications, a subsidized expansion of output in these categories could enable PRC firms to underprice foreign competitors and force them out of the market. If China succeeds in this gambit, it could starve foreign firms of the revenue that sustains the reinvestment in R&D needed to stay competitive over

Table 8.4. R&D as a Percentage of Sales (2020)

	UNITED STATES	EUROPE	JAPAN	CHINA	EMERGING MARKETS	GLOBAL
R&D as a percentage of sales	18.6%	17.1%	12.9%	6.8%	8.6%	13.7%

Source: Semiconductor Industry Association, 2021 State of the US Semiconductor Industry, September 2021, 18.

time; instead, that revenue would flow to China and finance the ascent of its own firms.

That strategy would play to China's strengths. To date, China's semiconductor industry has advanced with levels of R&D spending less than half the global average (table 8.4). While this model cannot support a bid for technological leadership, it can fund the establishment of a dominant position in mature technologies. Suppressing competition could slow innovation across the industry.[56]

Conclusion

Leadership and self-sufficiency in semiconductors are political goals without clear benchmarks. Yet Xi's determination to pursue them must not be underestimated, and his administration will bring to bear all the tools at its disposal, including diplomacy, IP theft, and espionage.

Semiconductors are market commodities for which reliability, costs, and features are paramount. Establishing technological leadership requires not just resources, discipline, and will, but also a model of development that fosters the organizational and cultural conditions to allocate inputs efficiently, innovate consistently at competitive prices, and earn the trust of clients. Self-sufficiency sets the bar still higher, suggesting not just a seamless indigenous production chain but also routine upgrades to it since the technology advances relentlessly.

By any measure, China's patchwork semiconductor industry is far from reaching these goals, and the hurdles before it are formidable. China's economy is slowing, the demographic and educational composition of its workforce is unfavorable, and the state is taking a firmer hand in the management of major technology firms, which may impair innovation and market discipline. Mercantilist policies, domestic repression, and rising geopolitical tensions are alienating foreign partners and amplifying calls to decenter China from global supply chains. And US export controls aim to halt China's advance by cutting off access to sought-after technology, equipment, and talent.

Against such headwinds, China may be able to bootstrap itself into a volume leader of mature products such as trailing-edge memory and logic. This feat alone would give China new leverage in its rivalry with the United States by establishing a chokehold on chips used in a wide array of products, including consumer goods, medical devices, automobiles, industrial systems, and military platforms. But absent breakthroughs that enable China's firms to leapfrog competitors—or state subsidies sufficient to cripple competitors—attaining broad self-sufficiency or leadership in semiconductors will likely remain out of reach for the foreseeable future.

NOTES

1. Semiconductor Industry Association, 2022 Factbook, 13.
2. IC Insights, "China-Based IC Production to Represent 21.2% of China IC Market in 2026."
3. Semiconductor Industry Association, "US Needs Greater Semiconductor Manufacturing Incentives," July 24, 2020.
4. Alex Capri, "China's Microchip Ambitions: Semiconductors Advance the Next Phase of Techno-Nationalism," Hinrich Foundation, June 22, 2021.
5. *Xinhua*, 习近平主持召开中央全面深化改革委员会第二十七次会议强调 健全关键核心技术攻关新型举国体制 全面加强资源节约工作 [Xi Jinping Presided over the 27th Meeting of the Central Committee for Comprehensively Deepening Reform, Stressed Improvement of the New Type Whole-Nation System of Core Research and Development, and Comprehensively Strengthening of the Work of Resource Conservation], September 6, 2022, http://www.news.cn /politics/leaders/2022-09/06/c_1128981539.htm; Max J. Zenglein and Anna Holzmann, "Evolving Made in China 2025: China's Industrial Policy in the Quest for Global Leadership," MERICS, July 2, 2019.
6. For instance, National Development and Reform Commission, "高技术产业化"十一五"规划 [11th Five-Year Plan for High-Technology

Industrialization]," April 10, 2008, http://www.mofcom.gov.cn/aarticle/b/g/200804/20080405470382.html.

7. Douglas Fuller, "Growth, Upgrading, and Limited Catch-Up in China's Semiconductor Industry," in *Policy, Regulation, and Innovation in China's Electricity and Telecom Industries*, edited by Loren Brandt and Thomas G. Rawski (New York: Cambridge University Press, 2019), 267–79; John VerWay, "Chinese Semiconductor Industrial Policy: Past and Present," *Journal of International Commerce and Economics*, July 2019, 9–12.

8. State Council, 国家中长期科学和技术发展规划纲 (2006–2020), December 20, 2005, http://www.gov.cn/gongbao/content/2006/content_240244.htm.

9. State Council, "《国家集成电路产业发展推进纲要》正式公布 [Guideline for the Promotion of the Development of the National Integrated Circuit Industry Officially Promulgated]," China Semiconductor Industry Association, October 30, 2019, http://www.csia.net.cn/Article/ShowInfo.asp?InfoID=88343.

10. Eastmoney Securities, "东方财富证券 [The First Phase of Fundraising Bears Fruit, The Second Phase is About to Begin]," 大基金一期投资硕果累累,二期蓄势待发, December 31, 2019, p. 9, https://pdf.dfcfw.com/pdf/H3_AP201912311373119321_1.pdf?1577789587000.pdf.

11. State Council of the PRC, "中华人民共和国国民经济和社会发展第十四个五年规划和2035年远景目标纲要 [Outline of the 14th Five-Year Plan and 2035 Vision for National Economic and Social Development of the PRC]," March 12, 2021, http://www.gov.cn/xinwen/2021-03/13/content_5592681.htm.

12. Beijing Municipal People's Government, "北京市国民经济和社会发展第十四个 五年规划和二〇三五年远景目标纲要 [Outline of the 14th Five-Year Plan and 2035 Vision for the National Economic and Social Development of Beijing]," January 27, 2021, http://fgw.beijing.gov.cn/fgwzwgk/zcgk/ghjhwb/wnjh/202104/P020220614554396990009.pdf; Shanghai Municipal People's Government, 上海市国民经济和社会发展第十四个五年规划 和二〇三五年远景目标纲要 [Outline of the 14th Five-Year Plan and 2035 Vision for the National Economic and Social Development of Shanghai]," January 27, 2021, https://www.shanghai.gov.cn/cmsres/8c/8c8fa1641d9f4807a6897a8c243d96ec/c70c2c6673ae425efd7c11f0502c3ee9.pdf; Zhejiang Province Development and Reform Commission, "浙江省国民经济和社会发展第十四个五年 规划和二〇三五年远景目标纲要 [Outline of the 14th Five-Year Plan and 2035 Vision for the National Economic and Social Development of Zhejiang Province]," February 23, 2021, https://zjjcmspublic.oss-cn-hangzhou-zwynet-d01-a.internet.cloud.zj.gov.cn/jcms_files/jcms1/web3185/site/attach/0/6abf4850723f40ce863f0a7d517072b4.pdf.

13. Semiconductor Industry Association, *SIA Whitepaper: Taking Stock of China's Semiconductor Industry*, July 2021, 3.

14. OECD Trade Policy Papers, *Measuring Distortions in International Markets: The Semiconductor Value Chain*, No. 234, December 12, 2019, p. 8.

15. Stephen Ezell, "Moore's Law under Attack: The Impact of China's Policies on Global Semiconductor Innovation," ITIF, February 18, 2021, p. 22, https:// itif.org/publications/2021/02/18/moores-law-under-attack-impact-chinas -policies-global-semiconductor/.

16. Antonio Varas, Raj Varadarajan, Jimmy Goodrich, and Falan Yinug, *Government Incentives and US Competitiveness in Semiconductor Manufacturing* (Boston, MA: Boston Consulting Group and Semiconductor Industry Association, September 2020), 1.

17. Semiconductor Industry Association, *SIA Whitepaper*, 3; Tianlei Huang, "Government-Guided Funds in China: Financing Vehicles for State Industrial Policy," Peterson Institute for International Economics, June 17, 2019; Yifan Wei, Yuen Yuen Ang, and Nan Jia, "The Promise and Pitfalls of Government Guidance Funds," June 21, 2022, abstract available at https://ssrn.com /abstract=3812796.

18. *Xinhua*, "十四五"先进制造业集群发展蓝图酝酿待出 [The Blueprint for the Development of Advanced Manufacturing Clusters in the '14th Five-Year Plan' Is Brewing and Ready to Come Out]," March 23, 2021, http://www.xinhuanet .com/techpro/2021-03/23/c_1127243005.htm; PRC Ministry of Industry and Information Technology, "先进制造业集群决赛优胜者名单公示 [Advanced Manufacturing Cluster Finalist List Announcement]," March 22, 2021, https:// www.miit.gov.cn/jgsj/ghs/gzdt/art/2021/art_c59a0995a34d4c26a850faae 580f0544.html.

19. Wei Sheng, "Where China Is Investing in Semiconductors, in Charts," TechNode, March 4, 2021.

20. Semiconductor Industry Association, *SIA Whitepaper*, 5.

21. Kensaku Ihara, "Taiwan Loses 3,000 Chip Engineers to 'Made in China 2025,'" *Nikkei Asia*, December 3, 2019.

22. Capacity is in terms of potential water starts per month, not necessarily outputs or value created. See Semiconductor Industry Association, *SIA Whitepaper*, 2.

23. Thomas Alsop, "Leading Semiconductor Foundries Revenue Share Worldwide from 2019 to 2022, by Quarter," Statista, June 20, 2022.

24. Dylan Patel, "2022 NAND–Process Technology Comparison, China's YMTC Shipping Densest NAND, Chips 4 Alliance, Long-Term Financial Outlook," *SemiAnalysis*, August 12, 2022.

25. Qianer Liu and Eleanor Olcott, "China's Chip Darling YMTC Thrust into Spotlight by US Export Controls," *Financial Times*, October 13, 2022.

26. IC Insights, "Top Suppliers Enjoy Big Gains in Small NOR Flash Market," June 21, 2022.

27. Dylan Patel, "Meet NETINT: The Startup Selling Datacenter VPUs to Byte-Dance, Baidu, Tencent, Alibaba, and More," *SemiAnalysis*, August 14, 2022.

28. For example, a US Cybersecurity and Infrastructure Security Agency (CISA) advisory in September 2022 pointed to a hard-coded backdoor password within a GPS chip used by motorcyclists produced by Shanghai-based MiCODUS that allowed for unpermitted access to location tracking. See Alexi Drew, "Chinese Technology in the 'Internet of Things' Poses a New Threat to the West," *Financial Times*, August 10, 2022.

29. Mathieu Duchâtel, *The Weak Links in China's Drive for Semiconductors*, Institut Montaigne (Paris: January 2021).

30. IC Insights, "China Forecast to Fall Far Short of Its 'Made in China 2025' Goals for ICs," January 6, 2021.

31. Scott Fulton III, "Arm Processors: Everything You Need to Know Now," *ZD Net*, March 30, 2021.

32. Will Hunt, Saif M. Khan, and Dahlia Peterson, "China's Progress in Semiconductor Manufacturing Equipment: Accelerants and Policy Implications," Center for Security and Emerging Technology, March 2021.

33. Julie Zhu, "Exclusive: China Readying $143 billion Package for Its Chip Firms in Face of US Curbs," Reuters, December 13, 2022.

34. "Implementation of Certain 2021 Wassenaar Arrangement Decisions on Four Section 1758 Technologies," *Federal Register* 87, no. 156, August 15, 2022, 49979–49986; "Revisions to the Unverified List: Clarifications to Activities and Criteria that May Lead to Additions to the Entity List," *Federal Register* 87, no. 197, October 13, 2022, 61971–61977.

35. IC Insights, "China-Based IC Production to Represent 21.2% of China IC Market in 2026," May 18, 2022; IC Insights, "China Forecast to Fall Far Short of Its 'Made in China 2025' Goals for ICs."

36. General Administration of Customs of the PRC, "2021年12月进口主要商品量值表(美元值) [December 2021 Table of Imports of Major Commodities in Terms of Volume and Value (in Dollars)]," January 18, 2022, http://www.customs.gov.cn/customs/302249/zfxxgk/2799825/302274; General Administration of Customs of the PRC, "2021年12月出口主要商品量值表(人民币值) [December 2021 Table of Exports of Major Commodities in Terms of Volume and Value (in RMB)]," January 18, 2022, http://www.customs.gov.cn/customs/302249/zfxxgk/2799825/302274. The Internal Revenue Service's average currency conversion rate for 2021 of 6.452 RMB to the dollar was applied.

37. Semiconductor Industry Association, *SIA Whitepaper*.

38. IC Insights, "China Forecast to Fall Far Short of Its 'Made in China 2025' Goals for ICs."

39. Jin Yezi, "集成电路人才缺口仍超20万，这些岗位最紧缺 [Integrated Circuit Talent Shortfall Still Exceeds 200,000, These Positions Are in the Shortest

Supply]," *Sina*, October 29, 2019, https://finance.sina.com.cn/roll/2021-10 -29/doc-iktzscyy2370774.shtml.

40. Sheng, "Where China Is Investing in Semiconductors"; Mark Lapedus, "China Accelerates Foundry, Power Semi Efforts," *Semiconductor Engineering*, November 22, 2021.

41. John Lee and Jan-Peter Kleinhans, *Mapping China's Semiconductor Ecosystem in Global Context: Strategic Dimensions and Conclusions*, Stiftung Neue Verantwortung and MERICS, June 2021, 40–51.

42. Song Jie and Guo Fang, "大跃进与烂尾潮同现 国产芯片路在何方? [Great Leap Forward and Rotten Tide at the Same Time: Where Does the Domestic Chip Road Lie?]," *China Economic Weekly*, November 2, 2020, 44–48, http://www.ceweekly.cn/2020/1102/318726.shtml.

43. Wei Sheng, "HSMC Promised China's First 7nm Chips: It Didn't Go Well," *TechNode*, September 9, 2020.

44. Sidney Leng, "US Semiconductor Giant Shuts China Factory Hailed as 'a Miracle,' in Blow to Beijing's Chip Plans," *South China Morning Post*, May 20, 2020; Emily Feng, "A Cautionary Tale for China's Ambitious Chipmakers," NPR, March 25, 2021.

45. Che Pan, "China's Tsinghua Unigroup Completes Debt Restructuring, Ownership Change to Keep Afloat Its Major Semiconductor Operations," *South China Morning Post*, July 12, 2022.

46. Joanne Lee-Young, "Analysis: The Digital Prince of China," CNN, March 6, 2001.

47. *Securities Times*, "千亿武汉弘芯：空壳股东障眼法 "芯骗" 团伙钻产业空子 [Hundred Billion Wuhan Hongxin: Shell Shareholders Cover Up 'Core Fraud,' Gang Exploits Industry Loopholes]," September 25, 2020, https://archive.ph /Zqliz.

48. Li Yuan, "Xi Jinping's Vision for Tech Self-Reliance in China Runs into Reality," *New York Times*, August 22, 2022.

49. Dan Macklin, "What's Driving China's Chip Sector Crackdown," *The Diplomat*, August 29, 2022.

50. Zhu, "Exclusive: China Readying $143 Billion Package."

51. Justice Bureau of Shenzhen Municipality, "深圳市关于促进半导体与集成电路产业高质量发展的若干措施 (征求意见稿) [Several Measures of Shenzhen City for the Promotion of High-Quality Development in the Semiconductor and Integrated Circuit Industry (Draft for Comment)]," October 8, 2022, http://sf.sz.gov.cn/ztzl/gfxwj/gfxwjyjzj_171008/content/mpost_10156478.html.

52. Takeshi Hattori, "ISSCC 2023 、論文採択件数で中国が北米を抜いて史上初の首位に [ISSCC 2023: China Surpassed North America in the Number of Papers Adopted for the First Time in History]," Tech+ , November 21, 2022, https://news.mynavi.jp/techplus/article/20221121-2519134/.

53. Coco Feng, "China Has Named Nearly 9,000 'Little Giants' in Push to Preference Home-Grown Technologies from Smaller Companies," *South China Morning Post*, September 9, 2022; Ministry of Industry and Information Technology, "工业和信息化部办公厅关于开展第四批专精特新"小巨人"企业培育和第一批专精特新"小巨人"企业复核工作的通知 [Notice of the General Officer of the Ministry of Industry and Information Technology on the Cultivation of the Fourth Batch of Specialized New 'Little Giant' Enterprises and the Review of the First Batch of Specialized New 'Little Giant' Enterprises]," Enterprise Letter no. 133, May 15, 2022, https://www.miit.gov.cn/jgsj/qyj/wjfb/art/2022/art_9d88f62a3c5d47bd8698e84d7a486274.html.

54. Che Pan and Ann Cao, "Tech War: Fresh Funding Pipeline Enables China's Sanctions-Hit Semiconductor Industry to Cope with Latest US Trade Restrictions," *South China Morning Post*, November 27, 2022.

55. Qianer Liu, Ryan McMorrow, Nian Liu, and Kathrine Hill, "Chinese Chip Designers Slow Down Processors to Dodge US Sanctions," *Financial Times*, November 6, 2022.

56. Ezell, "Moore's Law under Attack."

CHAPTER NINE

Mitigating the Impact of China's Nonmarket Behavior in Semiconductors

ROBERT DALY AND MATTHEW TURPIN

The United States and its partners should be on guard to mitigate nonmarket behavior by China's emerging semiconductor firms.

While starting from a weak position, China's leaders are aggressively pursuing their domestic semiconductor aims—first to reduce the country's dependence on imports and then to take global market share through chip supply chain exports. As witnessed in a raft of other industries, the variety of government targets and subsidies to this end imply a high likelihood that semiconductor firms in China operating under nonmarket incentives may undercut pricing of established US and partner semiconductor firms.

This nonmarket behavior by semiconductor firms in China could have negative near-term impacts on US or partner producers, for example in mature chip production. And over time, it could create new US or partner dependencies on China-based supply chains that do not exist today, impinging on US strategic autonomy.

The US government has a variety of tools to monitor and limit the impact of such export dumping. It should also be concerned with the risk of its partners developing new dependencies on chips from China.

• • •

Semiconductors are ground-zero in this technological competition.
—SECRETARY GINA RAIMONDO[1]

Since China produced its first integrated circuit in 1965, its semiconductor policies have been shaped by its need for material and technological development, its drive for great-power status, its relations with the United States, and, especially since 2015, its quest for technological autonomy. As in other industries, China was willing to accept dependence on global semiconductor supply chains during an unavoidable period of tutelage and adaptation. As it mastered or obtained key technologies in the mid-2010s, however, China began a campaign intended to take it from dependence to dominance.

American export controls imposed in 2019 and then again in 2022 shocked China's planners and caused China's semiconductor industry to turn its focus from dominance to survival. Its current goals are, first, to master advanced-node design and manufacturing to shield itself from continued decoupling in high-tech sectors; and second, to protect its supply chains from the impact of possible future sanctions. Only if China succeeds in meeting its own demand for both mature and advanced semiconductors will its dreams of industry dominance return to the forefront of policy. In the interim, its goals are defensive, and the mood in China's semiconductor industry wavers between determination and desperation.

Warning Signs

Technology acquisition in the service of national development and military power has been China's primary goal in its relations with the United States since the Qing Dynasty sent students to the United States in 1872.[2] Their suspicions that the United States was denying China access to its leading technologies—and US suspicions regarding the ends and means of China's technological strategy—have been a mainstay of bilateral relations ever since.

Persistent US concerns—both economic and strategic—were heightened in 2006 when China announced its Indigenous Innovation agenda, which coincided with Beijing pressuring the European Union to lift its Tiananmen arms embargo.[3] Indigenous Innovation was not a secret program. When China's ministries announced detailed plans for the project in 2009, it was hailed domestically as a comprehensive plan for industrial policy that would make the country "a technology powerhouse by 2020 and a global leader by 2050."[4] When foreign governments and corporations said the program was a threat to their interests and that China's methods violated global norms, Beijing seemed surprised and confused—China's leaders muted propaganda related to Indigenous Innovation but continued to implement the strategy at full force.

The pattern of declaration, blowback, and retrenchment was repeated in 2015 with the launch of Made in China 2025 (MiC 2025). MiC 2025 was a program of investment and research for China's corporations aimed at making the People's Republic of China (PRC) the world leader (defined as 70 percent of global market share) in ten industrial sectors: (1) information technology; (2) automated machine tools and robotics; (3) aerospace and aeronautical equipment; (4) maritime equipment and high-tech shipping; (5) modern rail transport equipment; (6) new-energy vehicles and equipment; (7) power equipment; (8) agricultural equipment; (9) new materials; and (10) biopharmaceuticals and advanced medical products. Though a source of pride for China, the program was viewed internationally as a brazen announcement that China would do whatever it took—relying on "discriminatory treatment of foreign investment, forced technology transfers, intellectual property (IP) theft, and cyber espionage"—to reduce China's dependence on the world and lock in the world's dependence on China.[5] Again, China seemed surprised by the criticism, as if its status as a strategically innocent developmental state was so firmly established that no one would question its motives. China's leaders spoke about the program less after 2018—but for foreign governments and corporations, the klaxon had already sounded.

Aptly named Military-Civil Fusion policies, which began in the 1990s, were another source of Western alarm. Instituted under the restrictions of the Tiananmen arms embargo, the program's goal was to achieve complete modernization of China's armed forces based on "informatization, intelligence, and mechanization" by 2027, the hundredth anniversary of the People's Liberation Army (PLA). Military-Civil Fusion required that any technology available to China's industry or academia be provided to the PLA. It was not surprising that China would have such a policy. The Four Modernizations—first proclaimed by Zhou Enlai in 1963, later amplified by Deng Xiaoping as the core of China's development strategy—highlighted the essential integration of China's agriculture, industry, science and technology, and defense. China's whole-of-government (举国制度) approach was reflected in a series of National Intelligence Laws enacted under Xi Jinping that required all domestic entities, including universities, to give the state any information it requested.[6]

The strategic logic of these programs—Indigenous Innovation, MiC 2025, Military-Civil Fusion, and the National Intelligence Laws—was explained to the satisfaction of many US lawmakers, especially on the Republican side of the aisle, by Michael Pillsbury's *The Hundred-Year Marathon*.[7] Published in 2015, the book claimed that China has long had a plan to eclipse the United States and dominate a new global order. The same point was made (perhaps to a more Democratic readership) in Rush Doshi's *The Long Game: China's Grand Strategy to Displace American Order*.[8] Business communities in the United States and Europe both took notice, as evidenced by the publication of reports by the US and European chambers of commerce in early 2017 pointing out the harm PRC policies would do to their members.[9]

US bipartisan focus on the looming technology race and great-power competition was heightened by milestones reached and investments made under Xi Jinping during his first two terms as Party general secretary. Not only was China the most populous nation and largest exporter on Earth—it quickly became the world's largest producer and consumer of electric vehicles and batteries, as well as the global leader in mobile payments, wind and solar power generation, patents awarded, research cited in peer-reviewed journals, and training of college STEM (science, technology, engineering, and mathematics) students. It is the world's fastest-growing manufacturer of the legacy semiconductors used in most electronic devices and automobiles.[10] And China has invested heavily in the hardware that will drive the next generation of discovery (including supercomputers), the world's largest radio telescope (arguably underused), and one of the world's most advanced wind tunnels, which Beijing uses to develop hypersonic weapons. In 2016, working with European partners, China launched the world's first quantum satellite, which completed a handshake with a quantum ground station.[11]

These advances all took place while China remained sanctioned under a comprehensive arms embargo by nearly all developed economies, as well as the target of multilateral dual-use export control regimes. As chapter 7 in this report notes, in the wake of the Cold War, the United States and its allies dismantled the Coordinating Committee for Multilateral Export Controls (COCOM) and replaced it with the Wassenaar Arrangement, which included states of the former Soviet Union and its Eastern Bloc satellites. Due to the Tiananmen arms embargo imposed on China in 1989, Beijing was not invited to join Wassenaar, and it still remains outside this multilateral regime.

Semiconductors—and the artificial intelligence (AI) and high-performance computing they enable—are essential to the PRC's commercial and military projects, as described in Indigenous Innovation, Made in China 2025, Military-Civil Fusion, and the National Intelligence Laws. China cannot achieve its MiC 2025 or military modernization goals, or master quantum computing, nanotechnology, or other emerging technologies, without a secure supply of advanced chips and without the designs, software, manufacturing equipment, and components needed to make them. Now that the era of US-China engagement is over, the problem for China is that no semiconductor supply chain can be secure unless it is within China, but most components of the advanced-semiconductor supply chain are in foreign—and especially US—hands.

Geopolitics/Geoeconomics

Semiconductors have once again become the key terrain of superpower rivalry, just as early semiconductors were in the rivalry with the Soviet Union.[12] This battleground, however, is a subset of a global contest between the superpowers, which has the hallmarks of a cold war. Long-term, comprehensive, "extreme" geopolitical competition between China and the United States will condition the strategies both sides employ to win the semiconductor battle.[13] Put another way, the logic of security—not technological progress or economic efficiency—will drive the contest, even if tech and finance are its principal battlegrounds.

Beijing perceives an existential threat from a United States that wants to contain it or even bring down the Chinese Communist Party (CCP).[14] It, therefore, sees an urgent need to become more secure, not only in its high-tech industries but in its food supply,[15] culture,[16] biopharmaceutical sector, and media. Moreover, the West's rapid response to Russia's February 2022 invasion of Ukraine spurred China to sanctions-proof its economy. China's inclination toward decoupling did not begin with the semiconductor war or even the trade war that President Trump launched in 2018. Rather, self-sufficiency has been a keystone of CCP thinking since 1921, and many of China's modern industries have never coupled to the West in the first place. Until recently, however, China seemed confident that it could decouple selectively and at its own pace. That is no longer its plan, although it is unclear whether Beijing has fully considered the costs of this decision to rapidly decouple across a variety of sectors, or calculated its likelihood of success.

Washington's view now is that an expansion of China's economic and technological power is not in the interests of the United States or the rules-based international order. The United States, therefore, will no longer sell China the rope it needs to hang the United States in the global marketplace or on the battlefield. In the parlance of this report's strategic scenario work, Washington accepts a world moving to the "western" quadrants—and if that means hampering China's continued educational, scientific, medical, and economic progress by denying advanced chips and artificial intelligence to China's military, so be it. If it means greater scarcity and higher prices for US consumers, lower profits for US corporations, and the decoupling of global supply chains, so be it.

Popularized by President Trump and largely unquestioned by President Biden, antiglobalist narratives—as opposed to increasing market access among partners with common values—have prepared the ground for costly decoupling. These narratives appear to reflect a broader geopolitical trend. When the founder of Taiwan

Semiconductor Manufacturing Corporation (TSMC), Morris Chang, spoke at the Phoenix, Arizona, site of a new TSMC fabrication facility ("fab") in December 2022, he said, "Twenty-seven years have passed and [the semiconductor industry] witnessed a big change in the world, a big geopolitical situation change in the world. Globalization is almost dead and free trade is almost dead. A lot of people still wish they would come back, but I don't think they will be back."[17]

Even so, barring a direct military conflict between the United States and China, it is far more likely that the complexion of what we call "globalization" will simply shift over time, becoming characterized by a greater distribution of economic activity across more countries and regions. In many ways, we have mislabeled the last quarter century as a period of "globalization"—it was really a period of hyperconcentration in one country: China.[18]

Given that many of the unique geopolitical circumstances that led to this hyperconcentration of economic activity in China have ended, companies and countries will likely diversify their supply chains and manufacturing to places other than China. As this process unfolds, there will be relative gains and also significant costs, both of which will produce winners and losers. And as some have started to point out, China will likely lose more from this process.[19]

China's Ends, America's Means

Before 2019, Beijing's semiconductor policy focused on increasing China's global market share in every phase of production—from design to packaging—and producing more-advanced nodes. This agenda was pursued aggressively, but it was premised on gradually weaning Chinese producers off from foreign suppliers and then surpassing them. In other words, China was realistic about its dependence on the global supply chain—it was not looking so much to decouple immediately from US and third-country technologies as it was looking to reduce its dependence on them over time. The unstated assumptions of this approach were that foreign companies would remain as involved in the domestic market as China permitted them to be and that China could be as integrated or as self-sufficient as its own capacities warranted. The attractiveness of China's vast market to tech multinationals would keep China in the driver's seat as long as the logic of technological progress and economic efficiency drove the semiconductor industry. That is to say, China assumed it would control the pace of decoupling to its advantage and that the rest of the world would be too dependent on China to prevent its success.

The placement of ZTE (in 2016) and Huawei (in 2019) on the Commerce Department's Entity List—subjecting them to US export controls—was a strong signal that Beijing's assumptions were wrong. Others could control the pace of decoupling, and China was not, in fact, the sole author of its technological future. This point was further underscored by the August 2022 passage of the CHIPS and Science Act. Also in August, Commerce banned the sale of electronic design automation software to China and informed chip designer Nvidia that, effective immediately, the company would need new licenses for the export to China of its A100 and H100 integrated circuits—both of which are essential to AI research and have a 95 percent market share in China.[20] Nvidia's DGX enterprise AI infrastructure systems (which incorporate A100 or H100) as well as "any future Nvidia integrated circuit achieving both peak performance and chip-to-chip I/O performance equal to or greater than . . . the A100, as well as any system that includes those circuits," were also covered by the order.[21] This move banned not only the sale of Nvidia's advanced graphics processing units (GPUs), but also any product of Advanced Micro Devices (AMD) or other American fabless chip design companies whose technology met the criteria detailed in the order. It ripped away the foundation on which China's AI and data analysis strategies had been built years before China was ready to stand on its own.

While the export controls of August 2022 were, as Gregory Allen of the Center for Strategic and International Studies (CSIS) wrote, aimed at "strangling large segments of the Chinese technology industry . . . with an intent to kill,"[22] from the US perspective they were actually restrained, as they left additional steps in the escalation ladder available to the United States. Rather than seeking a complete technological decoupling from China, the Biden administration's policy has sought to limit its controls to chips that train AI models with advanced military applications. That delicacy may not have been noticed by China, however, as it has no "immediate substitute for the Nvidia GPUs that train AI models for autonomous driving, semantic analysis, image recognition, weather variables, and big data analysis," and every buyer in China will be affected by the new rules.[23]

One of the difficulties for Nvidia and other US suppliers is that they have no immediate substitute for the China market. In the third quarter of 2022, Nvidia "had booked $400 million in sales of the affected chips . . . to China that could be lost if [Chinese] firms decide not to buy alternative Nvidia products."[24] That said, the impacts on these companies should not be viewed in isolation; China's loss of its pathway to technological superiority in advanced chips would generate national security and economic competitiveness costs that would dwarf the affected sales of companies like Nvidia.

If the Nvidia announcement destabilized the train of China's semiconductor strategy, changes in export controls announced by the Department of Commerce's Bureau of Industry and Security (BIS) on October 7, 2022, knocked it off the rails. The BIS rules on advanced computing and semiconductor manufacturing added new license requirements for any US products sent to China's fabs that support the domestic building of logic chips of 14nm or below, DRAM memory chips of 18nm half-pitch or less, or NAND Flash memory chips with 128 layers or more. As Gregory Allen explained, Biden was attempting to

> (1) strangle the Chinese AI industry by choking off access to high-end AI chips; (2) block China from designing AI chips domestically by choking off China's access to US-made chip design software; (3) block China from manufacturing advanced chips by choking off access to US-built semiconductor manufacturing equipment; and (4) block China from domestically producing semiconductor manufacturing equipment by choking off access to US-built components.[25]

The rules also restricted the ability of unlicensed US citizens or green card holders to support the design or production of advanced chips in China's fabrication facilities.[26] This class of restrictions meant that hundreds of Americans employed by the industry in China (no exact number is yet available), including forty-three senior executives, had to quit working immediately. Many of these executives were naturalized American citizens of Chinese origin with advanced degrees from the United States and long experience in Silicon Valley.[27]

China's Response

After the October 2022 export controls were released, China's strategy of steadily progressing toward industry dominance on its own timeline, with an assumption of ready access to foreign technology and talent along the way, had to be scrapped. Because the CCP's 20th National Congress closely followed the announcement—and itself was followed by a series of economic and social crises related to Xi Jinping's "dynamic zero"-COVID policy—it was not clear by year's end that Beijing had fully absorbed the impacts of the new export controls.

When Beijing felt attacked by US actions during the Trump administration, its response was to mirror US actions immediately. It made such shows of strength throughout the trade war, for example, when the United States required Chinese media outlets to register as foreign missions and when the PRC consulate in Houston was suddenly shut down in 2020. Given this tendency to counterpunch, some commentators expected China to hit back against the new US rules by banning the sale to the United States of products such as rare earths, medicine and medical precursors, or legacy chips. On a number of occasions involving science and technology over the last five to ten years, however, China lacked the leverage or capability to successfully respond. For example, a little more than a year after Huawei's Entity Listing, the National People's Congress passed and adopted the Export Control Law of China (ECL) in an effort to mirror US capabilities and deny China's advanced technologies to the United States.[28] Like the US Export Administration Regulations (EAR), which provide the legal basis for Commerce's and the State

Department's export controls, China's 2020 ECL establishes extra-territorial reach, directs the creation of control lists and blacklists, and defines controls for dual-use items and military products. Unfortunately for Beijing, this legislation remains an empty regulatory shell, as China lacks control over advanced technologies that surpass what is available to its rivals. One could imagine a future where Beijing responds in this domain with true reciprocity, but that time has not arrived.

To date, rather than hitting back against American export controls, China has adopted five broad, long-term strategies aimed at limiting their impact and, if possible, advancing its drive for technological security and dominance:

1. *Increasing investment* in China's semiconductor companies, large and small; in training personnel; and in building design and manufacturing hubs
2. *Encouraging workarounds* to existing technologies
3. *Discouraging third countries* from working with the United States
4. *Playing for time* in the hope that the costs of decoupling, the interest of US corporations, and pressure from US partners result in the watering down of export controls
5. *Controlling the international narrative* on technological decoupling

Strategy One: Increased Investment

China's commitment to achieving dominance in the semiconductor industry, based on the size of its domestic market and investment in its companies and universities, coincided with American policy makers' understanding of the challenge Beijing was posing.[29] As outlined in chapter 8 of this report, the current drive to fund the industry was launched in 2014.[30] In that year, China published its Guideline for the Promotion of the Development of the National Integrated Circuit Industry, "with the goal of establishing a world-leading semiconductor industry in all areas of the integrated circuit supply chain by 2030."[31] It also established the National Integrated Circuit Industry Investment

Fund (or "Big Fund") to provide an estimated $150 billion in state funds to support research. By 2020, China was home to more than ten thousand semiconductor companies,[32] a figure that more than doubled over the course of that same year.[33] Many of these enterprises were overnight operations that existed primarily to chase government subsidies. Some, like Tsinghua Unigroup, a company founded at Xi Jinping's alma mater that even bid to buy Micron in 2015 for $23 billion, were spectacular failures that spotlighted the waste that remains endemic in China's government investment programs.[34] Tsinghua Unigroup had received tens of billions of dollars in government support but still defaulted on its bonds in 2020. Others, like Wuhan's Yangtze Memory Technologies Co. (YMTC), which was founded in 2016 and is now China's leading memory chip maker, were spectacular successes.[35] TechInsights, a Canadian semiconductor and microelectronics analytics company, recently declared that "at their current rate of innovation, YMTC is poised to be the uncontested global NAND flash technology leader before 2030."[36] China's latest Five-Year Plan, unveiled in July 2021, committed to raising public and private R&D spending by 7 percent annually—a rate greater than the increase in its military spending—with semiconductors as a top priority.[37]

It is too soon to predict the scale at which Beijing will further increase its investments in the industry, but the speed with which major Chinese municipalities responded to the October 2022 export controls indicates that a major reinvestment is under way. In late October 2022, the Lingang Special Area (a free-trade zone), Shanghai University, and the city's Integrated Circuit Industry Association—all shocked by the BIS ban on US persons in China's semiconductor companies and buoyed by grants from the municipal government—set up a new campus to foster talent for the semiconductor industry.[38] Such training efforts garnered government support despite China's overall success in developing STEM talent broadly.

According to Georgetown University's Center for Security and Emerging Technology (CSET), "by 2025 Chinese universities will produce more than 77,000 STEM PhD graduates per year compared to approximately 40,000 in the United States. If international students are excluded from the US count, Chinese STEM PhD graduates would outnumber their US counterparts more than three-to-one."[39] Even so, that advantage may not be of much help in the semiconductor industry. The China Semiconductor Industry Association anticipates that China already has a shortage of two hundred thousand semiconductor engineers for the years 2022 and 2023, while one of China's leading educational talent organizations reports that most STEM students prefer work in AI and big data over the lower-paying semiconductor industry (ironically mirroring a trend observed among US STEM graduates, as outlined earlier in this report).[40]

In Shenzhen, the municipal government announced plans to reinvest in its semiconductor industry architecture on October 8, 2022, one day after BIS's bombshell. The city's Development and Reform Commission announced that it would cover 20 percent, or up to US$1.4 million annually, to subsidize the R&D expenses of companies chasing breakthroughs in the design and development of logic chips, including CPUs (central processing units) and GPUs.[41] Huawei, which is based in Shenzhen, is leveraging the established networks and talent in that city to invest in firms throughout China, including NAURA Technology Group (China's leading chipmaking equipment manufacturer), to build itself a complete China-only supply chain. The Fujian Jinhua Integrated Circuit Corporation (JHICC)—after being driven into bankruptcy in early 2019 after the Trump administration placed it on the Entity List in 2018 for stealing intellectual property from Micron Technology—has been resurrected to play a major role in this network.[42] Huawei engineers are reported to be working stealthily in JHICC's Quanzhou plant to help the telecom giant recover from its own placement on the Entity List in 2019[43]—albeit neither Huawei's nor JHICC's engineers have access to the most-advanced software, tools, or components that would help them to achieve these objectives.

Strategy Two: Work-Arounds

Writing in *American Affairs*, Geoffrey Cain claims that China's failure thus far to meet its MiC 2025 goals for chip development stems from its deeply entrenched "diplomatic isolation . . . oppressive top-down mandate(s) of selecting national champions . . . the weak position of starting generations behind industry leaders in America, Taiwan, South Korea, and Japan," and corruption.[44] Within China, most domestic commentators are similarly pessimistic about China's prospects for building an indigenous cutting-edge semiconductor supply chain using existing technologies. China is therefore searching for new technologies that can match the performance of systems developed and controlled by Western-oriented competitors.

For example, the Beijing Open Source Chip Research Institute—a group of research centers and companies that includes the Chinese Academy of Sciences, Tencent, and Alibaba[45]—is developing domestic semiconductor-related intellectual property using the RISC-V open-source chip design architecture created by the University of California, Berkeley. If it succeeds, the group's Xiangshan RISC-V architecture could free China from IP constraints imposed by ARM, the Cambridge-based company whose technology underlies most cell phones, including Apple products.[46] China may also hope to offset the need for US-designed advanced nodes by developing photonic chips (which use photons instead of electrons in integrated circuits[47]) and experimenting with nonsilicon substrates, such as cubic boron arsenide, graphene,[48] and silicon carbide.[49] As described in chapter 2 of this report, however, marketable breakthroughs in any of these areas are likely decades off, and China's pace of advancement even here may face acute threats after its stockpiles of banned chips, components, and manufacturing tools run out or require repairs in the next year or two.

Strategy Three: Outreach to US Allies

The ubiquity of essential US semiconductor designs, software, manufacturing tools, and components in the global supply chain makes it possible for the Department of Commerce to use its Entity List and Foreign-Direct Product Rule to compel allies and partners to support its ban on cooperation with China's semiconductor industry.[50] The Netherlands, Taiwan, South Korea, Japan, and most other suppliers share US concerns about China's threats to security, intellectual property, and global order—but they value their trade relations with China highly. China will be alert to any opportunities that such conflict provides to sow division within US partnerships and gain the chips and chip manufacturing equipment it needs to develop its industries and military.

China accounts for over 25 percent of the annual global demand for semiconductor equipment. It would doubtless buy as many of Advanced Semiconductor Materials Lithography's (ASML) $100 million extreme ultraviolet (EUV) lithography machines as the Dutch company could sell it, but the Netherlands agreed in 2016 that none of ASML's high-end machines would be sold to China. Bloomberg reported on December 7, 2022, that Amsterdam had agreed to enforce Washington's October 2022 export controls as well.[51] ASML will continue to sell its mature-node manufacturing equipment to China, however, and the knowledge that China is its greatest potential profit center will continue to nag at ASML's leadership, despite the firm's claim that under current market conditions, it can sell as many machines as it can produce to other customers.[52]

America's Asian partners in the "Chip 4" alliance will likely fall in line as well—but doing so will be costly for them, and China will exert as much pressure on them as it can to seek carve-outs and workarounds to US requirements. As outlined in chapter 6, US partners have their own substantial semiconductor supply chain strengths and ambitions, with sales to or production in China as part of them. In 2021, Taiwan's chip sales to China, worth $155 billion, constituted 62 percent of its exports to the mainland. The latest data, however, shows that Taiwan's export of chips to China and Hong Kong fell for a fourth month in a row in February 2023—a 31 percent drop in exports from a year earlier.[53] Semiconductor manufacturing machines and materials are Japan's second-largest export, and one-third of them are purchased by China—a trade worth $9.5 billion to Japan in 2021.[54] China buys 43 percent of South Korea's exported chips—58 percent including exports to Hong Kong—a trade worth over $49 billion ($66 billion including Hong Kong) to South Korea in 2022.[55] The US Commerce Department recently granted Samsung and SK hynix exceptions to its export controls, allowing them to provide otherwise banned capabilities to their facilities in China for one more year—but it is not likely that those exceptions will be granted again.

Taipei, Tokyo, and Seoul are all likely to be courted, hectored, coerced, and threatened by Beijing as they move toward full compliance with BIS rules. They may also compensate for cooperating with the United States on semiconductors by reassuring Beijing in other aspects of their political and trade relations, and Beijing will be attentive to such opportunities to weaken the will of, and widen the divisions between, America's Asian partners.

Assiduous attention to alliance management, therefore, will be essential to the success of US policy. Here again, we run across a ubiquitous theme of this report: the sustainability of US security-oriented efforts toward China will rely on the commercial attractiveness that the United States can offer its partners. Making the subsidies through the CHIPS and Science Act attractive to allied partners—and not saddled by non-security-related short-term US social or protectionist politics—is the first step.[56] Beyond those five years, like-minded partners need confidence that the United States will continue to offer market access and bidirectional investment.

Strategy Four: Play for Time

China domestic companies' most effective responses to US pressure may be to stockpile chips and equipment while they are still available (Nvidia, for example, will continue to ship AI chips from its Hong Kong logistics center through September 2023[57]); manage their capital reserves to weather the current slowdown in global chip demand; and hope that the current storm passes. At the moment, the United States' position seems certain, but its adamancy may not last. A change in administration in 2024 could also bring a change in priorities. Or the United States might blanch as the ban's full costs to US companies become clear. AMD, Intel, Nvidia, and Qualcomm all have enormous stakes in sales to China, as do US semiconductor manufacturing equipment companies such as Applied Materials, KLA, and Lam Research.[58]

Even though most US multinationals no longer lobby for expanded trade with China (as they did in the run-up to the PRC's ascension to the World Trade Organization [WTO] in 2001), executives and their shareholders are bound to ask Washington to take some of the roughest edges off its export controls.

Only two months after October 7, 2022, China already saw signs of a thaw in the American position and an opportunity to import advanced chips despite the export controls. Under the new BIS rules, thirty-one companies in China, including YMTC and NAURA Technology, were placed on an "unverified list" and given sixty days to prove that no controlled items they imported from the United States could be used in weapons manufacture or transferred to China's military. "Verification" involves on-site inspection of companies in China by US officials who conduct "end-use checks." Historically, the CCP has viewed these procedures as insults to its sovereignty and has refused the necessary access to Americans. During a December 6 event at the Center for Strategic and International Studies, however, Alan Estevez, the under secretary of commerce for industry and security, said that China's Ministry of Commerce had been cooperating on end-use checks since November, raising the possibility that firms currently on the unverified list might be verified as good actors and would therefore be eligible to import advanced US chips and equipment.

The United States has assumed, reasonably, that China's Military-Civil Fusion program and National Intelligence Laws were proof—if proof were needed at all—that any technology available anywhere in China that had a military application was certain to be put to that use. As the US-China rivalry expands and as military conflict becomes more imaginable, that assumption might seem to imply that US enforcement of export controls on China should be absolute and unwavering. Estevez's comments suggest, however, that China may now see a glimmer of light: cooperating with Commerce's end-use checks to get firms off the unverified list and stalling may be its best short-term strategy to keep open a channel for technology imports.

Despite this potential for near-term churn, over the long term, time may arguably be on the side of the United States and its allies in this realm. If—as characterized in the strategic scenario planning of chapter 1—trends toward supply chain diversification continue and companies like Apple reduce their dependency on China's manufacturing base and market, then the leverage Beijing now applies to get access to technology from foreign companies could dissipate.[59] As the world shifts from hyperconcentration to a more dispersed distribution of high-tech manufacturing with fewer dependencies on the PRC, then companies will have less incentive to place advanced capabilities in China. The current commercial logic for providing advanced-chip capabilities to China is that much of the world's electronics manufacturing takes place in China. As that condition changes, so too will the commercial rationale for providing the advanced chips. South and Southeast Asian nations likely stand to be the true beneficiaries of these trends. Manufacturing jobs and the attendant flows of infrastructure funding, science and technology know-how, and economic development will flow to them just as those same benefits flowed to the PRC over the past quarter century. Rather than being the grass trampled between two competing superpowers, the nearly 2.2 billion people of South and Southeast Asia could experience a dramatic increase in economic growth and prosperity.

Strategy Five: Frame Narratives

Building "discourse power" (话语权) is an essential component of China's "comprehensive national power" (国家综合势力). On September 1, 2022, after the announcement of restrictions on the sale of Nvidia GPUs to China, Foreign Ministry spokesman Wang Wenbin said:

> The US has been stretching the concept of national security and abusing state power. The US seeks to use its technological prowess as an advantage to hobble and suppress the development of emerging markets and developing countries. This violates the rules of the market economy, undermines international economic and trade order, and disrupts the stability of global industrial and supply chains.[60]

On October 8, Foreign Ministry spokesperson Mao Ning argued:

> In order to maintain its sci-tech hegemony, the US has been abusing export control measures to wantonly block and hobble Chinese enterprises. Such practice runs counter to the principle of fair competition and international trade rules. It will not only harm Chinese companies' legitimate rights and interests, but also hurt the interests of US companies. It will hinder international sci-tech exchange and trade cooperation, and deal a blow to global industrial and supply chains and world economic recovery.[61]

Such statements do not aim to convince Washington to change its policies. They are intended, first, to persuade the Chinese people that China is an innocent and righteous victim of a malign United States; and, second, to persuade third countries—the Global South and nondemocratic partners of China in particular—that the United States is a bully to developing nations and a threat to global order. These messages are conveyed around the world by the state-run broadcaster China Global Television Network (CGTN), which is a leading provider of news in Africa and the Pacific Islands.[62] China's critique of the United States has also gained traction in the Middle East, Latin America, and many countries that participate in the Belt and Road Initiative.

China has prepared domestic and foreign audiences to be receptive to these messages about the technology war by promulgating a master narrative over the past ten years—a narrative that forms the backbone of its rebuttals to the United States: *The United States has fundamentally misperceived China's intentions and policies because it fears that China's peaceful, globally beneficial rise and the success of its governance model threaten its own hegemony.* Global public opinion polling indicates, however, that China's well-resourced, carefully planned global public diplomacy campaign has had mixed results at best.[63] In developed democracies, it has failed entirely, but it has adherents in the Global South, where it is largely unchallenged by US messages.

Cowed but Unbowed

In addition to these five observable responses to the imposition of export controls, it would be wise to assume that China's established technology-acquisition methods have accelerated since 2022. These include IP theft, hacking campaigns, digital and traditional espionage, talent recruitment programs such as the Thousand Talents Plan, recruitment of third-country technology experts, and global influence operations designed to spread PRC narratives among foreign publics, including diaspora Chinese.

The PRC government was angered, but not surprised, by the United States' determined prosecution of a tech war in 2022. The Ministry of Commerce's cooperation with US end-use checks indicates that BIS now has Beijing's full attention, and many of China's semiconductor companies are desperate. Many will go under. It is too soon to predict the course of these developments, but it is already clear that China is adjusting in an attempt to limit damage; it is not reconsidering its national goals, however, and it has not used all of the weapons at its disposal.

Beijing is unlikely to abandon its dual objectives to assume a leadership position in the development of cutting-edge semiconductors and to become self-sufficient in the production of semiconductors for broader use. As outlined in this chapter, the first objective has become more difficult to achieve, given the actions taken by the United States and the likelihood that the United States can persuade others to squeeze the semiconductor choke points. China will seek to find work-arounds to these restrictions, but it appears that the United States is paying close attention to China's actions and has sufficient regulatory escalation space to continue to stymie Beijing. In pursuit of the second objective, however, state subsidies and other forms of encouragement now give China a path to build an increasingly dominant position in the manufacture of legacy chips. While economic on the surface, this pursuit will nonetheless also have important national security implications that the United States and its partners must consider.

The Next Challenge

Going forward, the United States and its partners must design policies to deal with two interrelated challenges caused by China's semiconductor industrial policies.

The first is *military*. The United States cannot afford to lose the unequal technological advantages it has long enjoyed. In an era in which a US-China conflict is becoming more likely, the United States will derive qualitative military advantages by denying the most-advanced semiconductors and AI applications to China.

The second is *economic*. Even if US export controls are enforced and expanded, China may be able to generate an overcapacity of legacy chips and dominate the global market for semiconductors that go into household appliances, automobiles, and the internet-of-things. Such dominance will create political and economic leverage for China, as its near monopoly on rare earth extraction and refining already do. As China floods global markets with low-cost, good-enough mature chips, the ability of the United States and other countries to manufacture them will be degraded, along with the profit margins that fuel further commercial R&D for the next generation of products. China's profits from legacy chips will be used to offset the impact of US export controls through greater investment in the education and research needed to design and manufacture advanced nodes.

The Biden administration's formally stated rationale for the ban on the sale of advanced chips, design software, manufacturing equipment, and components to China is that these technologies are employed in weapons that target the United States and in surveillance systems used to monitor and persecute Chinese citizens. But the economic arguments for limiting Chinese dominance of mature- and advanced-node markets are almost equally strong. If China achieves the goals it has set for its semiconductor industry, the global risks of technological lock-in and innovation drag are high. The instructive example is China's dominance of solar panel production. Studies by the Information Technology and Innovation Foundation[64] argue that, once China pushed other manufacturers out of the solar panel market, innovation in this young and vital technology sector all but ceased.[65] Chinese panel production, dominated by national champion companies controlled by the CCP, had neither the motivation nor the ability to develop the technology further. The same is possible if China dominates chip design and manufacture, particularly if done primarily through subsidized state-oriented enterprises.

China is, in fact, on track to become a major producer of legacy chips. If its behavior in other industry sectors is a model for its actions in legacy semiconductors, the world should expect massive overcapacity of these older chips, which would collapse the price for every other producer. Consumers who purchase commercial electronics will benefit from marginally lower prices, but Beijing's dumping of subsidized semiconductors will severely undermine companies that currently produce legacy chips in South Korea, Taiwan, Japan, the United States, Europe, and the Middle East. Those companies will lose the revenue needed to make capital improvements, as well as the revenue to conduct R&D for the next generation of semiconductors. This all could cause a consolidation of semiconductor manufacturers whereby foreign fabless chip design companies become increasingly dependent on mature-node PRC fabrication facilities. This dependency does not exist today.

Commercial consolidation and increased dependency on Chinese fabs for legacy semiconductors will have important national security implications. As outlined in chapter 2 of this report, advanced chips are crucial to military superiority—but the majority of semiconductors used in defense applications are legacy chips, drawn from both dedicated (for sensitive applications or chips with special attributes like radiation hardening) and off-the-shelf commercial chip suppliers. Losing access to a healthy global ecosystem of friendly commercial suppliers of mature chips could increase costs or drive the defense industrial base to rely on single-source producers, limiting innovation. While the defense industry may seem large, it is dwarfed by the commercial sector for legacy semiconductors. And even if countries can avoid dependencies on China for legacy chips in their defense industries, the wider economy will likely fall victim to overcapacity and dumping of legacy chips.

One potential mitigation against the worst harms of Beijing's semiconductor industrial policy would be to take preemptive action and impose antidumping/countervailing duties (AD/CVDs) on China-manufactured chips immediately. Traditionally, countries like the United States impose AD/CVDs only after the harm of dumping has taken place—that is, once companies go bankrupt and employees are laid off. Given the track record of China's industrial policies, however, the United States and other countries should act proactively by imposing those duties now, which would prevent Beijing's semiconductor policy from harming domestic chip manufacturers. Should those duties be insufficient, countries could also block the importation of China-manufactured legacy semiconductors. This move could force electronics manufacturers to require non-PRC legacy chips or further shift the manufacture of electronics outside the PRC.

While such actions would likely lead Beijing to bring suit at the WTO, China would be making these arguments in bad faith, given China's failure to fulfill its own obligations to other members of the WTO and the harm done to the global trade system in the process.[66] The United States and other countries should not shy away from confronting Beijing on this issue—to repeat a phrase that Chinese Foreign Ministry spokesman Zhao Lijian often deploys (albeit against Western nations), China's protest to the WTO would be like "a thief crying 'stop the thief' (贼喊捉贼)."[67]

While this threat may seem further off than the one posed by the acquisition and production of advanced chips, failure to take actions like these in the short term could endanger US abilities to constrain PRC efforts to develop cutting-edge semiconductors in the medium term. The semiconductor industry is first and foremost a commercial industry that is shaped by market forces, and it is hard to predict just how damaging Beijing's dumping of legacy chips would be to the health of the broader industry—particularly to those companies that spend massive amounts of money on building new fabs, buying new and more advanced tools, and investing in R&D. While it is possible that the effects of legacy chip dumping could be isolated to only a small number of semiconductor companies, it is also possible that there would be a contagion effect that would weaken even the most advanced manufacturers. Given these uncertainties, the United States and its allies should err on the side of strenuous and well-coordinated actions against Beijing's plans. It is understandable that companies and governments would want to take the least costly action—but again, given the complex commercial, geopolitical, and technological dynamics, it is nearly impossible to predict with accuracy what the perfect balance will be. In this critical and fast-moving sector, we should pursue an "all of the above" approach that seeks to deny China the capability to achieve its objectives. Under these conditions, we advocate being more exclusionary rather than less.

Would pursuing this approach encourage Beijing to double down on its objectives? If so, should we instead moderate our response to reassure Beijing and persuade them not to pursue their goals? To date, the United States and its allies have had a poor track record in reassuring the PRC and persuading it to abandon goals that undermine our interests. It would be naïve to place our faith in our powers of persuasion yet again. Rather than trying to reassure China, we should focus on a strategy of denial. That is the strategy that the October 2022 rules announced. Having crossed that Rubicon and knowing that China is now gearing up to compete with the United States on those terms, the time for cautious gradualism has passed.

In short, meeting the two challenges—military and economic—posed by China's semiconductor policies will require different tools, different groups of partners, and different strategies. The complexity of pursuing and coordinating these strategies, and the scale of investment and intensity of diplomacy required to succeed, will require government direction. It can't be left to the market, as the primary measure of success will not be profit. The United States' task is to hamper China's development of advanced AI that could help it win wars by restricting China's access to the world's most powerful chips—*without incentivizing its dominance of legacy semiconductor markets worldwide by doing so.*

NOTES

1. US Department of Commerce, "Remarks by US Secretary of Commerce Gina Raimondo on the US Competitiveness and the China Challenge," November 30, 2022.

2. See Robert Daly, "Thinkers, Builders, Symbols, Spies?: Sino-US Higher Educational Relations in the Engagement Era," in *Engaging China*, edited by Anne F. Thurston (New York: Columbia University Press, July 2021).

3. Peng Heyue, "China's Indigenous Innovation Policy and Its Effect on Foreign Intellectual Property Rights Holders," China Law Insight, September 9, 2010; and Kristin Archick, Richard Grimmett, and Shirley Kan, "European Union's Arms Embargo on China: Implications and Options for US Policy," Congressional Research Service, January 26, 2006.

4. James MacGregor, "China's Drive for 'Indigenous Innovation': A Web of Industrial Policies," APCO Worldwide, 2009.

5. James McBride and Andrew Chatzky, "Is 'Made in China 2025' a Threat to Global Trade?," Council on Foreign Relations, May 13, 2019.

6. Murray Scot Tanner, "Beijing's New National Intelligence Law: From Defense to Offense," Lawfare, July 20, 2017.

7. Michael Pillsbury, *The Hundred-Year Marathon: China's Secret Strategy to Replace America as the Global Superpower* (New York: Henry Holt and Co., 2015).

8. Rush Doshi, *The Long Game: China's Grand Strategy to Displace American Order* (New York: Oxford University Press, 2021).

9. European Union Chamber of Commerce in China, "China Manufacturing 2025: Putting Industrial Policy ahead of Markets," March 7, 2017; and US Chamber of Commerce, "Made in China 2025: Global Ambitions Built on Local Protections," March 16, 2017.

10. Semiconductor Industry Association, "China's Share of Global Chip Sales Now Surpasses Taiwan's, Closing In on Europe's and Japan's," January 10, 2022.

11. Karen Kwon, "China Reaches New Milestone in Space-Based Quantum Communications," *Scientific American*, June 25, 2020.

12. US General Accounting Office, "Export Controls: US Policies and Procedures Regarding the Soviet Union," May 24, 1990.

13. AP News, "Biden: China Should Expect 'Extreme Competition' from US," February 7, 2021.

14. Simultaneously, the United States perceives the PRC as "the only competitor with both the intent to reshape the international order and, increasingly, the economic, diplomatic, military, and technological power to advance that objective," replacing the liberal, rules-based order with an international system

that privileges authoritarian regimes. See the White House, Executive Office of the President, "National Security Strategy," October 2022.

15. Asim Anand, "What Xi Jinping Brings to the Table in China's Quest for Food Security," S&P Global, November 17, 2022.

16. Neil Renwick and Qing Cao, "China's Cultural Soft Power: An Emerging National Cultural Security Discourse," *American Journal of Chinese Studies* 15, no. 2 (January 2008): 69–86.

17. Cheng Ting-Fang, "TSMC Founder Morris Chang Says Globalization 'Almost Dead,'" *Nikkei Asia*, December 8, 2022.

18. As of 2015, the PRC produced or assembled 28 percent of the world's automobiles; 41 percent of the world's ships; more than 80 percent of the world's computers; more than 90 percent of the world's mobile phones; 60 percent of the world's color TV sets; more than 50 percent of the world's refrigerators; 80 percent of the world's air conditioners; and 50 percent of the world's steel. See European Chamber of Commerce in China, "China Manufacturing 2025: Putting Industrial Policy Ahead of Market Forces," March 2017.

19. George Magnus, "Why China Has More to Lose from Decoupling than the US," *South China Morning Post*, June 29, 2022; Minxin Pei, "China Can't Afford to Decouple from the West," *Bloomberg*, January 30, 2022; Kinling Lo, "Tech War: Beijing Will Come Out of Decoupling Worse Off than the US, Say Chinese Academics," *South China Morning Post*, February 1, 2022; and Shen Lu, "A Report Detailed the Tech Gap between China and the US—Then It Disappeared," *Protocol*, February 9, 2022.

20. Debby Wu, Ian King, and Vlad Slavov, "US Deals Heavy Blow to China Tech Ambitions with Nvidia Chip Ban," *Bloomberg*, December 2, 2022.

21. Nvidia, "Form 8-K," Securities and Exchange Commission, August 26, 2022.

22. Gregory C. Allen, "Choking Off China's Access to the Future of AI," CSIS, October 11, 2022.

23. Che Pan, "Tech War: Why the US Nvidia Chip Ban Is a Direct Threat to Beijing's Artificial Intelligence Ambitions," South China Morning Post, September 12, 2022.

24. Stephen Nellis and Jane Lee, "US Officials Order Nvidia to Halt Sales of Top AI Chips to China," Reuters, August 31, 2022.

25. Allen, "Choking Off China's Access to the Future of AI."

26. US Department of Commerce, Bureau of Industry and Security, "Commerce Implements New Export Controls on Advanced Computing and Semiconductor Manufacturing Items to the People's Republic of China (PRC)," October 7, 2022.

27. Liza Lin and Karen Hao, "American Executives in Limbo at Chinese Chip Companies After US Ban," *Wall Street Journal*, October 16, 2022.

28. Yujing Shu and Xiaotang Wang, "China Overhauls Its Export Control Regime: What China's New Export Control Law Changes and How to Respond," K&L Gates, December 7, 2020.

29. Within eighteen months of the PRC's launching of significant investments in semiconductors, the Obama administration published a strategy for dealing with the problem that carried over to the Trump administration (see *Report to the President Ensuring Long-Term US Leadership in Semiconductors*, Executive Office of the President, President's Council of Advisors on Science and Technology, January 2017), cabinet secretaries were making public speeches about the challenge (see "Semiconductors and the Future of the Tech Economy," speech by Secretary of Commerce Penny Pritzker, CSIS, November 2, 2016), and the United States had already blocked Chinese acquisitions of semiconductor companies in the United States and Europe (see Paul Mozur, "Obama Moves to Block Chinese Acquisition of a German Chip Maker," *New York Times*, December 2, 2016; and Ana Swanson, "Trump Blocks China-Backed Bid to Buy US Chip Maker," *New York Times*, September 13, 2017).

30. Paul Mozur, "Using Cash and Pressure, China Builds Its Chip Industry," *New York Times*, October 27, 2014.

31. Congressional Research Service, "China's New Semiconductor Policies: Issues for Congress," April 20, 2021.

32. Kathryn Hille and Sun Yu, "Chinese Firms Go from Fish to Chips in New Great Leap Forward," *Financial Review*, October 13, 2020.

33. *New York Times* ("The Failure of China's Microchip Giant Tests Beijing's Tech Ambitions," July 19, 2021) puts the number at 58,000, while the *Financial Times* ("Chinese Firms Go from Fish to Chips in New Great Leap Forward," reprinted in *Financial Review*, October 13, 2020) claims the number is 13,000. Both reports seem to cite the same Chinese government study.

34. *New York Times*, "The Failure of China's Microchip Giant."

35. At least until the United States began directing regulatory firepower against YMTC in October 2022. See Karen Freifeld and Alexandra Alper, "US Adds China's YMTC and 30 Other Firms to 'Unverified' Trade List," Reuters, October 7, 2022.

36. Che Pan, "China's Top Memory Chip Maker YMTC Takes Latest Step to Become a Global Market Leader, but US Sanctions Could Derail Its Ambitions," December 1, 2022.

37. Paul Mozur and Steven Lee Myers, "Xi's Gambit: China Plans for a World without American Technology," *New York Times*, March 10, 2021.

38. Ann Cao, "Tech War: Shanghai Launches New Campus to Train Personnel for Semiconductor Sector as US Curbs Decrease China's Chip Talent Pool," *South China Morning Post*, October 26, 2022.

39. Remco Zwetsloot, Jack Corrigan, Emily S. Weinstein, Dahlia Peterson, Diana Gehlhaus, and Ryan Fedasiuk, "China Is Fast Outpacing US STEM PhD Growth," CSET, August 2021.

40. Coco Feng, "China's Semiconductor Self-Sufficiency Drive Needs to Strengthen Development of Talent and Skills, Education Agency Executive Says," *South China Morning Post*, October 5, 2022.

41. Iris Deng, "Shenzhen Plans to Shower Cash on Local Chip Industry to Bolster Development after Intensified US Trade Restrictions," *South China Morning Post*, October 10, 2022.

42. Cheng Ting-Fang, "Huawei Dives into Chip Production to Battle US Clampdown," *Nikkei Asia*, September 22, 2020.

43. Cheng Ting-Fang and Shunsuke Tabeta, "China's Chip Industry Fights to Survive US Tech Crackdown," *Nikkei Asia*, November 30, 2022.

44. Geoffrey Cain, "The Purges That Upended China's Semiconductor Industry," *American Affairs* 6, no. 4 (Winter 2022).

45. Anna Gross and Qianer Liu, "China Enlists Alibaba and Tencent in Fight against US Chip Sanctions," *Financial Times*, November 30, 2022.

46. Ann Cao, "Tech War: China Bets on RISC-V Chips to Escape the Shackles of US Tech Export Restrictions," *South China Morning Post*, November 12, 2022.

47. Ann Cao, "China's Chip Executives Brace for Winter as US Sanctions Push Country's Semiconductor Industry to the Brink of Desperation," *South China Morning Post*, November 12, 2022.

48. Jason R. Wilson, "China Taps in Graphene Technology to Replace Silicon-Based Chips & Breaking the Monopoly with 10 Times the Performance," WCCF Tech, November 22, 2022.

49. Dave Yin, "China's Plan to Leapfrog Foreign Chipmakers: Wave Goodbye to Silicon," Protocol, November 8, 2021.

50. US Department of Commerca, Bureau of Industry and Security, "Foreign-Produced Direct Product (FDP) Rule as it Relates to the Entity List § 736.2(b)(3)(vi) and footnote 1 to Supplement No. 4 to part 744," October 28, 2021.

51. Reuters, "Netherlands Plans New Curbs on Chip-Making Equipment Sales to China—Bloomberg News," December 8, 2022.

52. Per a remark made in private conversation with one of the authors in 2022.

53. Dashveenjit Kaur, "Chip Alliance: The Hefty Price Taiwan Is Paying for Choosing US over China," TechWire Asia, October 11, 2022; and Yoshihiro Sato, "Taiwan Chip Exports to China Sputter on Tensions, Falling Demand," *Bloomberg*, March 19, 2023.

54. Kazuaki Nagata, "Following US on China Chip Export Curbs Would Hit Japan's Industry Hard," *Japan Times*, November 17, 2022.

55. As detailed in the Korea International Trade Association export database (integrated classification code HS 8542), http://kita.org/kStat/byCom_SpeCom.do.

56. Early reactions from Korea's chip industry participants to the US Department of Commerce's mooted additional requirements for CHIPS Act recipients, including childcare requirements and limitations on stock buybacks, is not encouraging in this regard. See, for example, Yonhap News Agency, "Trade Minister Leaves for US for Talks on Chips Act," March 8, 2023.

57. Kif Leswing, "Nvidia Says US Government Allows A.I. Chip Development in China," CNBC, September 1, 2022.

58. Alex He, "Beijing and Washington Joust over Semiconductors," Centre for International Government Innovation, November 9, 2022.

59. Yang Jie and Aaron Tilley, "Apple Makes Plans to Move Production out of China," *Wall Street Journal*, December 3, 2022.

60. Ministry of Foreign Affairs of the People's Republic of China, "Foreign Ministry Spokesperson Wang Wenbin's Regular Press Conference on September 1, 2022," September 1, 2022.

61. Ministry of Foreign Affairs of the People's Republic of China, "Foreign Ministry Spokesperson Mao Ning's Regular Press Conference on October 8, 2022," October 8, 2022.

62. Merriden Varall, "Behind the News: Inside China Global Television Network," Lowy Institute, January 10, 2020.

63. Laura Silver, Christine Wang, and Laura Clancy, "Negative Views of China Tied to Critical Views of Its Policies on Human Rights," Pew Research Center, June 29, 2022.

64. David M. Hart, "The Impact of China's Production Surge on Innovation in the Global Solar Photovoltaics Industry," ITIF, October 5, 2020.

65. Nigel Cory, Stephen Ezell, David M. Hart, and Robert D. Atkinson, "Innovation Drag: The Impact of Chinese Economic and Trade Policies on Global Innovation," ITIF, June 10, 2021.

66. China's Ministry of Commerce in fact filed such a WTO suit on December 12, 2022, over the October 7 BIS rules aimed at advanced chips. Orange Wang, "China Files WTO Suit against US over Chip Export Controls, Saying Policy Is 'Trade Protectionism,'" *South China Morning Post*, December 13, 2022.

67. Andrew Methven, "A Thief Crying 'Stop Thief!'—Phrase of the Week," *China Project*, May 20, 2022.

CONCLUSION AND DISCUSSION OF RECOMMENDATIONS

The preceding chapters have painted a rich and challenging portrait of the dynamic and rapidly evolving global competition in semiconductors that has swept up the US-Taiwan-China triangle as well as the rest of the world.

As our report has shown, this new phase of international competition over semiconductors has existential implications for the economic and national security of the United States, its allies and partners—and, especially, Taiwan, the remarkable and dynamic but vulnerable democratic society that leads the world in the production of semiconductors. This concluding chapter distills the principal insights and recommendations of the preceding chapters, emphasizing those that have garnered broad support among the participants in our Working Group on Semiconductors and the Security of the United States and Taiwan, organized by the Hoover Institution at Stanford University and the Center on US-China Relations at the Asia Society. In a few instances, we have noted areas of disagreement among the participants. While this chapter represents the editors' final judgments of what we have learned and concluded as a group, it has benefited from extensive input and feedback from many of our participants.

1. Domestic Resilience

As the chapters in this report explain, we are moving toward a world of intensified trade among like-minded nations and sharply reduced dependence on adversary nations for critical supply chains. Thus, a framing principle of US policy on semiconductors in the next few years should be to make voluntary participation in this emerging trading bloc as reliable and attractive for its participants—including the United States—as possible.

The United States should aim to ensure that, as much as possible, its imports of finished semiconductors and key inputs along the supply chain come from reliable trading partners with whom we share common values, such as the current foreign industry leaders Taiwan, Korea, and Japan, and from other countries where the political divide does not bode ill for continued cooperation.

A balanced US policy to that end should pursue efficiencies and growth through trade and increased market access within this still-incipient coalition of critical-technology trading partners. Our policy must also commit to investing in a major new effort to revive US domestic production of semiconductors, from design to fabrication. Toward this goal, US policy should work to level the playing field by reducing domestic tax and regulatory barriers to the competitiveness of the US semiconductor industry.

Even if this approach succeeds, the United States will still be heavily dependent on international partners for critical inputs, materials, components, and steps in its semiconductor supply chain. However, this approach will also leave us less vulnerable to pressure from unreliable suppliers. Moreover, increased US production—as well as other domestic resilience measures—will nurture talent and know-how and stimulate economic growth in the United States. The goal is to create an insurance policy against the kind of catastrophic foreign supply chain disruption that might occur after a People's Republic of China (PRC) blockade or attack on Taiwan, a conflict in the South China Sea, a military accident around the Korean peninsula, or a severe natural disaster.

We recommend the following steps to mitigate supply chain risk and strengthen the US industrial base in semiconductors.

1a. Onshoring Supply Chains

The US government (USG) should subsidize a modest amount of new semiconductor supply chain capacity in sectors where US industry now lacks capacity or global cost competitiveness, such as in advanced-semiconductor manufacturing or packaging. The implementation of the manufacturing-oriented elements of the CHIPS and Science Act of 2022 should be evaluated primarily by their ability to reduce the potential short-term costs of a sudden and severe semiconductor supply chain disruption. While the United States can and should never be entirely self-sufficient, added increments of production will be extremely important if a major crisis strikes.

Funding awards should be made to firms, whether headquartered domestically or in friendly jurisdictions abroad, that have the best chances of executing on this promise from a technology-risk and operational-efficiency perspective.

The National Environmental Policy Act's categorical exemptions (or expedited approvals) should be considered for these initial facilities, which are intended to rapidly produce a minimum viable domestic semiconductor supply chain. Furthermore, Congress and the executive branch should avoid imposing unnecessary new regulations or policies associated with manufacturing subsidies that would impede or delay new semiconductor projects in the United States or make investment less attractive for like-minded foreign partners.

1b. Information Sharing

The US government should fund—or itself establish—improved intelligence gathering, data analysis, economic modeling, and information sharing on the global semiconductor market that is analogous to the US Department of Energy's Energy Information Administration (EIA). Such a data fusion center could be either operated directly through a government agency such as the Department of Commerce, or supported by specialized contractors such as federally funded research and development centers (FFRDCs).

Drawing from existing industry data services as a starting point, the USG should work with industry to balance the value of this information with commercial sensitivities. Such data could be variously managed for both internal and public consumption as well as being made available to partners globally in return for their own participation.

Even without imposing these additional disclosure requirements on private firms, the US Department of Commerce could do more with the information on trade and intellectual property (IP) flows in the global semiconductor supply chain that it already has. For example, Commerce could share this information within the interagency process more widely as well as with Congress in a summarized and thus less commercially sensitive form.

1c. Stockpiling Chips

In total, US industries use a staggering number and variety of specific chips—far too many to stockpile the way we stockpile primary commodities such as oil. We do believe that the feasibility of a more limited "smart" strategic semiconductor stockpile—which could also improve market liquidity and be operated as a public-private partnership model—deserves further study. Meanwhile, the USG should also explore other effective options to buffer near-term domestic chip supplies in case global supply chains are suddenly disrupted.

First, the Department of Defense (DoD) should, as appropriate, target advance buys of those key semiconductors needed for critical weapons platforms over multiple years, even for the expected lifetimes of the systems (as has recently been done for one key platform). Second, the USG should encourage a private sector strategy of extended inventory management by creating a new 25 percent tax credit on semiconductor inventories exceeding forty-five days for chip-consuming and -integrating firms (e.g., automotive, aerospace, defense, machinery, electronics).

Resilience Q&A

Q: Should the USG be concerned about commercial market and investment cycles of the semiconductor industry, and the effects of those changes on supply and demand?

A: No. But we do believe that increased USG attention on the semiconductor industry is now warranted by new national security concerns that were less prominent a decade ago. The USG now has longer-term public interests in fostering technological competitiveness among critical technologies generally, including semiconductors. At the same time, we underscore that an open, competitive market is the basis of technological innovation, and USG policy interventions should be designed to avoid or minimize intrusions that might cause market distortions as much as possible.

Q: Should domestic chip industry subsidies intended to improve resiliency favor US-domiciled semiconductor firms?

A: No. They should be made available as equally as possible to any company in any partner country, but on a competitive basis to multiple awardees in order to maximize the chances for successful implementation.

Q: Should domestic chip industry subsidies be focused on manufacturing leading-edge logic chips?

A: No. They should seek to enable domestic production of leading- or near-leading-edge logic chips, but the security motivation extends to minimum viable production for mature logic nodes, memory, storage, and analog chips as well, including the support of upstream inputs as well as downstream packaging.

2. Business Environment

The United States must seek new capabilities in the semiconductor supply chain, especially in segments where it is not now seen as cost-competitive with other global trading partners. But efforts should not seek to compromise competitiveness of existing US areas of innovation and strength in the global semiconductor supply chain. Creating a welcome environment for investment and operations by US allies and partners that command significant semiconductor supply chain strengths and expertise—a business environment that extends beyond the five-year time frame of the CHIPS and Science Act subsidies—should be a high priority during this period. Ensuring fair business opportunities and market access for foreign technology firms operating within the United States will also sustain the ability of foreign allied and partner governments to align with otherwise costly controls on commerce with China. To that end, US federal and state governments should take steps to reduce the costs of doing business in the United States within this and other critical-technology sectors.

2a. Federal Tax Efficiency

Given the capital-intensity of the industry, private investment will be the primary route to scaling the US domestic semiconductor supply chain. Hence, private capital efficiency ultimately matters more in terms of driving siting decisions than comparatively small or uncertain government subsidies:

- For example, well over half of the cost of a new semiconductor fabrication plant ("fab") comes from the equipment purchased by the manufacturer to build production lines. Congress should consider extending 100 percent tax depreciation for short-lived capital assets beyond 2022 to improve the competitiveness of US semiconductor and semiconductor equipment manufacturers.
- Similarly, Congress should consider a preemptive extension of the 25 percent chip manufacturing tax credit passed in the CHIPS and Science Act beyond its 2027 sunset. Further, it should consider moderately expanding coverage domestically of upstream semiconductor material inputs and manufacture of semiconductor equipment including etching, deposition, lithography, and metrology tools.

- Modern semiconductor fabs and semiconductor equipment manufacturers reinvest significant portions of their revenue into research and development each year to sustain leading-edge capabilities. Yet since 2022, US firm research and development (R&D) spending deductions have been required to be taken over five years rather than immediately in the year in which they are incurred (as per the Tax Cuts and Jobs Act of 2017). We recommend reverting to full tax deductions of R&D expenses in the year incurred, which would stimulate a broad swath of knowledge investments in this and other critical research-intensive industries.
- Taking advantage of these deductions could require eliminating the alternative minimum tax and additional corporate taxes passed in the Inflation Reduction Act of 2022 (IRA), which have historically been seen as disincentivizing domestic manufacturing and other investments of multinational corporations. Even so, we believe eliminating those taxes is particularly important for the semiconductor industry and other strategic technologies where the restoration of some degree of domestic manufacturing is critical to US economic and national security.

2b. Federal Environmental Regulation

New chip manufacturing facilities receiving federal subsidies are expected to be subject to National Environmental Policy Act (NEPA) regulations and reviews. Given the industry's short two-year technology cycles, however, the roughly eighteen-month time frame required for a NEPA Environmental Review—let alone the four- to five-year timeline for a full Environmental Impact Statement—could in itself prevent the United States from ever producing the world's most advanced chips. Federal financing intended to speed the development of this sector should not have the inadvertent and perverse effect of slowing down the process. To mitigate this problem, the USG should consider additional fast-tracking and definitional authorities for the semiconductor and other critical industries.

Separately, a policy of timely Environmental Protection Agency (EPA) reviews for critical industries such as chip fabs (perhaps with a special three-month cap) could improve private investor confidence in project delivery schedules. This confidence is particularly important given large up-front capital outlays and the need to coordinate orders with long lead times from dozens of vendors. Flexible air permits— as with, for example, Oregon's Plant Site Emissions Limit (PSEL) program—could allow for flexibility in operations and investment across a company's facilities (as long as overall emissions limits are met) without triggering additional federal or state reviews.

Industry should also be consulted more closely to avoid inadvertently introducing new regulatory barriers for chip manufacturing alongside other existing state and federal government climate change or water quality regulations. Investments in this sector already face high total compliance costs in the United States compared to other globally attractive sites. Excessive environmental reviews or mitigation requirements could push a manufacturer abroad—emissions will simply occur elsewhere (and in any case become embedded in our own imports). Particular attention should be given to gases and other manufacturing inputs that lack viable domestic alternatives. Here, priority should be given to funding and incentives for the discovery and development of alternative, environmentally friendly replacement materials and processes.

2c. State-Level Business Environment

Semiconductor firms have a wide range of investment opportunities globally. The ease of doing business across the United States, therefore, remains a key consideration in decisions about where to invest. Taiwan Semiconductor Manufacturing Company's (TSMC) leadership, for example, estimates that of the approximately 50 percent cost premium to operate a leading-edge fab in the United States, perhaps half of that premium is due to the lack of geographic clustering of spare equipment, service firms, and workers who can help improve factory uptime and yields. Thus, it is in the broader national interest for individual states with advanced-manufacturing endowments to remain attractive places to do business—in terms of cost of living, cost and reliability of electricity, water rights, local taxes, and local building regulations.

The federal government should coordinate with state and local governments to create technology hubs by implementing opt-in policies that engender such favorable business environments. These state-sponsored hubs could also adopt beneficial tax and regulatory reforms of their own that may not be possible to pass at the national level. Fine-tuning the legislation that establishes such hubs should be encouraged through the experimentation and success of pilot projects.

Business Environment Q&A

Q: Should water availability limit semiconductor manufacturing activities in the American West?

A: No. Given water recycling and purification technology advancements, we do not believe that in most places endowed water resources should be a major barrier to modern semiconductor manufacturing. Reliable, affordable electricity and local infrastructure that permits clustering of associated suppliers and service firms are far more important.

Q: Should the semiconductor industry receive special tax and regulatory treatment, or should cost-of-doing-business reforms be pursued more broadly?

A: This is a matter of judgment. We recognize that there are many competing US industrial and commercial policy priorities. At the same time, the historical record is clear that the United States' semiconductor manufacturing and packaging business environment has not been cost-competitive, even compared to that of some allies and partners.

A middle path between targeted and broad reforms would be to prioritize the competitiveness of the US business environment for critical emerging technologies with security implications, such as chips, and where flows of investment and IP are likely to be increasingly limited among like-minded trade clubs.

3. Technological Competitiveness

In the shift to a world more defined by trade, investment, IP, and human capital flows among voluntary blocs of like-minded nations, long-term US leadership in a portfolio of critical technologies should significantly influence the prosperity and security of all participant countries of that bloc.

The United States should therefore pursue comprehensive, market-oriented industrial policy measures that are also mindful of the interests of US partners. To achieve strategic autonomy by means of technology and economic leadership, these policies should accomplish the following:

- Enhance value capture and commercialization of research through scaling innovation, alongside the incubation of complementary domestic manufacturing activity.
- Strengthen national and economic security by decreasing dependence on unreliable competitor nations and by diversifying geographic risk.
- Amplify value creation through investment in US research capacity for breakthrough technologies, a process that for semiconductors is strongly coupled to advanced manufacturing activities.
- Strengthen the global intellectual property regime through both domestic reforms and, in consultation with allies and partners, countering China's systematic theft of open-society technologies.

3a. Immigration and Workforce

Additional legislative skilled immigration and workforce measures can greatly enhance the impact of the CHIPS and Science Act and other recent private investments in domestic semiconductor manufacturing, and help smooth an otherwise rapid labor market transition.

The USG should provide worker-oriented tax incentives for the semiconductor industry and other strategic manufacturing sectors. The goal should be to boost their take-home income and help semiconductor companies to compete for high-skilled (master's and PhD) workers within the domestic labor force. Examples could include waiving student loans for US citizens who work in the industry for a period of time after graduation.

Meanwhile, community colleges and related industry apprenticeships located within the region of a semiconductor manufacturing cluster should be supported in providing the skilled trade and tool operators that compose the bulk of fabrication facility jobs. The training of technicians needs to be targeted to the regions in which the jobs are.

Finally, we recommend that H-1B visas be made available to all international students who complete a graduate program in science or engineering at an accredited US university, without numerical visa caps. Until the United States can dramatically increase its own domestic supply of relevant science and engineering talent—a task that will, at a minimum, take a decade or more—the only alternative for the United States to restore its international competitiveness in high-tech manufacturing is by finding new ways to retain the international talent that it has already educated and trained.

3b. Market-Oriented Public Infrastructure

Subsidies to encourage the onshoring of semiconductor manufacturing capabilities should be designed to minimize market distortions and be as complementary as possible with already-existing private enterprise capabilities.

For example, funding access by start-ups to otherwise cost-prohibitive prototyping facilities can help overcome the increasingly steep barriers to entry into chip design. That kind of access will encourage competition over time. Rather than building a single public facility to this end, however, the Department of Commerce's public-private National Semiconductor Technology Center (NSTC) should instead aim to facilitate a digital and physical network of new pathfinder fabs and facilities across the country. These could be focused on simulation, AI-enabled chip design, and the development of digital test environments that can mimic more-expensive physical chip manufacturing processes.

Similarly, Commerce should in particular use funding for the National Advanced Packaging Manufacturing Program of the CHIPS and Science Act to sponsor the development of technologies that boost automation. The goal here should be to increase the output efficiency per packaging employee by one to two orders of magnitude, as a way of ensuring economically sustainable operations over the long term. More broadly, given US labor-cost concerns, US semiconductor manufacturing should pursue employee productivity through automation.

Other subsidies for research and development should be awarded on a cost-competitive basis. For example, the USG might act as a customer of the capabilities being developed under the subsidy program and then require firms competing for the subsidies to raise additional private capital to supplement taxpayer dollars.

3c. Antitrust

The USG has in the past expressed concern over the potential consumer impacts of large internet technology firms becoming even larger and more monopolistic. We nonetheless believe that US antitrust policy must take into account a firm's broader impact on US economic competitiveness, innovation capacity, and effects on national security. It can do so by recognizing the importance of a firm's market size on its ability to undertake valuable research, invent, and then scale up new technologies—particularly capital-intensive ones—as well as on its ability to compete with the protected industries of other nations.

In particular, Congress could consider antitrust protections for semiconductor industry collaborations that may be undertaken in response to the CHIPS Act, but extend beyond the limiting scope of precompetitive R&D. US regulatory agencies need to appreciate that these firms compete globally with enormous firms from other countries, often aided by government subsidies, as opposed to their traditional antitrust concern of US companies competing only with one another.

3d. Business and National Security

The USG should consider incentives to provide better feedback between US corporate activity and US national security interests. For example, regulatory bodies such as the Federal Trade Commission (FTC), Federal Communications Commission (FCC), Securities and Exchange Commission (SEC), Environmental Protection Agency (EPA), and Federal Energy Regulatory Commission (FERC) could be instructed to weigh the national security implications of their regulatory decisions. This instruction might be modeled on the Biden administration's 2021 executive order requiring regulatory bodies to weigh the estimated social cost of carbon emissions in their decisions.

3e. Investment and National Security

New geopolitical circumstances are now creating the need to consider both inbound and outbound investment screening in critical-technology areas.

As we continue to closely monitor inbound investment by China, we should make a special effort to enhance greenfield foreign direct investment into the United States from allied and partner countries, including partner-country firms making mergers and acquisitions (M&A) as a normal part of doing business. The inbound investment review of the Committee on Foreign Investment in the United States (CFIUS) should be more transparent, and more actively engage and negotiate with prospective foreign investors from friendly nations. To do that, CFIUS should hire more staffers with technical backgrounds. The United States should encourage foreign direct investment in critical technological fields from allied countries to make these attractive sectors for entrepreneurs to do business in. At the same time, it should limit foreign investment in such fields from autocratic countries that pose a documented national security risk.

Some in our working group believe CFIUS or a new agency should be given additional authority to review and restrict outbound investment in critical technologies, such as building research and manufacturing centers, establishing joint ventures, and making financial investment in China and other autocracies, especially when such outbound investments are required by those countries for access to their own domestic markets. Should things become more hostile and fraught, the United States should be open to such a prospect.

3f. Research and Development

The United States should increase federal R&D funding in basic and applied research that spans established fields such as conventional semiconductors as well as frontier fields such as beyond-CMOS (complementary metal-oxide semiconductor) devices that could someday complement today's predominant logic chips. And once increased, such funding should be sustained indefinitely. We also recommend allocating a portion of federal R&D budgets to building and operating new research infrastructure, rather than research programs alone. This would lower barriers for innovation and technology development by start-ups in the private sector.

In particular, we recommend significant increases in applied research funding to develop technologies, as opposed to pure science—an approach our competitors (friendly or otherwise) have been embracing more fulsomely than has the United States. We must better organize our economy and society to value and nurture applied engineering research. Increasing support for the new Engineering Directorate of the National Science Foundation would help.

We also endorse the role of international semiconductor research organizations, such as Taiwan's Industrial Technology Research Institute (ITRI), the Berlin-based Fraunhofer Group, and Belgium's industry and academic semiconductor research consortium imec; we believe that the CHIPS Act's NSTC should reinforce, not displace, those institutions. Even so, we maintain that imec's future role hinges on it offering a trusted environment for researchers and firms operating in democratic and open societies.

3g. Education and Human Capital

The long-term solution to the critical shortage of home-grown science and engineering talent in the United States must include substantial enhancements of K–12 education. Students should be exposed to high-tech industries, including semiconductors, at an early age. We must find ways to convey both the excitement of innovation in this sector and its vital importance to the national and economic security of the United States, as was done for the defense and space industries in earlier eras. K–12 education should be strengthened to ensure that students have sufficient training in math and science to compete with global peers upon entry into universities or trade schools. Funding as well as teacher incentives are important here.

For those pursuing college degrees in semiconductor technology and related fields, we recommend increasing the number of funded scholarships with direct pathways to jobs—for example, a semiconductor-focused version of the DoD SMART Scholarship program in partnership with industry. Universities should also consider making it possible for their students to transfer into engineering majors from other fields as they discover the opportunities and excitement of developing and producing transformative technologies.

Broadly speaking, more thought should be given to how government policies and regulations could directly or indirectly affect profitability across the entire semiconductor value chain—from chip designers and software system developers to materials and equipment producers, and ultimately to chip manufacturers. After all, such concerns affect domestic investment and employee compensation that determine the career choices of US graduates. A healthy US semiconductor ecosystem will need to attract and retain the best talent in the field among even the least glamorous links in that chain.

3h. Tacit Knowledge

An essential pillar of improved US competitiveness in the semiconductor ecosystem—or in most other critical technologies—must be the attraction and retention of advanced talent.

Toward this end, we urge corporations, government agencies, universities, and society at large to make the pursuit of engineering and careers in critical technologies as rewarding, well compensated, and esteemed as pathways as possible. Put simply, we must retain our own talent once they are trained, while attracting as much international talent as we can.

The United States should also provide an expedited path to legal residency in the United States for skilled and critical-technology workers fleeing autocracies.

Given the great contributions that scholars and professionals from China continue to make to the US economy, our society, and our nation's technological advancement, the United States should continue to grant visas to scientists and engineers from China, even to work in critical technologies. These visas, however, must be subject to an evidence-based process for screening out those applicants with demonstrable ties to China's military-industrial base, security agencies, United Front organs, surveillance apparatus, and other PRC entities that steal or misappropriate technological know-how. The USG should also consider mechanisms to embrace individuals who seek to vacate China's authoritarianism system and remain in or permanently relocate to the United States.

Noncompete agreements among skilled technology workers are critical, if imperfect, legal instruments for deterring leakage of tacit knowledge and trade secrets through employee mobility. Some in the United States have proposed broadly limiting the use of noncompete clauses, justifying new limitations on the proliferation of noncompetes among trade workers. But limiting noncompetes for advanced-technology workers risks encouraging trade secret theft in semiconductors. Limiting noncompete agreements may also make it less attractive for foreign technology firms of partner countries to invest in the United States, as many of them rely on noncompetes to protect tacit knowledge. For example, Korean and Taiwanese firms should not be made to worry that, if they send their semiconductor manufacturing experts to the United States, they may be poached by competing firms (just as we worry about US technical workers being lured to competitors in China).

3i. IP and Incentives for US Innovation

The United States' intellectual property regimes should be made more efficient, competitive, and stable through consideration of the following measures:

- Clarify and stabilize patent eligibility criteria to promote a range of high-tech industries and to ensure that the United States is not placed at a competitive disadvantage.

- Make injunctive relief readily available in IP infringement cases of all types.
- Create a team within the US Patent and Trademark Office (USPTO) to address the relationship between intellectual property and strategic competitiveness.
- Appoint US IP officials in a timely manner.
- Ensure that countries with which the United States forms relationships (such as via trade and friend-shoring) have robust IP regimes to avoid repeating the problems that US companies have faced in protecting IP in China.

3j. Trade

In partnership with allies and friends who share common values and seek to counter China's market-distorting actions, the United States should pursue a comprehensive agenda to reform global trade rules that are focused on strong protections of IP, the rule of law, fairness, and reciprocity. The United States should start by focusing on signing market-access trade deals with as many partners as possible to establish a wider circumference of stronger trade relationships.

The United States should also rigorously evaluate what, if any, criteria should be imposed on foreign companies seeking to gain access to the US economy. But such policies should be evaluated from a strong baseline expectation of encouraging open commerce and foreign investment in the United States.

Our working group members are united in favoring some use of technology export controls to protect intellectual property developed in the United States. Some members of our group favor robust export controls on critical emerging technologies (see below), while others endorse the use of such controls only sparingly, such as for technologies that are difficult to copy (so that the controlled technology cannot simply be reproduced abroad, resulting only in lost market share for US firms) or for technologies that directly pertain to security matters.

Technology Competitiveness Q&A

Q: Should the USG sponsor large-scale professional training programs to ensure that new semiconductor manufacturing or packaging facilities have sufficient employees?

A: No. The track record for such state-sponsored programs is poor. While we believe that the currently envisioned domestic supply chain investments may create some labor market disruption, the spike can most sustainably be met by more flexible visa and employee tax treatment in the near term. Over the mid term, broader skilled-immigration reforms, coupled with natural labor market wage adjustments, should be used to encourage an adequate and sustainable stream of students and workers to enter this industry. For trade workers and operators, strengthening existing local community colleges is preferable to other government training schemes.

Q: Should the USG directly engage in semiconductor manufacturing or use its Defense Production Act Title I authority to compel activity in this area by the private sector?

A: No. That is neither a sustainable nor a scalable approach to improving US technology competitiveness over the long term.

Q: Are you advocating increased government intervention in US markets?

A: Yes, in some measure, but only for technologies critical to national security interests. The challenge will be to find the right balance in a constantly changing geopolitical climate. We recognize that commercial incentives and free-market forces are the prime sources of US technology competitiveness and innovation. But we also see increasing security and strategic interests that relate to these sectors and warrant new initiatives and guardrails.

Q: Could such an "industrial policy" do more harm than good?

A: Yes. The historical record of the USG in encouraging the development of certain technologies or industries is mixed. We advocate for an honest reckoning with that track record and consideration of the downside risk. Given the geopolitical shifts that appear to be moving us away from a flat, fully globalized world, some members of the working group favor a more ambitious industrial policy. The predominant view, however, emphasizes lowering barriers for technology innovation and for translating that innovation into applications for manufacturing—so as to maximize the benefits of a competitive market—and opposes using industrial policies as a vehicle for other political or social priorities.

4. Taiwan's Stability

Taiwan is one of Asia's most prosperous, successful liberal democracies and a trusted partner in critical supply chains. While it stands at the center of the global semiconductor economy, its broader political isolation from the international community contributes to its existential vulnerability.

Consequently, we believe it is in the interest not only of the twenty-four million people of Taiwan but also of the United States and the entire Indo-Pacific region to both militarily deter aggression against the island and fortify its autonomy and democracy through strengthened security and economic interactions.

While the necessary security engagements are beyond the scope of this report, we strongly endorse US arms sales to strengthen Taiwan's defenses—including through a "porcupine" strategy of deterrence through a large number of small weapons systems—and improving joint training and coordination among Taiwan, the United States, and those countries in the region that view the future of Taiwan as critical to their own security and prosperity.

Semiconductors, meanwhile, which have drawn enormous levels of American attention to Taiwan's current situation, now offer a unique

platform for deeper and sustained US-Taiwan economic and civil engagements. To that end, we endorse the following steps to create an environment that fosters deeper business-to-business, research, academic,
individual, and civil ties between the United States and Taiwan.

4a. R&D Collaboration

There is a unique opportunity for US research centers and universities
to partner with Taiwan on talent development. One goal should be to
incentivize leading Taiwan semiconductor firms and research organizations to grow their R&D efforts in the United States. In addition, the
United States can learn from the semiconductor manufacturing expertise that Taiwan's semiconductor industry has pioneered over the past
three decades, while Taiwan can learn from US strengths in chip design
and other areas, such as these:

- Taiwan's semiconductor technology leaders—such as TSMC,
  United Microelectronics Corporation (UMC), and MediaTek—
  and Korea's industry leader, Samsung, should be invited to join
  the public-private National Semiconductor Technology Center to
  accelerate a wide range of collaborations on US soil, from R&D
  to manufacturing.
- Taiwan's Industrial Technology Research Institute (ITRI, established in 1973) and the Taiwan Semiconductor Research
  Institute (TSRI, established in 2019 to engage in cooperation
  with international partners) are logical partners for collaboration with the United States on technology research and supply chain resilience. There is considerable overlap between
  the missions of the TSRI and the NSTC. Indeed, the NSTC is
  intended to conduct research in semiconductor technologies,
  manufacturing, design, packaging, and prototyping; strengthen
  the competitiveness and security of supply chains; and promote
  workforce training.
- In 2021, Taiwan established a collection of "semiconductor colleges" within the top universities on the island. A potential US
  partner could be the American Semiconductor Academy (ASA)

initiative, a proposed nationwide semiconductor education and training network of faculty at US universities and colleges engaged in semiconductor research and education.

- Cooperative US-Taiwan work on advanced-technology IP protection regimes and experiences is essential to support such deeper joint R&D on semiconductors.

4b. Workforce and Educational Exchange

Both Taiwan and the United States are concerned with the development of the kinds of student-worker pipelines necessary to strengthen today's semiconductor supply chains in both places:

- The 2022 initiative announced between Taiwan-based chip designer MediaTek and Purdue University to create a new chip design center should become a model for pairing up Taiwan's semiconductor firms and expertise with US engineering programs. Such agreements can provide industry with know-how, firms with access to engineering talent, and students with career opportunities in a win-win-win development initiative.
- Meanwhile, initiatives such as the US-Taiwan Education Initiative— which encourages American students to study Mandarin at Taiwan universities—and bidirectional summer internship programs for engineering, economics, and social science students should be expanded, particularly as China becomes a less attractive destination for US students.
- In turn, the Taiwan and US governments should take steps to reverse the decline in the number of Taiwanese students studying in US universities—a cohort that formed the original bedrock of Taiwan's chip industry, as well as its democratization experiment. One future opportunity is to increase the presence of Taiwanese undergraduates in US master's degree programs, which would in turn improve the pipeline to funded research PhDs. Another is to encourage English coursework options within Taiwanese universities.

4c. Joint Evaluations of Vulnerabilities

There is a need for regular evaluations of US semiconductor industry vulnerabilities to a range of threats, including natural and geopolitical disaster scenarios involving Taiwan. Such evaluations, including tabletop scenario exercises with US and Taiwan industry participation, could reveal supply chain weaknesses that need to be addressed, and they could develop plans for recovery after such potential incidents. A partnership between Taiwan's TSRI and the US's NSTC would be a potential institutional structure to conduct such evaluations.

4d. Energy Cooperation

A stable electricity supply is essential for semiconductor production. With the growth of the industry in Taiwan, power demand from the information and communications technology (ICT) subsector in Taiwan has quadrupled since 2000, with TSMC alone consuming 5 percent of the island's electricity supply. And yet, Taiwan maintains only a forty-day supply of coal and roughly a ten-day supply of natural gas and may close its nuclear plants altogether. Meanwhile, US chip buyers and other original equipment manufacturers (OEMs) are increasingly concerned with the emissions profiles of their suppliers. So, climate, resource adequacy, and electric grid security issues are fertile areas for US-Taiwan technical collaboration to improve the island's supply chain resiliency. The US Department of Energy and national labs should be directed to increase energy statistical and technical collaborations with Taiwan. Climate and energy are also good areas for subnational collaboration—for example, with California, which already pursues such policy and technical memoranda of understanding with China.

4e. Smoothing US-Taiwan Economic Frictions

Taiwan's government has made significant overtures to opening its domestic market to US exports, even at some political risk, and its semiconductor firms are now in the process of carrying out one of the largest foreign direct investments (FDI) in US history. Meanwhile, Taiwan is also undertaking a long and potentially costly but ultimately sound effort to realign its own trade and investments to be less dependent on

China. Lacking access to multilateral trade fora, bilateral agreements are particularly important for Taiwan—not just for lowering tariffs, but as a symbol of strategic partnership.

- The US Trade Representative should accelerate its ongoing efforts to complete a real US-Taiwan free-trade agreement for the benefit of US businesses and consumers and as a demonstration of US commitment to Taiwan's prosperity and stability.
- In the near term, US-Taiwan worker and trainee exchanges are needed to enable the timely opening of new manufacturing facilities such as TSMC's Arizona plant, which will involve the transfer of thousands of workers in both directions. And Taiwanese nationals already have a significant presence in US semiconductor technology clusters, including in Silicon Valley and Texas. Accordingly, the US Department of the Treasury should rapidly finalize an avoidance-of-dual-taxation agreement with Taiwan, mirroring the income tax treaties and totalization agreements already in place with thirty-seven other jurisdictions globally.

4f. Defense Industry Cooperation

The war in Ukraine has exposed the fragility and limited capacity of the US defense industrial base. The invasion has also contributed to multiyear backlogs in the delivery of US weapons systems to Taiwan that would materially improve its deterrence posture. At the same time, Taiwan's capabilities in precision manufacturing, electronics, and defense-grade semiconductors make it—if given a green light—a promising contributor to the manufacture of key weapons systems and ammunitions for its own defense and even for export.

The USG can and should materially improve regional deterrence by partnering with Taiwan's manufacturing firms to rapidly scale up local production of a large number of mobile, distributed, resilient weapons. These efforts could include the authorization of IP transfer and other use provisions of the US International Traffic in Arms

Regulations (ITAR). Supported by defense firms in both the United States and Taiwan, the USG should sponsor a joint industry working group to identify opportunities and then work through the thicket of interagency barriers to allow greatly scaled weapons coproduction and codevelopment within Taiwan, and possible later indigenization. This is the most sustainable way to align Taiwan's deep will to defend itself with its capabilities to do so.

Taiwan Q&A

Q: Are there other areas ripe for semiconductor collaboration with Taiwan beyond manufacturing chips?

A: Yes, we believe that US collaboration with Taiwan on semi-conductors should also extend to technology research and development, and to parts of the supply chain where the US has considerable strengths as well, including chip design.

Q: Do US efforts to attract domestic investment by Taiwan semi-conductor firms compromise Taiwan's "silicon shield"?

A: No, we believe that potential semiconductor-related costs or benefits do not weigh heavily in Beijing's calculus regarding military force against Taiwan. US-Taiwan business and civil collaborations on semiconductors would therefore strengthen, not undermine, deterrence.

Q: Should the threat of semiconductor supply chain disruption be the motivation for US military involvement in a Taiwan contingency scenario?

A: No. A US decision to intervene militarily should be motivated by the defense of common values and broader regional security considerations, not by a failure to maintain the semiconductor supply chain. A test of proposed US domestic resilience efforts should be whether or not access to Taiwan's semiconductor exports is a significant factor motivating US decision makers in the event of a Taiwan contingency.

5. Dealing with China

There are two dimensions to any form of engagement with China on semiconductors. First is the need to mitigate emerging economic and supply chain vulnerabilities that could make us more dependent on China. While starting from a relatively weak position, China is now aggressively pursuing its own domestic semiconductor aims—first to reduce its dependence on imports, and then to seize an ever-larger share of the global market through steadily growing exports of chips and other elements in the global chip supply chain. But the variety of PRC government targets and subsidies to China's semiconductor firms make it likely that these firms, lavishly aided by nonmarket mechanisms, will undercut the pricing of established semiconductor firms in the US and its trading allies. However, anticompetitive behavior by firms in China could, with state assistance, severely and unfairly harm US or ally and partner producers through, for example, the production of legacy or specialized chips and then flooding the global market at discount prices. Over time, this could create new dangerous US or partner dependencies on China-based supply chains, with ominous consequences for US strategic autonomy.

Second is the option for the United States and allies to use their strengths in the semiconductor supply chain, and China's current reliance on them, as a form of economic deterrence against dangerous military or geopolitical pressure and actions by China. Aggression toward Taiwan is a key threat in this regard, but not the only one. As our relations with China morph, a deeper role for a more deliberate economic deterrence strategy may arise, especially given China's reliance on the United States and allies as trading partners. The critical question to keep asking is: What could help diminish the impulse of China's leadership to use force, economic coercion, or other punitive actions to achieve its geopolitical goals in both Taiwan and the world?

US and allied policy stances to deny China technological supremacy should remain flexible and preserve options for both escalation and deescalation, based upon principles of reciprocity and adherence to a rules-based order. The following recommendations should therefore be considered as points along a sliding scale that could offer such flexibility depending on China's own choices and behaviors.

5a. Supply Chain Diversification

As part of a long-term process of engagement and partnership, the US government and private industry should, with their counterparts in Taiwan, more clearly articulate the case for semiconductor manufacturers to diversify their operations beyond any single region. Doing so would effectively hedge against the risk of economic or military coercion by China. This messaging should be paired with a strong operational commitment to assist in the defense of a fellow liberal democracy. We believe this kind of engagement improves deterrence by making global decisions to oppose China's use of force over Taiwan less transactional. South Korea, likewise, should be incentivized to shift more of its production of memory chips to places other than China, where a large share of the world's memory chips is presently made by South Korean firms.

Beyond logic and memory chip production aims, China is already on course to attain significant market share in chip supply chain and related segments, including printed circuit boards, ingots, and the assembly, packaging, and testing that accompany them. US policy makers should dig deeper into their tool kits to mobilize more private capital, such as through investment partnerships with the US International Development Finance Corporation, to actively push more of these generally lower-skill and lower-margin production lines to Southeast Asia, India, Mexico, and other countries without the same political complexities as China.

5b. Multilateral Export Control Regime

Our working group members broadly endorse developing or reforming new institutional mechanisms to better coordinate multilateral export controls for semiconductors and other critical technologies. Members have proposed a host of different strategies to that end.

One view takes inspiration from the voluntary, informal Cold War–era Coordinating Committee for Multilateral Export Controls (COCOM) as a model to revive now as a way to confront China,

Russia, Iran, and North Korea. Proponents of this strategy observe that the Biden administration's October 2022 export controls, which involved preconsultation but were essentially unilateral, were undertaken before reaching agreement with other substitute suppliers—especially the Netherlands and Japan. They also placed few controls on these countries' firms exporting subsystems directly to China's equipment manufacturers. Accordingly, firms in China reacted by buying the equipment piecemeal and seeking to do assembly themselves. Our recommendation is therefore that future talks on semiconductor controls should be elevated to the level of the national security advisors and select cabinet officials of the United States, the Netherlands, and Japan to make it easier for new export controls to be multilateral and comprehensive from the start.

In parallel, the USG could also build a grouping of partners that additionally includes South Korea, Germany, Israel, Taiwan, the United Kingdom, and India to discuss semiconductor supply chain resiliency. That slightly broader but still nimble consortium could commission studies of existing and planned fab capacity at advanced and mature nodes, as well as of related segments of the semiconductor industry, such as chip packaging and testing.

Just as COCOM's coordination was done discreetly, such an approach would leave room for partners to agree on a shared goal—for example, limiting China's domestic chip manufacturing capabilities below 16nm—but leave the form of implementation up to each participating country, thus minimizing disagreement and domestic political or commercial costs.

A second view from our working members recommends a more expansive multilateral regime. These members note that at the end of the Cold War, the informal COCOM mechanism was replaced with the consensus-based Wassenaar Arrangement on arms and dual-use technologies, and was expanded to include the Russian Federation and the former members of the Eastern Bloc. Wassenaar, however, no longer serves its purpose, given each member's veto ability. Indeed, nearly all of the export control actions taken against Russia since its 2022 invasion of Ukraine have been outside this multilateral regime.

Accordingly, these working group members recommend that for the ongoing export controls imposed on Russia as well as concerns about coordinating export controls on China, the United States and its partners should retire the Wassenaar Arrangement, replacing it with a new multilateral regime that takes elements of COCOM, incorporates lessons from Wassenaar, and includes new members that were not a part of either regime. Such a mechanism could be used not just for semiconductors but for a variety of other critical technologies, too. High-technology powers such as Israel and Taiwan (members of neither COCOM nor the Wassenaar Arrangement) should be members of this new multilateral regime.

5c. USG Dependence on China's Chips

A provision of the 2023 National Defense Authorization Act strengthened the security of defense systems by prohibiting USG procurement of products that contain semiconductors from chipmakers with ties to the Chinese Communist Party, including Semiconductor Manufacturing International Corp. (SMIC), Yangtze Memory Technologies Co. (YMTC), and ChangXin Memory Technologies (CXMT). The legislation also requires the USG and its suppliers to understand their supply chains better—for example, external audits could help US defense contractors and end users identify their products' potential reliance on chips from China. But Congress should close several loopholes in this important bill by expanding its scope beyond "national security systems"—an outdated construct limited to weapons and certain equipment required for defense and intelligence activities—to include "critical infrastructure." Provisions should also be expanded to cover the procurement of not just critical goods but also critical software, inputs such as critical minerals or chemicals, and services.

5d. BIS

Congress should allocate the Department of Commerce's Bureau of Industry and Security (BIS), which has responsibilities in technology export controls, more funding for more staff to handle its growing plate of responsibilities in this more challenging era.

The Bureau reportedly has at times had only two officers to conduct end-use export checks in China. BIS also urgently needs to upgrade its technical systems to private sector standards; its current databases are too outdated and fragile for its new responsibilities. And BIS should make better use of private providers of market intelligence and abandon the flawed "end use" paradigm when it comes to China. US officials cannot be expected to reasonably determine the ultimate end user of chips under such a system, and the presumption should be that, if a sensitive technology can be diverted to or co-opted for an undesired end use, it will be.

BIS will increasingly also be tasked with addressing the phenomenon of US persons working or consulting for China's chip firms. For example, beyond the most advanced manufacturers covered by the October 2022 export control rules, US persons with expertise and know-how for mature chips may also indirectly, but substantially, impact China's chipmaking capabilities on leading-edge nodes. BIS should seek to creatively but firmly encourage US talent to leave China's semiconductor industry and work in allied and partner countries or in the United States, where numerous fabs are now under construction.

5e. Expand the Blacklist

The Foreign Direct Product Rule (FDPR) blacklist currently includes twenty-one firms in China to which both US and foreign firms are prohibited from selling goods that contain US technology and equipment. Given the ease with which targeted companies in China can evade export controls via affiliates, the blacklist should be expanded to include the subsidiaries and affiliates of listed PRC companies. The blacklist should also incorporate China's semiconductor manufacturing equipment firms.

As of the end of 2022, the FDPR blacklist (which limits the exports of products containing US technologies from all countries) includes Huawei and forty-nine other firms involved in advanced computing and supercomputing or military computing applications in China. Some in our working group urge that this strictest blacklist be expanded to include all BIS Entity Listed companies and their affiliates. The BIS

Entity List, a broader list that numbers hundreds of firms in China, is less strict and requires licenses only for exports from the United States (firms in third countries are generally not restricted from sales to China). Accordingly, this sort of expansion of the FDPR blacklist would more directly affect businesses operating in allied and partner countries; with the costs that entails, this should be viewed as a potential further step for consideration along a sliding scale as the changing geopolitical situation may demand.

5f. Import Restrictions/Antidumping

As a defensive step, the US could mitigate the potential harm of Beijing's semiconductor industrial policy by taking note of its track record in other sectors—in particular, creating a market reliance on China via overcapacity and global trade distortions through under-priced goods. Such defensive actions would be intended first to signal to US or partner manufacturers that their future investments to expand chip manufacturing capacity within the United States will be shielded from imports from China that are priced lower due to state subsidies. Additional actions could later protect existing domestic manufacturers from dumping (once it occurs and is formally demonstrated).

The USG could begin imposing incremental import restrictions contemporaneously with CHIPS Act investments. For example, despite potential punitive retaliation by China, some in our working group nevertheless support import restrictions that could, in the near term, be self-initiated by the USG under Section 301 of the Trade Act of 1974, as amended, and Section 232 of the Trade Expansion Act of 1962, as amended. In this scenario, restrictions would be low in the first year to allow imports to continue to fill domestic demand while US or partner firms invest in US domestic capacity. These measures, when initiated, should make available to industry and the public a tariff/quota sched-ule that shows how restrictions would be ratcheted up over time. The goal would be to give domestic manufacturers market certainty, that is, knowing their immense investments will be protected in the long term.

As domestic production capacity grows and ongoing harm can be shown, the USG should be ready to initiate more conventional antidumping/countervailing duties (AD/CVDs) against China to address any unfair trading practices. Traditionally, the United States has imposed AD/CVDs only after the harm of dumping has occurred. Moreover, even if they are self-initiated by the USG, AD/CVDs require individual US firms to prosecute at the International Trade Commission, which would open the door to retaliation. Such actions, while useful, can be seen as one tool within a larger portfolio of defenses.

Importantly, while it is possible that the effects of China's mature logic, memory, or power electronic chip dumping could be isolated to a small number of US or partner semiconductor companies, it is also possible that there would be a contagion effect, weakening even the most advanced manufacturers. A majority of members in our working group believe that, given these uncertainties, the United States and its allies should err on the side of more strenuous and well-coordinated actions in response to PRC plans both to become self-sufficient in microchips and to expand the global market reach of its microchip sector. Their view is that, in this critical and fast-moving sector, it is better to be more exclusionary rather than less.

5g. Target Mature Nodes

A more strenuous, and controversial, approach to mitigating the global risks of China's chip ambitions would be not just to defend against dumping through duties, but also to seek to hobble—or at least not further actively enable—China's ability to mass-produce commercially competitive mature chips.

Current Biden administration rules restrict US exports of technologies and tools that would help China make advanced-logic chips with transistor architectures of 16nm or smaller. But lagging node and specialized logic chips (e.g., in the 28nm range), as well as radio frequency (RF) chips, wide-bandgap chips, and analog sensors, are used to power consumer electronics, vehicles and transportation equipment, high-capacity energy-storage systems, and many of our most advanced weapons systems. Some in our working group recommend that the United States and its allies expand the scope of regulations to prohibit the export of equipment that China could use to make 28nm or smaller logic chips—specifically, the sale of deep ultraviolet (DUV) lithography tools and the skilled labor (from Dutch, Japanese, and US firms) that is essential to keep these machines running and with upgraded software. The trade-off of doing so could be revenue losses to Western firms likely exceeding the levels already expected from today's 16nm export restrictions.

China Q&A

Q: How do existing allied and partner technology coordination mechanisms, such as the US-EU Trade and Technology Council (TTC), fit into a modernized multilateral export control regime?

A: Our working group members expressed some skepticism about the US-EU TTC. Some believe that the effort has been worthwhile, even given the significant time and resources the Biden administration has put into it, but they argue that the true test of its value would be whether it becomes a venue for Europe to work more closely with the United States on coordinating semiconductor and other critical-technology export controls toward China. Others argue that placing too much emphasis on the TTC mechanism risks being ineffective, since the EU does not exercise authority over relevant member-state decisions.

Q: Should the US and partners continue to sell semiconductors to China?

A: Yes. A "constraining" strategy, as advocated by some in our group, would not entail stopping the sale of all chips to China, but rather would focus on preventing the sale of manufacturing equipment, subsystems, and other essential materials to China. The goal would be to prevent China from indigenizing advanced-semiconductor production capabilities domestically, or then possibly dominating certain trailing-edge chip markets instead. That said, sale of advanced chips should be prohibited.

Q: Would pursuing this approach further encourage Beijing to pursue its objectives, and should we instead moderate our response to reassure Beijing and persuade them not to pursue their semi-conductor goals?

A: No. The United States and its allies have a poor track record when using reassurance to persuade the PRC to abandon goals that it believes support its interests or undermine our own. The PRC leadership will undoubtedly try to respond to any steps the United States and allies may take, and it may produce some surprising outcomes, including potential parallel technology advances (such as in advanced packaging). But at a high level, we believe that China's perception of the United States as a "hostile foreign force" has already predisposed it to take every measure it can to pursue not just semiconductor autonomy but also greater global influence and dominance of the global chips market. This pattern is evident today, for example, through the PRC's twinning of production lines using both foreign and domestic semiconductor manufacturing equipment. Rather than trying to reassure China, it is now time for us to start focusing on a new strategy of denial.

Q: Regarding mature nodes, doesn't China already have DUV and the other manufacturing equipment it would need to produce chips at 28nm? Would further export controls have any meaningful effect?

A: Yes. True, China already has much of this equipment, and has even been a major buyer from Western equipment firms in recent years. But further controls could still have an effect. Scale matters. The concern among those in our working group about 28nm logic chips (or more mature memory or power management chips) is not to foreclose all of China's capability to produce them—it already does—but that it not be able to build the scale of its production to produce these chips at sustained, commercially competitive yields that would lead to massive exports and potential dumping.

Q: Would 28nm equipment export limits be commercially ruinous to Western semiconductor manufacturers or otherwise constrain their own R&D budgets and innovative potential?

A: There are different views on this question within our working group. These firms were competitive and profitable before the surge in recent demand from China, and there are many fabs in Taiwan and elsewhere outside China that are now on multiyear waiting lists to receive ASML's or other firms' DUV machines. The chip manufacturers that buy such equipment make investment decisions based on expectations of competing investment within China. As a result, they may choose to increase their own equipment orders if they expect that they will not be competing for global chip customers with an expected glut of new entrants from China. The Netherlands could effectuate a "soft ban" on China by simply delivering current orders, by delaying new orders from China's firms, by reprioritizing sales of DUV machines to non-China companies, or by not undertaking new firmware update or maintenance contracts for machines it has already sold to China.

Q: The October 2022 BIS export controls and subsequent allied and partner outreach emphasized the national security implications of China's chip manufacturing at advanced nodes (e.g., 16nm or smaller). With 28nm, are you arguing that there should in fact be a higher threshold for national security concerns, or is this predicated on more of an economic/protectionist justification?

A: We recognize that this is a matter of sensitivity and judgment, and our working group does not have a unanimous view on this matter. As discussed in our scenario-planning exercise and in subsequent analysis within this report, we feel that the separation between commercial and security considerations is less distinct in a world shifting toward the intensification in trade, investment, human capital, and IP flows among like-minded coalitions of nations—as opposed to the flatter, globalized vision of recent decades. In such a world, we believe that leadership of respective trade networks in critical technologies has major implications for the attractiveness of participation in them by otherwise nonaligned nations. And the vitality of those networks, in turn, affects both economic and military strength. What is economic today could become security tomorrow, and US policy must constantly make course corrections to keep up with changing trends.

This shift has profound implications for relations among US partners that have not yet been fully appreciated in semiconductors—or in other critical sectors where principles of economic freedom and national security intersect.

• • •

If the United States is to retain and strengthen its global leadership in semiconductors, or even to preserve its most vital economic and national security interests in this sector, it will need to revive the competitiveness of its workforce and business environment. It is not enough to simply constrain China's malign behavior and intentions. It is not even enough to innovate in design. The United States must run faster, harder, and with longer-term vision.

And in this increasingly globalized world, the United States cannot run alone. Restoring US leadership requires close cooperation with reliable partner countries as we work to strengthen and reconfigure global semiconductor supply chains. It also requires an international talent pool of scientists and engineers from around the world, and immigration rules that welcome and retain this talent.

To win this race, we will need both vigilance and agility. We will need the focus and enhanced information systems to detect important new trend lines, and the agility to respond to these changing forces as quickly as possible. We will also need the flexibility and humility to understand that our partners and friends will sometimes hold different views, and that their policies will sometimes evolve at a different pace than our own.

The key for the United States will be to deepen and nurture these cooperative relationships. Such cooperation will ensure that innovation can thrive through multilateral collaboration, so that our supply chains for semiconductors and other critical commodities can be secure, and so we cannot be held to ransom by our adversaries.

Above all, we must remain steadfast both in our commitment to the common values that undergird these partnerships and in our resolve that open societies can and must win the technological competition with authoritarian states.

WORKING GROUP PARTICIPANTS

A team of more than two dozen economists, strategists, industry veterans, and regional policy experts came together as the Hoover Institution–Asia Society Working Group on Semiconductors and the Security of the United States and Taiwan in the fall of 2021 to study the "silicon triangle." Some working group participants authored signed chapters in this book; others contributed to our collective deliberation through their participation in more than a dozen roundtables and review meetings.

The participants listed here have contributed in their individual capacities and not as representatives of affiliated institutions or of the US government; some have requested anonymity. While each has substantively impacted the resulting work, their participation does not imply endorsement of all arguments or depictions in this book. Going forward, however, we as coeditors and the working group's convenors recommend each of them to readers for their ability to provide informed counsel as new priorities and questions of policy emerge in this field.

Amb. Charlene Barshefsky is a nonresident senior fellow at Yale University's Paul Tsai China Center. She was formerly a senior international partner at WilmerHale and was US trade representative from 1997 to 2001.

Steve Blank is an adjunct professor at Stanford University and a co-founder of its Gordian Knot Center for National Security Innovation. A technology entrepreneur, he cocreated the Lean Startup movement.

Mark Cohen is a distinguished senior fellow and director of the Berkeley Center for Law and Technology at the University of California–Berkeley. He was formerly senior counsel, China, for the US Patent and Trademark Office.

Robert Daly is director of the Wilson Center's Kissinger Institute on China and the United States. Having served as an interpreter for both American and Chinese diplomats, he was formerly director of the Johns Hopkins-Nanjing University Center for Chinese and American Studies.

Larry Diamond is the William L. Clayton Senior Fellow at the Hoover Institution, the Mosbacher Senior Fellow in Global Democracy at the Freeman Spogli Institute, and a Bass University Fellow in Undergraduate Education at Stanford University.

Adm. James O. Ellis Jr., USN (Ret.), is an Annenberg Distinguished Visiting Fellow at the Hoover Institution. In 2004, he completed a distinguished thirty-nine-year navy career, including as commander of US Strategic Command.

Stephen Ezell is vice president for global innovation policy at the Information Technology and Innovation Foundation.

Niall Ferguson is the Milbank Family Senior Fellow at the Hoover Institution and a senior faculty fellow of the Belfer Center at Harvard.

Christopher Ford is a visiting fellow at the Hoover Institution and a fellow of the MITRE Corporation, where he is founding director of its Center for Strategic Competition. From 2018 to 2021 he was assistant secretary for international security and nonproliferation at the US State Department.

Jimmy Goodrich is vice president for global policy at the Semiconductor Industry Association. He has worked across the tech sector in China and serves on the board of the American Mandarin Society.

Yasheng Huang is the Epoch Foundation professor of international management at MIT's Sloan School of Management. He founded and runs MIT's China Lab, ASEAN Lab, and India Lab.

Edlyn V. Levine is chief science officer and cofounder at America's Frontier Fund and a research associate at Harvard University's department of physics. She was formerly chief technologist for the MITRE Corporation's Acceleration Office, where she architected MITRE's 2021 semiconductor strategy.

Greg Linden is a research associate at the Institute for Business Innovation at the UC Berkeley's Haas School of Business. He analyzes global value chain dynamics, the effect of foreign direct investment on economic growth, and collaboration in the semiconductor industry.

Mary Kay Magistad is deputy director of the Asia Society's Center on U.S.-China Relations. She is an award-winning journalist who lived and reported in Asia for more than two decades, including in China for NPR and PRI/BBC's *The World*, and in Southeast Asia for NPR and the *Washington Post*.

Anja Manuel is a partner at Rice, Hadley, Gates & Manuel and executive director of the Aspen Strategy Group. From 2005 to 2007 she was a special assistant at the US State Department.

Oriana Skylar Mastro is a center fellow at Stanford University's Freeman Spogli Institute and a nonresident senior fellow at the American Enterprise Institute. She continues to serve in the US Air Force Reserve, for which she works as a strategic planner at US Indo-Pacific Command.

Lt. Gen. H.R. McMaster, USA (Ret.), is the Fouad and Michelle Ajami Senior Fellow at the Hoover Institution. He was formerly US national security advisor and for thirty-four years was a commissioned officer in the US Army.

Nazak Nikakhtar is a partner at Wiley Rein LLP. From 2018 to 2021 she was the US Department of Commerce assistant secretary for industry and analysis at the International Trade Administration.

Jim Plummer is the John M. Fluke Professor of Electrical Engineering at Stanford University. From 1999 to 2014 he was the Frederick Emmons Terman dean of Stanford's School of Engineering. Formerly the director of Stanford's Nanofabrication Facility, he has graduated more than ninety PhD students.

Matthew Pottinger is a distinguished visiting fellow at the Hoover Institution. He served for four years in senior roles on the National Security Council staff, including as deputy national security advisor (2019–21). Formerly a Reuters and *Wall Street Journal* reporter based in China, he fought in Iraq and Afghanistan as a US Marine.

Gary Rieschel is founding managing partner of Qiming Venture Partners, a firm he launched in Shanghai in 2006. He is chair of the Asia Society of Northern California.

Don Rosenberg is a fellow in residence at the UC San Diego School of Global Policy and Strategy's Center on Global Transformation. He recently retired as executive vice president, general counsel, and corporate secretary at Qualcomm and was formerly senior vice president, general counsel, and corporate secretary at both Apple and IBM.

Danny Russel is vice president for international security and diplomacy at the Asia Society Policy Institute. He was formerly assistant secretary of state for East Asian and Pacific affairs and was National Security Council senior director for Asian affairs.

Orville Schell is the Arthur Ross director of the Asia Society's Center on U.S.-China Relations and former dean of the UC Berkeley Graduate School of Journalism.

Jacquelyn Schneider is Hoover Fellow at the Hoover Institution, where she directs its Wargaming and Crisis Simulation Initiative.

David J. Teece is the Thomas W. Tusher Professor at the Institute for Business Innovation at UC Berkeley's Haas School of Business. He is also the faculty director of the school's Tusher Initiative for the Management of Intellectual Capital and cofounder of the Berkeley Research Group.

Kharis Templeman is a research fellow at the Hoover Institution and program manager of the Hoover Project on Taiwan in the Indo-Pacific. A political scientist with research interests in Taiwan's politics, democratization, and security, he is a lecturer in Stanford University's Center for East Asian Studies.

Glenn Tiffert is a research fellow at the Hoover Institution and co-chairs its project on China's Global Sharp Power. A historian of modern China, he works closely with government and civil society partners around the world to document and build resilience against authoritarian interference with democratic institutions.

James Timbie is an Annenberg Distinguished Visiting Fellow at the Hoover Institution. From 1983 to 2016 he was a senior advisor at the US State Department.

Matthew Turpin is a visiting fellow at the Hoover Institution and a senior advisor at Palatir Technologies. From 2018 to 2019 he was US National Security Council director for China and the senior advisor on China to the US secretary of commerce focused on interagency coordination of US policy toward China. Prior to joining the White House, Turpin served over twenty-two years in combat units in the US Army.

Laura Tyson is a distinguished professor at the UC Berkeley Haas School of Business. From 1993 to 1995 she was chair of the Council of Economic Advisers, and from 1995 to 1996 she was director of the National Economic Council.

Lawrence Wilkinson is Chairman of Heminge & Condell and cofounder of the Global Business Network (GBN). He and GBN cofounders have been central to the development and spread of the Scenario Planning technique.

H.-S. Philip Wong is a professor of electrical engineering and the Willard R. and Inez Kerr Bell professor in the Stanford University School of Engineering, where he is the founding faculty director of its SystemX Alliance and director of the Stanford Nanofabrication Facility. From 2018 to 2020 he was vice president for corporate research at TSMC, where he remains as chief scientist in an advisory role.

Chenggang Xu is a visiting fellow at the Hoover Institution, a senior research scholar at the Stanford Center on China's Economy and Institutions, and a visiting professor at Imperial College London.

Amy Zegart is the Morris Arnold and Nona Jean Cox Senior Fellow at the Hoover Institution and is a senior fellow at Stanford's Freeman Spogli Institute.

Philip Zelikow is a distinguished visiting fellow at the Hoover Institution and the White Burkett Miller Professor of History and the J. Wilson Newman Professor of Governance at the Miller Center of Public Affairs, both at the University of Virginia.

ACKNOWLEDGMENTS

A number of participants in our Hoover Institution–Asia Society Working Group on Semiconductors and the Security of the United States and Taiwan volunteered individual chapters in this book. All advanced our group's collective education through active contributions to reviews and a series of roundtable meetings held on Stanford campus from the fall of 2021 to the spring of 2023. Those roundtables were enriched through expert commentary from guests across the United States. We are grateful for their efforts, which were brought to bear solely by a shared concern for the gravity of this subject.

The thinking of our working group participants and the writing of the authors was informed by two years of background research produced by an exceptional team of Hoover student fellows and other student research assistants and advisees: from Stanford University, Sam Chetwin George, Will Hallisey, Ruei-Hung Alex Lee, Sean Khang Lee, Omar Jose Pimentel Marte, Neelay Trivedi, Alex Tingxun Wei, and Caroline Zhang; and from the University of Chicago, Keishi Kimura and Aatman Vakil. In many cases, their words and ideas appear directly in this report.

We offer special thanks to Lawrence Wilkinson for his expert leadership of a working group team that undertook an intensive scenario planning exercise to consider alternative trajectories for US-China relations, from the perspective of these nations' intensifying technological competition.

We are grateful to many leaders and analysts in the public, private, and civil sectors in Taiwan, who generously shared their time and insights with us during an August 2022 research delegation and in other exchanges. We also benefited from the counsel of colleagues from a variety of backgrounds in China, some of whom have chosen to remain anonymous.

Stanford East Asian Studies program graduate Nicholas Welch was a heroic outside editor of the resulting manuscript; his efforts were joined by Mary Kay Magistad from the Asia Society Center on U.S.-China Relations. Jeffery Sequeira, also at the Asia Society, offered key research and logistical support. And Barbara Arellano, Alison Law, and Danica Michels Hodge at the Hoover Institution Press labored greatly to produce the final product at the speed of relevance.

As executive editor of this project, the Hoover Institution's David Fedor shepherded the various stages of meetings and report drafting with exemplary efficiency, dedication, and judgment. The completion of this report owes greatly to his substantive knowledge, attention to detail, and skill at project management.

We are in debt to each of these contributors, whose sense of responsibility and shared purpose produced this report on an issue of paramount strategic significance at a crucial historical juncture.

LARRY DIAMOND
JAMES O. ELLIS JR.
ORVILLE SCHELL

ABBREVIATIONS

AD/CVD	Anti-dumping/countervailing duty
ASEAN	Association of Southeast Asian Nations
ASICS	Application-specific integrated circuits
ASML	Advanced Semiconductor Materials Lithography (firm)
BIS	(US Department of Commerce) Bureau of Industry and Security
BRI	Belt and Road Initiative
CAA	Clean Air Act (1970 and 1992)
CCP	Chinese Communist Party
CFIUS	Committee on Foreign Investment in the United States
CHIPS Act	Creating Helpful Incentives to Produce Semiconductors and Science Act of 2022
CMOS	Complementary metal-oxide semiconductor (technology)
COCOM	Coordinating Committee for Multilateral Export Controls
CPTPP	Comprehensive and Progressive Agreement for Trans-Pacific Partnership
CPU	Central processing unit
CXMT	ChangXin Memory Technologies (firm)
DoD	(US) Department of Defense
DPP	Democratic Progressive Party (ROC)
DRAM	Dynamic random access memory
DUV	Deep ultraviolet (lithography)
EDA	Electronic design automation (software)
EPA	(US) Environmental Protection Agency

EUV	Extreme ultraviolet (lithography)
FDI	Foreign direct investment
FDPR	Foreign Direct Product Rule of 1959
FFRDC	Federally funded research and development center
FPGA	Field-programmable gate arrays
GPU	Graphics processing unit
IC	Integrated circuit
ICT	Information and communications technology
IDM	Integrated device manufacturer
IP	Intellectual property
IPEF	Indo-Pacific Economic Framework for Prosperity
IRA	Inflation Reduction Act of 2022
ITAR	(US) International Traffic in Arms Regulations
ITRI	Taiwan Industrial Technology Research Institute
KMT	Kuomintang / Nationalist Party of China (ROC)
MiC 2025	Made in China 2025
NAND	NAND Flash memory
NEPA	National Environmental Policy Act of 1970
NSTC	National Semiconductor Technology Center
OECD	Organisation for Economic Co-operation and Development
OEM	Original equipment manufacturer
OSAT	Outsourced assembly packaging and testing
PLA	People's Liberation Army
R&D	Research and development
RF	Radio frequency
RISC	Reduced instruction set computer
RMB	Renminbi / Chinese Yuan
SMIC	Semiconductor Manufacturing International Corp.
TSMC	Taiwan Semiconductor Manufacturing Company
TSRI	Taiwan Semiconductor Research Institute
TTC	(EU-US) Trade and Technology Council
UMC	United Microelectronics Corporation
USPTO	US Patent and Trademark Office
WTO	World Trade Organization
YMTC	Yangtze Memory Technology Co.

INDEX